T0345056

The Biological Foundations of
Organizational Behavior

THE BIOLOGICAL
FOUNDATIONS OF
ORGANIZATIONAL
BEHAVIOR

Edited by Stephen M. Colarelli
and Richard D. Arvey

The University of Chicago Press
Chicago and London

Stephen M. Colarelli is professor of psychology at Central Michigan University. Richard D. Arvey is head of the Department of Management and Organization at the National University of Singapore.

The University of Chicago Press, Chicago 60637
The University of Chicago Press, Ltd., London
© 2015 by The University of Chicago
All rights reserved. Published 2015.
Printed in the United States of America

24 23 22 21 20 19 18 17 16 15   1 2 3 4 5

ISBN-13: 978-0-226-12715-6 (cloth)
ISBN-13: 978-0-226-12729-3 (e-book)
DOI: 10.7208/chicago/9780226127293.001.0001

Library of Congress Cataloging-in-Publication Data

The biological foundations of organizational behavior / edited by Stephen M. Colarelli and Richard D. Arvey.
   pages cm
  Includes bibliographical references and index.
  ISBN 978-0-226-12715-6 (cloth : alkaline paper)—ISBN 978-0-226-12729-3 (e-book) 1. Organizational behavior. I. Colarelli, Stephen M., 1951– editor. II. Arvey, Richard D., editor.
  HD58.7.B545 2015
  302.3′5—dc23

                                      2014010240

♾ This paper meets the requirements of ANSI/NISO Z39.48-1992 (Permanence of Paper).

CONTENTS

This book would have never been written without the efforts of many people. Our first debt of gratitude is to David Pervin, the editor at the University of Chicago Press who approached us asking if we would be interested in writing a book about biology and organizational behavior. David was a champion of this book from the beginning. We also owe a tremendous debt of gratitude to of the book's contributors. They kindly and patiently worked through revisions to produce a marvelous set of chapters.

The School of Business of the National University of Singapore (NUS) hosted a week-long conference in the spring of 2011, during which the book's contributors discussed the first drafts of their chapters and solidified a common thematic vision for the book. We would like to thank NUS's Business School and its dean, Bernard Yeung, for their gracious hospitality and generosity in bringing authors from around the world to Singapore for a week. Several staff members and graduate students from NUS's Department of Management and Organization worked very hard to make the conference a success. Our thanks go to Don Jia Qing Chen, Sally Han, and Wendy Lim.

Joe Jackson took over for David as our editor once the second round of drafts was in. During this transition, Christie Henry, the Press's editorial director for the social sciences, helped keep communication and revisions moving forward. Joe guided us through responding to the outside reviewers' comments on the entire book and making subsequent revisions. Joe also did final editing on all of the chapters. Our outside reviewers gave us excellent feedback on the initial proposal and on the first draft of the book.

Steve spent a sabbatical semester at the Department of Management and Organization at NUS while he and Rich completed the book. Steve is grateful for the support and hospitality he received from Rich and the Business School at NUS. Thanks also go to Central Michigan University for additional travel assistance for Steve and sabbatical support. Particular thanks go to his dean, Pamela Gates, and his department chair, Hajime Otani. Shanna Palmer and Robin Decker ably assisted with word processing.

We are grateful to Kingsley Browne, who graciously read and commented on the entire manuscript. Kingsley is a scholar's scholar, with a wide grasp of the literature in evolutionary psychology and its intellectual history. His perceptive comments were invaluable.

Finally, we are grateful to the University of Chicago Press. It has a reputation as one of the great university presses, and our experience confirms this. Our editors were flexible and supportive of creativity and scholarly independence, while also maintaining an ethos of quality, intellectual rigor, and interdisciplinary scholarship.

ONE

Introduction: Biology and Organizational Behavior

Stephen M. Colarelli and Richard D. Arvey

It has been more than two hundred years since Charles Darwin's birth, and his theory of evolution by natural selection has had an incalculable impact on science and society. A majority of nonscientists (except in the United States) and virtually all scientists in industrialized countries now regard all life as the product of evolution by natural selection (Miller, Scott, and Okamoto 2006). Prior to Darwin, from Aristotle to the nineteenth century, people believed that forms of life were created whole in a matter of moments and never changed. Darwin turned all this on its head, showing that life forms evolve and change over eons of time.[1] What Newton and Einstein did for the way we think about space, time, and matter, Darwin did for the way we think about life and time. Darwin's theory did more than change our epistemology of life: it had a tremendous scientific and practical impact. Together with Mendel's discovery of the mechanism of inheritance (genetics), the theory of evolution by natural selection shaped the modern life sciences—biology, medicine and pharmacology, genetics, and neuroscience.[2] In addition to exponential advances in plant genetics, basic research in both evolutionary biology and genetics has yielded equally remarkable advances in animal husbandry, medicine, and pharmacology (Carroll et al. 2003; Dekkers and Hospital 2002). While startling results from these theories (such as

We would like to thank Glenn Carroll, David Pervin, and Kingsley Browne for their helpful comments on earlier drafts of this chapter.

animal cloning) make headlines, many practical advances go unnoticed because, like the air we breathe, they are all around us.

Given the impact of biology on so many areas of science and the economy, it seems odd that modern genetics and the theory of evolution by natural selection have had such a small impact on the study of organizational behavior (OB). In four leading journals in OB from the years 2005 through 2012, we found just six articles with biological, evolutionary, or genetic orientations.[3] Although the literature on occupational stress and occupational health refers to biological mechanisms of stress, there is little mention of evolution and genetics (Ganster and Rosen 2013), despite the obvious linkages (e.g., Hadany et al. 2006; Hoffman and Parsons 1993). Likewise, the organizational literature on sex differences eschews biological explanations (Powell 2010), something that most biologists would most certainly find strange.

We are biological creatures, and therefore our biological makeup influences our behavior—not entirely, but most certainly in important ways. Organizational scholars are missing a significant piece of the puzzle by overlooking biological mechanisms. Just as other social sciences have benefited by incorporating a biological perspective, the field of OB can benefit by incorporating a biological perspective into its theoretical and research toolkits. We are not claiming to know precisely how biological factors may influence theory and research in OB or that we can draw a blueprint of the biological implications for management practice. But, given the evidence, it would be prudent to take stock of what we do know about biology and behavior in organizations and to begin to think about biology's potential relevance for management practice.

WHY SO LITTLE BIOLOGY IN ORGANIZATIONAL BEHAVIOR?

Much of OB is still dominated by what Tooby and Cosmides (1992) call the "standard social science model" (SSSM), and this has slowed the acceptance of biological perspectives. The SSSM holds that most of the variation in human behavior is due to culture and socialization, and that humans are unique among species in that biological and instinctual constraints play a relatively small role in their behavior. The SSSM is evident in theories of sex differences (e.g., Hyde 2007), learning and training (e.g., Luthans 1975; Meichenbaum 1977), organizational culture (e.g., Schein 1985), and newcomer socialization (Ashkanasy, Wilderom, and Peterson 2003; Feldman and Bolino 1999). Cognitive psychology (which also views the mind as highly malleable, fallible, and shaped primarily by cultural inputs) has had a powerful impact on OB in many areas—ranging from individual and organizational learning (Crossan et al. 1995) to planning and decision making (Choo 1998).

The SSSM's prominence in the social sciences began in the early twentieth century and, though diminished, persists today. The SSSM arose from a confluence of intellectual and social trends: the rise of the social sciences and debates about how they could improve society, social Darwinism and its antagonists, intellectual turf battles in anthropology, and the rise of behaviorism in psychology. At the same time there were heated debates about the causes of, and solutions to, social problems and economic inequality. In one camp were the reformers, attributing social problems to the environment and advocating social and economic changes to remedy these problems. In the other camp were social Darwinists and eugenicists. Social Darwinists (a label popularized by the historian Richard Hoffsteader in the 1940s) refers to scholars who equated survival of the fittest with socioeconomic status, took a laissez-faire approach to social policies, and did not support social welfare programs. They felt that aiding those in need would violate a fundamental biological law (Richards 1987). Eugenics (a term coined by Francis Galton) advocated selective breeding as a means to improve society (e.g., see Brookes 2004).

These were not fringe movements led by crackpots; they were popular social philosophies articulated by prominent intellectuals and academics (e.g., Yerkes at Harvard; Thorndike at Columbia; William Graham Sumner at Yale) who, unfortunately, did not understand evolutionary theory and genetics. For example, equating survival of the fittest with socioeconomic status reveals a misunderstanding of Darwinian fitness. Fitness in the classical Darwinian sense refers to the number of offspring surviving to reproductive age, not one's standing in the pecking order. By the 1930s the intellectual tide began to turn against the social Darwinists and eugenicists, and this trend continued until the late twentieth century—so that *any* evolutionary perspective on human nature became tainted by association. The wrongheaded association of evolutionary theory with social Darwinism and eugenics constricted discourse and scientific progress in evolutionary approaches in the social sciences, and these associations still influence the thinking of some management and OB scholars.

Another reason that management scholars may be hesitant to embrace a biological perspective is that biology may seem uncontrollable. *Management*, on the other hand, implies control. Managers are supposed to plan and manipulate organizations to achieve the desired results. Management scholars may believe that biological factors are inherently unmanageable because they are more or less fixed and therefore less amenable to change (Sewell 2004). However, this is not necessarily the case. Consider aging. People grow old; aging is an inevitable biological process. However, understanding the nature of that biological process enables us to have some effect on how quickly we age. We know that aging is caused by the body's loss of ability to repair routine (and nonroutine) cell damage. Taking care of our health will minimize cell damage and can slow down the aging process. Quitting smoking, eating sensibly, and exercising all affect cell health and can keep people youthful longer. Most scholars in any field, we presume, believe in using medical interventions based on modern biological science because they implicitly accept the causal connection between biology and health and the efficacy of treatments based on that knowledge. The same logic applies to organizationally relevant biological factors. So why not accept that biological factors also influence people's behavior in organizations and that the use of that knowledge can positively influence the management of people in organizations?

A biological perspective on OB is simply part of the universe of *information* that managers can use in making decisions about organizational design and goals (Richerson, Collins, and Genet 2006; Tooby, Cosmides, and Price 2006). Biological knowledge is another level of knowledge for managers and management scholars. Managers (or anyone else who works in an organization) will be empowered by a deeper understanding of biological influences and motivations. If biology provides useful insights about how people respond to dominance hierarchies (Nicholson 1998) or leaders (Van Vugt, Hogan, and Kaiser 2008), about what types of environments are most compatible with the human animal (Foley 2005), or about the products or services to which people are most likely to respond positively (Colarelli and Dettman 2003; Miller 2009), then it can be a useful addition to the manager's and management scholar's toolkit.

INCORPORATING BIOLOGICAL EXPLANATIONS INTO ORGANIZATIONAL BEHAVIOR

Advancing Theory

A biological understanding of human behavior is very much a part of modern science now, making it all the more timely for management and OB scholars to incorporate biological influences into their work. A biological explanation will help us to identify mechanisms that account for regularities in organizational behavior. The addition of biological theory and research to OB will increase its explanatory and predictive power by providing a meta-theoretic foundation.

OB is an interdisciplinary field, and adding a biological lens should encourage broader interdisciplinary collaboration. Interdisciplinary collaboration among biologists and social scientists is becoming increasingly important as we learn more about the biological mechanisms that influence human behavior (Cacioppo et al. 2000). A deeper interdisciplinary understanding of the physiological and neurological mechanisms (and their adaptive functions) can augment our ability to enhance learning, engineer suitable environments, and integrate technology with the human body and mind.[4] Furthermore, biology and evolutionary psychology can help bring a strong comparative perspective to OB. How is the organization of human groups similar to the organization of groups in other species? What might be common mechanisms? How do we differ?

Consider sex differences. Although men and women share many physiological and psychological similarities, they also differ (Geary 1998). Evolutionary and biological perspectives can help identify the differences that are salient in organizational settings, and this can have positive effects for women (Colarelli, Spranger, and Hechanova 2006). One well-documented result of not taking sex differences into account is the increase in anterior cruciate ligament (ACL) injuries among women. The past twenty years have witnessed dramatic increases in women's participation in organized athletics (Women and Sport Commission 2012), but adjustments in training and technique to compensate for anatomical differences have been insufficient. Because the female femur angles more sharply at the knee than the male femur, women's ACLs may be more affected by excess strain, which can result in devastating injuries. Such injuries are less likely, however, if training practices and techniques are adjusted for this difference (Hutchinson and Ireland 1995). Studying sex differences in leadership, one finds human groups dominated by male leaders. In other social species, however (bonobos, elephants, hyenas, wild horses), females are the leaders. What are the contextual or biological mechanisms that lead to female leadership in those species? What are the characteristics of female leadership in those species, and what implications might this knowledge have for understanding leadership in human organizations?

Advancing Practice

Interventions are much more likely to work when they are based on an accurate view of human nature. If our fundamental assumptions about human nature or human systems are inaccurate, interventions based on those assumptions are likely to be ineffective. To use an example from psychiatry, almost no progress was made in treating autism, depression, bipolar disorder, and schizophrenia when the understanding and treatment of these illnesses were based on Freudian theories. The causal mechanisms that Freudians proposed (e.g., unconscious conflict, bad parenting) were incorrect. Major advances in treating these illnesses occurred only after scientists began to gain an accurate understanding of the mechanisms (psychological and biological) that cause these illnesses (Charney and Nestler 2004). For example, Bruno Bettelheim, a neo-Freudian, argued that cold (what became known as "refrigerator") mothers caused autism (Bettelheim and Sylvester 1950). Bettelheim's prescription for "curing" autism, therefore, was family therapy, principally directed at improving mothering. Not only was his causal explanation incorrect and his treatment ineffective, but his treatment had a devastating effect on many well-meaning and good mothers—making them feel personally responsible for their child's autism. We now know that a complex of genetic and other biological factors causes autism (Morrow et al. 2009; Sutcliffe 2009) and that training women to be "better mothers" will have no effect. Other approaches, based on a more accurate understanding of the etiology of the illness, are more appropriate (Gaines et al. 2010).

A better biological understanding of people's behavior in organizations should also improve the design and execution of organizational interventions. An evolutionary and biologically based understanding should increase the probability of designing successful interventions. Organizational interventions will not succeed if they are based on an inaccurate understanding of human nature.

WHY THIS BOOK?

Biology needs to be a part of the conversation in OB. Our aim is to provide a conceptual and empirical underpinning so that biology can become a full and recognized part of the levels of analysis in OB. The purposes of this book, therefore, are to (1) start a dialogue between OB and biology, (2) encourage research on links between biology and OB, (3) provide an initial framework for biological bases of OB, and (4) stimulate discussions about potential applications. The contributors are preeminent scholars who have each done seminal work in a specific intersection of biology and OB. While the chapters contain enough background to orient readers who may have little knowledge of biology, they also provide substantive contributions that advance our understanding of specific areas of biology and human behavior in organizations. They are both synthetic and forward-looking.

The scope of this volume is necessarily limited. On the one hand, a primary goal of this book is to examine the extant literature integrating OB and biology—but this literature is relatively sparse. On the other hand, we also wanted to explore new ideas about the confluence of OB and biology, and because these are potentially quite numerous, we had to impose limitations. We felt that it was prudent to work from areas where *some* linkage could be reasonably inferred—particularly (but not limited to) areas that would have traction with OB scholars, such as work attitudes and decision making. Inevitable limitations on space compelled us to exclude some topics that by all rights should have been included—like sex differences and neuroeconomics.

Overview

All of the chapters taken together embody Tinbergen's (1963) typology of an integrated explanation of behavior. That is, they reflect different levels of the analysis of behavior—ranging, for example, from molecular genetics and life history to psychological and physical adaptations.

The chapters that follow this introduction are organized into four sections. In the first section, "Genetics, Individual Differences, and Work Behavior," Zhaoli Song, Wendong Li, and Nan Wang review fundamental concepts in molecular genetics and genomic methods; Remus Ilies and Nikos Dimotakis review and explain linkages between genetics and work attitudes. Scott Shane and Nicos Nicolaou examine a specific occupational area, entrepreneurship, and show how genetics can provide a powerful framework for understanding why some people choose particular occupations and are adept at them; and Tim Judge and Robert Hogan suggest how natural selection has sculpted individual differences, particularly those that matter the most in organizational life. In the second section, "Physiology and Organizational Behavior," Jayanth Narayanan and Smrithi Prasad examine the neurobiology of three motivational systems that are particularly relevant to behavior in organizations: threat, reward, and affiliation. Zhen Zhang and Michael Zyphur's chapter examines the relationship between human physiology and employee health in organizations, using mismatch theory as an organizing framework. The third section, "Evolution and Organization," examines the influence of biology and evolved psychological mechanisms in relation to organizational processes and structure. Michael Price and Mark Van Vugt examine adaptations that enable both consensual and coercive leader-follower relationships. Peter DeScioli, Robert Kurzban, and Peter M. Todd argue that managerial decisions are based on a modular toolkit of fast and frugal heuristics that were sculpted during the course of human evolution, and that understanding the dynamics of fast and frugal decision making has important implications for OB. Nigel Nicholson's chapter shows how family-owned businesses can exemplify the integrative capacity of evolutionary theory—linking broad social forces with the interaction of kinship and organizational forms. Rod White and Barbara Decker Pierce link human cooperation in organizations with biological and social evolutionary processes in a multilevel selection framework. They show how both biological and cultural processes have interacted over time to forge the human propensity to cooperate with both kin and non-kin and in both small groups and large organizations. In the last section, "Challenges Ahead," Glenn Carroll and Kieran O'Connor provide a critical assessment of the potential intellectual value, limitations, and challenges of a biological approach to organizational studies.

Areas of Conceptual Congruence

After reading the following chapters, we hope you will realize that, in addition to providing new explanatory mechanisms and areas for theoretical integration, the authors have demonstrated that OB and biology have several broad levels of commonality. Drawing on the idea that there is a natural progression from the biological to the organizational, the chapters in this volume reflect an "extended phenotype" view of human organizations (a phenotype is the outward expression—observable characteristics—of an organism's genetic makeup). Richard Dawkins (1999) coined the term *extended phenotype* to mean that an organism's phenotype should not be confined to discrete packages (i.e., the biological body of the organism). Rather, an organism's behavior, potential for physical and symbolic creation, and relations with other organisms (of the same or different species) are all part of its (extended) phenotype. He used the analogy of a Necker cube: look at it from one angle, and it appears to be one thing; look at it from another angle and it appears to be something different. Look at a human being from one viewpoint, and you see a phenotype—a unique individual of certain proportions, coloration, facial features, and so on. Look at this individual from another perspective, and you see a genotype—20,000–25,000 genes that, combined with environmental input, gave expression to the phenotype. Looking from yet another perspective, you see this individual as a member of groups and organizations (e.g., a family, musical group, work organization).

Now, more than thirty years after Dawkins coined the term *extended phenotype*, connections among genes, organisms, behavior, and organization are no longer just speculation or a metaphor for viewing reality (Cacioppo et al. 2000). Each individual is a physical phenotype that is an expression of his or her genotype. Not only does the genotype influence an individual's physical phenotype, but genotypes influence predispositions, emotions, and behavior. Phenotypes in turn extend themselves, in combination with culture, to produce artifacts, symbols, and organization. In this volume you will see the interplay and interrelations among genotypes, phenotypes, and extended phenotypes in the context of humans working in organizations. This approach fits within OB's tradition of using multiple levels of analysis and also extends it to the biological level.

"Fit" is a key assumption in both OB and biology. Scholars from both disciplines are interested in what happens when there is a lack of fit and in what can bring more congruence to those situations. In OB, fit refers to the alignment of an organization's components (structure, technology, human resources, and culture) internally and with its environment. There are extensive literatures on person-organization fit, person-job fit, organization-environment fit, and structure-strategy fit—and how to make lack-of-fit adjustments. In biology, "fit" can refer to how well an organism's features are adapted to its environment (e.g., camels have three eyelids that function to protect their eyes from blowing sand). When the environment changes too rapidly for species to adapt, they decline or go extinct (consider the rapid cooling sixty-five million years ago that resulted in the extinction of the dinosaurs). Fit (i.e., adaptation) to the environment is a fundamental premise of the theory of evolution by natural selection.

Organizations and organisms must adapt to their environments. If they fail to adapt, they are unlikely to survive. Leaders can consciously adapt by aligning organizations' goals, strategies, structures, and processes to the characteristics of the environments they face. Perhaps more typically, organizations adapt through trial and error—by chance some changes fit and become embedded in organizational routines (Hannan and Freeman 1977). Like people, organizations that are better adapted to their environments are more likely to survive and reproduce, sending their genes into the future. Genes carry the information for the replication of organisms. In organizations, *memes* carry the information for replication. A meme is a coherent set of linguistic information that can be transferred from person to person—for example, information about an organization's parts, how they are organized, and how they interact with the environment. Thus, the basic evolutionary framework of variation, selection, and retention is applicable to the process of organizations adapting (or failing to adapt) to their environments.

Biology and the Scope of Organizational Behavior

The chapters in this volume stay, for the most part, within the broad scope of OB—organization, "fit," goals, collective action, leadership and hierarchy, decision making, and individual differences—but are also informed by a biological or evolutionary perspective.

By definition, OB begins within an organization. Complex organizational life is by no means unique to humans, which implies a biological component. The eusocial insects, such as the honeybee (*Apis mellifora*), form complex organizations. Hives can range from ten thousand to sixty thousand bees, and a hive can exist for years. In the complex social structure of a hive, different bees perform different roles (scouts, guards, nursery workers). Honeybee hives undergo major organizational change when a hive swarms (a group of bees split from the hive and form a new hive; see Green 2002; Michener 1974). Male emperor penguins form an organization every winter. Its purpose is to help each individual stay warm in the brutal cold, while each male is incubating his mate's egg (Gilbert et al. 2006). A wild horse herd can include more than a hundred animals. A typical herd is made up of bands (15–35 animals), each led by a dominant female (Salter and Hudson 1982). Similarly, elephant herds, led by a dominant matriarch, are made up of family groups, often with subunits with specific functions (infant care, juvenile care); adult males are excluded from the herds, unless they are with cows in estrus (Fowler and Mikota 2006; Poole 1994). Chimpanzee and bonobo troops can consist of about a hundred individuals, who typically separate during the day into small foraging groups. Chimpanzee groups are led by a dominant male (Parish 1994); bonobos are led by a dominant female (White and Wood 2007).

What is the social glue that *binds individuals together in organizations*? Individuals in nonhuman animal groups and organizations are bound together largely by instinct (Hamilton 1987; Wilson 2012). Explanations of the glue that binds humans together have tended to be sociological and psychological. The sociologist Emile Durkheim (1984), for example, posited that tradition and kinship ties—what he called "mechanical solidarity"—bound people together in simple, small societies; in more complex societies with an intricate division of labor, he proposed that people are bound by the exchange of services, which he called "organic solidarity." Durkheim argued that sociological phenomena are "social facts"—facts that cannot be reduced to psychological or biological underpinnings. In the first half of the twentieth century, organizational scholars (e.g., Max Weber, Frederick Taylor, and Kurt Lewin) relied on bureaucratic and social-psychological explanations, also avoiding biology. Lewin used analogies from physics. His "field theory" posited that group and organization members were bound together by a psychological force field. Social-psychological explanations persisted into the latter half of the twentieth century. Amitai Etzioni (1975) suggested that, depending on the type of organization, people are bound together by common values and norms or by contractual obligations. More recent work on organizational commitment (e.g., Meyer and Allen 1984) suggests similar forces that bind people to organizations.

In chapter 10 of this volume, Nigel Nicholson describes how the bonds of kinship still remain an important part of the glue of most organizations on the planet: family businesses. These bonds enable our most basic form of cooperative systems—the family and, by extension, family firms. Family firms typically begin from kin-based altruism (i.e., kin selection—the propensity to be altruistic toward close kin, without necessarily expecting tit-for-tat exchange). However, for family firms to grow and prosper, family members must engage in reciprocal altruism and cooperate with nonfamily members. These dual modalities of cooperation in family firms constitute a prime example of multiple levels of analysis and multilevel selection that, as White and Pierce (in chapter 11) and Nicholson argue, is inherent in an evolutionary perspective on organizational behavior. They show that cooperation is the glue of large-scale (non-kin-based) organizations. While reminiscent of Durkheim's notion of the exchange of specialized services and Etzioni's calculative commitment, White and Pierce tie human cooperation in organizations to evolutionary processes. Promising results are now appearing in the literature indicating that there is a genetic basis for sociality and cooperation among a variety of organisms.[5] Less is known about the genetics and neurology of social behavior among humans; however, empirical evidence is accumulating that shows biological substrates of human cooperation (Benkler 2011). Studies reviewed by Rilling and his colleagues (2008; Rilling 2011) describe the evidence for neurobiological correlates of social behavior, particularly cooperation, among humans. In particular, reward centers of the brain (e.g., the caudate nucleus) are activated or deactivated in response to cooperation or lack of reciprocation, respectively. Empathy and trust are important components of cooperation. Mirror neurons appear to be a biological foundation of empathy (Rizzolatti and Craighero 2004; Singer et al. 2004). Through mirror neuron pathways, areas of a person's brain that feel pain and pleasure will activate just when viewing another person display pain or pleasure (Rilling 2011). Also, the neuropeptide oxytocin has been found to be a critical biological element involved in social bonding and trust (MacDonald and MacDonald 2010). These findings clearly indicate a biological basis for cooperation.

Goals and Collective Action

Goals are an integral feature of organizations, and goal-directed behavior is a significant part of individuals' behavior in organizations. Typically, the organizational literature looks at goals and collective action from a cognitive perspective—intentions, plans, expected future states. However, goals also have a biological basis. Goals or goal states are associated with specific neural activity and regions of the brain (D'Argembeau et al. 2010; Fincham et al. 2002). Goals reflect what people value and find important (Bandura 1997), and biology plays a role in what people value. Ilies and Dimotakis point out in chapter 3 that a person's genetic makeup influences work values and fundamental choices in life, such as occupations, careers, and avocations; even political preferences are all influenced by a person's genetic makeup (Eaves, Eysenck, and Martin1989; Nicolaou and Shane 2010; Smith et al. 2011). Clearly, there are not genes for particular careers or occupations, and so forth. However, genetic makeup influences a person's personality, cognitive and physical abilities, appearance, and health. These in turn are very likely to influence, *although not determine*, long-term goals. Shane and Nicolaou, in chapter 4, describe how biologically based traits (e.g., sensation-seeking) and pathways have been linked to the probability that an individual will choose an entrepreneurial career. Individuals with the constellations of traits associated with entrepreneurship tend to start organizations, and thus—because organizational goals reflect the founder's values and goals—a founder's genetic makeup has some influence on an organization's goals.

Hierarchy

Hierarchy is a fact of organizational life. Even organizations with egalitarian values have some hierarchy. The macro OB literature is replete with research on the functions of hierarchy and its effects on organizational and individual outcomes (Anderson and Brown 2010; Cole and Bruch 2006). At the micro level, considerable attention has been given to attributes that differentiate those who get to the top of hierarchies and the processes and skills employed by those at and on their way to the top (e.g., Cavazotte, Moreno, and Hickmann 2012; Howard and Bray 1990; Judge, Piccolo, and Kosalka 2009; Strang 2007).

Evolutionary psychology and anthropology can bring an added perspective to how we think about hierarchy in organizations. The structure of hunter-gatherer societies (in which humans lived for more than 99% of their time on earth) is relatively flat (Boehm 1999). While there is typically a dominant male (or head man), his authority is often more informal than formal, based on respect and leadership skills. Usually, whenever a leader in a hunter-gatherer group becomes too demanding, too authoritarian, group members employ a variety of tactics (e.g., humiliation, etc.) to take him down a few pegs. If he continues, he is typically replaced (Boehm 1999). More complex hierarchies emerged with the first civilizations, approximately between five and six thousand years ago. The precipitating event was the development of agriculture. Agriculture provided surplus food and led to sedentary communities, which in turn enabled individuals to specialize and some classes of individuals to accumulate more resources than others (Price 1995). Some hierarchy is functional, because it minimizes conflicts about position and resource distribution, and facilitates collective action. However, studies in anthropology and evolutionary psychology suggest that different ecological conditions influence the nature of hierarchies. When organizational members have viable exit options, or when it is difficult for any group or organizational member to accumulate resources, hierarchies tend to be flat.

Genetically inherited characteristics have a significant effect on who becomes a leader. Genotypes explain more than 20% of the variance in leadership occupancy, for both male and female leaders, and genotypes probably explain more variance in leadership occupancy than is explained by any of the traditional leadership variables in the social science literature (Arvey et al. 2006; De Neve et al. 2013). As Judge and Hogan point out in chapter 5, many phenotypic characteristics that are highly heritable are associated with leadership, including personality, intelligence, and, for males, height and facial structure. Judge and Hogan, as well as Price and Van Vugt (chapter 8), suggest likely ecological pressures that, over our evolutionary history, have sculpted psychological mechanisms that enable leadership and hierarchy in human groups.

Our hominid ancestors emerged about two million years ago, and the basic genotype for *Homo sapiens* emerged about two hundred thousand years ago. Thus, our psychology and physiology evolved under conditions that were, in many ways, quite different than they are today. This is the background behind the notion of "mismatch": that our evolved psychology and physiology do not fit with the modern environment in which we currently live (Gluckman and Hanson 2006; Markham 2012). Changes in our genotype inevitably lag behind changes in culture and technology, and this has important implications for OB.[6]

Zhang and Zyphur make a convincing case in chapter 7 that the modern workplace is mismatched to human physiology—with frequently disastrous effects on human health. For example, although humans evolved in environments that were relatively quiet, allowed regular exposure to direct sunlight (Boubekri, Hull, and Boyer 1991; Holick 2004) and the natural world (Kaplan 1993; Vischer 2007), and where people had opportunities for daily physical exercise as well as daytime rest (Anthony and Anthony 2005), the modern workplace has little of this. More obvious, perhaps is the mismatch of the sedentary, repetitive, and controlling modern work environment with the active, physically diverse, and flexible work life of our hunter-gatherer ancestors (Aronoff and Kaplan 1995). Our implicit models of effective leaders, as Judge and Hogan point out, also appear to be mismatched to our current environment. Some of the traits we associate with leaders—such as height and a masculine visage—seem more relevant to past conditions, when the strength, aggression, and physical formidability of a leader were more important to group survival than they are now.

Other common examples of mismatch in modern organizations include stress responses, decision cues, and aggregations of people. In the Pleistocene, stress responses were typically functional—they were acute responses to immediate threats, arming our physiology to take action by fighting or fleeing. In modern organizations stressors are typically chronic rather than acute, and the resulting chronic stress responses play a significant role in many of the physical and mental maladies common to employees of modern organizations. Mismatch in decision making can occur because we use eco-logic rather than pure logic: context and framing influence how people interpret and make decisions. How else could one explain the fact that intelligent, organizationally savvy, and experienced CEOs, generals, and politicians have love affairs with employees, when organizational policies typically prohibit such affairs and when, if discovered, such affairs prove ruinous for their careers?

The mismatch between the size of modern organizations and the size of the groups in which humans evolved is also striking. Large, modern corporations have thousands of employees who are dispersed geographically. Humans, however, evolved in small groups of no more than 150 people, where people were acquainted with each other, had regular face-to-face contact, and minimal interaction with outsiders (Dunbar 1993; 1998). Therefore, it is likely that human (intra-) group psychology is still primarily based on relatively close-knit associations. The resulting mismatch between the size of modern organizations and our evolved group psychology has implications for organizational communication, solidarity, identity, cooperation, and corruption.

CONCLUSION

At this point, OB and organizational studies are social sciences. Their concepts and theories have not strayed far from Durkheim's dictum of "social facts." Similarly, our interventions derive primarily from social sciences. As the chapters in this volume suggest, it is no longer far-fetched to believe that the field will witness a sea change. In the coming decades, biological and evolutionary mechanisms are likely to become part of the conceptual foundations of OB. How soon this happens depends on changing attitudes of organizational scholars toward incorporating biology into the discipline, increasing biologically based research in OB, and greater exposure of organizational scholars to biological and evolutionary interpretations of organizational phenomena. It is our hope that this book contributes to each of these factors.

Just as the twentieth century was the century of physics, the twenty-first century could be the century of biology. One of the most exciting areas of biology is the biology of social behavior. Although worthwhile results in this field were long considered a pipe dream, scientists now have solid theoretical frameworks, empirical studies, and tools to advance our knowledge of biological influences on social behavior, all improving at an accelerating pace. For both practical and scholarly reasons, we believe that OB can and should make better use of the biological and evolutionary psychological knowledge of social behavior. More than at any other time in human history, people are spending their working hours in organizations. We therefore need a better understanding of how biology influences behavior at work and how modern organizational life influences people's biology. The chapters in this book provide a point of departure for organizational scholars who are interested in these two broad questions.

Notes

1. Alfred Wallace, contemporaneous with Darwin, was the codiscoverer of evolution by natural selection.

2. Although Darwin understood that traits were passed on from parents to offspring through some biological mechanism of inheritance, he did not know what it was. In 1866, Mendel published his famous research on inheritance of color and texture in peas, in which he made the case that biological "particles" (later called "genes") were the means of transmission of traits from parents to offspring. Unfortunately, Darwin was not aware of Mendel's discovery. It was not until 1924 that British biologist J. B. S. Haldane (1924) saw the connection between Darwin's and Mendel's theories and realized that genes were the mechanisms responsible for the transmission and evolution of traits. The combination of these theories was called "the grand synthesis."

3. The articles appeared in *Administrative Science Quarterly, Academy of Management Journal, Academy of Management Review,* and *Journal of Applied Psychology.*

4. A deep understanding of the nature of gorillas enabled Penny Patterson to train Koko (a gorilla) to communicate with sign language; a deeper understanding of human nature has enabled engineers to design environments in which people can live and work in outer space and accounts for extraordinary advances in biotechnology (automatic insulin monitors and regulators) and electronic social networking.

5. Wang et al. (2013) recently found a sequence of genes that is responsible for the social behavior among fire ants.

6. This is not to say that human evolution stopped after the Pleistocene. For example, lactose tolerance in adults probably emerged about ten thousand years ago, after the invention of animal husbandry. However, much of our evolved psychology and physiology has remained the same.

References

Anderson, C., and Brown, C. E. 2010. The functions and dysfunctions of hierarchy. *Research in Organizational Behavior* 30:55–89.

Anthony, W. A., and Anthony, C. W. 2005. The napping company: Bring science to the workplace. *Industrial Health* 43 (1): 209–12.

Aronoff, S., and Kaplan, A. 1995. *Total workplace performance: Rethinking the office environment.* Ottawa, ON, Canada: WDL Publications.

Arvey, R. D., Rotundo, M., Johnson, W., Zhang, Z., and McGue, M. 2006. The determinants of leadership role occupancy: Genetic and personality factors. *Leadership Quarterly* 17 (1): 1–20.

Ashkanasy, N. M., Wilderom, C., and Peterson, M. F. W., eds. 2003. *Handbook of organizational culture and climate.* Thousand Oaks, CA: Sage, 365–69.

Bandura, A. 1997. *Self-efficacy in changing societies.* New York: Cambridge University Press.

Benkler, Y. 2011. The unselfish gene. *Harvard Business Review* 89 (7–8): 77–85.

Bettelheim, B., and Sylvester, E. 1950. Delinquency and morality. *Psychoanalytic Study of the Child* 5:329–42.

Boehm, C. 1999. *Hierarchy in the forest: The evolution of egalitarian behavior.* Cambridge, MA: Harvard University Press.

Boubekri, M., Hull, R. B., and Boyer, L. L. 1991. Impact of window size and sunlight penetration on office workers' mood and satisfaction: A novel way of assessing sunlight. *Environment and Behavior* 23 (4): 474–93.

Brookes, M. 2004. *Extreme measures: The dark visions and bright ideas of Francis Galton.* New York: Bloomsbury.

Cacioppo, J. T., Berntson, G. G., Sheridan, J. F., and McClintock, M. K. 2000. Multilevel integrative analyses of human behavior: Social neuroscience and the complementing nature of social and biological approaches. *Psychological Bulletin* 126 (6): 829–43.

Carroll, P. M., Dougherty, B., Ross-Macdonald, P., Browman, K., and FitzGerald, K. 2003. Model systems in drug discovery: Chemical genetics meets genomics. *Pharmacology and Therapeutics* 99 (2): 183–220.

Cavazotte, F., Moreno, V., and Hickmann, M. 2012. Effects of leader intelligence, personality and emotional intelligence on transformational leadership and managerial performance. *Leadership Quarterly,* 23 (3): 443–55.

Charney, D. S., and Nestler, E. J. 2004. *Neurobiology of mental illness.* New York: Oxford University Press.

Choo, C. W. 1998. *The knowing organization.* New York: Oxford.

Colarelli, S. M. , Spranger, J. L., and Hechanova, M. 2006. Women, power, and sex composition in small groups: An evolutionary perspective. *Journal of Organizational Behavior* 27 (2): 163–84.

———, and Dettman, J. R. 2003. Intuitive evolutionary perspectives in marketing. *Psychology and Marketing* 20 (9): 837–65.

Cole, M. S., and Bruch, H. 2006. Organizational identity strength, identification, and commitment and their relationships to turnover intention: Does organizational hierarchy matter? *Journal of Organizational Behavior* 27 (5): 585–605.

Crossan, M. M., Lane, H. W., White, R. E., and Djurfeldt, L. 1995. Organizational learning: Dimensions for a theory. *International Journal of Organizational Analysis* 3 (4): 337–60.

D'Argembeau, A., Stawarczyk, D., Majerus, S., Collette, F., Van der Linden, M., Feyers, D., and Salmon, E. 2010. The neural basis of personal goal processing when envisioning future events. *Journal of Cognitive Neuroscience* 22 (8): 1701–13.

Dawkins, R. 1999. *The extended phenotype: The long reach of the gene.* 2nd ed. Oxford: Oxford University Press. Orig. pub. 1982.

Dekkers, J. C. M., and Hospital, F. 2002. The use of molecular genetics in the improvement of agricultural populations. *Nature Review Genetics* 3 (1): 22–32.

De Neve, J., Mikhaylov, S., Dawes, C. T., Christakis, N. A., Fowler, J. H. 2013. Born to lead? A twin design and genetic association study of leadership role occupancy. *Leadership Quarterly* 24 (1): 45–60.

Dunbar, R. I. M. 1998. *Grooming, gossip, and the evolution of language*. Cambridge, MA: Harvard University Press.

———. 1993. Coevolution of neocortical size, group size and language in humans. *Behavioral and Brain Sciences* 16 (4): 681–735.

Durkheim, E. 1984. *The division of labor in society*. New York: Free Press. Orig. pub. 1893.

Eaves, L. J., Eysenck, H. J., and Martin, N. G. 1989. *Genes, culture and personality: An empirical approach*. San Diego, CA: Academic Press.

Etzioni, A. 1975. *A comparative analysis of complex organizations*. Rev. ed. New York: Free Press.

Feldman, D. C., and Bolino, M. C. 1999. The impact of on-site mentoring on expatriate socialization: A structural equation modeling approach. *International Journal of Human Resource Management* 10 (1): 54–71.

Fincham, J. M., Carter, C. S, van Veen, V., Stenger, A., and Anderson, J. R. 2002. Neural mechanisms of planning: A computational analysis using event-related fMRI. *PNAS* 99 (5): 3346–51.

Foley, R. 2005. The adaptive legacy of human evolution: A search for the environment of evolutionary adaptedness. *Evolutionary Anthropology: Issues, News, and Reviews* 4 (6): 194–203.

Fowler, M., and Mikota, S. 2006. *Biology, medicine, and surgery of elephants*. Ames, IA: Blackwell.

Gaines, K., Curry, Z., Shroyer, J., and Amor, C. 2010. Brain-compatible learning environments for students with autism spectrum disorders. *IDEC Proceedings*, 388–95. Available online at http://knowledgecenter.iida.org/AssetDetails.aspx?assetGuid=bb349aa4-082a-4b11-bf5d-8bb372c359e6

Ganster, D. C., and Rosen, C. C. 2013. Work stress and employee health: A multidisciplinary review. *Journal of Management* 39 (5): 1085–1122.

Geary, D. C. 1998. *Male/female*. Washington, DC: American Psychological Association Press.

Gilbert , C., Robertson, G., Le Maho, Y., Naito, Y., and Ancel, A. 2006. Huddling behavior in emperor penguins: Dynamics of huddling. *Physiology and Behavior* 88 (4–5): 479–88.

Gluckman, P., and Hanson, M. 2006. *Mismatch: Why our world no longer fits our bodies*. Oxford: Oxford University Press.

Green, R. 2002. *Apis mellifera, a.k.a. honeybee*. Boston, MA: Branden Books.

Hadany, L., Beker, T., Eshel, I., and Feldman, M. W. 2006. Why is stress so deadly? An evolutionary perspective. *Proceedings of the Royal Society B* 273:881–85.

Haldane, J. B. S. 1924. A mathematical theory of natural and artificial selection, part 1. *Transactions of the Cambridge philosophical society* 23 (2): 19–41.

Hamilton, W. 1987. Kinship, recognition, disease, and intelligence: Constraints of social evolution. In *Animal Societies: Theories and Facts*, ed. Y. Itô, J. L. Brown, and J. Kikkawa, 81–102. Tokyo: Japan Science Society Press.

Hannan, M. T., and Freeman, J. H. 1977. The population ecology of organizations, *American Journal of Sociology* 82 (5): 929–64.

Hoffmann, A. A., and Parsons, P. A. 1993. Direct and correlated responses to selection for desiccation resistance: A comparison of *Drosophila melanogaster* and *D. simulans*. *Journal of Evolutionary Biology* 6 (5): 643–57.

Holick, M. F. 2004. Sunlight and vitamin D for bone health and prevention of autoimmune diseases, cancers, and cardiovascular disease. *American Journal of Clinical Nutrition* 80 (6): 1678–88.

Howard, A., and Bray, D. W. 1990. Predictions of managerial success over long periods of time: Lessons from the Management Progress Study. In *Measures of leadership*, ed. K. E. Clark and M. B. Clark, 113–130. West Orange, NJ: Leadership Library of America.

Hutchinson, M. R., and Ireland, M. L. 1995. Knee injuries in female athletes. *Sports Medicine* 19 (14): 114–26.

Hyde, J. S. 2007. *Half the human experience: The psychology of women*. 7th ed. Boston, MA: Houghton Mifflin.

Judge, T. A., Piccolo, R. F., and Kosalka, T. 2009. The bright and dark sides of leader traits: A review and theoretical extension of the leader trait paradigm. *Leadership Quarterly* 20 (6): 855–75.

Kaplan, R. 1993. The role of nature in the context of the workplace. *Landscape and Urban Planning* 26 (October): 193–201.

Luthans, F. 1975. *Organizational behavior modification and beyond*. Upper Saddle River, NJ: Celebration Press.

MacDonald, K., and MacDonald, T. M. 2010. The peptide that binds: A systematic review of oxytocin and its prosocial effects in humans. *Harvard Review of Psychiatry* 18 (1): 1–21.

Markham, S. E. 2012. The evolution of organizations and leadership from the ancient world to modernity: A multilevel approach to organizational science and leadership (OSL). *Leadership Quarterly* 23 (6): 1134–51.

Meichenbaum, D. 1977. Cognitive-behavior modification: An integrative approach. New York: Plenum.

Meyer, J. P., and Allen, N. J. 1984. Testing the "side-bet theory" of organizational commitment: Some methodological considerations. *Journal of Applied Psychology* 69 (3): 372–78.

Michener, C. D. 1974. *The social behavior of the bees*. Cambridge, MA: Harvard University Press.

Miller, G. 2009. *Spent*. New York: Viking.

Miller, J. D., Scott, E. C., and Okamoto, S. 2006. Science communication: Public acceptance of evolution. *Science* 313:765–66.Morrow, E. M., Yoo, S., Flavell, S. W., Kim, T., Lin, Y., Hill, R., and Barry, B. 2009. Identifying autism loci and genes by tracing recent shared ancestry. *Science* 321:218–23.

Nicholson, N. 1998. Personality and entrepreneurial leadership: A study of the heads of the UK's most successful independent companies. *European Management Journal* 16 (5): 529–39.

———, and Shane, S. 2010. Entrepreneurship and occupational choice: Genetic and environmental influences. *Journal of Economic Behavior and Organization* 76 (1): 3–14.

Parish, A. R. 1994. Sex and food control in the "uncommon chimpanzee": How bonobo females overcome a phylogenetic legacy of male dominance. *Ethology and Sociobiology* 15 (3): 157–79.

Poole, J. H. 1994. Sex differences in the behavior of African elephants. In *The Differences between the Sexes*, ed. R. V. Short and E. Balaban, 331–46. Cambridge: Cambridge University Press.

Powell, G. N. 2010. *Women and men in management*. 4th ed. Los Angeles: Sage.

Price, T. D. 1995. Social inequality at the origins of agriculture. In *Foundations of social inequality*, ed. T. D. Price and G. M. Feinman, 129–51. New York: Plenum Press.

Richards, R. J. 1987. *Darwin and the emergence of evolutionary theories of mind and behavior*. Chicago: University of Chicago Press.

Richerson, P. J., Collins, D., and Genet, R. M. 2006. Why managers need an evolutionary theory of organizations. *Strategic Organization* 4 (2): 201–11.

Rilling, J. K. 2011. The neurobiology of cooperation and altruism. In *Origins of altruism and cooperation, developments in primatology: Progress and prospects*, ed. R. W. Sussman and C. R. Cloninger, 295–306. New York: Springer.

———, King-Casas, B., and Sanfey, A. G. 2008. The neurobiology of social decision-making. *Current Opinion in Neurobiology* 18 (2): 159–65. doi:10.1016/j.conb.2008 .06.003.

Rizzolatti, G., and Craighero, L. 2004. The mirror-neuron system. *Annual Review of Neuroscience* 27:169–92.

Salter, R. E., and Hudson, J. 1982. Social organization of feral horses in western Canada. *Applied Animal Ethology* 8 (3): 207–23.

Schein, E. H. 1985. Coming to a new awareness of organizational culture. *Sloan Management Review* 12 (2): 3–16.

Sewell, G. 2004. Yabba-dabba-doo! Evolutionary psychology and the rise of Flintstone psychological thinking in organization and management studies. *Human Relations* 57 (8): 923–55.

Singer, T., Seymour, B., O'Doherty, J., Kaube, H., Dolan, R. J., and Frith, C. D. 2004. Empathy for pain involves the affective but not sensory components of pain. *Science* 303:1157–62.

Smith, K. B., Oxley, D. R., Hibbing, M. V., Alford, J. R., and Hibbing, J. R. 2011. Linking genetics and political attitudes: Reconceptualizing political ideology. *Political Psychology* 32 (3): 369–97.

Strang, K. 2007. Examining effective technology project leadership traits and behaviors. *Computers in Human Behavior* 23 (1): 424–62.

Sutcliffe, J. S. 2009. Insights into the pathogenesis of autism. *Science* 321:208–9.

Tinbergen, N. 1963. On aims and methods in ethology. *Zeitschrift für Tierpsychologie* 20 (4): 410–33.

Tooby, J., and Cosmides, L. 1992. The psychological foundations of culture. In *The Adapted Mind: Evolutionary Psychology and the Generation of Culture*, ed. J. Barkow, L. Cosmides, and J. Tooby, 19–136. New York: Oxford University Press.

———, Cosmides, L., and Price, M. E. 2006. Cognitive adaptations for *n*-person exchange: The evolutionary roots of organizational behavior. *Managerial and Decision Economics* 27 (2–3): 103–29.

Van Vugt, M., Hogan, R., and Kaiser, R. B. 2008. Leadership, followership, and evolution: Some lessons from the past. *American Psychologist* 63 (3): 182–96.

Vischer, J. C. 2007.The effects of the physical environment on job performance: Towards a theoretical model of workspace stress. *Stress and Health* 23 (3): 175–84.

Wang, J., Wurm Y., Nipitwattanaphon, M., Riba-Grognuz, O., Huang, Y., Showmaker, D., and Keller, L. 2013. A Y-like social chromosome causes alternative colony organization in fire ants. *Nature* 493:664–68.

White, F. J., and Wood, K. D. 2007. Female feeding priority in bonobos, *Pan paniscus*, and the question of female dominance. *American Journal of Primatology* 69 (8): 837–50.

Wilson, E. O. 2012. *The social conquest of earth*. New York: Liveright.

Women and Sport Commission. 2012. Olympic.org: Official website of the Olympic Movement. Retrieved from http://www.olympic.org/women-sport-commission.

TWO

Progress in Molecular Genetics and Its Potential Implications in Organizational Behavior Research

Zhaoli Song, Wendong Li, and Nan Wang

Virtually all human behavioral traits are heritable, which means that traits are genetically transmitted from parents to offspring. Although it sounds bold, decades of empirical research in the social sciences have accumulated abundant evidence largely supporting this claim (Turkheimer 2000; Turkheimer and Gottesman 1991). Organizational behaviors are no exception. We have reached a general consensus, mainly through studies involving twins, that work-related behaviors and experiences are partially influenced by genetic factors. For instance, the heritability of job satisfaction is estimated to be about 30% (Arvey et al. 1989; Arvey, et al. 1994). Genetic factors are also estimated to explain, on average, 36% of the variance in vocational interests (e.g., Bouchard 2004) and about 30% of the variance in work values (Keller et al. 1992). These figures mean that a certain portion of variance of the trait difference among individuals can be explained by their genetic compositions. The rest of the variance then can be attributed to environmental factors.

The major material foundation of inheritance of living organisms is deoxyribonucleic acid (DNA), which contains genetic instructions to produce specific proteins. In recent years, with the successes of the Human Genome Project and subsequent HapMap projects, which developed a haplotype map of the human genome for investigations of genes associated with human disease and response to pharmaceuticals, we have obtained the full sequence of the human genome. This knowledge has led to an unprecedented succession of discoveries in the genomics of complex traits, including leukemia, obesity, type 2 diabetes, prostate cancer, and breast cancer, to name a few (Guo 2008). Individuals differ not only in genetic susceptibilities to diseases, but also in genetic propensities for other psychological traits and work-related behaviors. After they published a series of pioneering studies on heredity of job satisfaction and work values, Arvey and Bouchard hopefully suggested that "perhaps certain genes or constellations of genes will be identified as being associated with such phenotypic variables such as IQ, personality, and even job satisfaction" (Arvey and Bouchard 1994, 75). Indeed, just two years after the publication of their review, breakthroughs in molecular genetics research on personality appeared in *Nature* and *Science* (e.g., Benjamin et al. 1996; Cloninger, Adolfsson, and Svrakic 1996; Ebstein et al. 1996; Lesch et al. 1996). Since then, hundreds of studies have examined relationships between genes and psychological traits, such as personality, temperament, and cognitive ability (Bouchard and McGue 2003; Ebstein et al. 2010).

We have gained great insights into human behaviors by linking molecular genetics with social-science approaches. These insights and how they have been arrived at, although mainly based on basic research in areas such as human genomics and biological psychology, have important implications for management scholars. We intend this chapter to serve as a primer on molecular genetics approaches to organizational behavior (OB) research. We first introduce some basic concepts and approaches in molecular genetics. Then we discuss some conceptual issues and tentatively propose a model to link genes with work behaviors. We also review findings on the relationship between genes and some psychosocial variables that are most relevant to work behaviors. In the last section, we suggest several future research directions.

AN INTRODUCTION TO BASIC CONCEPTS OF GENETICS

What Is DNA?

The structure of the material foundation of inheritance, DNA, was proposed to be a double helix by James D. Watson and Francis Crick in 1953. Since then, modern genetics has advanced dramatically. We now know that DNA is organized and contained in chromosomes. The human genome consists of one pair of sex chromosomes and twenty-two pairs of other chromosomes, or "autosomes." DNA can be divided into discrete functional regions called *genes* that contain instructions to produce specific proteins. DNA exists as a pair of long polymers in the shape of a double helix that are made from repeating units of four types of nucleotides:

adenine (abbreviated as A), cytosine (C), guanine (G), and thymine (T). The two strands of the DNA double helix are connected to each other by chemical pairing of complementary bases: Adenine (A) always pairs with thymine (T), and guanine (G) always pairs with cytosine (C). Because of this complementary base-pairing structure, one strand of DNA can act as a template for the production of a complementary strand. The continuous synthesis of DNA strands allows genetic information to be copied into new cells within the live organism and passed on to new generations. The combination of these four nucleotides in DNA includes coding instructions to produce proteins that are essential parts of organisms. The heredity that resides in replicable DNA codes ensures the functional stability of organisms and species.

Genetic Variants

Humans have three billion nucleotide base pairs, and 99.9% of them are exactly the same in all individuals. The remaining 0.1%, or three million human nucleotide bases are called *single-nucleotide polymorphism* (SNP) markers, which are vital in determining differences among individuals. In addition to SNPs, there are other structural differences in DNA that can be functional, including the insertion/deletion of particular portions of the DNA sequence (those insertion/deletion variations ranging from one thousand bases to several megabases are often called *copy number variation*, or CNV), a variable number of tandem repeats (VNTR, also called *microsatellite*), and small tandem repeats (STR, also called *minisatellite*). A VNTR or STR is a polymorphism marker that consists of various repeated sequences (10–200 bases of repeating units for a VNTR and 2–5 bases of repeating units for an STR), that vary from one individual to another. Tens of thousands of human VNTR or STR markers have been identified. The different forms of these genetic structures are called *alleles*. A combination of alleles at different places (*loci*) that are transmitted together is called a *haplotype*. The specific allele makeup of an individual is called a *genotype*, while the observed traits are called *phenotype*. One of the primary assumptions of genetic analysis is that there is a unidirectional causal relationship between these two: the genotype of a person influences or determines his or her phenotype, not vice versa. Most genetic studies aim to identify a corresponding genotype with a given phenotype. The relationship between genotypes and phenotypes is most likely not simply one-to-one. Although some phenotypes involve only a single gene, such as Huntington's disease (HD) and phenylketonuria (PKU), most phenotypes involve multiple genes. Most psychological traits, such as personality and cognitive ability, are polygenetic phenotypes. Pheno-types that vary in degree and can be attributed to polygenetic effects are called *quantitative traits*. In the eyes of genetic researchers, most variables studied in the OB area, such as personality, job satisfaction, and leadership, are quantitative traits.

Genotyping Methods

Given the potential importance of genetics in determining phenotypes that we are interested in, OB research can benefit from knowing the genotypes of research participants. There are multiple genotyping methods that can determine the DNA sequence or types. The most often-used methods include polymerase chain reaction (PCR), allele-specific oligonucleotide (ASO) probes, microarray, and DNA sequencing. PCR is a widely used biological method to amplify a section of DNA and generate thousands to millions of copies of it. PCR often is used with ASO probes, which are short pieces of synthetic DNA complementary to the sequence of target DNA sections, to test for the presence of a mutation in a DNA sample. A DNA microarray comprises tens of thousands of microscopic spots of probes. Microarrays are also called *gene chips* because their appearance resembles microtransistor chips. Microarrays can be used to type up to a million SNPs of a human genome in one round. DNA sequencing includes a variety of methods that can determine the actual sequence of all base pairs of a section of DNA or even the whole genome. Genotyping is a rapidly evolving technical area that has been providing faster, cheaper, and more comprehensive analysis of genes. It is expected that with the advancement of genotyping technology, we will soon be able to conduct the whole genome sequencing of all three billion base pairs of a human being at an affordable price for most people. Such technology will profoundly influence our ways of living in the near future.

Human Genetic Studies

Human genetic studies aim to identify genetic variants that are important in shaping phenotypes. In general, they can be divided into two categories: linkage studies and association studies. Linkage analysis aims to find out the rough location of the target gene that is related to a phenotype, in a region between 1 and 5 million base pairs in length, relative to another genetic marker whose position is already known. Linkage analysis was the most commonly used method to search for genes until very recently, but it is much less common now, partially because it lacks precision. Instead, most contemporary genetic studies that try to establish relationships between genetic variants and human traits use association analysis. Association studies are conducted to determine whether a genetic variant is associated with a disease or trait. Association is present when a particular allele, genotype, or haplotype of a polymorphism or polymorphisms appears together with an observable trait in a person more often than we would expect by chance. The association method has been used recently to conduct a genome-wide analysis of up to one million SNPs to identify novel SNPs in the whole human genome that are associated with a certain disease or trait. This method is called the genome-wide association study (GWA study/studies, or GWAS). It is particularly suited to hunting for novel genes that may be relevant to a trait or disease, because it can examine up to one million SNPs across the human genome at the same time. Breakthroughs have been made with GWAS of many diseases, such as diabetes, cancer, and bipolar disorder. However, limited progress has been made on identifying novel genes with GWAS for psychological traits, such as IQ and personality (Davis et al. 2010; Terracciano et al. 2010; Verweij et al. 2010).

POTENTIAL PATHWAYS THROUGH WHICH GENETICS MAY INFLUENCE WORK-RELATED OUTCOMES

How would genes shape our work-related behaviors and attitudes? This is a complicated issue, because it is impossible for genes to have direct effects on work-related outcomes. Genetic influence must be mediated by multiple pathways, such as physiological and psychological mechanisms. Generally speaking, there are multiple pathways through which genes can shape human behaviors and attitudes. Arvey and Bouchard (1994) have provided a generic framework articulating the potential pathways (see fig. 2.1). Drawing from this framework and recent work from molecular genetic research, we present a model diagram of the unfolding process of genetic influence on work-related outcomes.

In essence, genetic variables may shape work-related outcomes through at least three phases by modulating protein formation in the biochemical processes (e.g., hormones), physiological traits and functions (e.g., height, weight, brain structure and function), and psychological traits and functions (e.g., general mental abilities, personality, interests, and values). Genetic variables could be variations in the number

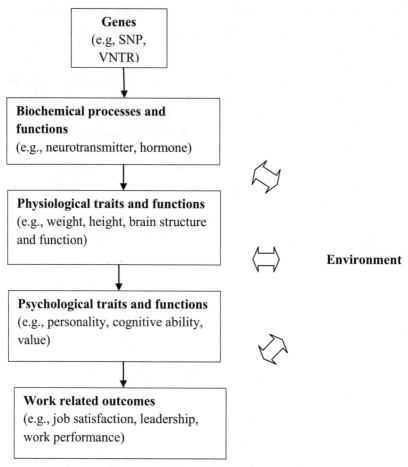

Fig. 2.1 Pathways from genes to work-related outcomes

of a specific allele located at one DNA polymorphism or several DNAs of the same region, or CNVs, to name a few. Work-related outcomes would incorporate such variables as leadership, work attitudes and affect (e.g., job satisfaction), entrepreneurship, job performance, health/well-being, job/occupational choice, job characteristics, career success, socialization, and work environment (e.g., organizational climate and culture). Simply put, genetic variations are likely to drive individual differences in protein formation, which in turn trigger divergent biochemical and physiological processes and brain functions. The different biochemical and physiological processes and brain functions then would yield individual differences in psychological traits, which would impact work-related outcomes. The last process (from psychological traits to work-related outcomes) has been mostly studied in industrial organizational (IO) psychology and OB. The previous three processes (from genetic variables to psychological traits) are relatively understudied or under-represented in the OB literature.

Bear in mind that during all the possible processes, environmental influence can kick in and play an essential role, so that gene-environment interaction may figure in. Moreover, behavioral outcomes under genetic influences may further serve as environmental influences that modulate genetic impacts (Freese 2008). For example, work-related outcomes (e.g., selection into a more or less stressful position), though they may subject to genetic influence, can also be taken as environmental variables to further investigate gene and environment interaction (e.g., well-being at work in the selected work environment for people with different genotypes). In this sense, there may exist a dynamic process through which genetic factors influence work-related outcomes.

Gene and Environment Interplays

These processes present one perspective that can enrich our understanding of how genetic factors influence work-related outcomes. *Gene and environment* interplay (GE interplay; Plomin, DeFries, and Loehlin 1977) is a generic term and covers a broad range of concepts that can be subsumed under GE correlation and GE interaction. GE correlation occurs when there is congruence between an individual's genetic makeup and her environment. According to Plomin and colleagues (1977), there are three types of GE correlations: passive, reactive, and active. Passive GE correlation arises when there is an association between children's family environment and their genetic architecture, which are both conferred by their parents. Reactive GE correlation refers to the fact that an individual is treated differently from other individuals due to his genetic makeup. For instance, leaders are likely to treat employees with high levels of competence well, resulting in a positive correlation between employees' competence and leader-member relationship (Gerstner and Day 1997). Active GE correlation occurs as a result of an individual actively seeking or building an environment compatible with his genetic propensities. For instance, people with high levels of proactive personality are likely to proactively shape their work environment, resulting in a high level of job control and an active relationship with their supervisor (Fuller and Marler 2009). GE correlation maps onto several theories in OB on the fit or match between the person and the environment, such as person-environment fit (Kristof-Brown and Guay 2010), occupational choice (Holland 1997), and the gravitational hypothesis of abilities (McCormick, Jeanneret, and Mecham 1972).

GE interaction means that genetic influence on work-related outcomes, for instance, is contingent upon environmental factors; that is, the same environmental variables may have different effects on work-related outcomes, depending on an individual's genetic makeup. In the multiple pathways from genes to work-related outcomes, GE interaction may occur in a number of processes. For instance, environmental factors may influence gene expression (i.e., the correlation between genes and protein formation). An emerging stream of research on epigenetics mainly centers on the issue of what environmental factors may "switch off" the genetic influence on outcomes (Meaney 2010). Neurofeedback training has been reported to influence brain function (e.g., Egner and Gruzelier 2003); thus, by extension, it is possible that neurofeedback may moderate the effect of genes on brain functions and even performance. Interaction between psychological traits and the environment has been the focus of several areas of research in OB, such as situational strength (Meyer, Dalal, and Hermida 2010) and trait-activation (Tett and Burnett 2003), to name a few.

Molecular Genetics Studies of Psychosocial Variables

In this section, we review existing literature that links molecular genetics and psychosocial variables. Particularly, we select studies on personality, social attitudes, and cognitive ability. We chose to focus on these three aspects for two reasons. First, OB researchers are particularly interested in individual behaviors and the motivations behind them. Second, genetics can influence individual behaviors only through the body (Freese 2008), through either physical or psychological pathways, or both. Moreover, variables from these three pathways have been well incorporated into the OB area (e.g., Fiedler 1986; Judge et al. 2008).

Personality is a fundamental concept that refers to "the individual psychological aspects of people that make them 'recognizable'" (Ebstein and Israel 2009). It is of mutual interest in both OB and behavioral genetic research. Personalities are important antecedents of individual differences in various organizational attitudes and behaviors (e.g., Judge, Heller, and Mount 2002; Organ 1994; Weiss and Adler 1984). To illuminate the genetic basis of personality, the properties of relative stability and reported heritability (Floderus-Myrhed, Pedersen, and Rasmuson, 1980; Jang, Livesley, and Vemon, 1996) suggest significant genetic bases.

In fact, this line of research has become the recognizable scientific field of personality genetics, which is driven not only by twin studies, but also by molecular genetics (Ebstein, 2006) and evolutionary perspectives (e.g., Verweij et al. 2010).

In OB research, a wide range of focused behaviors, such as leadership and teamwork, are all pertinent to social interactions (Entin and Serfaty 1999; Wayne, Shore, and Liden 1997). Social attitudes are inherent motivational "directors" that guide individuals' behaviors and responses regarding social interactions (e.g., Triandis 1964). Moreover, some social attitudes could be reflective of certain personalities in terms of social interactions (e.g., Wilson and Brazendale 1973).

General cognitive ability, also known as IQ (intelligence quotient) or the general factor, g, has remarkable psychological credentials as a successful predictor of educational achievement, occupational success, or even longevity and many aspects of illness and health behaviors (Deary 2008; Strenze 2007). At the same time, cognitive ability is one of the most heritable dimensions of psychological traits (Plomin and Neiderhiser 1992), making the question of its biological origins an attractive one.

The Molecular Genetics of Personality

Personality measures are developed in different ways, and can therefore reflect the molecular gene's influence in different ways. According to Ebstein and Israel (2009), a practical theory of personality should include a set of manageable dimensions that relate to universal and fundamental aspects of personality and account for most of the variance. In genetic studies, either pencil-and-paper questionnaires or direct laboratory observations are used to evaluate personality. In their review, Ebstein and Israel also note that the dimensions in the pencil-and-paper measurements of personality are usually developed in three ways. One is the approach based on psychopathology, where the personality traits are derived from psychiatric illnesses. That is, a particular behavioral abnormality is observed, and an explanation is sought in patterns of responses to a set of questions, in terms of how those who are abnormal respond differently from those who are normal. Such measurement takes the perspective that psychiatric illnesses represent the extreme variants of normal personalities. An example is the Minnesota Multiphasic Personality Inventory (Butcher 2001), although this measure is not as widely applied in genetic research as in popular discourse.

The "everyday speech" method measures personality through descriptions of daily expression. Thousands of descriptors from everyday language are listed and then reduced to a few dimensions through factor analysis. The most popular example of this approach is the NEO Personality Inventory (Costa and McCrae, 1997). It includes five dimensions of personality (known as the "Big Five"): neuroticism, extraversion, openness to experience, agreeableness and conscientiousness.

The third method is the theoretical approach. This approach develops personality dimensions based on biological models, which are built upon empirical animal and human findings regarding the association between personality dimensions and neurological system functions. Cloninger's Tridimensional Personality Questionnaire (TPQ) (Cloninger 1986) is an example of this approach. The traits measured in the TPQ include novelty-seeking, harm avoidance, and reward dependence (Cloninger, Przybeck, and Švraki 1991). They are hypothesized to be based on neurochemical and genetic influences. For example, dopaminergic (DA) pathways are implicated in drug use, curiosity, sensation-seeking and explorative behaviors, and these features correspond to novelty-seeking in the TPQ. Individuals with a high level of novelty-seeking are risk-takers and impulsive. Serotonin has been tied to harm avoidance and escape from punishment. Lower levels of serotonin result in high harm avoidance, or a "neurotic" personality. Noradrenaline is implicated in reward dependence. Individuals high in harm avoidance are more sentimental and affectionate; people with low reward dependence are more tough and pragmatic. All these personality factors reflect certain degrees of heritable biases, and some traits in the TPQ and the NEO correspond to each other. For example, harm avoidance correlates with neuroticism, while novelty-seeking correlates with extraversion. This provides some evidence for the cross-validation of each measure in terms of its ability to capture fundamental human personalities. The second and third approaches are relatively more popular in molecular genetic studies of personality. The current developments of molecular genetics in relation to personality sprout from several remarkable studies. Ebstein et al. (1996) found a significant association between novelty-seeking and the dopamine receptor gene DRD4 (or D4DR). Such a finding corresponds to Cloninger's earlier argument that individual variance in novelty-seeking was likely to be associated with genetic variation in dopamine transmissions (Cloninger, Svrakic, and Przybeck 1993). In the other study, Benjamin and colleagues found an association between the Big Five factor extraversion and the dopamine receptor gene DRD4 (Benjamin et al. 1996). These studies were quickly followed by another finding by Lesch et al. (1996) that showed an association between another Big Five factor, neuroticism, and the serotonin transporter genetic marker 5-HTTLPR. The nice fit of these findings to previous assumptions has attracted a large school of curious researchers.

Despite earlier success, methodological issues became a major concern in later studies. People began to notice that replications of the earlier findings were not as consistent as expected. Meta-analyses of the following studies regarding the relationship between DRD4 and novelty-seeking/extraversion and the relationship between the serotonin transporter and neuroticism/harm avoidance showed no strong evidence (e.g., Munafo et al. 2003; Sen et al. 2004; Willis-Owen et al. 2005). Some researchers have proposed that the inconsistency of results could be due to excessive dependence on self-reported measures (Ebstein 2006; Munafo et al. 2003). They argue that self-report questionnaires can be psychologically robust but are not powerful enough to capture the small effects of single genes. Instead, measurements of lower-level expressions of individual psychological traits, such as the imaging of brain functioning, neurological activity patterns, and observed behaviors, may be more informative in illustrating the inherent relationship between molecular genes and personality.

Encouraging findings from neuroimaging studies provide support to such lower-level measurements. For example, mice with their serotonin transporter genes knocked out show increased anxiety (Murphy et al. 2001), consistent with the findings in human studies. Genetically altered mice with the DRD4 gene knocked out reduce their response to novel environments and become more responsive to the effects of alcohol and cocaine in locomotor activities (Rubinstein et al. 1997). Functional magnetic resonance imaging (fMRI) studies have shown that the short allele in the serotonin transporter gene is associated with increased activity of the amygdala (part of the brain involved in detection of threats and emotional regulation) under threatening stimuli (such as fearful faces) (Hariri et al. 2002). These findings support the role of genes as a biological basis of personality, despite the prevalent failures of the pencil-and-paper method. We do not encourage researchers to abandon the pencil-and-paper method, given its robustness and considerable impact in personality studies. Rather, we suggest that researchers be more open-mined and creative in terms of selecting the proper measures—for example, the repeated diary measures (Gunthert, et al. 2007).

Dopamine receptor gene DRD4 and serotonin transporter gene 5-HTTLPR polymorphisms have been the focus in the development of personality genetics. At the same time, researchers are also engaged in identifying more genes that are related to personality. In the serotonin system, two other genes have been studied in relation to personality, namely the serotonin receptor 2A (5-HT2A) and the serotonin receptor 2C (5-HT2C). The studies failed to associate 5-HT2A with the dimension of harm avoidance (e.g., Blairy et al. 2000). However, Ebstein and colleagues (1997) found that for individuals who had the long version of the D4DR exon III repeat polymorphism, the effect of the 5-HT2C polymorphism on the personality trait of reward dependence was accentuated remarkably. Reward dependence, as referred to in the TPQ, is the tendency to respond intensely to reward and succorance and to learn to maintain rewarded behavior (Cloninger 1986), especially behaviors rewarded by social cues such as social support and approval. Low reward dependence is exhibited by programmatic and detached tough-mindedness. This result has been successfully replicated (Kühn et al. 1999).

Two groups applying GWAS to look for specific genes associated with Big Five personality traits and personalities from the Temperament and Character Inventory (TCI, an outgrowth of the TPQ) respectively (Terracciano et al. 2010; Verweij et al. 2010) have failed to find significant results. However, by bundling single-nucleotide polymorphisms (SNPs) in groups instead of focusing on single SNPs, McCrae and his colleagues (2010) reanalyzed the data from the GWAS of Terracciano et al. and found significant associations between certain groups of SNPs and Big Five personality dimensions, with successful replication.

Molecular Genetics and Cognitive Ability

Studies have shown that the heritability of human intelligence ranges from 30% to 80% (Deary, Johnson, and Houlihan 2009). There are two key findings in this area (Plomin and Spinath 2004). One is that the heritability of intelligence increases through the life span; genes account for more variations in intelligence level for older individuals, other things being equal. A possible explanation of the increasing heritability through the life span is that genetic effects may unfold over time and manifest themselves through GE interactions. The second important finding is that specific genes may not only account for a specific ability but may also be responsible for a range of different abilities. Despite the interest in identifying specific genes related to cognitive ability, molecular genetic studies have made little progress in providing consistent findings. Many specific genes are examined because of the primary interest in their associations with mental retardation or other brain disorders, and it has been found that among approximately three hundred identified genes associated with mental retardation, about 20% are located in the X chromosome (Ropers and Hamel 2005).

The limited progress in finding associations between particular genes and cognitive ability in normal samples may result from the small effect size of single genes. Especially for the complex construct of cognitive ability, multiple genes and numerous environmental factors are likely to be influential. Researchers used to deal with this problem by studying the quantitative trait locus (QTL), where genes in the multiple gene systems are considered to result in quantitative continua rather than qualitative dichotomies (Plomin and Spinath 2004). The systems are considered to influence cognitive ability through the combined action of many genes, possibly several on each chromosome. In their study of the distribution of QTL among groups of children with high and average cognitive abilities, Chorney and colleagues (1998) found unique genetic distributions in the high cognitive ability group. Fisher et al. (1999) found that significant QTL associations emerge on chromosome 4.

Nonetheless, QTL assumes the additive effects of alleles, where the functional genes are considered relatively independent in their effects. Recent interest in non-additive genetic effects and epistasis in genetic personality studies aims to challenge such assumptions. *Epistasis* refers to the interaction between genes, where the effect of a certain gene depends on the genotype of a second gene. Thus, the phenotype of a certain genotype cannot be predicted by the sum of the single-locus genetic effects only. As an example of epistasis, Sen et al. (2004) have found that the association between 5-HTTLPR and neuroticism depends on the genotype of a polymorphism named GABA(A). Interested readers are referred to Ebstein and Israel (2009) for more relevant examples.

Molecular Genetics and Social Attitudes

Oxytocin and vasopressin are two kinds of peptide hormones considered to regulate a range of complex social behaviors. Different levels of these hormones in the brain can lead to different brain activities and subsequent perceptions and reactions to social settings. Kosfeld et al. (2005) have shown oxytocin to be part of the biological basis of trust among humans; thus it plays an important role in social attachment and affiliation. They found that intranasal administration of oxytocin causes a substantial increase in trust. In particular, oxytocin has no effect on a general increase in the readiness to bear risks, but specifically affects the willingness to bear social risks through interpersonal interactions. At the molecular level, recent findings have shown that the 1a receptor gene in the promoter region of vasopressin (AVPR1a) is associated with sibling relationships and autism (Bachner-Melman et al. 2005; Kim et al. 2002).

Some recent association studies have also successfully linked prosocial behaviors with the oxytocin receptor gene (OXTR) and AVPR1a (e.g., Israel et al. 2009). A more recent study also found that the COMT val158Met, a polymorphism involved in the dopaminergic system, played a positive role in altruism (Reuter et al. 2010).

Genes have also been identified in many other important areas. For example, genes can influence one's social experience, such as popularity and network composition; they can also influence one's political attitudes and decision making styles. Burt (2009) showed that the genetic variants in serotonin receptor gene 5-HT2A are associated with different behavioral tendencies for rule-breaking, which has been found to contribute to increased popularity among peers of late-adolescent boys. Interesting studies by Fowler and his colleagues revealed that there are correlated genotypes in networks. For example, in the friendship network, DRD2 exhibits significant homophily and CYP2A6 exhibits significant heterophily (Fowler, Settle, and Christakis 2011). Genes have also been associated with political attitudes. One interesting study found that the 7R variant of the dopamine receptor D4 gene (DRD4) may influence one's political ideology, moderated by the number of friendships one has in adolescence (Settle et al. 2010). Specifically, Settle et al. found that the number of friends one has had in adolescence is significantly associated with liberal political ideology. There is no such association among those without the gene variant. The argument is that friendship offers a psychological context for social belonging, and more friends offer a greater diversity of viewpoints; these contexts together support the expression of the novelty-seeking tendency associated with the dopamine gene and lead an individual to be more open to new experiences, more likely to form a liberal political ideology. The risk-taking tendency in decision making is another hot topic in genetic studies, since decision making is a commonly encountered task with increased importance under risk and uncertainty. A recent study indicates that the genetic variation in the serotonin transporter gene (5-HTTLPR) may mediate bias in decision making (Roiser et al. 2009). The genotypes with double short alleles are associated with heightened amygdala reactivity and lack of prefrontal regulatory control, which in turn relate to one's susceptibility to context and risk in decision making. In particular, they found that individuals with short versions of the serotonin transporter gene are more susceptible to the "framing-effect"; that is, they exhibit a strong bias toward choosing the certain option when the decision is phrased in terms of gains and toward choosing more risky options when the decision is phrased in terms of losses, even though the difference is only in the manner of framing rather than in the expected results. Kuhnen and Chiao (2009) found that the 5-HTTLPR s/s allele carriers took 28% less risk than those carrying the s/l or l/l alleles of the gene, while DRD4 7-repeat allele carriers took 25% more risk than individuals without the 7-repeat allele. Additionally, risk-taking and impulsivity seem to share some genetic influences with drug or alcohol addiction. Risk-taking is characterized by behaviors conducted under uncertainty that have the potential to be harmful or dangerous. Impulsivity is characterized by behavioral disinhibition, with sudden actions conducted in an unplanned manner to satisfy a desire. Both risk-taking and impulsivity have some association with dopaminergic and serotoninergic genes that account for a propensity to addiction. Interested readers are referred to a comprehensive review by Kreek et al. (2005).

Genes and the Environment

The important perspective of GE interaction has been emphasized by the work of Caspi and his colleagues (2003), which shows that the influence of environmental effects depends on the genotypes of individuals. For example, they found that the short allele of the serotonin transporter gene (5-HTTLPR) did not show a higher level of association with the onset of depression than the long allele, unless the subjects had experienced major stressful life events. Another study found that a more hostile childhood environment (strict discipline, emotional distance, low tolerance of a child's normal activity) may lead to a higher risk for novelty-seeking in people with D4.2 or D4.5 alleles in the DRD4 gene, while those without such genes but with similar environmental precursors did not differ from their counterparts of other genotypes in manifesting such behavior (Keltikangas-Järvinen et al. 2003). Gene-environment correlations show that a strict separation between "nature" and "nurture" is untenable.

POSSIBLE AVENUES USING A MOLECULAR GENETICS
APPROACH IN ORGANIZATIONAL BEHAVIOR RESEARCH

The complex nature of the potential pathways from genes to work-related outcomes allows for ample ways in which molecular genetic thinking may contribute to OB research. Below we outline a few avenues that we believe may be fruitful in future research. Since very little work has been done in applying the molecular genetic approach in OB research, we refer mainly to findings from more basic research for possible explanations linking genetics to work-related outcomes.

Identifying Associations between Work-Related Outcomes and Particular Genes

Associating specific genes with work-related outcomes might be the easiest way, or the first step, in OB research using molecular genetics approaches. One prerequisite for studies of this kind is that there should be substantial heritability in the work-related outcome of interest. Behavioral genetics research generally supports the notion that almost all human traits are heritable (Turkheimer 2000; Turkheimer and Gottesman 1991), thus encouraging further exploration of specific genes that may be responsible for heritability. Many genetic approaches are available in the toolkit for researchers to select, such as "candidate gene approach," GWAS, and CNV, to name a few. Using molecular genetic information obtained with these methods, OB researchers can examine the associations between genetic variants and targeted work-related outcomes. For instance, one of our studies found significant correlations between two genes, dopamine receptor DRD4 and serotonin transporter gene 5-HTTLPR, and job satisfaction (Song, Li, and Arvey 2011).

Behavioral genetics research has found that some constructs of similar nature share the same genetic influences. For instance, different types of cognitive abilities and disabilities are reported to share generalist genes (Plomin and Kovas 2005). In the OB area, researchers also found that different constructs of leadership (e.g., transformational leadership and leadership role occupancy) share the same genetic influence (Li et al. 2012). It would be interesting in future research to search for such generalist genes associated with constructs of similar nature.

Gene-Environment Correlation

Studying GE correlation is conducted essentially to test mediating mechanisms by which genes may affect work-related outcomes. Research of this kind can shed light on two lines of inquiry. First, it can enhance our understanding of the underlying mechanisms through which genes may modulate work-related outcomes. For instance, based on the findings that genetic factors are associated with characteristics of social networks (Fowler, Dawes, and Christakis, 2009), it is conceivable that social networks may be the conduit for genetic influence on work-related outcomes. Second, and perhaps more importantly, inquiry of this kind can help confirm a causal relationship between two variables that are assumed to have a causal relationship. For instance, job characteristics such as job demands, job control, and work-social support are regarded as exogenous influences from work and organization, which affect job attitudes and behaviors (Hackman and Oldham 1980). However, recent research suggests that the characteristics of a job that one is likely to hold are partially heritable (Li and Arvey 2010), thus casting doubt on the assumed causal relationship between job characteristics and job satisfaction, for instance. This is because job satisfaction is also partially heritable (Arvey et al. 1989); thus the relationship between job characteristics and job satisfaction may be accounted for by overlapping genetic factors. The true environmental effects in the relationship between job characteristics and work-related outcomes may be established after partialling out genetic influences.

Gene-Environment Interaction

The existence of GE interaction may diminish the chance of observing the main effect of genes. GE interaction has been receiving more and more research attention in recent molecular genetics research, for instance, on antisocial behavior (Caspi et al. 2002), support-seeking (Kim et al. 2010), and political attitudes (Settle et al. 2010). Although there have been few endeavors in the OB area, GE interaction seems to be a fruitful route to take. Drawing from previous research in other areas (e.g., Moffitt, Caspi, and Rutter 2006), we suggest a few strategies for researchers interested in conducting such research in the OB area.

A first step would be to consult behavioral genetics studies on the heritability of and possible GE interactions on work-related outcomes. For instance, previous research found that heritability of being an entrepreneur and a leader depends upon family environment (Zhang and Ilies 2010; Zhang, Ilies, and Arvey 2009). This line of research has laid the foundation for future studies in identifying interactions of specific DNA polymorphisms and environmental variables on leadership and entrepreneurship.

A second step would be to identify candidate genes and environmental factors that are empirically or theoretically associated with work-related outcomes of interest. Current molecular genetics research has uncovered several candidate genes that might be relevant for OB researchers. For instance, dopamine receptor genes have been shown to be related to human behavioral traits. With respect to environmental factors, OB researchers have examined numerous variables that tend to prompt or inhibit work-related outcomes, such as social relationship within organizations, leadership, job design, human resource practices, and so forth. A careful match between specific genes and environmental factors is essential in this step. It is noteworthy that experimental designs appear suitable for testing such interactions between specific genes and environmental factors, given their sophisticated methodology in manipulating environmental influence.

An ensuing third step would be to put the interaction between specific genes and environmental factors to an empirical test. Large sample sizes are necessary in order to have sufficient statistical power to detect significant interactions. If significant GE interactions are observed, researchers can further examine whether the results can be replicated in other samples and with other genes or environmental variables. If primary studies can be accumulated, then a meta-analytic synthesis would solidify research findings. Obviously, multidisciplinary collaborations are needed to pursue such aims with GE interactions.

Gene-Environment Correlation and Interaction on Human Development in Longitudinal Studies

Recently, much research has been devoted in longitudinal studies to determine how genes and the environment interdependently shape human development. For instance, our research team examined the association between one SNP (rs1438A/G) on the HTR2A gene and momentary job satisfaction in an experience-sampling study (Wang and Song 2010). We collected DNA samples from blood from more than one hundred Chinese couples living in Singapore and rates of momentary job satisfaction through their cell phones four times a day for seven days. We found that this particular SNP was significantly related to their reported momentary job satisfaction, and this genetic variation also moderated the relationship of momentary job satisfaction with momentary and major life stressors. As exemplified in this study, we believe introducing a temporal framework can greatly enhance the likelihood of observing GE correlations and interactions. Previous research has found that self-esteem facilitates leadership role occupancy and leadership advancement (i.e., trajectory) in terms of leaders' supervisory scope (Li, Song, and Arvey 2011). Thus it might be interesting to examine whether specific DNA polymorphisms may shape leader advancement through individual traits and developmental experience, or whether work experience might moderate the impact of genes on leader development. More complicated models (e.g., mediated moderation and moderated mediation) can also be adopted to unravel how GE interplay modulates work-related outcomes dynamically.

Individuals' genetic makeup is a fundamental individual-difference variable that has its root in biological materials developed through human evolution. The molecular genetics approach opens up a number of new opportunities for OB research on the interdependence between the person and the environment. We believe that findings from psychological studies linking genetics with psychological traits such as personality, cognitive ability, and attitudes will serve as a stepping-stone for connecting genes with work-related outcomes. Such empirical studies have appeared in the literature more recently, but many more are needed to establish the research field. We believe molecular genetics has theoretical implications for enhancing our understanding of organizational behavior, which is one purpose of organization science. This kind of research also has implications for management practices. For example, although it might seem far-fetched to suggest that specific genes can help us identify talents with higher precision than the tests and inventories commonly used today, knowledge about an individual's genetic profile may have the potential to augment existing test batteries to help select suitable people for tasks such as combat and firefighting, which are physically and psychologically very demanding. At this stage, however, we need to accumulate more evidence on whether the genetic information can help predict work-related outcomes before we can speak with confidence about its general implications.

References

Arvey, R. D., and Bouchard, T. J. 1994. Genetics, twins, and organizational behavior. In *Research in Organizational Behavior*, vol. 16, ed. L. L. Cummings and B. Staw, 47–82. Greenwich, CT: JAI Press.

——, Bouchard, T. J., Segal, N. L., and Abraham, L. M. 1989. Job satisfaction: Environmental and genetic components. *Journal of Applied Psychology* 74 (2): 187–92.

——, McCall, B. P., Bouchard, T. J., Taubman, P., and Cavanaugh, M. A. 1994. Genetic influences on job satisfaction and work values. *Personality and Individual Differences* 17 (1): 21–33.

Bachner-Melman, R., Zohar, A. H., Bacon-Shnoor, N., Elizur, Y., Nemanov, L., Gritsenko, I., et al. 2005. Link between vasopressin receptor AVPR1A promoter region microsatellites and measures of social behavior in humans. *Journal of Individual Differences* 26 (1): 2–10.

Benjamin, J., Li, L., Patterson, C., Greenberg, B. D., Murphy, D. L., and Hamer, D. H. 1996. Population and familial association between the D4 dopamine receptor gene and measures of novelty seeking. *Nature Genetics* 12 (1): 81–84.

Blairy, S., Massat, I., Staner, L., Le Bon, O., Van Gestel, S., Van Broeckhoven, C., et al. 2000. 5 HT2a receptor polymorphism gene in bipolar disorder and harm avoidance personality trait. *American Journal of Medical Genetics* 96 (3): 360–64.

Bouchard, T. J. 2004. Genetic influence on human psychological traits. *Current Directions in Psychological Science* 13 (4): 148–51.

———, and McGue, M. 2003. Genetic and environmental influences on human psychological differences. *Journal of Neurobiology* 54 (1): 4–45.

Burt, A. 2009. A Mechanistic Explanation of Popularity: Genes, Rule Breaking, and Evocative Gene-Environment Correlations. *Journal of Personality and Social Psychology* 96 (4): 783–94.

Butcher, J. N. 2001. *MMPI-2: Minnesota Multiphasic Personality Inventory-2: Manual for administration, scoring, and interpretation.* Minneapolis: University of Minnesota Press.

Caspi, A., McClay, J., Moffitt, T. E., Mill, J., Martin, J., Craig, I. W., et al. 2002. Role of genotype in the cycle of violence in maltreated children. *Science* 297 (5582): 851–54.

———, Sugden, K., Moffitt, T., Taylor, A., Craig, I., Harrington, H., et al. 2003. Influence of life stress on depression: Moderation by a polymorphism in the 5-HTT gene. *Science* 301 (5631): 386.

Chorney, M. J., Chorney, K., Seese, N., Owen, M. J., Daniels, J., McGuffin, P., et al. 1998. A quantitative trait locus associated with cognitive ability in children. *Psychological Science* 9 (3): 159–66.

Cloninger, C. R. 1986. A unified biosocial theory of personality and its role in the development of anxiety states. *Psychiatric developments* 4 (3): 167.

———, Adolfsson, R., and Svrakic, N. M. 1996. Mapping genes for human personality. *Nature Genetics* 12 (1): 3–4.

———, Przybeck, T. R., and Švraki, D. M. 1991. The Tridimensional Personality Questionnaire: US normative data. *Psychological Reports* 69:1047–57.

———, Svrakic, D. M., and Przybeck, T. R. 1993. A psychobiological model of temperament and character. *Archives of General Psychiatry* 50 (12): 975.

Costa, P. T., and McCrae, R. R. 1997. Stability and change in personality assessment: The revised NEO Personality Inventory in the year 2000. *Journal of Personality Assessment* 68 (1): 86–94.

Davis, O., Butcher, L., Docherty, S., Meaburn, E., Curtis, C., Simpson, M., et al. 2010. A three-stage genome-wide association study of general cognitive ability: Hunting the small effects. *Behavior Genetics* 40 (6): 759–67.

Deary, I. J. 2008. Why do intelligent people live longer? *Nature* 456 (7219): 175–76.

———, Johnson, W., and Houlihan, L. 2009. Genetic foundations of human intelligence. *Human Genetics* 126 (1): 215–32.

Ebstein, R. 2006. The molecular genetic architecture of human personality: Beyond self-report questionnaires. *Molecular Psychiatry* 11 (5): 427–45.

———, and Israel, S. 2009. *Molecular genetics of personality: How our genes can bring us to a better understanding of why we act the way we do.* New York: Springer.

Ebstein, R. P., Segman, R., Benjamin, J., Osher, Y., Nemanov, L., and Belmaker, R. H. 1997. 5-HT2C (HTR2C) serotonin receptor gene polymorphism associated with the human personality trait of reward dependence: Interaction with dopamine

D4 receptor (D4DR) and dopamine D3 receptor (D3DR) polymorphisms. *American Journal of Medical Genetics* 74 (1): 65–72.

———, Israel, S., Chew, S. H., Zhong, S., and Knafo, A. 2010. Genetics of human social behavior. *Neuron* 65 (6): 831–44.

———, Novick, O., Umansky, R., Priel, B., Osher, Y., Blaine, D., et al. 1996. Dopamine D4 receptor (D4DR) exon III polymorphism associated with the human personality trait of novelty seeking. *Nature Genetics* 12 (1): 78–80.

Egner, T., and Gruzelier, J. H. 2003. Ecological validity of neurofeedback: Modulation of slow wave EEG enhances musical performance. *NeuroReport* 14 (9): 1221–24.

Entin, E. E., and Serfaty, D. 1999. Adaptive team coordination. *Human Factors: The Journal of the Human Factors and Ergonomics Society* 41 (2): 312.

Fiedler, F. E. 1986. The contribution of cognitive resources and leader behavior to organizational performance. *Journal of Applied Social Psychology* 16 (6): 532–48.

Fisher, P. J., Turic, D., Williams, N. M., McGuffin, P., Asherson, P., Ball, D., et al. 1999. DNA pooling identifies QTLs on chromosome 4 for general cognitive ability in children. *Human Molecular Genetics* 8 (5): 915.

Floderus-Myrhed, B., Pedersen, N., and Rasmuson, I. 1980. Assessment of heritability for personality, based on a short-form of the Eysenck Personality Inventory: A study of 12,898 twin pairs. *Behavior Genetics* 10 (2): 153–62.

Fowler, J. H., Dawes, C. T., and Christakis, N. A. 2009. Model of genetic variation in human social networks. *Proceedings of the National Academy of Sciences* 106 (6): 1720–24.

———, Settle, J. E., and Christakis, N. A. 2011. Correlated genotypes in friendship networks. *Proceedings of the National Academy of Sciences* 108 (5): 1993.

Freese, J. 2008. Genetics and the social science explanation of individual outcomes. *American Journal of Sociology* 114 (S1): 1–35.

Fuller, B., and Marler, L. E. 2009. Change driven by nature: A meta-analytic review of the proactive personality literature. *Journal of Vocational Behavior* 75 (3): 329–45.

Gerstner, C. R., and Day, D. V. 1997. Meta-analytic review of leader-member exchange theory: Correlates and construct issues. *Journal of Applied Psychology* 82 (6): 827–44.

Gunthert, K., Conner, T., Armeli, S., Tennen, H., Covault, J., and Kranzler, H. 2007. Serotonin transporter gene polymorphism (5-HTTLPR) and anxiety reactivity in daily life: A daily process approach to gene-environment interaction. *Psychosomatic Medicine* 69:762–68.

Guo, G. 2008. Introduction to the Special Issue on Society and Genetics. *Sociological Methods and Research* 37 (2): 159–63.

Hackman, J. R., and Oldham, G. R. 1980. *Work redesign*. Reading, MA: Addison-Wesley.

Hariri, A., Mattay, V., Tessitore, A., Kolachana, B., Fera, F., Goldman, D., et al. 2002. Serotonin transporter genetic variation and the response of the human amygdala. *Science* 297 (5580): 400.

Holland, J. L. 1997. *Making vocational choices: A theory of vocational personalities and work environments*. 3rd ed. Odessa, FL: Psychological Assessment Resources.

Israel, S., Lerer, E., Shalev, I., Uzefovsky, F., Riebold, M., Laiba, E., et al. 2009. The oxytocin receptor (OXTR) contributes to prosocial fund allocations in the dictator game and the social value orientations task. *PLoS One* 4 (5): 5535.

Jang, K., Livesley, W., and Vemon, P. 1996. Heritability of the big five personality dimensions and their facets: A twin study. *Journal of Personality* 64 (3): 577–92.

Judge, T. A., Heller, D., and Mount, M. K. 2002. Five-factor model of personality and job satisfaction: A meta-analysis. *Journal of Applied Psychology* 87 (3): 530.

———, Klinger, R., Simon, L. S., and Yang, I. W. F. 2008. The contributions of personality to organizational behavior and psychology: Findings, criticisms, and future research directions. *Social and Personality Psychology Compass* 2 (5): 1982–2000.

Keller, L. M., Bouchard, T. J., Arvey, R. D., Segal, N. L., and Dawis, R. V. 1992. Work values: Genetic and environmental influences. *Journal of Applied Psychology* 77 (1): 79–88.

Keltikangas-Järvinen, L., Räikkönen, K., Ekelund, J., and Peltonen, L. 2003. Nature and nurture in novelty seeking. *Molecular Psychiatry* 9 (3): 308–11.

Kim, H. S., Sherman, D. K., Sasaki, J. Y., Xu, J., Chu, T. Q., Ryu, C., et al. 2010. Culture, distress, and oxytocin receptor polymorphism (OXTR) interact to influence emotional support seeking. *Proceedings of the National Academy of Sciences* 107 (36): 15717–721.

Kim, S. J., Young, L. J., Gonen, D., Veenstra-VanderWeele, J., Courchesne, R., Courchesne, E., et al. 2002. Transmission disequilibrium testing of arginine vasopressin receptor 1A (AVPR1A) polymorphisms in autism. *Molecular Psychiatry* 7 (5): 503–7.

Kosfeld, M., Heinrichs, M., Zak, P. J., Fischbacher, U., and Fehr, E. 2005. Oxytocin increases trust in humans. *Nature* 435 (7042): 673–76.

Kreek, M. J., Nielsen, D. A., Butelman, E. R., and LaForge, K. S. 2005. Genetic influences on impulsivity, risk taking, stress responsivity and vulnerability to drug abuse and addiction. *Nature Neuroscience* 8 (11): 1450–57.

Kristof-Brown, A. L., and Guay, R. P. 2010. Person-environment fit. In *APA handbook of industrial and organizational psychology*, vol. 3, ed. S. Zedeck, 3–50. Washington, DC: American Psychological Association.

Kühn, K. U., Meyer, K., Nöthen, M. M., Gänsicke, M., Papassotiropoulos, A., and Maier, W. 1999. Allelic variants of dopamine receptor D4 (DRD4) and serotonin receptor 5HT2c (HTR2c) and temperament factors: Replication tests. *American Journal of Medical Genetics Part B: Neuropsychiatric Genetics* 88 (2): 168–72.

Kuhnen, C. M., and Chiao, J. Y. 2009. Genetic determinants of financial risk taking. *PLoS One* 4 (2): e4362.

Lesch, K. P., Bengel, D., Heils, A., Sabol, S. Z., Greenberg, B. D., Petri, S., et al. 1996. Association of anxiety-related traits with a polymorphism in the serotonin transporter gene regulatory region. *Science* 274 (5292): 1527–31.

Li, W. D., and Arvey, R. D. 2010. The heritability of work design characteristics. Paper presented at the Annual Academy of Management Meeting, Montréal, Québec, Canada.

———, Arvey, R. D., Zhang, Z., and Song, Z. 2012. Do leadership role occupancy and transformational leadership share the same genetic and environmental influences? *Leadership Quarterly* 23 (2): 233–43.

———, Song, Z., and Arvey, R. D. 2011. The influence of general mental ability, self-esteem and family socioeconomic status on leadership role occupancy and leader advancement: The moderating role of gender. *Leadership Quarterly* 22 (3): 520–34.

McCormick, E. J., Jeanneret, P. R., and Mecham, R. C. 1972. A study of job characteristics and job dimensions as based on the Position Analysis Questionnaire (PAQ). *Journal of Applied Psychology* 56 (4): 347–68.

McCrae, R. R., Scally, M., Terracciano, A., Abecasis, G. R., and Costa, P. T. 2010. An alternative to the search for single polymorphisms: Toward molecular personality scales for the five-factor model. *Journal of Personality and Social Psychology* 99 (6): 1014–24.

Meaney, M. J. 2010. Epigenetics and the biological definition of gene × environment interactions. *Child development* 81 (1): 41–79.

Meyer, R. D., Dalal, R. S., and Hermida, R. 2010. A review and synthesis of situational strength in the organizational sciences. *Journal of Management* 36 (1): 121–40.

Moffitt, T. E., Caspi, A., and Rutter, M. 2006. Measured gene-environment interactions in psychopathology: Concepts, research strategies, and implications for research, intervention, and public understanding of genetics. *Perspectives on Psychological Science* 1 (1): 5–27.

Munafo, M., Clark, T., Moore, L., Payne, E., Walton, R., and Flint, J. 2003. Genetic polymorphisms and personality in healthy adults: A systematic review and meta-analysis. *Molecular Psychiatry* 8 (5): 471–84.

Murphy, D. L., Li, Q., Engel, S., Wichems, C., Andrews, A., Lesch, K. P., et al. 2001. Genetic perspectives on the serotonin transporter. *Brain Research Bulletin* 56 (5): 487–94.

Organ, D. W. 1994. Personality and organizational citizenship behavior. *Journal of Management* 20 (2): 465–78.

Plomin, R., DeFries, J., and Loehlin, J. C. 1977. Genotype-environment interaction and correlation in the analysis of human behavior. *Psychological Bulletin* 84 (2): 309–22.

———, and Kovas, Y. 2005. Generalist genes and learning disabilities. *Psychological Bulletin* 131 (4): 592–617.

———, and Neiderhiser, J. 1992. Quantitative genetics, molecular genetics, and intelligence. *Intelligence* 15 (4): 369–87.

———, and Spinath, F. M. 2004. Intelligence: Genetics, genes, and genomics. *Journal of Personality and Social Psychology* 86 (1): 112–29.

Reuter, M., Frenzel, C., Walter, N. T., Markett, S., and Montag, C. 2010. Investigating the genetic basis of altruism: The role of the COMT Val158Met polymorphism. *Social Cognitive and Affective Neuroscience* 6 (5): 662–68

Roiser, J. P., de Martino, B., Tan, G. C. Y., Kumaran, D., Seymour, B., Wood, N. W., et al. 2009. A genetically mediated bias in decision making driven by failure of amygdala control. *Journal of Neuroscience* 29 (18): 5985–91.

Ropers, H. H., and Hamel, B. C. J. 2005. X-linked mental retardation. *Nature Reviews Genetics* 6 (1): 46–57.

Rubinstein, M., Phillips, T. J., Bunzow, J. R., Falzone, T. L., Dziewczapolski, G., Zhang, G., et al. 1997. Mice lacking dopamine D4 receptors are supersensitive to ethanol, cocaine, and methamphetamine. *Cell* 90 (6): 991–1001.

Sen, S., Villafuerte, S., Nesse, R., Stoltenberg, S. F., Hopcian, J., Gleiberman, L., et al.

2004. Serotonin transporter and GABA (A) alpha 6 receptor variants are associated with neuroticism. *Biological Psychiatry* 55 (3): 244–49.

Settle, J. E., Dawes, C. T., Christakis, N. A., and Fowler, J. H. 2010. Friendships moderate an association between a dopamine gene variant and political ideology. *Journal of Politics* 72 (4): 1189–98.

Song, Z., Li, W. D., and Arvey, R. D. 2011. Associations between dopamine and serotonin genes and job satisfaction: Preliminary evidence from the Add Health Study. *Journal of Applied Psychology* 96 (6): 1223–33.

Strenze, T. 2007. Intelligence and socioeconomic success: A meta-analytic review of longitudinal research. *Intelligence* 35 (5): 401–26.

Terracciano, A., Sanna, S., Uda, M., Deiana, B., Usala, G., Busonero, F., et al. 2010. Genome-wide association scan for five major dimensions of personality. *Molecular Psychiatry*, 15 (6): 647–56.

Tett, R. P., and Burnett, D. D. 2003. A personality trait-based interactionist model of job performance. *Journal of Applied Psychology* 88 (3): 500–17.

Triandis, H. C. 1964. Exploratory factor analyses of the behavioral component of social attitudes. *Journal of Abnormal and Social Psychology* 68 (4): 420.

Turkheimer, E. 2000. Three laws of behavior genetics and what they mean. *Current Directions in Psychological Science* 9 (5): 160–64.

———, and Gottesman, I. I. 1991. Is $H^2 = 0$ a null hypothesis anymore? *Behavioral and Brain Sciences* 14 (3): 410–11.

Verweij, K. J. H., Zietsch, B. P., Medland, S. E., Gordon, S. D., Benyamin, B., Nyholt, D. R., et al. 2010. A genome-wide association study of Cloninger's temperament scales: Implications for the evolutionary genetics of personality. *Biological Psychology* 85 (2): 306–17.

Wang, N., and Song, Z. 2010. The relationships between HT2RA gene, negative mood and job satisfaction in daily life. Paper presented at the Annual Academy of Management Meeting, Montréal, Québec, Canada.

Wayne, S. J., Shore, L. M., and Liden, R. C. 1997. Perceived organizational support and leader-member exchange: A social exchange perspective. *Academy of Management Journal* 40 (1): 82–111.

Weiss, H. M., and Adler, S. 1984. Personality and organizational behavior. *Research in Organizational Behavior* 6:1–50.

Willis-Owen, S. A. G., Turri, M. G., Munaf , M. R., Surtees, P. G., Wainwright, N. W. J., Brixey, R. D., et al. 2005. The serotonin transporter length polymorphism, neuroticism, and depression: A comprehensive assessment of association. *Biological Psychiatry* 58 (6): 451–56.

Wilson, G. D., and Brazendale, A. H. 1973. Social attitude correlates of Eysenck's personality dimensions *Social Behavior and Personality: An International Journal* 1 (2): 115–18.

Zhang, Z., and Ilies, R. 2010. Moderating effects of earlier family environment on genetic influences on entrepreneurship. Paper presented at the Annual Academy of Management Meeting, Montréal, Québec, Canada.

———, Ilies, R., and Arvey, R. D. 2009. Beyond genetic explanations for leadership: The moderating role of the social environment. *Organizational Behavior and Human Decision Processes* 110 (2): 118–28.

THREE

Genetic Influences on Attitudes, Behaviors, and Emotions in the Workplace

Remus Ilies and Nikolaos Dimotakis

In this chapter we make the case that biology influences organizational behavior because work attitudes and emotional states experienced at work, as proximal influences on work behavior, have substantial genetic components. As a result, we contend that the genetic makeup of individuals has profound implications for how people experience their workplaces and for their attitudinal and behavioral reactions to work. Given the important implications of genetics for individuals and organizations, evidence documenting the genetic effects of work attitudes and behaviors is accumulating rapidly, along with the development of more sophisticated models for explaining the links between genetics and work attitudes. Management and organizational scholars will increasingly have to integrate this knowledge into theories of organizational behavior (but see Shane 2009).

The chapter proceeds as follows. First, we provide a brief primer of behavioral genetics and traditional methods used to examine the influence of genetics on attitudes. Second, we discuss how evolution, inheritance, behavioral genetics, and individual differences in attitudes, emotional states, and behavioral tendencies are related, and we propose specific explanations linking evolution and genetics with work attitudes and emotions. Third, we examine the available scientific evidence with respect to the genetic basis of work attitudes and more complex links between genetics, work attitudes, and organizational behaviors. Finally, we review the most recent methodology used in studies aimed at explaining how genetics influences organizational attitudes and behaviors, and we provide directions for future research.

A PRIMER ON BEHAVIORAL GENETICS

Research on behavioral genetics ultimately aims to distinguish between and explain genetic and environmental influences on individual differences in behavior. Examining genetic influences on both general and work attitudes starts from the assumption that people's personal characteristics (e.g., personality traits) influence their attitudes (e.g., see Judge, Heller, and Mount 2002) and that these personal characteristics are influenced by people's genotypes (the biochemical codes providing their genetic composition) through biological processes and through development. Even though individual phenotypes (observed and/or measured individual characteristics) are influenced by genetic composition, they include environmental influences. In turn, scholars are interested in estimating genetic and environmental influence on work attitudes because attitudes influence decisions and behaviors (e.g., Ilies et al. 2009). That is, research is investigating how individuals' genetic composition can affect both stable individual differences (such as personality and behavioral dispositions) as well as mean levels of fluctuating states (such as moods, emotions, or attitudes).

In its simplest form, behavioral genetics research attempts to partition the variance in some measured phenotypic construct—a trait, attitude, or behavior—among individuals (phenotypic variance) into genetic and environmental components. For an attitude A, for example, a parameter of interest is the heritability (h_A^2) of the attitude. This statistic estimates the proportion of phenotypic variance (between individuals) accounted for by genetic differences (Ilies, Arvey, and Bouchard 2006; McGue and Bouchard 1998).

Nevertheless, because heredity and environment have a complexly intertwined influence on human development, it is important to note that behavioral genetics designs can only estimate the extent to which differences between individuals in a particular attitude, attribute, or characteristic reflect environmental or genetic variation. That is, behavioral genetics methods cannot estimate the impact of genetics in an absolute sense, over the entire range of possible variations in environmental factors and genetic backgrounds (e.g., Olson et al. 2001).

Genetic influences on a behavioral trait or any individual-difference construct can be decomposed into *additive genetic effects* (transmissible across generations) and *non-additive genetic effects* (dependent on specific configurations of genes, and nontransmissible). Individual differences caused by environmental variation can also be further decomposed into differences caused by *shared environments* (e.g., common family environments that would cause unrelated individuals reared together as siblings to become similar), and differences caused by *unshared environments* (i.e., environmental influences that are unique for each individual).

The simplest way to estimate the magnitude of the genetic influence on an attitude (or any other individual-difference construct) is to examine whether the scores on that attitude (e.g., *A*) of monozygotic (MZ) twins who were reared apart (i.e., given up for adoption at birth) are correlated with each other. The assumption here is that if the attitude scores of MZ twins (who share, on average, 100% of their genetics; dizygotic [DZ] twins, share, on average, 50% of their genetic material) who were raised in different environments are similar, then this similarity must be the result of genetics. More sophisticated univariate genetic models compare the covariance among twins' scores on the variable of interest across four types of twin pairs (MZ reared apart, MZ reared together, DZ reared apart, DZ reared together). In these univariate models, the variance of each of the variables is decomposed into additive genetic variance, shared environmental variance, and nonshared environmental variance (which includes measurement error). As shown in figure 3.1, additive genetic effects (latent variable *A*) reflect effects of the summation of genes across loci, while shared (latent variable *C*) and nonshared (latent variable *E*) environmental effects refer to environmental effects that contribute to twin similarities and differences, respectively. The four groups involve different patterns of constraints as follows: across pairs of twins, variable *A* was correlated 1.0 or 0.5 for MZ and DZ pairs, respectively (because MZ and DZ twins share, on average, 100% and 50% of their genes), whereas variable *C* was correlated 1.0 for twins reared together and uncorrelated for twins reared apart. The latent variable *E* was uncorrelated in all groups because *E* represents nonshared environmental effects.

Using the notations from figure 3.1, the total variance in *A* (V_A) can be decomposed into additive genetic variance (a^2), shared environmental variance (c^2), and nonshared environmental variance (e^2).

(1) $$V_A = a^2 + c^2 + e^2$$

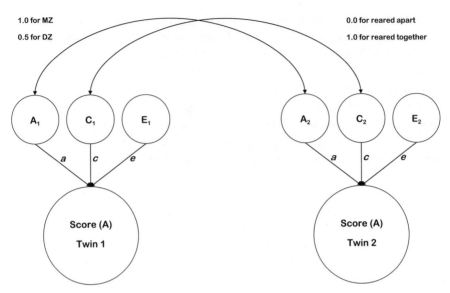

Fig. 3.1 Conceptual univariate ACE model for an attitude (*A*). (Note: MZ = monozygotic twins. DZ = dizygotic twins.)

Heritability is then estimated as the proportion of the total variance that reflects additive genetic influences:

$$(2) \qquad\qquad h^2 = a^2 / V_A$$

After estimating the full, or the ACE, model (containing all the three types of effects), the paths estimated are examined for significance, and the model is tested against alternative (simpler) models (e.g., the AE model, which eliminates shared environment effects; see Arvey et al. 2007).

EVOLUTION, INHERITANCE, AND BEHAVIORAL GENETICS

For quite a long time, it was difficult to understand how the existence of individual differences in particular characteristics of humans (i.e., traits, attitudes) fit within the broad framework of evolutionary theory. Gregor Mendel's discoveries regarding the mechanisms of hereditary transmission and, later, evolutionary synthesis (Mayr and Provine 1980) addressed this important question.[1] Within species, the evolutionary perspective of individual differences stipulates that dispositions have evolved because they contributed to solving specific adaptation problems (e.g., Buss 2001; see also Buss and Hawley 2010). Individual differences in personality traits or stable attitudes, for example, represent ranges of viable evolutionary strategies for humans, reflecting evolved motive dispositions (Buss 1991; Lusk, MacDonald, and Newman 1998; MacDonald 1991; 1995; 1998).

As Ilies, Arvey, and Bouchard (2006) explain, this perspective proposes that variation in individual characteristics within a population represents a continuous distribution of phenotypes that matches a continuous distribution of strategies for survival. In other words, each particular environment across time can be successfully negotiated with a variety of adaptive strategies, each of which might have a differing chance of success, and each of which can also support a particular proportion of the population engaging in it. It then follows that variation in a specific characteristic produces a wide range of variation that facilitates the occupation of a wide range of possible niches in the environment (Lusk, MacDonald, and Newman 1998). The fact that a certain individual characteristic is heritable indicates that it can be subject to sexual or natural selection, although it is difficult to establish the consequences of traits or other individual characteristics for fitness—that is, the relationship between a trait and the advantage it can offer is not always clear (Ilies, Arvey, and Bouchard 2006). Nevertheless, the evolutionary perspective on human differences reflected in heritable characteristics anchors individual-difference theories within a much broader and perhaps more meaningful context that governs all life: "the organizing forces of evolution by natural selection" (Buss 1991, 461).

To illustrate some of the mechanisms that could be at work, Nettle (2006) discussed how different broad personality factors each provide individuals with evolutionary fitness costs and benefits, with no trait (or configuration of traits) being optimally suited for survival across all situations, environments, or conditions. In other words, selection pressures fluctuate, creating pressures for different trait levels across time. While this argument does not necessarily hold for all psychological traits and average states, it suffices to explain variation across a number of factors important to organizational behavior.

THE GENETIC BASIS OF WORK ATTITUDES, EMOTIONALITY, AND BEHAVIORS

Since the first studies on the inheritance of "talent" by Galton (1865), scientific examinations of the extent to which individual differences in behavioral traits are inherited have consistently shown that such individual differences have important genetic components (e.g., Plomin and Daniels 1987). Therefore, given that behavioral traits such as those comprising the personality framework of the "Big Five" factors are known to predict work attitudes and behaviors (e.g., Ilies et al. 2009), it is reasonable to expect that (and therefore to investigate whether) work attitudes and behaviors are influenced by genetic makeup. Once sufficient evidence from research in support of such influences is found, further study will be needed to explore why these genetic influences exist and how they operate.

Though the existence of individual differences in job satisfaction has been recognized for as long as job satisfaction has been formally studied (e.g., Hoppock 1935; Weitz 1952), the dispositional approach to job satisfaction has been the focus of major research efforts only since the mid 1980s (House, Shane, and Herold 1996). Evidence is accumulating. Staw and Ross (1985) found that job satisfaction scores were stable over moderate time periods and that these scores showed significant consistency across situations (changes in occupations and in employers). Similarly, Staw, Bell, and Clausen (1986) found that affective disposition, assessed at childhood, influenced ratings of job satisfaction that were reported more than forty years later.

However, it was impossible to determine from the results of these early studies on the dispositional source of job satisfaction whether these influences have genetic or social-developmental (early childhood experiences) causes. Also, these studies offer only indirect evidence for the dispositional source of job satisfaction, because they do not document any direct relationship between job satisfaction and dispositional characteristics of individuals (Judge 1992). Nevertheless, we must recognize their importance, because these early studies did lead to research efforts that examined what specific dispositional characteristics best predict individual differences in job satisfaction.

The definition of job satisfaction as "a pleasurable or positive emotional state resulting from the appraisal of one's job or job experiences" (Locke 1976, 1300) clearly states that job satisfaction has a strong affective (i.e., emotional) component in other words, the extent to which a person is satisfied by her job is not simply the result of cognitive processes and judgments, but also depends on how she feels about her position. Research linking personality traits to job satisfaction has therefore employed a large variety of personality measures in attempts to capture the affective dispositions underlying job satisfaction. Judge and Hulin

(1993) and Judge and Locke (1993) found that employees' affective disposition, measured as their responses to a series of neutral objects common to everyday life, was significantly correlated with facets of job satisfaction. The measure used by Judge and colleagues asked individuals to indicate their satisfaction with a list of neutral objects common in everyday life (your telephone number, your first name, the neighbors you have, $8\frac{1}{2}'' \times 11''$ paper). The premise of using this measure to predict job satisfaction was that individuals predisposed to be dissatisfied with such ostensibly neutral items are likely to be unhappy with most aspects of their lives, including their jobs.

An emotionality-based framework that has often been studied in relating affective disposition to job satisfaction comprises the traits of positive affectivity (PA) and negative affectivity (NA; see Watson, Clark, and Tellegen 1988). NA reflects individual tendencies to experience aversive emotional states such as fear, hostility, and anger, whereas PA measures characteristic differences in the propensity to experience positive states, such as enthusiasm, confidence, and cheerfulness (Watson et al. 1999). Several studies have related PA and NA to job satisfaction, and they have consistently shown moderate relationships of PA and NA with job satisfaction (see Brief 1998; Spector, 1997; Watson 2000). Cumulating research findings on the topic, Connolly and Viswesvaran's (2000) meta-analysis of these relationships found true score correlations (corrected for unreliability) between PA and NA and job satisfaction of .49 and $-.33$, respectively.

Although it reflects a broad conception of human personality from a behavioral trait perspective (compared to the PA-NA framework), the Big Five (Goldberg 1990) framework, alternatively referred to as the five-factor model of personality, provides a comprehensive taxonomy to organize traits relevant to job satisfaction (Ilies and Judge 2003; Judge, Heller, and Mount 2002). The Big Five framework comprises the dimensions of neuroticism, extraversion, openness to experience, agreeableness, and conscientiousness, with neuroticism and extraversion being considered the traits most relevant to the experience of emotions and thus thought to reflect affective dispositions. Neuroticism (the opposite pole of emotional stability) , is characterized by poor emotional adjustment and the frequent experience of negative affective states, such as anxiety and stress, as well as depression and lack of confidence. Individuals high on the extraversion dimension tend to be sociable, talkative, dominant, and exhibit positive emotions. Openness to experience is the propensity of individuals to be imaginative, autonomous, nonconforming, and unconventional. Agreeable persons are characterized as trusting, compliant, caring, and gentle, while conscientiousness is indicated by two facets: achievement-orientation and dependability.

Nettle (2006) describes a variety of potential fitness costs and benefits of each of these factors from an evolutionary perspective. The important implication is that to some extent they can all contribute to individual success in occupying specific niches, thus providing a reason for the existence of variation among these traits across individuals. These general factors, however, are linked to important organizational variables in a variety of studies that have been used to relate genetic factors influencing personality to variables of interest to organizational scholars.

Judge, Heller, and Mount (2002) used the Big Five framework to organize previous research studies that investigated relationships between personality traits and job satisfaction by means of meta-analysis. These authors found that four of the Big Five traits were related to job satisfaction. Based on 335 correlations between personality traits and job satisfaction reported in 135 research projects using categories corresponding to the Big Five traits, they computed true score correlations (corrected for unreliability in the measures) between each of the Big Five traits and job satisfaction. The true score correlations were $-.29$, $.25$, $.02$, $.17$, and $.26$ for neuroticism, extraversion, openness to experience, agreeableness, and conscientiousness, respectively. Though the Big Five traits vary in their relevance to job satisfaction (with openness being the least relevant), they concluded that organizing personality traits according to the Big Five model leads to substantial support for the dispositional source of job satisfaction.

As shown above, there have appeared studies that demonstrate significant stability in job satisfaction (indirectly suggesting a dispositional source of job satisfaction), as well as direct studies showing job satisfaction to be related to various personality traits. While there is no expected theoretical or conceptual explanation for why genetics would influence work and non-work contexts differently, we constrain our discussion mostly to the work domain, as this is of most proximal interest to organizational studies. In the next section, we review research that has directly examined the link between genetics and job satisfaction, as well as other attitudes important for organizations and employees. We begin with an investigation of a variety of attitudes important to organizational behavior; in this section, satisfaction with one's work and life is arguably the most important as well as the most closely studied attitude. We then move on to investigate genetic influences on the way people affectively experience their work and life, and then to examine the genetic bases of manifested behavior.

Behavioral Genetics Research on Job and Life Satisfaction

Job satisfaction, although sometimes examined as a fluctuating state, has been found to have variance components that are significantly stable over time. In an initial effort to examine whether genetic factors could potentially account for a part of this stable component of job satisfaction, Arvey et al. (1989), in a study of thirty-four pairs of monozygotic twins raised apart (MZA), found significant intraclass correlations for general job satisfaction (.31) and intrinsic satisfaction (.32), indicating that genetic factors accounted for a significant proportion of variance. Moreover, they found that monozygotic twins tended to hold similar jobs in terms of job complexity, motor skills required, and physical demands (intraclass correlation coefficients .44, .36, and .34, respectively), indicating that genetic influences might be related to the jobs that individuals gravitate toward, suggesting an additional pathway for these effects. The introduction of this paper to applied psychology and organizational behavior generated substantial debate (for discussion, see Cropanzano and James 1990; Bouchard et al. 1992) and provided some interesting preliminary evidence for the role of genetic influences in determining workplace attitudes.

As additional evidence for such conclusions, similar results were found by Arvey et al. (1994), who reported that, across two studies (involving 95 monozygotic and 80 dizygotic pairs of male twins from the Minnesota Twin Family Registry, and 1,236 monozygotic and 1,165 dizygotic male twins from a National Academy of Sciences and National Research Council twin sample), genetic influences were again found to play an important role in predicting job satisfaction. Specifically, the first study indicated a significant genetic influence on intrinsic job satisfaction ($a = .23$) and a modest genetic influence on general job satisfaction ($a = .16$). The second study by Arvey et al. (1994) indicated that genetic factors accounted for 27% of the variance in overall job satisfaction.

Not all investigations of job satisfaction have supported the role of genetic influences, however. Hershberger, Lichtenstein, and Knox (1994), using a sample of twins from the Swedish Adoption/Twin Study of Aging (including 146 monozygotic twins raised together, 74 monozygotic twins raised apart, 146 dizygotic twins raised together, and 164 dizygotic raised apart), found no significant genetic influences on job satisfaction, although their job satisfaction items related to intrinsic satisfaction were indeed influenced by genetics, echoing the results of Arvey et al. (1989) to some extent. Moreover, these authors did report a significant role for genetic influences in predicting other work-related attitudes, such as perceptions of supportive climate and annoyances experienced (with genetic effects accounting for 22% and 27% of the variance in these variables, respectively).

In terms of life satisfaction, a general attitude thought to be related to job satisfaction, Stubbe et al. (2005), in a study involving 2,219 monozygotic and 2,110 dizygotic twins, found that non-additive genetic factors explained 38% of the variance in life satisfaction scores. These results are similar to the ones reported by Harris et al. (1992), who found that 32% of variation in life satisfaction was attributable to genetic factors in a study involving elderly subjects from the Swedish Adoption/Twin Study of Aging, and to the ones reported by Tellegen et al. (1988), who reported a heritability estimate of 48% for general subjective well-being.

Similarly, Johnson and Krueger (2006), using a sample of 719 twin pairs from the National Survey of Midlife Development, found that genetic effects accounted for a substantial amount of variance in individual levels of life satisfaction, and that the proportion of variance explained by genetic effects was moderated by the level of financial position and the level of perceived control. Specifically, both of these moderating variables served to enhance the proportion of life satisfaction associated with genetic influences (with 17% and 30% of the variance in life satisfaction associated with genetic influences at low levels of financial position and perceived control, respectively, and 32% and 45% of the variance in life satisfaction being associated with genetic influences at high levels of financial position and perceived control, respectively).

In general then, genetic influences were found to play an important role in fundamental judgments about quality of work and life. Further work expanded on these findings to investigate whether other attitudes of interest to the workplace could also have a genetic component.

Attitudes toward Work Values

To investigate attitudes about work values, Keller and colleagues (1992) administered the Minnesota Importance Questionnaire (MIQ; a questionnaire measuring the importance of various work values, including six higher-order factors) to twenty-three monozygotic and twenty dizygotic pairs of twins reared apart. Using the intraclass correlation as the indicator of heritability, results of this behavioral genetic study indicated that genetic influences were indeed present for half the MIQ scales (ten out of twenty), Moreover, approximately 40% of the variance in the six higher-order value factors in the sample was associated with genetic factors, with the remainder being associated with environmental differences and measurement error. Similar results were reported by Arvey et al. (1994), who reported finding a substantial genetic influence on a representative sampling of different work values (with an average heritability estimate across fifteen work values of .35). In other words, many categories of work values seem to have a substantial genetic component, although this is perhaps not universal—and of course all such attitudes are subject to a variety of other influences.

While studies of work values might not directly assess genetic influences on attitudes per se, the insight they provide on how individuals' desired work outcomes are influenced by their genes can be useful in understanding specific aspects of work attitudes though the valences associated with different outcomes.

Other Attitudes

Genetic influences are of course not limited to work attitudes, nor are they expected to be, since neither phenotypes nor genotypes differentiate between work and non-work activities. Other research has demonstrated the importance of genetic factors in explaining variation across various attitudes, and these studies provide insights that can be of use in workplace investigations as well. For example, in a study of non-work attitudes and dispositions involving 195 pairs of monozygotic and 141 pairs of same-sex dizygotic twins, Olson et al. (2001) found that six out of the nine general attitude factors tested had significant genetic components (with estimates ranging from .27 to .66), and also found significant genetic components for three out of five personality factors in their sample (ranging from .13 to .43). Moreover, personality factors were found to mediate the relationship between genetics and attitudes in all these cases, with dispositional sociability having an especially strong mediating role.

In a similar vein, Tesser (1993) reported that a wide variety of attitude items had a substantial heritable component across two studies, and also argued that several factors might explain why attitudes are heritable, including temperament, conditionability, and sensory structures. Moreover, he argued that attitudes with a stronger heritable component should also be more enduring and more easily accessible. This contention was supported in a subsequent study involving forty-two female and twenty male subjects (Tesser et al. 1998), where high heritability attitudes were found to be more resistant to change and associated with greater electrodermal and cardiovascular responses. Relationships have also been reported between genetics and other attitudes, such as conservatism (see Bergen, Gardner, and Kendler 2007).

Furthermore, Conway et al. (2011), administering a variety of attitude items to a sample of 2,237 individuals and using heritability estimates for these items from previous studies (Eaves, Eysenck, and Martin 1989; Martin et al. 1986; Olson et al. 2001), found that attitude complexity was associated with increased heritability. This relationship between heritability and complexity persisted even when controlling for a variety of mediating processes (such as attitude importance or cognitive effort associated with the attitude), indicating that genetic factors can operate under a multitude of pathways, not all of which have yet been accounted for or even investigated in the literature.

Emotional Traits and States

Affective traits, such as the broad positive affectivity (PA) and negative affectivity (NA) factors from the Positive and Negative Affect Schedule (PANAS; Watson, Clark, and Tellegen 1988), are enduring dispositional characteristics of individuals that predispose them to experience certain emotions, emotional reactions, or moods; PA generally relates to positive feelings such as pride, interest, and happiness, while NA generally relates to negative feelings such as anger, fear, and anxiety (Watson et al. 1999; Watson 2000). These dispositional traits represent individual differences in affective temperament. They have been conceptualized as reflecting differences among individuals in bio-behavioral systems that regulate sensitivities to rewards and punishments and thus control appetitive and aversive motivation (the behavioral approach system and the behavioral inhibition system, respectively; see Fowles 1987; Gray 1981, 1990; Watson et al. 1999).

These two bio-behavioral systems are thought to have evolved through natural selection and thus to have adaptive value (MacDonald 1995; Nesse 1991; Watson et al. 1999). As noted earlier, two of the five traits from the five-factor model, neuroticism and extraversion, have also been traditionally associated with the experience of affect and emotion (Watson 2000), and there is evidence for the genetic bases of these two traits. Loehlin (1992), for example, estimated various path models on personality data reported in several behavioral genetics studies of personality conducted in multiple countries (e.g., Britain, the United States,

Sweden, and Australia). The broad heritabilities of neuroticism and extraversion, estimated by a path model that fit the data well (and included all five factors), were .41 and .49, .respectively.

The positive and negative emotionality high-order traits from the Multidimensional Personality Questionnaire (MPQ; Tellegen 1985) are perhaps the most closely associated with the broad PA and NA factors from the PANAS. Finkel and McGue (1997) report broad heritabilities of .50 and .44 for positive and negative emotionality, and another study has found heritabilities of .43 and .47 (Bouchard and McGue 2003, table 6). Because the experience of affective states, or moods, is influenced by affective traits, and these traits are heritable, one can reasonably conclude that affective experiences are influenced by genetic factors. Indeed, there is some research examining the influence of genetics on affective states. Unlike affective traits, which are relatively stable, affective states fluctuate substantially across time (Watson 2000), including when people are at work (e.g., Ilies and Judge 2003). These temporal changes are, at least in part, determined by the situation in which the respondents are when the affective state is assessed. Thus, if general affective tendencies are determined by affective traits (which are in turn influenced by genetics), and the actual affective experience is influenced in part by situations, the change in affective experience across situations represents, in fact, a person-situation interaction (Riemann et al. 1998). On this topic, Riemann et al. examined positive and negative mood experiences of twin pairs across five situations. Their results showed that genetic effects on aggregate mood measures were substantial and also that there were genetic influences on the consistency of moods across situations.

Work and Non-work Behaviors

Genetic influences can have a significant effect on a wide range of behaviors, some of them with important implications for workplace functioning. For example, McCall et al. (1997), in a sample of 1,236 monozygotic and 1,165 dizygotic twin pairs, found that genetic differences accounted for 36% of job-change frequency and 26% of occupation-change frequency. As turnover is a particularly costly part of human resource management (see Tziner and Birati 1996), the implications of genetic influences on such work behaviors for organizations can be quite important.

In terms of variables that can relate directly to employee performance (another variable of particular interest to organizational behavior scholarship and practice), Deater-Deckard et al. (2005), in a sample of 92 monozygotic and 139 dizygotic pairs of twin children, found that task persistence had a significant heritable component ($h^2 = .59$) and that this estimate tended to increase over time (that is, the heritable component of task persistence increased as people aged). Even though this sample was of course not representative of (nor directly generalizable to) adult employees, their findings can provide some initial insight into the differences that exist between people in terms of motivation, effort expended, and (perhaps ultimately) performance on the job.

In addition to performance, behaviors that organizations consider undesirable can also be influenced by genetic factors. For example, in a meta-analysis of genetic influences across time, Bergen, Gardner, and Kendler (2007) reported that genetics can have an impact on aggressive behaviors manifested by individuals, which could potentially have implications for organizational safety and the psychological and physical well-being of employees. Specifically, the authors found a significant heritability index for externalizing behavior (a domain associated with antisocial behavior, conduct disorder, and similar behaviors), as well as a tendency for this effect to increase over time.

Similarly, Cates et al. (1993), in a study of hostility-related traits, attitudes, and behaviors involving 109 pairs of female twins (77 monozygotic, 21 dizygotic) recruited from the Midwest Twin Register, found significant heritability for verbal and indirect hostility, as well as trait-anger (i.e., a trait indicating chronic anger and the tendency to anger easily) and irritability. However, no significant genetic component of hostility-related attitudes or physical aggression was found. These results may suggest that demographics (such as gender) can represent important moderating variables in the study of genetic effects, or that more interactive effects need to be considered and examined. They also indicate that, from a broader perspective, gene–environment (GE) interaction investigations can provide significant insights. Moreover, such insights can also arise from more basic investigations that look into components of the environment, such as gender roles, stratification effects, and so forth.

Entrepreneurial behaviors have also been the focus of recent investigations. Zhang et al. (2009), in a study involving 1,285 monozygotic and 849 pairs of dizygotic pairs of twins (for a total of 449 male and 836 female pairs, and 283 male and 566 female pairs, respectively), found strong heritability for entrepreneurship for females but not for males. Similarly, Nicolaou et al. (2009), using a sample consisting of 851 pairs of monozygotic and 855 pairs of dizygotic female twins raised together, found that a substantial part of opportunity-recognition abilities had a genetic component (.45 estimate) and that genetic factors accounted for a large percentage (53%) of the relationship between recognizing opportunities and the tendency to be an entrepreneur.

These results mirror investigations in other areas of behavior that have indicated important genetic influences on a host of human behaviors that could potentially be of interest to scholarship and practice in a variety of fields. For example, Harlaar et al. (2008), in a sample of 2,334 twin pairs (including 297 male monozygotic, 446 female monozygotic, 438 male dizygotic, 664 female dizygotic, and 489 opposite-sex dizygotic pairs) demonstrated that parenting styles have a significant genetic component, with genetic factors accounting for 17% to 30% of the variance in parenting styles, including physical affection, control, responsiveness, and abusiveness. It is reasonable to conclude, therefore, that genetic factors play an important role in determining individual behavior as well as attitudes.

STUDIES EXAMINING CAUSAL GENETIC MODELS THAT LINK ATTITUDES AND BEHAVIORS

Two decades ago, Arvey et al. (1989) and Judge (1992) speculated that heritability in job satisfaction could be explained by personality factors, and recent investigations have begun to develop more sophisticated models investigating the relationships between genetics, attitudes, and behavior. Such approaches are particularly important not only in establishing the presence of these phenomena of interest, but also in illustrating how these effects might operate. They may therefore give us a clear understanding of the mechanisms and intermediate variables involved and are thus invaluable in promoting knowledge in this field.

Indeed, personality variables in particular have shown great promise in explaining the relationships between genetics and attitudes. These variables are ideally positioned in that role, as they have been shown to be significantly influenced by genetics and also have demonstrated relationships with workplace attitudes and behavior, thus being theoretically and conceptually well positioned to explain causal mediated models. For example, Loehlin (1992) reported mean narrow heritability estimates of .34, and broad heritability estimates of .45 for the five-factor model, perhaps the most commonly used personality framework (Goldberg, 1992). Bouchard (1994) reported similar estimates of heritability (average of .41) in a combined analysis of twins raised together and apart from the Minnesota Study of Twins Reared Apart.

In a more explicit examination of a mediated model, Ilies and Judge (2003) investigated the degree to which individual dispositions (including the five-factor model of personality and positive/negative affectivity) might mediate the relationship between genetics and job satisfaction. Using a method that involved correlation estimates derived from previous meta-analytic investigations of the five-factor model, positive and negative affectivity, as well as the heritability of these variables and their relationships with job satisfaction, these authors found that approximately 45% of genetic influences on job satisfaction were mediated by positive and negative affectivity, and approximately 24% were mediated by the personality dimensions of the five-factor model. Similar results were reported by Zhang et al. (2009), who found a mediating effect of personality on entrepreneurial tendencies (with extraversion and neuroticism mediating the effects of genetic influences on women's entrepreneurial tendencies). These results support the argument that at least part of the genetic component of job satisfaction and other attitudes and tendencies of interest to organizational psychologists is represented by individual affective and personality dispositions by providing examinations of specific potential pathways linking genetic influences and workplace attitudes and behaviors.

Other authors, however, have followed a different pathway, investigating whether genetic factors can mediate the relationship between other variables of interest (i.e., outside of personality and attitudes). For example, Bergeman et al. (1991), utilizing a sample of 424 older twin pairs (64 monozygotic pairs raised apart, 95 monozygotic pairs raised together, 132 dizygotic pairs raised apart, and 133 dizygotic pairs raised together), found that genetic influences mediated a substantial part of the relationship between perceived adequacy of social support and subjective well-being (including depression and life satisfaction). Specifically, genetic factors accounted for 65% of the relationship between the social support and depression and 56% of the relationship between perceived social support and life satisfaction. These results indicate that alternative conceptualizations of genetic influences in the causal structure linking attitudes and behaviors can also be supported by data, and they highlight the importance of investigating these phenomena from a variety of viewpoints.

Apart from theoretical and conceptual approaches such as the ones described above, progress in the field is also aided by novel and sophisticated methodologies that enable researchers to gain a more accurate and specific understanding of the effects of genetic influences. For example, advances in statistics have enabled researchers to conduct multigroup structural equation modeling, allowing more precise and less biased estimates of effects across groups with different genetic similarities. Other advances have introduced multivariate methods that are capable of estimating the heritability of multiple variables simultaneously. Such methods can be invaluable in testing complex mediated models that aim to investigate how genetics and environment affect variables of interest through (potentially multiple) intervening pathways. They allow us to identify the variables that mediate the linkages between genetic and latent or phenotypic variables, and also to test the relative importance of multiple variables of those kinds. This in turn allows researchers to simultaneously test competing hypotheses and ultimately to test complex theoretical approaches as a whole.

Similarly, other advances in statistical methodology and research design have made possible the estimation of genetic and environmental correlations, thus allowing researchers to investigate whether particular genetic influences tend to coincide with particular environmental characteristics or specific experiences and thus to conduct further investigations into the ways in which genetics and environment relate to each other. Such approaches can ultimately make the investigation of interactive gene and environmental effects much more accurate and feasible, allowing for more research that investigates the interplay between these two factors and how one can alter the effects of the other. In general then, the aforementioned theoretical, conceptual, and methodological advances have already allowed for much more nuanced investigations and insights, and their contribution to organizational and other disciplines is expected to increase.

OPERATIONAL AND LEGAL IMPLICATIONS

The various streams of research that we have reviewed provide conclusions that can significantly affect a variety of facets of organizational life. From an operational standpoint, they speak to a need for organizational and human-capital professionals to take the characteristics of individual differences (and traits in general) seriously. While broad personality traits have been a source of controversy in the organizational literature (see Morgeson et al. 2007), the genetic bases of other individual factors with potentially important implications for organizational life (such as aggression and risk-taking) warrant a more careful approach in organizational practices. Whereas personnel selection would seem to be the prime function for such considerations, training and development, performance management, and retention would also need to take into account the existence of stable traits, their behavioral and attitudinal outcomes, and the capacity (or lack thereof) of these relationships to change.

Such considerations, however, might not long remain free from controversy. In terms of legal concerns, overt investigations that include genetic information are not well accepted. For example, in the United States the Genetic Information Nondiscrimination Act (GINA) of 2008 made it illegal to discriminate against individuals on the basis of genetic tests. Of course, this law was mainly intended to protect individuals from discrimination based on medical conditions with a genetic component; however, with increasing sophistication in genetic research (and from the perspective of legal professionals), it does seem possible that organizational practices that touch upon individual differences could become increasingly controversial in the future. For example, selection tests that capture a trait that has been demonstrated to have a strong genetic component could at some point be challenged in court as indirectly assessing protected genetic information, with potentially unforeseen yet important implications for organizational practice.

CONCLUSIONS AND DIRECTIONS FOR FUTURE RESEARCH

In this chapter, we suggest that organizational researchers examine genetic influences on work behavior and develop and test explanatory models linking genetics to work behaviors through personality, attitudes, emotions, or other constructs relevant to organizational behavior. In addition, more complex models that include GE interactions and GE correlations could be developed to explain behavioral and emotional tendencies that are relevant to on-the-job behaviors. Towards that end, there are examples of research from other areas that have successfully studied such GE effects on constructs that are indirectly relevant to organizational behavior (e.g., popularity; Burt 2009).

We suggest that the greatest contributions at this point may come from researchers who utilize methodological and conceptual advances to outline, develop, and test theoretically grounded models of the pathways (including affective, dispositional, and perceptual processes) by which genetics can influence conceptually linked clusters of organizational variables (such as work-related attitudes [e.g., job satisfaction], behaviors, or performance). Such approaches can serve not only to advance our understanding of genetic effects, but also to do so in a way that is well suited to the accumulation of knowledge and the building of interdisciplinary consensus. Moreover, such attempts can further magnify their contributions to academia, practice, and society at large by paying increased attention to the potential implications for application, with an eye toward the organizational, individual, and legal ramifications of accumulated findings. Such increased attention is mandated by the need to link future study of genetic influences to existing bodies of knowledge (much of it in more applied areas such as industrial/organizational psychology), as well as by the increasing number of laws that can affect both how studies are conducted and how their results might be implemented (see the Genetic Information Nondiscrimination Act of 2008 in the United States).

Notes

1. Evolutionary synthesis also helped answer the question of how species originate, a question that has been difficult to answer within the tenets of Darwin's theory of natural selection (by itself, evolution through natural selection as a gradual and continuous process is seemingly at odds with the discontinuity between species). Mayr (1942; 1991) proposed that when populations of organisms become separated, they develop different characteristics, and thus can no longer interbreed.

References

Arvey, R. D., Bouchard, T. J., Segal, N. L., and Abraham, L. M. 1989. Job satisfaction: Environmental and genetic components. *Journal of Applied Psychology* 74:187–92.

———, McCall, B. P., Bouchard, T. J., Taubman, P., and Cavanaugh, M. A. 1994. Genetic influences on job satisfaction and work values. *Personality and Individual Differences* 17:21–33.

———, Zhang, Z., Avolio, B. J., and Krueger, R. F. 2007. Developmental and genetic determinants of leadership role occupancy among women. *Journal of Applied Psychology* 92 (3): 693–706.

Bergeman, C. S., Plomin, R., Pedersen, N. L., and McClearn, G. E. 1991. Genetic mediation of the relationship between social support and psychological well-being. *Psychology and Aging* 6:640–46.

Bergen, S. E., Gardner, C. O., and Kendler, K. S. 2007. Age-related changes in heritability of behavioral phenotypes over adolescence and young adulthood: A meta-analysis. *Twin Research and Human Genetics* 10:423–33.

Bouchard, T. J., Jr. 1994. Genes, environment and personality. *Science* 264:1700.

———, Arvey, R. D., Keller, L. M., and Segal, N. L. 1992. Genetic influences on job satisfaction: A reply to Cropanzano and James. *Journal of Applied Psychology* 77:89–93.

———, and McGue, M. 2003. Genetic and environmental influences on human psychological differences. *Journal of Neurobiology* 54 (1): 4–45.

Burt, S. A. 2009. A mechanistic explanation of popularity: Genes, rule breaking, and evocative gene-environment correlations. *Journal of Personality and Social Psychology* 96:783–94.

Buss, D. M. 1991. Evolutionary personality psychology. *Annual Review of Psychology* 42:459–91.

———. 2001. Human nature and culture: An evolutionary psychological perspective. *Journal of Personality* 69:955–78.

———, and Hawley, P. H., eds. 2010. *The evolution of personality and individual differences*. New York: Oxford University Press.

Cates, D. S., Houston, B. K., Vavak, C. R., Crawford, M. H., and Uttley, M. 1993. Heritability of hostility-related emotions, attitudes, and behaviors. *Journal of Behavioral Medicine* 16:237–56.

Connolly, J. J., and Viswesvaran, C. 2000. The role of affectivity in job satisfaction: A meta-analysis. *Personality and Individual Differences* 29 (2): 265–81.

Conway, L. G., Dodds, D. P., Towgood, K. H., McClure, S., and Olson, J. M. 2011. The biological roots of complex thinking: Are heritable attitudes more complex? *Journal of Personality* 79:101–34.

Cropanzano, R., and James, K. 1990. Some methodological considerations for the behavioral genetic analysis of work attitudes. *Journal of Applied Psychology* 75: 433–39.

Deater-Deckard, K., Petrill, S. A., Thompson, L. A., and DeThorne, L. S. 2005. A cross-sectional behavioral genetic analysis of task persistence in the transition to middle-childhood. *Developmental Science* 8:21–26.

Eaves, L. J., Eysenck, H. J., and Martin, N. G. 1989. *Genes, culture, and personality: An empirical approach*. London: Academic Press.

Finkel, D., and McGue, M. 1997. Sex differences and nonadditivity in heritability of the Multidimensional Personality Questionnaire scales. *Journal of Personality and Social Psychology* 72:929–38.

Fowles, D. C. 1987. Application of a behavioral theory of motivation to the concepts of anxiety and impulsivity. *Journal of Research in Personality* 21:417–35.

Galton, F. 1865. Hereditary talent and character. *Macmillan's Magazine* 12:157–66, 318–27.

Goldberg, L. R. 1990. An alternative "description of personality": The Big-Five factor structure. *Journal of Personality and Social Psychology* 59:1216–29.

———. 1992. The development of markers for the Big-Five factor structure. *Psychological assessment*, 4 (1): 26–42.

Gray, J. A. 1981. A critique of Eysenck's theory of personality. In *A model for personality*, ed. H. J. Eysenck, 246–76. New York: Springer.

———. 1990. Brain systems that mediate both emotion and cognition. *Cognition and Emotion* 4:269–88.

Harlaar, N., Santtila, P., Björklund, J., Alanko, K., Jern, P., Varjonen, M., von der Pahlen, B., and Sandnabba, K. 2008. Retrospective reports of parental physical affection and parenting style: A study of Finnish twins. *Journal of family psychology*, 50: 605–13.

Harris, J. R., Pedersen, N. L., Stacey, C., McClearn, G. E., and Nesselroade, J. R. 1992.

Age differences in the etiology of the relationship between life satisfaction and self-rated health. *Journal of Aging and Health* 4 (3): 349–68.

Hershberger, S. L., Lichtenstein, P., and Knox, S. S. 1994. Genetic and environmental influences on perceptions of organizational climate. *Journal of Applied Psychology* 79:24–33.

Hoppock, R. 1935. *Job Satisfaction.* Oxford: Harper.

House, R. J., Shane, S. A., and Herold, D. M. 1996. Rumors of the death of dispositional research are vastly exaggerated. *Academy of Management Review* 21 (1): 203–24.

Goldberg, L. R. 1993. The structure of phenotypic personality traits. *American Psychologist* 48 (1): 26–34.

Ilies, R., Arvey, R. D., and Bouchard, T. J., Jr. 2006. Darwinism, behavioral genetics and organizational behavior: A review and agenda for future research. *Journal of Organizational Behavior* 27:121–41.

———, and Judge, T. A. 2003. On the heritability of job satisfaction: The mediating role of personality. *Journal of Applied Psychology* 88:750–59.

———, Fulmer, I., Spitzmuller, M., and Johnson, M. 2009. Personality and citizenship behavior: The mediating role of job satisfaction. *Journal of Applied Psychology* 94:945–59.

Johnson, W., and Krueger, R. F. 2006. How money buys happiness: Genetic and environmental processes linking finances and life satisfaction. *Journal of Personality and Social Psychology* 90:680–91.

Judge, T. A. 1992. The dispositional perspective in human resources research. *Research in Personnel and Human Resource Management* 10:31–72.

———, Heller, D., and Mount, M. K. 2002. Five-factor model of personality and job satisfaction. *Journal of Applied Psychology* 87:530–41.

———, and Hulin, C. L. 1993. Job satisfaction as a reflection of disposition: A multiple source causal analysis. *Organizational Behavior and Human Decision Processes* 56 (3): 388–421.

———, and Locke, E. A. 1993. Effect of dysfunctional thought processes on subjective well-being and job satisfaction. *Journal of Applied Psychology* 78:475–90.

Keller, L. M., Bouchard, T. J., Jr., Arvey, R. D., Segal, N. L., and Dawis, R. V. 1992. Work values: Genetic and environmental influences. *Journal of Applied Psychology* 77:79–88.

Loehlin, J. C. 1992. *Genes and environment in personality development.* Newbury Park, CA: Sage.

Locke, E. A. 1976. The nature and causes of job satisfaction. In *Handbook of industrial and organizational psychology,* ed. M. D. Dunette, 1279–1343. Chicago: Rand McNally.

Lusk, J., MacDonald, K., and Newman, J. R. 1998. Resource appraisals among self, friend and leader: Implications for an evolutionary perspective on individual differences and a resource/reciprocity perspective on friendship. *Personality and Individual Differences* 24:685–700.

MacDonald, K. B. 1991. A perspective on Darwinian psychology: The importance of domain-general mechanisms, plasticity, and individual differences. *Ethology and Sociobiology* 12:449–80.

———. 1995. Evolution, the five-factor model, and levels of personality. *Journal of Personality* 63:525–67.

———. 1998. Evolution, culture, and the five-factor model. *Journal of Cross-Cultural Psychology* 29:119–49.

Martin, N. G., Eaves, L. J., Heath, A. R., Jardine, R., Feingold, L. M., and Eysenck, H. J. 1986. Transmission of social attitudes. *Proceedings of the National Academy of Science* 83, 4364–68.

Mayr, E. 1942. *Systematics and the Origin of Species.* New York: Columbia University Press.

———. 1991. *One long argument: Charles Darwin and the genesis of modern evolutionary thought.* Cambridge, MA: Harvard University Press.

———, and Provine, W., eds. 1980. *The evolutionary synthesis.* Cambridge, MA: Harvard University Press.

McCall, B. P., Cavanaugh, M. A., Arvey, R. D., and Taubman, P. 1997. Genetic influences on job and occupational switching. *Journal of Vocational Behavior* 50:60–77.

McGue, M., and Bouchard, T. J. 1998. Genetic and environmental influences on human behavioral differences. *Annual Review of Neuroscience* 21:1–24.

Morgeson, F. P., Campion, M. A., Dipboye, R. L., Hollenbeck, J. R., Murphy, K., and Schmitt, N. 2007. Are we getting fooled again? Coming to terms with limitations in the use of personality tests for personnel selection. *Personnel Psychology* 60:1029–49.

Nesse, R. M. 1991. What good is feeling bad? The evolutionary benefits of psychic pain. *The Sciences* (November/December): 30–37.

Nettle, D. 2006. The evolution of personality variation in humans and other animals. *American Psychologist* 61 (6): 622–31.

Nicolaou, N., Shane, S., Cherkas, L., and Spector, T. D. 2009. Opportunity recognition and the tendency to be an entrepreneur: A bivariate genetics perspective. *Organizational Behavior and Human Decision Processes* 110:108–17.

Olson, J. M., Vernon, P. A., Harris, J. A., and Jang, K. L. 2001. The heritability of attitudes: A study of twins. *Journal of Personality and Social Psychology* 80:845–60.

Plomin, R., and Daniels, D. 1987. Why are children in the same family so different from one another? *Behavioral and Brain Sciences* 10:1–16.

Riemann, R., Angleitner, A., Borkenau, P., and Eid, M. 1998. Genetic and environmental sources of consistency and variability in positive and negative mood. *European Journal of Personality* 12:345–64.

Shane, S. 2009. Introduction to the focused issue on the biological basis of business. *Organizational Behavior and Human Decision Processes* 110:67–69.

Spector, P. E. 1997. *Job satisfaction: Application, assessment, causes, and consequences.* Vol. 3. Thousand Oaks, CA: Sage.

Staw, B. M., Bell, N. E., and Clausen, J. A. 1986. The dispositional approach to job attitudes: A lifetime longitudinal test. *Administrative Science Quarterly* 31:56–77.

———, and Ross, J. 1985. Stability in the midst of change: A dispositional approach to job attitudes. *Journal of Applied Psychology* 70 (3): 469–80.

Stubbe, J. H., Posthuma, D., Boomsma, D. I., and De Geus, E. J. C. 2005. Heritability of life satisfaction in adults: A twin-family study. *Psychological Medicine* 35:1581–88.

Tellegen, A. 1985. Structures of mood and personality and their relevance to assessing anxiety, with an emphasis on self-report. In *Anxiety and the anxiety disorders*, ed. A. H. Tuma and J. D. Maser, 681–706. Hillsdale, NJ: Erlbaum.

————, Lykken, D. T., Bouchard, T. J., Wilcox, K. J., Segal, N. L., and Rich, S. (1988). Personality similarity in twins reared apart and together. *Journal of Personality and Social Psychology* 54 (6): 1031–39.

Tesser, A. 1993. The importance of heritability in psychological research: The case of attitudes. *Psychological Review* 100:129–42.

————, Whitaker, D., Martin, L., and Ward, D. 1998. Attitude heritability, attitude change, and physiological responsivity. *Personality and Individual Differences* 24:89–96.

Tziner, A., and Birati, A. 1996. Assessing employee turnover costs: A revised approach. *Human Resource Management Review* 6:113–22.

Watson, D. 2000. *Mood and temperament.* New York: Guilford Press.

Watson, D., Clark, L. A., and Tellegen, A. 1988. Development and validation of brief measures of positive and negative affect: The *PANAS* scales. *Journal of Personality and Social Psychology* 54:1063–70.

————, Wiese, D., Vaidya, J., and Tellegen, A. 1999. The two general activation systems of affect: Structural findings, evolutionary considerations, and psychobiological evidence. *Journal of Personality and Social Psychology* 76:805–19.

Weitz, J. 1952. A neglected concept in the study of job satisfaction. *Personnel Psychology* 5:201–5.

Zhang, Z., Zyphur, M. J., Narayanan, J., Arvey, R. D., Chaturvedi, S., Avolio, B. J., et al. 2009. The genetic basis of entrepreneurship: Effects of gender and personality. *Organizational Behavior and Human Decision Processes* 110:93–107.

FOUR

The Biological Basis of Entrepreneurship

Scott Shane and Nicos Nicolaou

During the past fifty years, academics have tried to understand the factors that influence the tendency of people to engage in entrepreneurial activity. Research has identified a number of factors that affect this tendency, ranging from the industry they are in (Taylor 1996) to sociocultural factors (Aldrich 1990), the economic environment (Audretsch and Acs 1994), and individual differences and aspects of personality (Shane 2003). Recently, researchers have examined whether there is a genetic predisposition to entrepreneurship. By dint of our genetic makeup, are some of us more likely than others to come up with new business ideas, start companies, and engage in the other activities that entrepreneurs undertake? This new research suggests that the answer is yes. There is a biological component to entrepreneurial activity.

This chapter provides a framework to explain how human biology affects the tendency of people to become entrepreneurs and their performance at entrepreneurial activity. While understanding the biological basis of business activity is in its infancy, researchers have some clues about how this process works. Human biology exerts its influence in large part through genetic variation among individuals, which affects

We are grateful to Richard Arvey, Steve Colarelli, Joe Jackson, and the anonymous reviewers for their helpful comments and suggestions. We are grateful as well for funding from Philip Zepter grant no. ucy 31028.

appearance, personality, intelligence, cognitive style, brain function, and hormones.

Human beings vary in their genetic composition. These genetic differences lead to variation in entrepreneurial activity in four ways.[1] First, genetic differences lead to variation in physiological attributes that influence the tendency of people to become entrepreneurs. For instance, some researchers believe that genetic variation in dopamine receptors makes some people more likely than others to engage in activities, like starting businesses, that provide greater stimulation of the dopaminergic system. Genetic variation affects the *predisposition* of people to develop different physiological attributes, such as brain structure, neurotransmitter system function, hormone levels, physical strength, physical attractiveness, and so on (Plomin et al. 2008). While researchers have yet to explore many of these pathways, the evidence for genetic effects on their variation coupled with the plausibility of their influence on entrepreneurial activity suggests that genetic differences could influence entrepreneurial activity directly through a number of physiological attributes.

Second, genetically influenced variation also affects the tendency of people to develop psychological characteristics, attitudes, and preferences, which, in turn, affect their tendency to choose entrepreneurship as a vocation and their performance at it (See Shane et al. 2010. This mechanism differs from the first [direct *physiological* effects on hormones, brain activity, and appearance] in that it involves mediation through *psychological* characteristics, attitudes, and preferences.) For instance, genetic variation influences the tendency of some people to be more sensation-seeking than others. This tendency toward sensation-seeking, in turn, influences the propensity of people to start businesses.

Third, genetic factors also influence the tendency to be an entrepreneur and performance at entrepreneurship through gene-environment (GE) interactions. Most researchers believe that genes interact with the situations in which people find themselves to influence their behavior. The tendency to start a business may follow this pattern. For example, some people are born with variants of genes that make them more likely than others to seek novelty. Being born with these genetic variants may not lead a person to become an entrepreneur, because she could pursue novelty in many different ways. The person might start a business, but could also take up hang gliding, travel the world, or seek novelty in many other ways. Thus, the decision to start a business is unlikely to come just from having the versions of certain genes; rather, it is likely to arise from the interaction between those genetic variants *and* the right environmental triggers (Nicolaou and Shane 2009).

Fourth, genes may also influence the odds of becoming an entrepreneur through GE correlations (Nicolaou and Shane 2009). These correlations occur when a person's genetic composition influences the environments in which he operates. That is, the environments that people face are partly endogenously determined by their genetic propensities. By affecting the tendency of people to select into entrepreneurship-rich environments, our genes may influence the odds that we become entrepreneurs and our performance at this activity.

We discuss how researchers have learned about genetic effects on entrepreneurial activity and how they have identified the physiological pathways through which biological factors influence business behavior. We describe the two primary ways in which researchers seek to identify genetic effects on entrepreneurial activity: quantitative and molecular genetics studies. We also discuss how researchers use cognitive neuroscience and studies of hormones to examine the physiological mechanisms through which biological factors operate. Finally, we discuss the complexity of measuring genetic effects when many genes may influence entrepreneurship: those genes may have additive or multiplicative effects; genes may exert their influence through a variety of mechanisms; different genes may influence different aspects of entrepreneurial activity; and genes may have different effects over time.

Before we turn to a more detailed discussion of how genes affect entrepreneurial activity and how researchers have found evidence of these effects, we must first discuss the boundaries of the biological basis of entrepreneurial activity. While early research indicates that biology matters, it does not determine outcomes. Recognizing the difference between biology mattering and biology determining is crucial to understanding this new area of inquiry.

BOUNDARIES OF A BIOLOGICAL PERSPECTIVE ON ENTREPRENEURSHIP

Biological factors influence all aspects of human behavior and are solely responsible for none of them. This axiom undergirds why we start our discussion of a biological perspective on entrepreneurship with the boundaries of the perspective.

Human biology influences entrepreneurship, but does not determine it. This central assumption leads to six subpropositions about what we expect to find from investigations into the biological basis of entrepreneurial activity. First, genetic factors affect the *probability* that some individuals and not others will become entrepreneurs, but they do not *cause* people to do so. Stated differently, genetics does not have a deterministic effect on entrepreneurship; it has a probabilistic effect.

Second, genetics operates through many mechanisms, each of which is influenced by many genes. As a result, the effect of any single-nucleotide polymorphism (SNP) on entrepreneurial activity is likely to be very *small*, accounting for less than 1% of the variance in the phenomenon. This is consistent with molecular genetic findings on most behavioral variables for which a large number of genes are likely to be influential (Plomin et al. 2008).

Third, genetic influences on entrepreneurship are very likely to be *polygenic*: certain versions of many genetic polymorphisms are needed to increase the likelihood that an individual will become an entrepreneur. As a result, entrepreneurship, like any other behavioral outcome, is different from single-gene diseases such as Huntington's disease and phenylketonuria, in which a single gene is responsible for the disease. Thus, the presence of a particular polymorphism associated with entrepreneurship is neither necessary nor sufficient for an individual to engage in this activity.

Fourth, the influence of any given gene on entrepreneurship is very likely to be *pleiotropic*. This means that the same gene that increases the probability that people will engage in entrepreneurship also is likely to also increase the probability that they engage in other social activities. Therefore, genetic effects on entrepreneurship are likely to involve interactions between genes and environmental factors.

Fifth, the presence of genetic effects does not negate other influences on entrepreneurial activity. Genetic influences are *complementary* to the role of the environment in increasing the likelihood that some people and not others will engage in entrepreneurship. Therefore, the explanations that account for the most variance in why some people and not others engage in entrepreneurial activity or why some people perform better than others at it are likely to involve a mix of genetic and environmental factors.

Sixth, the likelihood that certain genes influence all aspects of entrepreneurial activity is very low. Rather, different combinations of genes probably influence different aspects of entrepreneurship. For instance, the genes that influence opportunity recognition may be different from the genes that affect opportunity exploitation.

Heritability is "the proportion of phenotypic differences among individuals that can be attributed to genetic differences in a particular population" (Plomin et al. 2008, 416). It describes the amount of variation due to genetic differences at a particular point in time and in a particular population. For example, evidence that the heritability of height is .90 means that 90% of the difference in height among people is due to genetic factors (Ward 2010).

Entrepreneurship is heritable (Nicolaou et al. 2008b; Zhang et al. 2009). Examining a variety of different measures of entrepreneurship—from starting a company to being self-employed—for a sample of 1,740 monozygotic (MZ) twins and 1,704 dizygotic (DZ)[2] twins from the United Kingdom, Nicolaou et al. (2008b) found a heritability of .41 for starting a business. (This indicates that 41% of the differences in starting a business among the people in the population studied were due to genetic factors.) These authors also found heritability estimates of .42 for number of businesses started, .37 for being an owner-operator and for the number of companies owned and operated, .48 for being self-employed, .39 for years self-employed, .41 for having engaged in a start-up effort, and .42 for the number of start-up efforts.[3] The findings of this UK study were replicated in two other studies. In a study of Swedish twins, Zhang et al. (2009) found a heritability estimate of .60 for entrepreneurship among females, and, in a study of US twins, Shane et al. (2010) found a heritability estimate of .48 for self-employment.

An important aspect of entrepreneurship is recognizing opportunities for new businesses. Indeed, one of the most fundamental questions for the field of entrepreneurship is why, when, and how some people and not others recognize the potential to generate an entrepreneurial profit (Shane and Venkataraman 2000; Shane 2003). Nicolaou et al. (2009) investigated whether the recognition of entrepreneurial opportunities has a genetic component. Measuring opportunity recognition using a five-item scale composed of questions like, "I enjoy thinking about new ways of doing things"; "I frequently identify opportunities to start-up new businesses (even though I may not pursue them)"; "I frequently identify ideas that can be converted into new products or services (even though I may not pursue them)," they found a heritability of .45 for opportunity recognition.

Studies have also found evidence of the heritability of entrepreneurial performance. For instance, in an investigation of self-employed MZ and DZ twins, Shane and Nicolaou (2013) found that the heritability of self-employment income was .74, which means that 74% of the differences in entrepreneurial performance among the people studied were due to genetic factors.

This estimate is quite large and may be a result of the small sample size in that particular study. Therefore, additional studies using much larger samples are required to corroborate this evidence. Nevertheless, the finding shows that entrepreneurial performance has a genetic component.

MECHANISMS THROUGH WHICH GENETIC DIFFERENCES INFLUENCE ENTREPRENEURSHIP

If entrepreneurship has a genetic component, an important question is *how* genes exert their influence. As mentioned in the introduction, researchers believe that genetic factors may affect the likelihood of engaging in entrepreneurship in four primary ways: (1) direct physiological effects, (2) genetic covariation with individual-level attributes; (3) GE interactions, and (4) GE correlations (Nicolaou and Shane 2009; White, Thornhill, and Hampson 2006). While these mechanisms could also apply to most vocations and professions, we focus specifically on entrepreneurship in this chapter.

Direct Genetic Effects on Physiology

Genetic factors may influence entrepreneurial activity through direct physiological effects. These include the effects of genes on appearance, hormones, and brain function.

Genes may affect entrepreneurial activity by influencing appearance. Genetics affects hair color, eye color, height, weight, and body shape. Because these factors collectively influence how attractive people are to others, genetics clearly influences physical attractiveness. Genetically influenced physical attractiveness, in turn, affects several aspects of entrepreneurial activity. Baron, Markman, and Bollinger (2006) found that both entrepreneurs and their products were viewed more positively by others if the entrepreneurs were judged to be physically attractive. Baron, Markman, and Bollinger (2006) also found that observers thought entrepreneurs who were more attractive made better presentations to investors. Finally, Baron and Markman (1999) found that people who were judged to be physically attractive earned more money from running their own businesses than those judged to be less physically attractive.

Genes may affect entrepreneurial activity by influencing hormones.

While relatively little research has examined how this mechanism operates, initial work on three hormones—testosterone, oxytocin, and cortisol—suggests several pathways. Testosterone, an androgenic hormone produced in the testes, ovaries, and, in lower amounts, in the adrenal glands of both men and women, has been shown to have a strong genetic predisposition (Harris, Vernon, and Boomsma 1998; Meikle et al. 1988a). Genetically influenced testosterone levels have been associated with greater odds that people will engage in entrepreneurial activity. Specifically, White, Thornhill, and Hampson (2006) found that testosterone levels were higher among individuals with start-up experience than among those with no start-up experience in an analysis of 110 male MBA students.

Oxytocin is a hormone generated by the hypothalamus that also has a strong genetic predisposition (Meikle et al. 1988b). While no research has yet examined the direct effect of oxytocin on entrepreneurial activity, research findings on the effect of oxytocin on human behavior suggest the plausibility of such an effect. Experimental evidence shows that oxytocin increases the tendency to trust others (Kosfeld et al. 2005). Because entrepreneurs tend to be more skeptical and less trusting than others (Fraboni and Saltstone 1990; Zhao and Seibert 2006), it is plausible that genetically influenced levels of oxytocin are responsible for the difference. Those with a genetic predisposition to high levels of oxytocin may select out of entrepreneurial activity due to their tendency to act in more trusting and less skeptical ways.

Cortisol is a third hormone that plausibly could affect entrepreneurial activity. While no studies have yet tested the hypothesis, cortisol levels, which are partly influenced by a person's genetic composition, affect a person's perception of the time value of money. People whose genetic makeup leads them to have higher cortisol levels tend to be more prone to stress and anxiety about the future. As a result, they engage in more severe time discounting and may be less likely to engage in entrepreneurship because entrepreneurship involves delayed gratification.

Genetics also may influence entrepreneurial activity by influencing brain function. While little research has yet to explore the relationship between genetically influenced aspects of brain function and entrepreneurial activity, indirect evidence suggests two likely avenues: attention deficit hyperactivity disorder (ADHD) and dyslexia.

Several studies show that ADHD is highly heritable (Thapar et al. 2000; McLoughlin et al. 2007) and other studies have identified specific genes associated with ADHD (Faraone and Mick 2010). The genetic predisposition to develop ADHD might affect the tendency to engage in entrepreneurship because people with ADHD are disproportionately likely to own their own companies (Mannuzza et al. 1993). Jet Blue's founder, David Neeleman has ADHD and posits a causal mechanism for this genetic effect (Low 2009). He says, "My ADD brain naturally searches for better ways of doing things. With the disorganization, procrastination, inability to focus, and all the other bad things that come with ADD, there also come creativity and the ability to take risks." Thus the way that particular genetic variations influence brain function might influence the ability to see new business opportunities, which, in turn, influences the odds of being an entrepreneur.

The influence of genes on the functioning of the language centers of the brain may also influence the tendency of people to be entrepreneurs. Indeed, those with dyslexia have been found to be more than twice as likely to be in business for themselves as those without the disorder (Pinker 2008). Research has shown a high level of heritability to dyslexia, and specific genes have been found to be associated with the disorder (Plomin and Kovas 2005; Olson 2002; Hannula-Jouppi et al. 2005). Genetic effects on the way the brain processes language may motivate some people to select into occupations that demand less reading and writing of words and numbers, which would include running one's own business.

Genetic Covariation with Individual Attributes

Genetic factors may influence entrepreneurial activity through genetic covariation with individual-level attributes associated with entrepreneurial activity. These attributes include, but are not limited to, personality characteristics. They also include cognitive factors, attitudes, skills, and abilities (Baron 2004).

Although researchers have not yet begun to look at the genetic covariation between cognitive factors, attitudes, skills, or abilities and the tendency to engage in entrepreneurship, they have begun to examine the genetic covariation between entrepreneurship and a number of psychological attributes. Nicolaou et al. (2008a) found that sensation-seeking (Zuckerman 1994; Stephenson et al. 2003), a personality characteristic associated with a desire for novelty and change, accounts for part of the genetic predisposition to entrepreneurship.

Shane et al. (2010) examined whether the Big Five personality characteristics of extraversion, agreeableness, emotional stability, openness to experience, and conscientiousness mediated the heritability of entrepreneurship in two samples of UK and US twins. They utilized bivariate genetics techniques to determine the degree to which the correlation between each of the Big Five and the tendency to be an entrepreneur is a function of genetic factors. The study examined the cross-characteristic, cross-twin correlations between each of the Big Five and the tendency to be an entrepreneur across MZ and DZ twin pairs. Greater MZ than DZ cross-characteristic, cross-twin correlations suggest that genetic factors account for part of the correlation between each of the Big Five and the tendency to be an entrepreneur. Shane et al. (2010) found that genetic factors accounted for 80% and 74% of the correlation between openness to experience and the tendency to be an entrepreneur in the US and UK samples, respectively, and between 60% and 62% of the correlation between extraversion and the tendency to be an entrepreneur in the US and UK samples, respectively.

Scholars have also investigated whether there is genetic covariation between individual attributes and opportunity recognition and between individual attributes and entrepreneurial performance. Using a sample of 1,740 MZ and 1,714 DZ twins, Shane et al. (2010) found that genetic factors accounted for 62% of the correlation between openness to experience and opportunity recognition. Shane and Nicolaou (2013) found that genetic factors accounted for 38%, 61%, and 100% of the correlation between openness to experience, extraversion, agreeableness, and entrepreneurial performance, respectively.

Gene-Environment Interactions

Genetic factors may influence entrepreneurial activity through interactions with environmental factors (Nicolaou and Shane 2009). GE interaction means that the effect of environmental factors is contingent upon the presence of certain genotypes (Rowe 2003; Moffitt, Caspi, and Rutter 2005). That is, environmental stimuli have different effects on people depending on their genetic makeup. For example, in a sample of 835 pairs of MZ and 565 pairs of DZ Swedish twins, Zhang and Ilies (2010) showed that unfavorable family environment at childhood lowered the degree to which genetic factors influenced the propensity to engage in entrepreneurship in adulthood. Similarly, a study by White, Thornhill, and Hampson (2007) found that high levels of a strongly heritable steroid hormone, testosterone, interacted with family business background to increase the odds that people engaged in entrepreneurial activity.

Although there are no GE studies in entrepreneurship that have interacted a specific genetic polymorphism with an environmental trigger, other related studies show the plausibility of this mechanism in entrepreneurship. For example, Keltikangas-Järvinen et al. (2004) found that the DRD4 gene moderated the impact of the rearing environment on novelty-seeking. Because entrepreneurship involves seeking novel products and applications, the DRD4 gene may moderate the impact of a supportive environment on the likelihood of engaging in entrepreneurial activity.

Gene-Environment Correlations

Genetic factors may influence entrepreneurial activity through GE correlations (Nicolaou and Shane 2009). The environments that people experience are partly influenced by their genotypes, suggesting that genetic factors may influence entrepreneurship by increasing the odds that they will experience environments where the likelihood of engaging in entrepreneurship is greater.

There are three types of GE correlations: active, evocative, and passive (Plomin, DeFries, and Loehlin 1977; Ulbricht and Neiderhiser 2009). Active GE correlations occur when people seek and create environments associated with their genetic propensities (Plomin et al. 2008). Consider, for example, genetically influenced variation in mechanical aptitude. This genetically influenced capability is likely to affect the choices that people make throughout their lives. Those with mechanical aptitude will be more likely than those without it to choose activities in which they can exploit their skills. They might, for instance, be more likely to take a course in auto repair than those who have less mechanical aptitude. Learning automobile repair skills, in turn, increases the odds that one will work as an auto mechanic, because people tend to work in jobs for which they have received the requisite training. Because auto repair is an occupation for which running one's own business is more likely than many others (e.g., postal worker or elementary school teacher), a genetic endowment of mechanical aptitude ultimately affects one's odds of starting a business through active GE correlations.

Evocative GE correlations occur when people evoke reactions from others because of their genetic proclivities (Plomin et al. 2008). For example, people whose genetic makeup increases their sociability may elicit warmer responses from business angels and financiers when discussing their ventures.

Passive GE correlations occur "when children passively inherit from their parents family environments that are correlated with their genetic propensities" (Plomin et al. 2008, 319). For instance, if entrepreneurship is heritable, entrepreneurially gifted children are more likely to have entrepreneurially gifted parents who provide them both with the genes and with an environment supportive of entrepreneurship. For example, they might own a family business or discuss the issues they face in the business with their children.

RESEARCH DESIGNS FOR STUDYING BIOLOGICAL EFFECTS ON ENTREPRENEURIAL ACTIVITY

A variety of research techniques can be used for studying biological effects on entrepreneurial activity. They include quantitative genetics, molecular genetics, cognitive neuroscience, and studies of hormones.

Research Designs Employing Quantitative Genetics

Researchers have conducted two broad categories of research to obtain evidence of genetic effects on entrepreneurial activity: quantitative and molecular genetics. With quantitative genetics, researchers have used twins, an experiment of nature, and adopted children, an experiment of nurture, to separate genetic from environmental influences.

Twin studies investigate monozygotic (MZ; also known as identical) twins, and dizygotic (DZ; also known as nonidentical) twins. MZ twins are entirely genetically identical; DZ twins share, on average, 50% of their segregating genes (genetically, biological siblings and DZ twins are thus equivalent).

Comparing twin concordances for entrepreneurship between MZ and DZ twin pairs allows researchers to identify genetic differences in entrepreneurship. If there is no difference between MZ and DZ twin concordances for entrepreneurship, this would imply that genetic factors do not account for any part of the variance in entrepreneurship. Alternatively, greater MZ than DZ twin concordances would indicate that genetic factors are influential (Nicolaou et al. 2008b).

To examine whether genetic factors influence both entrepreneurship and a mediating variable, such as a personality trait or cognitive ability, researchers look at genetic correlations. By separating out the portion of a phenotypic correlation that comes from environmental and genetic factors, researchers can determine how much of the correlation between different variables is accounted for by genetic rather than environmental factors.

Quantitative genetics also includes studies of adoptive children, because these children share the genes of their biological parents but experience the environments of their adoptive parents. The different correlations between the entrepreneurial activities of children and their biological and adoptive parents allow researchers to identify the degree to which entrepreneurial activity is affected by genetic and environmental factors.

Research Designs Involving Molecular Genetics

Recently researchers have begun to examine entrepreneurship from a molecular genetics perspective. Molecular genetics tries to identify how specific variations in DNA increase the likelihood that some individuals and not others will engage in entrepreneurial activity. This search for genes that might influence the tendency to engage in entrepreneurial activity centers on two major approaches: candidate gene studies and genome-wide association studies (GWAS).

The candidate gene approach involves a hypothesis-driven design in which a number of genes are, a priori, hypothesized to influence the likelihood of engaging in entrepreneurship. For instance, using a candidate gene design, Nicolaou et al. (2011) examined the association between nine genes (five dopamine receptor genes [DRD1, DRD2, DRD3. DRD4, DRD5] and four genes associated with attention deficit hyperactivity disorder [SLC6A3, SNAP25, HTR1B, HTR1E]) and the likelihood of engaging in entrepreneurship in a sample of 1,335 people from the United Kingdom. The authors argued that because dopamine receptor genes have been associated with novelty/sensation-seeking (Benjamin et al. 1996; Noblett and Coccaro 2005) and sensation-seeking has been associated with entrepreneurship (Nicolaou et al. 2008a), it is plausible that dopamine receptor genes are associated with entrepreneurship. Similarly, as ADHD is more common among entrepreneurs than among others (Mannuzza et al. 1993), ADHD-related genes could also be associated with entrepreneurship. The study found that the rs1486011 polymorphism of the DRD3 gene was significantly associated with the tendency to become an entrepreneur.

In another study, Wernerfelt et al. (2012) examined the impact of specific polymorphisms in the DRD4, AVPR1a, and MAOA genes on the likelihood of being a serial entrepreneur. They found that individuals who had the long repeat of the RS3 microsatellite in the AVPR1a gene were more likely to be serial entrepreneurs (operationalized as those who started more than one company) than nonserial entrepreneurs (those who started only one or no companies).

A GWAS is a hypothesis free, gene-agnostic approach (Yeo 2011) in which the entire genome is tested for associations with entrepreneurship.

A recent GWAS of entrepreneurship found that the most encouraging genetic variant (rs10791283 of the OPCML gene) was only significant at the 6×10^{-7} level (Quaye et al. 2012). This is short of the genome-wide threshold for significance (10^{-8}), suggesting that very large sample sizes will be required to identify genes that reach genome-wide significance.

Research Designs Involving Cognitive Neuroscience

Cognitive neuroscience techniques can be useful in demonstrating the actual physiological processes that underlie entrepreneurial decision making. They may also help to explain *how* genetic factors influence entrepreneurship, because most genetic influences on entrepreneurship are likely to be mediated by some aspect of brain function.

The two most prominent methods in cognitive neuroscience that can be used in the study of entrepreneurship are functional magnetic resonance imaging (fMRI) and electroencephalography (EEG). Functional MRI detects hemodynamic changes in the brain while an individual is involved in a cognitive task that has a temporal resolution of no more than a few minutes. The technique utilizes the fact that blood flow increases in the activated parts of the brain and measures the ratio of oxygenated to deoxygenated hemoglobin, or blood oxygenated level-dependent (BOLD) effect (Gazzaniga, Russell, and Senior 2009). By contrast, electroencephalography (EEG) captures electrical recordings of the scalp and has a temporal resolution of milliseconds (Niedermeyer and Silva 1982).

Although neuroscience research has been conducted in financial decision making (Kuhnen and Knutson 2005), creativity (Fink, Graif, and Neubauer 2009), and decision making in the Ultimatum Game (Sanfey et al. 2003), we are unaware of any empirical research that has used neuroscientific techniques in entrepreneurship. At present researchers have only proposed areas where these techniques could contribute to understanding entrepreneurship (Holan 2014; Nicolaou and Shane 2014). For instance, Krueger and Day (2010) argue that these techniques could be used to investigate the role of emotions (Baron and Ward, 2004) in entrepreneurial decision making, or how entrepreneurs "connect the dots" in pattern recognition when they are recognizing entrepreneurial opportunities.

Research Designs Involving Hormones

Researchers can examine the effect of hormones on entrepreneurial activity. For example, as White et al. (2006) showed, researchers can measure hormone levels of entrepreneurs and non-entrepreneurs and use regression analysis to evaluate the impact of the hormone levels on entrepreneurial activity, either directly or in interaction with other factors. While research has examined the role of testosterone on entrepreneurial activity (White et al. 2006), there are no studies that examine the role of other hormones, such as cortisol or oxytocin, on entrepreneurial activity.

CONCLUSION

A number of studies have contributed to a biological perspective on entrepreneurship. While still in its infancy, this perspective incorporates and integrates research that has adopted quantitative genetic, molecular genetic, hormonal, and neuroscience approaches in studying the phenomenon.

The biological perspective has the potential to change many long-held beliefs about what explains certain long-observed empirical patterns in entrepreneurship. For instance, the biological perspective suggests that role modeling and learning may not be the only explanations for why the children of entrepreneurs are more likely than other people to become entrepreneurs. This empirical pattern may also result, at least in part, from genetic influences on entrepreneurship.

A biological perspective also suggests the use of different research designs to study the phenomenon than have been common in the entrepreneurship literature. If genetic factors influence entrepreneurship, for example, the use of non-experimental data to investigate the impact of environmental factors can lead to confounded estimates, because unobserved genetic factors may simultaneously influence both the dependent and independent variables (Kohler, Behrman, and Skythe 2005). One way to overcome the estimation problems caused by the effect of genetic factors on the environmental factors is by using co-twin control designs. Such designs use pairs of MZ twins to control for a wide range of factors (such as capabilities due to genetic predispositions, family background, cohort effects, neighborhood effects, etc.) that can otherwise lead to biased estimates. Such approaches will enable entrepreneurship scholars to conduct more rigorous empirical analyses of the relationship between environmental factors and the tendency to engage in entrepreneurial activity.

A biological perspective on entrepreneurship might point out *how* we can best influence entrepreneurial activity. It could someday help us to develop targeted "treatments" for entrepreneurship, just as we have developed targeted treatments for medical problems. Identifying treatments—such as specific incentive plans—that are designed to fit the biology of particular individuals might allow researchers to identify ways to encourage entrepreneurship among people whose biological attributes demand different approaches.

A biological perspective on entrepreneurship may someday have implications for career counseling. For example, people with ADHD or dyslexia may have an advantage in entrepreneurship. Therefore, such individuals could be encouraged to pursue entrepreneurial careers and turn what others may have considered a disadvantage into an asset for entrepreneurial success.

A biological perspective may also someday be important for policymakers. For instance, government officials might want to increase the number of people creating productive new businesses and decrease the number of people committing crimes. If genetic predispositions toward the pursuit of an opportunity interact with environmental triggers to account for which of these activities people undertake, then understanding interactions between genetic predispositions and environmental triggers might help policymakers to increase the amount of productive new businesses. The biological basis of entrepreneurship is a new and fascinating research area that holds the potential for creating new insights into our understanding of this important phenomenon.

Notes

1. A general argument for a biological basis for entrepreneurship could be made for most vocations and professions.

2. Monozygotic (MZ) twins share 100% of their genes, while dizygotic (DZ) twins share, on average, 50% of their segregating genes. Differences in the twin concordances for entrepreneurship between the pairs of the MZ and DZ twins can be attributed to genetic factors.

3. The entrepreneurship field does not agree on a definition of entrepreneurship. Some of the definitions that have been proposed include self-employment (Burke et al. 2000; Parker 2004), starting a new business (Gartner 1988; Delmar and Davidsson 2000), being an owner-operator (Ahmed 1985; Bitler et al. 2005) and being engaged in the start-up process (Reynolds et al. 2004; Ruef et al. 2003).

References

Aldrich, H. E. 1990. Using an ecological perspective to study organizational founding rates. *Entrepreneurship: Theory and Practice* 14 (3): 7–24.

Audretsch, D. B., and Acs, Z. J. 1994. New firm start-ups, technology and macroeconomic fluctuations. *Small Business Economics* 6 (6): 439–49.

Baron, R. A. 2004. Potential benefits of the cognitive perspective: Expanding entrepreneurship's array of conceptual tools. *Journal of Business Venturing* 19 (2): 169–72.

———, and Markman, G. D. 1999. The role of personal appearance in entrepreneurs' financial success: Effects and mediating mechanisms. (Working paper).

———, Markman, G. D., and Bollinger, M. 2006. Exporting social psychology: The effects of attractiveness on perceptions of entrepreneurs, their ideas for new products and their financial success. *Journal of Applied Social Psychology* 36 (2): 467–92.

———, and Ward, T. B. 2004. Expanding entrepreneurial cognition's toolbox: Potential contributions from the field of cognitive science. *Entrepreneurship Theory and Practice* 28 (6): 553–74.

Benjamin, J., Li, L., Patterson, C., Greenberg, B. D., Murphy, D. L., and Hamer, D. H. 1996. Population and familial association between the D4 dopamine receptor gene and measures of novelty seeking. *Nature Genetics* 12 (1): 81–84.

Faraone, S. V., and Mick, E. 2010. Molecular genetics of attention deficit hyperactivity disorder. *Psychiatric Clinics of North America*, 33 (1): 159–80.

Fink, A., Graif, B., and Neubauer, A. C. 2009. Brain correlates underlying creative thinking: EEG alpha activity in professional vs. novice dancers. *NeuroImage* 46 (3): 854–62.

Fraboni, M., and Saltstone, R. 1990. First and second generation entrepreneur typologies: Dimensions of personality. *Journal of Social Behavior and Personality* 5 (3): 105–13.

Gazzaniga, M.S., Russell, T., and Senior, C. 2009. *Methods in mind*. Cambridge, MA: MIT Press.

Hannula-Jouppi, K., Kaminen-Ahola, N., Taipale, M., Eklund, R., Nopola-Hemmi, J., Käariäinen, H., and Kere, J. 2005. The axon guidance receptor gene ROBO1 is a candidate gene for developmental dyslexia. *PLoS Genetics* 1 (4): 50.

Harris, J. A., Vernon, P. A., and Boomsma, D. I. 1998. The heritability of testosterone: A study of Dutch adolescent twins and their parents. *Behavior Genetics* 28 (3): 165–71.

Holan, P. M. 2014. It's all in your head: Why we need neuroentrepreneurship. *Journal of Management Inquiry* 23 (1): 93–97.

Keltikangas-Järvinen, L., Raikkonen, K., Ekelund, J., Peltonen, L. 2004. Nature and nurture in novelty seeking. *Molecular Psychiatry* 9 (3): 308–11.

Kohler, H.-P., Behrman, J. R., and Skytthe, A. 2005. Partner+Children=Happiness? The effect of fertility and partnerships on subjective well-being. *Population and Development Review* 31 (3): 407–45.

Kosfeld, M., Heinrichs, M., Zak, P. J., Fischbacher, U., and Fehr, E. 2005. Oxytocin increases trust in humans. *Nature* 435:673–76.

Krueger Jr, N. F., and Day, M. 2010. Looking forward, looking backward: From entrepreneurial cognition to neuroentrepreneurship. In *Handbook of entrepreneurship research*, ed. Z. J. Acs and D. B. Audretsch, 321–57. New York: Springer.

Kuhnen, C. M., and Knutson, B. 2005. The neural basis of financial risk taking. *Neuron* 47 (5): 763–70.

Low, K. 2009. Famous People with ADD: Meet David Neeleman. *About.com*, February 11. Online at http://add.about.com/od/famouspeoplewithadhd/a/davidneeleman.htm

Mannuzza, S., Klein, R. G., Bessler, A., Malloy, P., and La-Padula, M. 1993. Adult outcome of hyperactive boys: Educational achievement, occupational rank, and psychiatric status. *Archives of General Psychiatry*, 50 (7): 565–76.

McLoughlin, G., Ronald, A., Kuntsi, J., Asherson, P., and Plomin, R. 2007. Genetic support for the dual nature of attention deficit hyperactivity disorder: Substantial genetic overlap between the inattentive and hyperactive-impulsive components. *Journal of Abnormal Child Psychology* 35:999–1008.

Meikle, A. W., Stringham, J. D., Bishop, D. T., and West, D. W. 1988a. Quantitating genetic and nongenetic factors influencing androgen production and clearance rates in men. *Journal of Clinical Endocrinology and Metabolism* 67 (1): 104–9.

———, Stringham, J. D., Woodward, M. G., and Bishop, D. T. 1988b. Heritability of variation of plasma cortisol levels. *Metabolism* 37 (6): 514–17.

Moffitt, T. E., Caspi, A., and Rutter, M. 2005. Strategy for investigating interactions between measured genes and measured environments. *Archives of General Psychiatry* 62 (5): 473–81.

Nicolaou, N., Shane, S., Adi, G., Mangino, M., and Harris, J. 2011. A polymorphism associated with entrepreneurship: Evidence from dopamine receptor candidate genes. *Small Business Economics* 36 (2): 151–55.

———, and Shane, S. 2009. Can genetic factors influence the likelihood of engaging in entrepreneurial activity? *Journal of Business Venturing* 24 (1): 1–22.

———, and Shane, S. 2014. Biology, neuroscience and entrepreneurship. *Journal of Management Inquiry* 23 (1): 98–100.

———, Shane, S., Cherkas, L., and Spector, T. D. 2008a. The influence of sensation seeking in the heritability of entrepreneurship. *Strategic Entrepreneurship Journal* 2 (1): 7–21.

———, Shane, S., Cherkas, L., and Spector, T. D. 2009. Opportunity recognition and the tendency to be an entrepreneur: A bivariate genetics perspective. *Organizational Behavior and Human Decision Processes* 110 (2): 108–17.

———, Shane, S., Cherkas, L., Hunkin, J., and Spector, T. D. 2008b. Is the tendency to engage in entrepreneurship genetic? *Management Science* 54 (1): 167–79.

Niedermeyer, E., and Lopes da Silva, F. H. 1982. *Electroencephalography, basic principles, clinical applications, and related fields.* Baltimore, MD: Urban and Schwarzenberg.

Noblett, K. L., and Coccaro, E. F. 2005. Molecular genetics of personality. *Current Psychiatry Reports* 7 (1): 73–80.

Olson, R. K. 2002. Dyslexia: Nature and nurture. Dyslexia 8 (3): 143–59.

Pinker, S. 2008. *The sexual paradox: Men, women, and the real gender gap.* New York: Scribner.

Plomin, R., DeFries, J. C., and Loehlin, J. C. 1977. Genotype-environment interaction and correlation in the analysis of human behavior. *Psychological Bulletin* 84 (2): 309–22.

———, DeFries, J. C., McClearn, G. E., and McGuffin, P. 2008. *Behavioral Genetics.* 5th ed. New York: Worth.

———, and Kovas, Y. 2005. Generalist genes and learning disabilities. *Psychological Bulletin* 131 (4): 592–617.

Quaye, L., Nicolaou, N., Shane, S., and Mangino, M. 2012. A. Discovery Genome-wide association study of entrepreneurship. *International Journal of Developmental Science* 6 (3–4): 127–35.

Rowe, D. C. 2003. Assessing genotype-environment interactions and correlations in the postgenomic era. In *Behavioral Genetics in the Postgenomic Era*, ed. R. Plomin, J. C. DeFries, I. W. Craig, and P. McGuffin, 71–86. Washington, DC: American Psychological Association.

Sanfey, A. G., Rilling, J. K., Aronson, J. A., Nystrom, L. E., and Cohen, J. D. 2003. The neural basis of economic decision-making in the ultimatum game. *Science* 300:1755–58.

Shane, S. 2003. *A general theory of entrepreneurship: the individual-opportunity nexus*, Aldershot, UK: Edward Elgar.

———, and Nicolaou, N. 2013. The genetics of entrepreneurial performance. *International Small Business Journal* 31(5): 473–95.

———, Nicolaou, N., Cherkas, L, and Spector, T. 2010. Genetics, the Big Five, and the tendency to be an entrepreneur. *Journal of Applied Psychology* 95:1154–62.

———, and Venkataraman, S. 2000. The promise of entrepreneurship as a field of research. *Academy of Management Review* 25 (1): 217–26.

Taylor, M. P. 1996. Earnings, independence or unemployment: Why become self-employed? *Oxford Bulletin of Economics and Statistics* 58 (2): 253–66.

Thapar, A., Harrington, R., Ross, K., and McGuffin, P. 2000. Does the definition of ADHD affect heritability? *Journal of the American Academy of Child and Adolescent Psychiatry* 39 (12): 1528–36.

Ulbricht, J. A., and Neiderhiser, J. M. 2009. Genotype-environment correlation and family relationships. In *Handbook of Behavior Genetics*, ed. Y. K. Kim., 209–22. New York: Springer.

Ward, J. 2010. *The student's guide to cognitive neuroscience*. New York: Psychology Press.

Wernerfelt, N., Rand, D., Dreber, A., Montgomery, C., and Malhotra, D. K. 2012. Arginine vasopressin 1a receptor (AVPR1a) RS3 repeat polymorphism associated with entrepreneurship. Working paper, Harvard University. Available at SSRN: http://ssrn.com/abstract=2141598 or http://dx.doi.org/10.2139/ssrn.2141598.

White, R., Thornhill, S., and Hampson, E. 2006. Entrepreneurs and evolutionary biology: The relationship between testosterone and new venture creation. *Organizational Behavior and Human Decision Processes* 100 (1): 21–34.

———, Thornhill, S., and Hampson, E. 2007. A biosocial model of entrepreneurship: The combined effects of nurture and nature. *Journal of Organizational Behavior* 28 (4): 451–66.

Yeo, G. S. H. 2011. Where next for GWAS? *Briefings in Functional Genomics* 10 (2): 51.

Zhao, H., and Seibert, S. 2006. The big five personality dimensions and entrepreneurial status: A meta-analytic review. *Journal of Applied Psychology* 91 (2): 259–71.

Zhang, Z., and Ilies, R. 2010. Moderating effects of earlier family environment on genetic influences on entrepreneurship. Symposium presentation at the annual conference of the Academy of Management, Montréal, Canada.

Zhang, Z., Zyphur, M., Narayanan, J., Arvey, R., Chaturvedi, S., Avolio, B., et al. 2009. The genetic basis of entrepreneurship: Effects of gender and personality. *Organizational Behavior and Human Decision Processes*, 110 (2): 93–107.

Zuckerman, M. 1994. *Behavioral expressions and biosocial bases of sensation seeking.* Cambridge: Cambridge University Press.

FIVE

Fitness, Adaptation, and Survival:
The Role of Socio-Anthropic Characteristics,
Personality, and Intelligence in Work Behavior

Timothy A. Judge and Robert Hogan

INTRODUCTION

Many pioneers of modern psychology—Francis Galton, William James, William McDougall, G. Stanley Hall, Sigmund Freud—were enthusiastic Darwinians who believed the study of human behavior should begin with identifying the key biological tendencies underlying each behavior, tendencies that are themselves rooted in our evolutionary history as a species. Although many modern psychologists believe evolutionary psychology is largely speculative, we believe progress in understanding the behavior of people in organizations will require framing that behavior in an evolutionary context. In fact, we would argue that the workplace is often a compacted microculture wherein human behavior reflects behavior from evolutionarily earlier social settings. The elements are similar between the modern workplace and ancient groups of people: a need to gather into packs for survival, competition within and between packs, threats from outside the organization, and a need for leadership for survival. When it comes to the workplace, then, it seems we are all animals, some of us more evolved than others. A study of the evolution of human society can illuminate many of our work-behavior tendencies and suggest how to survive and thrive.

A review of the literature in sociology, anthropology, and primate field research (Chapais 2008) reveals four broad themes running through every society, and these themes point to the existence of important innate drivers of human behavior. The first and most important theme is that people evolved as animals living in groups (Wade 2006). About this generalization there is no dispute: we are social animals. This allows the inference that, at a deep and unconscious level, people are innately responsive to other people; we need social acceptance/approval and fear criticism/rejection (Baumeister and Leary 1995). Since there are, by nature, individual differences in this need, we can draw an interesting conclusion: people at the low end of the distribution (those low in need for social acceptance) will lack social support. While evolutionary study concludes that these individuals are therefore less likely to find life partners and, from an evolutionary perspective, reproduce—a catastrophic outcome for that line of the species—the more subtle but equally telling implications for organizational behavior are clear, since any organization is a study in group living.

The second theme running through every society is that throughout the course of our evolutionary history, human groups have been involved in almost constant warfare (Bowles 2009; Bowles and Gintis 2011; Keeley 1996; McNeill 1982). Although the level of intragroup violence in the last century has been severe, research proves that modern combat has not been as disastrous to our species as were earlier conflicts. In fact, violence actually is lower in modern society than in ancient times (Pinker 2010). Keeley (1996) estimates that if the wars of the twentieth century were as vicious as those "before civilization," there would have been more than two billion casualties as opposed to 180 million. While group living and warfare were probably the two most powerful influences on earlier stages of human evolution, the residue of those experiences has important implications for understanding peoples' behavior in organizations. For example, people need more than mere social acceptance from others; in the face of deadly external threats, they depend on the cooperation of others for their sheer survival. In addition, the natural history of leadership can be traced to our group history of violence, showing that effective leadership and membership cooperation have always been responsible for the survival of groups, whether on the battlefield or on the streets (see Van Vugt, Hogan, and Kaiser 2008).

But most importantly, in our view, human history of continuous tribal warfare provides a concrete path to understanding organizational effectiveness. Organizational effectiveness has been traditionally conceptualized in three ways: (1) as the match with an ideal type (e.g., Max Weber's bureaucracy); (2) as the match between organizational characteristics and environmental demands; or (3) as the match between organizational performance and the values of key constituencies (e.g., the quality movement)—see Whetton and Cameron (1994). Note that each of these definitions involves comparisons of certain aspects of organizations, wherein effectiveness is determined by harmonious fit. Yet, human history shows that human groups have been in continuous competition with one another, which suggests an alternative but perfectly straightforward definition of organizational effectiveness—the effective organization is a winner, not a loser, in competition (Kaiser, Hogan, and Craig 2008). In evolutionary history, the stakes were high—losers disappeared from the gene pool; in modern organizations, corporations face similar extinction with bankruptcy.

The third theme running through every society, as revealed by a review of sociology, anthropology, and ethnography literature, is that every human group has a status hierarchy, no matter what the purpose of the group. Since status differences have foundationally powerful implications for the ability to reproduce (Eibl-Eibesfeldt 1989; Marmot 2004), which is the ultimate test of species survival, we can conclude that status has been an innate human motivator since the earliest evolution of our species. While the reasons or outcomes may not be procreation, the motivation for status is ingrained. This suggests that, at a deep, unconscious level, people need power, status, and the control of resources, tendencies that most people associate with "ambition." With few exceptions (see Ashby and Schoon 2010; Hansson et al. 1983; Hogan and Holland 2003; Jansen and Vinkenburg 2006), ambition has been rarely studied in industrial-organizational psychology and management research. Nonetheless, the fundamental dynamic in every organization is the individual search for power (Hogan 2006). Of course, there are substantial individual differences in people's need for power and in their ability to acquire it. It is also important to note that the need for social acceptance, discussed above, and the need for status are antagonistic: to maximize acceptance, one must conform and comply; to maximize status, one must outperform others. Life in human groups requires a careful balancing act, and all human relationships are fundamentally ambivalent. That is, every human relationship contains a mixture of two opposing impulses: (1) the desire to form a bond with the other person; and (2) the desire to outperform the other person.

The fourth and final theme in society is that every human group has a religion.[1] This suggests that a need to find structure and order in reality serves important psychological functions (Hamer 2004) that have roots in human evolutionary history. Research shows that being required to perform in ambiguous or unpredictable environments is highly stressful for animals at every level in the phylogenetic sequence, and we are no exception: people have created societal structures since the beginning. In fact, the argument can be made that the very reinforcement throughout the ages for constant human group living, in light of the complicating factors of warfare and jostling for status while looking for acceptance, is the underlying need for survival, attainment, and communion, none of which are feasible when living in isolation. Even in the modern world, where priorities are perhaps more sociologically refined, it is rare for individuals to live removed from society. Culture in all its manifestations—religion, art, technology—is driven by (or satisfies) the powerful human need for predictability and order, a need that plays out in organizational life—which consists of a sequence of role performances in accordance with well-defined norms (see Hogan and Blickle, in press). By looking to our evolutionary past, we can understand the powerful role that organizations play in our lives and shape these organizations to better meet human innate needs.

So what do these four themes important to human society since its inception mean, taken together? From an evolutionary perspective, they mean the following. We live our lives in groups in which we strive to maximize the amount of respect and status we can receive while minimizing the loss of these same resources. We do this by means of ingratiation and competition within the context of established cultural rules of behavior. Our ability to do this has consequences for our reproductive success. The issue of intergroup aggression (attacking or being attacked by other groups) will arise periodically, and this may threaten the existence of the groups in which we live or earn our livelihoods. Our ability to deal with external threats has consequences for our collective reproductive success. All of this means that other people are the most consequential and often the most dangerous forces in our lives. And this brings us to the subject of modern personality.

Personality is defined in two ways (MacKinnon 1944). We refer to these two definitions as: (1) how people think about themselves (their *identity*); and (2) how others think about them (their *reputation*). There are very few reliable generalizations about identity to report, and the reason seems obvious—to study identity, we need to rely on people's reports regarding how they think about themselves, but these reports are, by definition, unverifiable. Identity is very difficult to study.

In contrast, reputation is easy to study using rating forms, Q sorts, 360-degree appraisals, and assessment-center exercises. Reputation is immensely consequential—it is the basis on which people marry you, hire you, promote you, loan you money, confide in you, or reject you. Smart organizational players care about their reputations and try to maintain them. The best predictor of future behavior is past behavior; reputation is a summary of past behavior and is the best data source available regarding a person's future behavior. In addition, we have a robust taxonomy of reputation—the Five-Factor Model (FFM; Wiggins 1996), which is based on the factor-analytic study of observer ratings (by definition, observer ratings are the litmus test of reputation, since reputation is in the eye of the beholder, after all). Research organized in terms of the FFM has been highly enlightening in identifying the unique blends of the five pillars of human personality: emotional stability/neuroticism, conscientiousness, agreeableness, openness, and extraversion.

The FFM seems to be a cultural universal; it is found in every language that has been studied. Why might this be the case? The answer, we believe, is also the point of this chapter: our evolutionary history as social animals is encoded in our modern behavioral repertoire in various ways. One of these involves cognitive prototypes—mental maps or ways of perceiving the world—that allow us to organize experiences and navigate the social landscape. We believe the FFM is a cultural universal because it concerns key characteristics that make people more or less valuable members of their groups. For example, observable performance reflecting an individual's emotional stability ranges from fearfulness and cowardice at the low end to serenity and courage at the high end.

The FFM dimension of conscientiousness concerns performance that ranges from deceitfulness, carelessness, and delinquency at the low end to probity and reliability at the high end. Research has shown that conscientiousness is perhaps the single greatest predictor of job performance. We can expect that individuals at the high end of conscientiousness may be perceived as the most valuable members of their groups. Conversely, the individual exhibiting conscientiousness at the low end (deceitfulness, carelessness, and delinquency) is likely to be considered a less valuable member of the group and, from an evolutionary perspective, the group could distance itself from this individual, whose traits may endanger survival. Yet, like the highly neurotic individual, this person may have much to contribute in knowledge and skill. Organizations can benefit by understanding individual tendencies and employing organizational behavior techniques to increase, in this case, accountability.

The dimension of agreeableness concerns behavior that ranges from irritability and hostility at the low end to tact, diplomacy, and charm at the high end. In many groups, although irritability and hostility may have evolutionary advantages in terms of willingness to compete, disagreeable individuals are not valued for exhibiting that tendency. In fact, as we discussed, this is particularly true in the modern workplace, where the need for status and the competition necessary to achieve it are often best described by the advice to "walk softly and carry a big stick." Yet research conflicts with the idea that high agreeableness predicts workplace success: almost the opposite is true. As Judge, Livingston, and Hurst (2012) found, individuals lower in agreeableness are often more successful, particularly in terms of extrinsic success (of which perhaps the best marker is earnings). The reasons for this may be complex, but then again, they may be rooted in evolutionary history, as human beings acknowledge inherently the need for fight.

The dimension of openness concerns performance that ranges from literal-mindedness and intellectual self-satisfaction at the low end to curiosity and creativity at the high end. The implications of high openness versus low openness are perhaps more difficult to relate to a group's perception of a member's value than the implications of high or low emotional stability, conscientiousness, and agreeableness. Indeed, research has not shown openness to be a strong predictor of job performance. On the surface, it would be easy to conclude that a group would not therefore consider this a valuable trait for an individual; perhaps, though, it is a matter of evolutionary theory principles.

The significance of the FFM dimension of extraversion is perhaps hardest to grasp—some argue that it concerns shyness versus exhibitionism; others argue it reflects needs for social attention; still others maintain that its core is reward sensitivity. In any case, people at the low end may be perceived as less valuable to the group simply because they are not "out there" broadcasting a need for social acceptance and status or exhibiting a willingness to fight. Research does support the theory that strong extraverts are initially regarded as capable by groups. Whether or not extraversion is actually helpful in meeting the need for status and acceptance depends in part upon how extraversion is defined, but from an evolutionary history perspective, it may be reasonable to conclude that high extraversion confers an advantage at the starting gate, while other traits determine long-term success. Our global point is that there must be a reason that we find the dimensions of the FFM in most languages of the world. The reason is that the FFM codes personalities for behavior that contributes to group functioning, behavior that makes a person an attractive and useful member of a group, or makes a person a candidate for transfer. Without a doubt, there are evolutionary anchors for the cross-culturally validated dimensions of reputation known as the FFM. Yet there are other factors to consider in evaluating the realities of group and organizational success, perhaps best illustrated by cognitive prototypes that illuminate certain truths to provide a full picture.

A significant cognitive prototype is evident in Odysseus's comment at the end of *The Iliad*, as he watched Achilles fall in battle: "So much for Greek courage, now for Greek cunning." The army of Agamemnon ultimately relied on the cunning of Odysseus, not the courage of Achilles, to conquer Troy, and this captures an important point. The success of any group enterprise depends on the existence of group members with a talent for strategic thinking and innovation. In modern psychology, talent for strategy and innovation is assumed to covary with intelligence, so the group or team with the most intelligent members is the one most likely to outthink the competition.

Our other example of important cognitive prototypes derived from our evolutionary history, in which decisive group action often determined survival against the threats of animals, nature, and other groups, appears in our current implicit theories of leadership (Lord, Foti, and DeVader 1984). As Van Vugt et al. (2008) argued, leadership is a resource for group survival in the face of hostile incursions. Because leadership is so important for group survival, people have prototypes for evaluating the leadership claims of "candidates." The relevant dimensions of leadership evaluation include (1) integrity—can the person be trusted? (2) good judgment—can the person's judgment be trusted? (3) competence—can the person contribute productively to group functioning? and (4) vision—does the person have an inspiring view of the group's past history and possible future?

This discussion of evolutionary history informs our contemporary human organizational experience in terms of four points. First, success in life (potential for reproductive success) can be defined in terms of two criterion variables: (1) how well a person is liked, respected, and accepted in his group, tribe, or culture; and (2) the amount of status, power, and control of resources a person enjoys in her group, tribe, or organization. We believe that an important goal for psychological research is to explain individual differences in people's performance in terms of these two dimensions. Second, explanations of the links between our evolutionary history and contemporary observations are initially framed in terms of surface-level characteristics such as the FFM and anthropometric variables; this is a descriptive or predictive level of analysis. Third, we will frame more profound explanations of the carryover of traits from our evolutionary roots in terms of certain deep-level traits or characteristics whose epistemological status is less clear-cut but is nonetheless vital and interesting. Finally, we believe an analysis from this perspective is cross-culturally valid in a manner that other approaches have failed to provide.

Modern culture often seems banal and superficial—a fleeting captivation with celebrities, entertainment, and appearances, based on attributes no one explicitly admits valuing, despite ample evidence to the contrary. The most salient individuals in culture—movie stars, television celebrities, and professional athletes—are rarely the best or the brightest that society has to offer when judged by the values society professes to hold. The work on which their fame rests is rarely as important as the work of social workers, company leaders, health-care providers, and educators. Indeed, when comparing fame and egotism with real accomplishment, it is easy to caricature celebrities as self-centered identities forged from and depending on trivialities.

So why are celebrities so influential and well compensated? Their fame chiefly rests on surface characteristics: Celebrities tend to be young, attractive, and physically fit (lean and athletic).[2] To a lesser but still important degree, other leaders (in government or business) are similarly promoted based on surface-level traits. For instance, Gladwell (2005) shows that 58% of *Fortune 500* CEOs are more than six feet fall, compared to 14.5% of the general population. Culture tends to confer fame, fortune, and influence on those who *look good*, often at the expense of those who *do good*. As one of many examples, consider Norman Borlaug. Borlaug is credited with saving the lives of more than one million people because of his invention of semi-dwarf wheat, a grain that greatly increased food production (up to sevenfold in some countries) and fed starving populations in impoverished, heavily populated, and now rapidly progressing countries like Mexico, China, and India. Judging by the values America espouses, Borlaug should have been a household name, a veritable superstar. Yet Borlaug died in 2009 after a lifetime of service for which he never gained worldwide notoriety, sums of money worth his stature, or influence on the world stage. This is in stark contrast to the status and media coverage of celebrities who have raised funds for the relief of world hunger, often to promote themselves as much as to promote the cause.

Surface-level characteristics are important for both forms of evolutionary fitness: (1) reproductive fitness and (2) survival fitness. First, animal mating decisions happen very quickly. Given that, genetically speaking, humans resemble other primates, human mating decisions also happen quickly and are based, especially for males, on surface-level characteristics (Hill and Buss 2008). Second, accurate "fight or flight" responses often depend on quick impressions. Early in human evolution, tall hunter-gatherers would, for example, find it easier to see predators (or prey) on the savannah. Also, the perception of height or strength in others might provide important input into accurate fight or flight decisions in human-to-human and human-to-animal confrontations. This would help people who possessed the surface-level anthropometric trait of physical tallness to survive, and it would also make them most likely to be chosen as group leaders.

Humans, like other animals, evolved to act after brief (fast and frugal) appraisals of available information. The fact that society (and reality) is intricate and complex does not change the fact that we survived and evolved by making decisions rapidly on the basis of available (surface) information. It is possible that this conflict in contemporary culture—between, on the one hand, disavowing the primacy of surface-level characteristics while, on the other hand, placing high value on them in actual decision making—will be resolved by the slow hand of natural selection. Have the advantages of surface-level processing been diminished by changes in the environment (technology, social mores, etc.)? Or have these environmental changes simply provided a complementary context for natural selection to occur based on the same surface-level traits? The ultimate answer, of course, is provided by natural selection.

The importance of anthropometric characteristics can also be explained on the basis of behavioral genetic evidence. It is not surprising that surface characteristics are highly heritable, and indeed are among the most heritable of all individual differences (Bouchard 2004). As anthropometric traits, they are also observable and measurable. In contrast, not only are deep-level traits less observable/measurable, which complicates the study of evolutionary effects, but genetic effects are somewhat less strong for individual differences such as intelligence, personality, values, and attitudes. Moreover, it is easier to bolster one's standing by feigning to hold a particular value or attitude than by manipulating surface-level traits (it is easier to falsely profess a value or attitude than to undergo cosmetic surgery to manipulate the appearance of age). However, even for these variables, genetic effects are so strong and pervasive that Turkheimer (2000) has labeled the proposition "All human characteristics are heritable" as the First Law of Genetics. In short, we may be culturally predisposed to *value* surface-level characteristics, but there remain enduring individual differences in deep-level traits that are largely genetic. In evolutionary terms, then, survival has always been determined by more than physically measurable advantages. The deep-level trait differences go a long way toward explaining why there are genetic differences in career and life success and other outcomes. A whole host of organizational behavior variables have been found to be heritable, including job satisfaction (Arvey et al. 1989; Arvey et al. 1994), work values (Keller et al. 1992), job and occupational switching (McCall et al. 1997), entrepreneurship (Zhang et al. 2009), and leadership emergence (Arvey et al. 2007). Very little research has been focused on why these genetic effects exist, but more should be done. As noted by Ilies, Arvey, and Bouchard (2006), "Specific operational models explaining the mechanisms through which genetics influence certain organizational outcomes can and should be developed and tested" (135). Although, of course, some of these mediated effects are likely to be explained by outside variables, such as personality and intelligence, we would also argue that anthropometric characteristics play an important explanatory role.

Our hypothesizing notwithstanding, how important are these anthropometric or surface-level traits? Surprisingly so, the literature suggests. Below, we review four anthropometric characteristics: age, height, weight, and physical attractiveness. Of course, these are not the only measurable surface characteristics that subconsciously affect our perception of others, and many of our instant judgments may have evolutionary roots. These traits include masculine and feminine features, vocal characteristics, gait, and various proportional measurements drawn from what we consider as ideals of the human form. Research shows that people have strong preferences for stereotypical ideals, but conforming to them does not always bring success in organizations. For instance, male facial structure predicts cooperation (Stirrat and Perrett 2012); as we have discussed, the perception of agreeableness by others can be an asset or a liability for the individual in the workplace. A growing research literature on the subject has also shown that male facial structure predicts winning elections (Todorov et al. 2005) and organizational financial success among male CEOs (Rule and Ambady 2008; Wong, Ormiston, and Haselhuhn 2011). We do not include gender or race here due to the exhaustive literatures on these variables, as well as to the "reason for being," or ontological controversies, surrounding them.

Age

Age, of course, is a multifaceted concept—true chronological age is purely temporal, but individuals age differently, and individuals of the same chronological age may be perceived as being of different ages. Here, we consider age as an anthropometric characteristic in terms of its surface qualities—how old someone looks or acts as judged by others. Like the aging process itself, the role of age in career success and employment decisions is complex. Although age is weakly related to job performance

(McEvoy and Cascio 1989; Waldman and Avolio 1986), there is ample evidence that older employees are less likely to engage in counterproductive behaviors at work (Rhodes, 1983). Age is positively related to extrinsic career success, in that older employees reliably earn more and occupy higher-level positions than do younger employees (Judge, Klinger, and Simon 2010). Nonetheless, the evidence suggests that organizational decision makers are often biased against hiring or promoting older employees (Bennington 2001). How can these pieces of evidence be reconciled?

To integrate these phenomena, we need two related distinctions. First, we must decouple age from experience. The two are highly correlated, but in this case it is critical not to confound them. As employees gain experience, their pay generally increases, particularly when merit raises are progressively applied to the current salary. However, that does not mean that age per se is a career advantage. To make that distinction, one would need to perform two different comparisons: (1) two employees of the same age working in the same field—one with considerable experience, the other with little experience; (2) two employees with the same experience in the field—one older than the other. If we made these comparisons, we suspect the employee's age would not be an advantage.[3]

For example, assume that we work in an economy with no real wage growth (a reasonable assumption over the past generation in Western democracies), and wherein a manager received annual merit raises based on performance in the previous year. If we further assume that the manager started her career with a salary of $66,000, and received an annual merit raise of 4% per year (high in the 2008–12 economy, but a reasonable historical average), her pay would be $180,000 after twenty-five years in that same position. Compared to a younger employee, newly hired at the opening $66,000 mark, the older employee would be earning a dramatically higher salary than the younger employee—for the same position—simply through the compounding interest applied to salaries over time. Even if the annual inflation rate is taken into account, and is, say, 1.5%, pay will still double in real terms.[4]

Second in integrating the effect of age on workplace outcomes, we must separate stocks from flows (trajectories). If we compare an older employee to a younger employee, it may well be true that the older employee has greater career success than the younger. However, generally our interest is in prediction (predicting future career success). In that case, we would predict that the future is brighter for the younger employee, and indeed may be relatively dim for the older. Yet our point of perspective is mismatched for the two.

As a result of these factors, age is often a double-edged sword as far as employment is concerned. Due to the compounding value of merit raises, older employees usually earn more than younger employees; this is true even if their level of job performance is the same. However, if an older employee competes against a younger employee for a position, there is reason to believe that the advantage rests with the younger employee. Here society seems to suffer from a neurosis: we advertise to and about youth, and we may favor younger individuals in hiring decisions, and yet we pay older individuals more and limit access to certain positions on the basis of age.

Height

It is surely uncontroversial to state that, given the choice, many more people would choose to be taller than would choose to be shorter. Research confirms that height is a socially desirable asset (Roberts and Herman 1986). Taller people are seen as more persuasive (Young and French 1996), considered more attractive and desirable as mates (Freedman 1979; Harrison and Saeed 1977; Lerner and Moore 1974), and are more likely to emerge as leaders of groups (Higham and Carment 1992; Stogdill 1948). Indeed, it has been well more than a century since US citizens have elected a president whose height was below average (William McKinley, 5 feet, 7 inches tall and ridiculed in the press as a "little boy," was elected president in 1896 despite being slightly shorter than average).

In a quantitative review of forty-four studies, Judge and Cable (2004) found that height was positively related to extrinsic career success. Analyzing data from several large American and British data sets, they found that, controlling for gender, weight, and many other human-capital characteristics, each inch in height led to a predicted increase of $786 in annual earnings. The effect was somewhat stronger for men, but it was significant and nearly as strong for women. The positive effect of height was not due to higher self-esteem, suggesting that height may work primarily through the perceptions of others. The importance placed on height in contemporary society is interesting because one would be hard-pressed to find jobs in which height was a bona fide occupational qualification. Moreover, Judge and Cable (2004) found no evidence for a diminishing returns relationship—height appeared to positively predict earnings as well at the high end of the height distribution as at the low end.

Like most values, and in accord with the idea that greater height would benefit survival for early humans, the value placed on height even today convincingly shows evolutionary origins. Like human beings, animals use height as an index for power and strength when making fight-

or-flight decisions. As noted by Freedman (1979), "Throughout nature the rule is the bigger, the more dangerous" (92). Thus, from a sociobiological perspective, height equals power and therefore demands respect, which translates to group behavior in any organizational setting, however misplaced. Added to the perceived fitness advantage, there is evidence that height has reproductive fitness advantages as well (Shepperd and Strathman 1989). Tall men, in particular, are more likely to be seen as attractive, are more likely to marry, and more likely to have children when they do marry (Pawlowski, Dunbar, and Lipowicz 2000). As with the idea that height and power inherently require respect, the application of reproductive fitness to the workplace is perhaps limited and controversial, but the clear implications for contemporary organizational behavior of our evolutionary realities invite us to identify the roots of phenomena we universally acknowledge as factors.

Weight

Despite evidence that 80% of the variation between individuals in body mass index (BMI) is heritable (Bouchard et al. 1998), Roehling's (1999) comprehensive review suggests that obese individuals are rated as less desirable as subordinates, coworkers, and bosses, and they are viewed as less conscientious, less agreeable, less emotionally stable, and less extraverted than their "normal-weight" counterparts. Even though these stereotypes are inaccurate (Roehling, Roehling, and Odland 2008), it appears that obese employees are seen by employers as lazy and lacking self-discipline (Puhl and Brownell 2003). Roehling's (1999) review also revealed that overweight women are consistently judged more harshly in the workplace than overweight men, and Griffin (2007) reported that 60% of overweight women and 40% of overweight men describe themselves as having been discriminated against in the course of employment.

Why does being obese lead to negative evaluations by employers and other employees? From the perspective of evolutionary psychology, being overweight may lead to lower estimated reproductive fitness by others, a phenomenon that appears to exist for both men and women (Barber 1995). Thus, overweight individuals may be viewed in generally negative terms by others, and this negative appraisal generalizes to nonmating decisions (a process of generalization that may apply to other anthropometric characteristics as well).

Culture may also play a role here. Judge and Cable (2011) reviewed evidence showing that, over time, models, actors, and celebrities—especially female ones—have been portrayed as increasingly thin. In two large samples of individuals from the United States and Germany, they showed that the negative effect of weight on earnings was stronger for women than for men and that the effects were particularly strong as women moved off of the "model thin" standard. The highest-earning men where those who were above-average in weight but not obese, whereas the highest-earning women were very thin.[5] This exposes a cultural neurosis—although society gets progressively fatter, it continues to worship thinness and punish those who deviate from a standard few people actually meet.

Physical Attractiveness

Ratings of physical attractiveness are highly consensual within cultures. But what is physical attractiveness? Here, various cultures differ, which may explain the debate between researchers. Some researchers have argued that facial symmetry underlies attractiveness judgments. Others argue that other aspects of facial structure are more important, such as eye size, baby-facedness, and so on. Still others investigate body shape, hair color, and other characteristics. While these studies are important for understanding what causes perceived attractiveness, as far as implications for organizational behavior are concerned, the causes of those judgments may not be critical, since people tend to agree in their attractiveness ratings.

That attractiveness positively affects income has been well established in research. In their meta-analysis, Langlois et al. (2000) revealed that 68% of attractive adults were above the mean on occupational success—which included income—versus 32% of unattractive adults. Other research provides further support for the relationship between attractiveness and earnings (Harper 2000). Judge, Hurst, and Simon (2009) found that independent evaluations of physical attractiveness were positively related to later-career earnings, and the effects for men and women did not differ significantly. This is good news for women, who were not afforded leadership and workplace opportunities equal to those available to men throughout time and therefore struggled to define workplace competence. Why is attractiveness so valuable in the labor market? We can offer two explanations: (1) how attractiveness influences people's self-image and (2) how it affects others' perceptions of them.

First, attractive people may simply be more self-confident, and the self-confidence translates into career success. Harter (1993) described the correlations between appearance and self-esteem throughout life as "staggeringly high" (95). Langlois et al. (2000) found a more modest relationship, but attractiveness was still positively related to observed self-confidence/self-esteem in children and self-reported self-confidence, competence, and mental health in adults. In longitudinal samples of adolescents and adults, Zebrowitz, Collins, and Dutta (1998) found that men judged as attractive in their thirties were more emotionally stable than those judged as average or unattractive, although they did not find the same results for adult women or for adolescents of either gender. Judge, Hurst, and Simon (2009) found that core self-evaluations (CSE) mediated a significant part of the relationship between attractiveness and income, further supporting the positive influence of attractiveness on self-esteem, in that feedback from self and others that one is attractive (or not) can raise (or lower) CSE.

Second, the way others perceive attractive individuals affects how they treat them. Hosoda, Stone-Romero, and Coats (2003) showed in their meta-analysis that decision makers are biased against unattractive people in employment contexts such as interviews, performance evaluations, and so forth. Mulford et al. (1998) found that others are more likely to cooperate with attractive people, partly because the latter are expected to be more cooperative. Attractive people tend to be seen as higher in intelligence (Jackson, Hunter, and Hodge 1995), despite the fact that the actual relationship between attractiveness and intelligence is nonexistent ($r = .03$; Langlois et al. 2000). The answer to this apparent riddle—why do people perceive and react positively to attractive people, even when their ascriptions are inaccurate?—likely lies in evolutionary history.

DEEP-LEVEL PERSONALITY CHARACTERISTICS

Successful group living, status-seeking, and group defense depend on how people perceive and relate to one another. Because other people are such consequential forces in human lives, we have acquired certain cognitive prototypes (height, attractiveness, the FFM, implicit leadership theory) that we use to evaluate other people in an automatic and unconscious way. Within each person's group, the most important criteria concern how much respect and affection a person enjoys, as well as how much power and resources he controls, and these criteria are related to reproductive success. A person's reputation is an index of her standing on these outcome variables. Between groups, the most important criteria concern team, group, or organizational effectiveness, and the coordination needed to bring about such effectiveness is largely a function of leadership (Spisak, Nicholson, and Van Vugt 2011). Within the group, personality matters; between groups, leadership matters.

We use surface-level traits (height, the FFM, etc.) to describe and predict other people's behavior. This section puts forth our best guesses regarding the deep-level individual-difference characteristics that explain these observed tendencies. Specifically, we suggest that key life outcomes (getting along and getting ahead) can be explained in terms of three deep-level personality traits that are also rooted in biology and our evolutionary history: (1) relations to authority; (2) social sensitivity; and (3) competitiveness.

Relations to Authority

The ability of infants of all mammalian species to survive depends on their willingness to comply with adult commands (alarm calls, etc.). The ability of human infants to acquire language depends on acquiring adult rules of speech. Hogan and Henley (1970) suggested that the socialization process, which occurs during the critical ages of three to five, depends on the existence of a hypothetical rule-acquisition device. This device is potentiated by a child's relationship with parents/caregivers, and the process parallels Freud's discussion of the origins of the superego.

Parents who are warm and restrictive—who love their children but put firm limits on their behavior (as contrasted with warm and permissive, cold and permissive, or cold and restrictive parents)—produce children who accommodate easily to adult authority, quickly acquire the rules of their culture and, in the developed world, do well in school and in life (Roberts et al. 2007).[6] Children who can accommodate easily to authority are able to fit in with their social group and family, find adult protectors, acquire mentors, and learn the rules of the culture. Children who do not make this accommodation are at serious risk for social failure. Individual differences in relations to authority are captured by any well-validated measure of conscientiousness, and these measures are powerful predictors of positive life outcomes (Roberts et al. 2007).

Social Sensitivity

George Herbert Mead (1934), an avid Darwinian, argued that role-taking ability—the ability to anticipate another person's expectations—is the "g-factor," or general intelligence, in social life. According to him, role-taking ability accounts for language acquisition, the socialization process, the development of a self-concept, and moral conduct. In short, Mead used the development of role-taking ability to explain exactly the same phenomena that Freud explained with the development of the superego. Social sensitivity is a combination of the dimensions of the FFM; Hogan (1969) developed a psychometric measure based on Mead's ideas about role-taking, and the scale is a robust predictor of a wide range of positive career outcomes (Hogan and Grief 1973). The employability literature (e.g., Hogan and Chamorro-Premuzic 2011) indicates that employers place a high value on interpersonal sensitivity for any job requiring social interaction. In addition, Woolley et al. (2010), in a study of team performance, show that the effectiveness of problem-solving teams is directly related to the average level of social sensitivity of the team members.

The literature on mirror neurons (Rizzolatti and Craighero 2004) suggests that there is a reasonably well defined neural architecture underlying the human capacity for role-taking ability or empathy (De Waal 2006) and that social sensitivity has played a key role in human evolution and group functioning (Ramachandran 2006). Ramachandran argues, for example, that social sensitivity based on mirror neurons is the factor responsible for the so-called great leap forward in human evolution. The reality and potency of this deep-level trait is beyond dispute.

Social sensitivity enables or potentiates altruism and cooperation, two of the most distinctive but puzzling human characteristics, when considered from the perspective of "the selfish gene." Bowles and Gintis (2011) argue that altruism and cooperation are best understood from the perspective of multilevel selection (Wilson, Van Vugt, and O'Gorman 2008), where group differences—in addition to and beyond individual differences—may be responsible for selection (e.g., cooperative groups may reproduce better and survive longer than uncooperative groups [Wilson and Sober 1994]). But, more importantly, they argue that the capacity for altruism and cooperation is a by-product of intergroup warfare—like Darwin, they found that groups whose members were better able to coordinate their actions and more willing to sacrifice themselves for the group had an adaptive advantage (Darwin 1871).

Competitiveness

The tradition of realpolitik, as exemplified by Bismarck (Steinberg 2010), maintains that the fundamental question in human affairs is, "Who shall rule?" All social animals, including chickens, rhesus monkeys, and humans, organize their groups in terms of status hierarchies, and there are clear benefits to being at the top. High-status female chimpanzees, for instance, forage in the best parts of the forest and kill the babies of low-status females. Genghis Khan fathered tens of thousands of children, and the offspring of high-status parents do much better in life than the children of low-status parents (Marmot 2004). Status hierarchies emerge very early in children's play groups—high-status children are the ones other children watch. Some form of status striving must be innate; William James, William McDougall, and even Charles Darwin speculated about the universality of "rivalrous tendencies."

The Hogans developed psychometric measures of a competiveness cluster (ambition, power, and recognition). The scales are not concerned with dominance or aggression; rather they concern desires to compete and win, desires to create a legacy and make a difference, and desires for status and control. The Hogans provide ample data to support the validity of these scales in predicting performance in managerial and leadership roles (J. Hogan and R. Hogan, 2010; R. Hogan and J. Hogan, 2007).

We think that individual differences in the ability to get along and get ahead can be partially accounted for in terms of individual differences in three deep traits: people's ability to adjust to authority, their sensitivity to the intentions of other group members, and their competitiveness. The three may come together under the rubric of the broad psychometric construct of core self-evaluations (Judge, Locke, and Durham, 1997). That is, the demonstrated predictive power of this construct may reflect the fact that core self-evaluations sample broadly from all three domains.

ANOTHER DEEP-LEVEL TRAIT: INTELLIGENCE

One might argue, as did fifty-two prominent psychologists in the *Wall Street Journal*, that: "IQ is strongly related, probably more so than any other single measurable human trait, to many important educational, occupational, economic, and social outcomes" (Arvey et al. 1994a, A18). Little has changed with respect to the state of science regarding the practical importance of intelligence since then (e.g., Deary et.al. 2007; Lubinski 2004). After studying general intelligence (general mental ability, or GMA) for more than one hundred years, psychologists from a variety of disciplines have identified many important correlates of this "very general mental capability that, among other things, involves the ability to reason, plan, solve problems, think abstractly, comprehend complex ideas, learn quickly and learn from experience" (Gottfredson 1997, 13). Psychologists agree that general intelligence predicts educational and occupational attainment, as well as performance within occupations or jobs (see Kuncel, Hezlett, and Ones 2004; Schmidt and Hunter 2004).

There is evidence that general intelligence is associated with physical and psychological health (e.g., subjective well-being), although the evidence for the former outcome is relatively recent and for the latter is tentative and mostly indirect (Campbell, Converse, and Rodgers 1976; Gottfredson 2004; Sigelman 1981). Perhaps the most impressive test of the relationship between GMA and health is a study that links the Scottish Mental Survey of 1932, which assessed intelligence in childhood, to health outcomes assessed later in life (see Deary et al. 2004; Gottfredson and Deary 2004). This study found a clear connection between GMA and health: GMA scores collected at eleven years of age influenced survival and hospital admissions for illnesses up to age sixty-five (Deary et al. 2004). Thus, as far as survival is concerned, it appears that intelligence helps individuals solve the adaptive problem of living longer.

The reason *why* general intelligence predicts a broad array of criteria is much less understood. Ostensibly, intelligence facilitates learning and decision making so that smart people learn more, and more quickly (about their jobs, health, crime and punishment), and use that knowledge to make better decisions. It is also possible that intelligence enhances motivation. If smart people perceive themselves as more able to execute a plan of action, or set more ambitious goals, they are likely to work harder. The motivational aspects of intelligence, however, are largely unexplored in research.

Notwithstanding the numerous advantages intelligence brings, alone it is insufficient for job, career, or leadership success. People must also be motivated to use their abilities, and, depending on the job, they also need social and self-management skills in order to leverage their abilities to their best advantage (Kaiser et al. 2008). Many promising careers have been undone by poor self-management skills. Organizations also too often assume that competence in a previous role assures success in a future role (which may have little to do with the skills of the previous role), or that the best leader is the "smartest person in the room." Intelligence matters for career success and leadership effectiveness, but the correlation is not so strong as to assure it. Personality and social skills are just as important. Moreover, in contemporary society, intelligence is not helpful in either predicting subjective well-being or reproductive success (indeed, intelligent couples tend to have smaller, not larger, families). Thus, intelligence is quite important to some aspects of life and work, but it is not the only, nor always the most important, predictor of every criteria.

Importance of General versus Specific Abilities

Research in industrial-organizational psychology shows rather conclusively that the variance attributable to the general mental ability or general intelligence factor overwhelms the variance contributed by more specific abilities in predicting job performance (Olea and Ree 1994; Ree, Earles, and Teachout 1994), training success (Ree and Earles 1991), and other criteria (Lubinski 2004). Although past research clearly supports the importance of general mental ability for predicting a host of consequential criteria, it does not render inconsequential the validity of specific abilities. As Lubinski (2009) notes, "Specific abilities add value to forecasts based on general cognitive ability in multiple real-world settings" (351). Gottfredson (2003, 119), in reviewing evidence demonstrating that "general ability, g, predicts performance to some extent in all jobs," also notes that "this is not to say that specific skills are unimportant. Far from it. This is to say only that more general abilities are more broadly useful across the great variety of tasks and settings that we encounter in the workplace." Certainly, there are cases where specific abilities matter, as shown in a recent study (Lang et al. 2010).

There is not much dispute that general mental ability is of substantial importance to many spheres of life, but this does not preclude the potential importance of specific abilities for many narrower criteria. Rather than engaging in an infinite round of "either-or" thinking ("either general mental ability is important, or specific abilities are important"), it would be more productive to frame future research and understanding around "yes-and" thinking ("yes, general mental ability is important, and we have found that, in some cases, specific abilities add to prediction"). In fact, this "yes-and" thinking should be applied across the board to all the traits when predicting organizational outcomes. In an always-turning kaleidoscope of perceptions and feedback from anthropometric characteristics, personality dimensions, intelligence, and other factors influencing opportunity and performance in the workplace, it is always the interaction of these characteristics with the situation that determines an individual's success.

Emotional Intelligence

In considering the implications of intelligence for evolutionary psychology and organizational behavior, the reader may wonder about social forms of intelligence. Some people have argued that "emotional intelligence" is as important for career success as general mental ability. Although a careful review of the emotional intelligence literature is beyond the scope of this essay, a few comments are in order. First, unless one subscribes to the view that in order to justify a new concept, one must attack an existing one, there is nothing about emotional intelligence that challenges the importance of general mental ability. Depending on the measures used and aspects of emotional intelligence considered, there are some correlations between the measures, but their magnitude is not great (Joseph and Newman 2010). Being able to "read" others' faces, for example, is correlated with general mental ability, but not very strongly (Wilhelm et al. 2010).

Furthermore, emotional intelligence is an ambiguous concept. Are "emotionally intelligent" individuals able to recognize facial expressions? Understand emotional undertones in social interaction, art, literature, and so forth? Successfully regulate their emotions? Provide supportive counsel to others? As Joseph and Newman's (2010) important study shows, these are not the same processes. If one views specific aspects of emotional recognition and regulation as components of a more general ability, perhaps it is possible to argue for the importance of an overall ability. We suspect, however, that future research will show that the neural substrates governing emotion recognition are distinct from those underlying emotional regulation.

CONCLUSION

The newfound interest in the biological foundations of organizational behavior represented by the contributors to this book is an important and innovative turn in applied psychology. The specific research topics in organizational behavior all share a common underlying concern— every topic concerns some aspect of human nature. Unless and until organizational researchers agree on the proper conceptual context for their research, that research will be little more than "stamp collecting," pointillism, and ad hoc aggregation of empirical facts.

Many organizational researchers (and business managers) will agree with Frederick Winslow Taylor's (1911) assumption that organizational processes (1) can and should be based on the needs of the organization and (2) that the motives and desires of employees can (even should) be ignored. But the emerging research on engagement (Harter, Schmidt, and Hayes 2002) indicates that paying attention to staff morale is the path to enhanced productivity, customer satisfaction, and profitability—Taylor (1911) was simply wrong.

Research on employee engagement can be sharpened and focused by a better understanding of human nature. The first great challenge to Taylor (1911) came from precisely this perspective. Argyris (1960), Herzberg (1959), and especially McGregor (1960) criticized Taylor (1911) and existing management practices for ignoring, stultifying, or violating basic human needs. They then argued that better business results would be obtained by paying attention to human nature (i.e., personality—which concerns "the nature of human nature"). We agree with the formal thrust of their argument, but the three books ultimately fail for precisely the reasons that prompted the writing of the present book—they adopted an indefensible model of human nature. They were correct to ground their ideas on assumptions about personality and to argue that violating basic human needs would be bad for business. But they started with a wrong-headed model of human nature.

So, finally, although books such as this run the risk of engaging in fantasy theory, as Alfred North Whitehead once said, "To set limits to speculation is treason to the future." Successful organizational practices must be based on the best understanding of human nature that we can possibly derive. For that, the wisest path is to begin at the beginning, when human beings first walked on Earth and learned to survive over many millennia. This book is an important first step toward understanding how the modern workplace has, in many ways, replaced the tribe and the savannah in how these forces play out.

Notes

1. We define religion broadly here: "A particular system of faith and worship" or a collective "devotion to some principle" (*Oxford English Dictionary*, 2011, s. v. "religion."). In many cases, this most fundamentally is a belief in God, gods, mysticism, and so forth, but that need not be the case. It could mean, for example, a shared belief and devotion to central aspects of one's culture.

2. Following the diversity literature (see Bell 2007), we make a distinction between surface-level characteristics (e.g., height, weight, age, and attractiveness) that are easily seen and appraised, and deep-level characteristics (e.g., personality, intelligence, and values).

3. Of course, it is possible to make this distinction statistically by including separate measures of age and experience in predicting a criterion (e.g., career success).

4. Calculated using the formula: $FW = PW (1 + mr)^Y$, where FW = future value of wages, P = present wage, mr = merit raise annually, and Y = number of years.

5. In this case, results do not perfectly conform to evolutionary psychology;

evolutionary psychologists would expect a brawny, muscular man to be most desirable (for reproductive and protective purposes), whereas a fit or plump woman should be seen as most desirable (for reproductive fitness). In short, evolutionary psychology would predict that, for reproductive fitness, thinness is not highly desirable. That does not explain, however, contemporary Western cultures desire for thinness in mates.

6. We recognize that the possible transmission mechanism here may be genetic ("nature of nurture" [Plomin and Bergeman 1991]).

References

Argyris, C. 1960. *Personality and organization*. New York: Harper.

Arvey, R. D., Bouchard, T. J., Jr., Carroll, J. B., Cattell, R. B., Cohen, D. B., Dawis, R. W., et al. 1994a. Mainstream science on intelligence. *Wall Street Journal*, December 13, A18.

———, Bouchard, T. J., Segal, N. L., and Abraham, L. M. 1989. Job satisfaction: Environmental and genetic components. *Journal of Applied Psychology* 74:187–92.

———, McCall, B. P., Bouchard, T. J., Taubman, P., and Cavanaugh, M. A. 1994b. Genetic influences on job satisfaction and work values. *Personality and Individual Differences* 17:21–33.

———, Zhang, Z., Avolio, B. J., and Krueger, R. F. 2007. Developmental and genetic determinants of leadership role occupancy among females. *Journal of Applied Psychology* 92:693–706.

Ashby, J. S., and Schoon, I. 2010. Career success: The role of teenage career aspirations, ambition value and gender in predicting adult social status and earnings. *Journal of Vocational Behavior* 77:350–60.

Barber, N. 1995. The evolutionary psychology of physical attractiveness: Sexual selection and human morphology. *Ethology and Sociobiology* 16:395–424.

Baumeister, R. F., and Leary, M. 1995. The need to belong: Desire for interpersonal attachments as a fundamental human motivation. *Psychological Bulletin* 17:497–529.

Bennington, L. 2001. Age discrimination: Converging evidence from four Australian studies. *Employee Responsibilities and Rights Journal* 13:125–34.

Bouchard, C., Prusse, L., Rice, T., and Rao, D. 1998. The genetics of human obesity. In *Handbook of obesity*, ed. G. A. Bray, C. Bouchard, and W. James, 157–90. New York: Marcel Dekker.

Bouchard, T. J., Jr. 2004. Genetic influence on human psychological traits: A survey. *Current Directions in Psychological Science* 13:148–51.

Bowles, S. 2009. Did warfare among ancestral hunter-gatherers affect the evolution of human social behaviors? *Science* 324:1293–98.

———, and Gintis, H. 2011. *A cooperative species: Human reciprocity and its evolution*. Princeton, NJ: Princeton University Press.

Campbell, A., Converse, P. E., and Rodgers, W. L. 1976. *The quality of American life: Perceptions, evaluations, and satisfactions*. New York: Russell Sage Foundation.

Chapais, B. 2008. *Primeval kinship*. Cambridge, MA: Harvard University Press.

Darwin, C. 1871. *The descent of man*. London: John Murray.

De Waal, F. 2006. The animal roots of human morality. *New Scientist* 192:60–61.

Deary, I. J., Strand, S., Smith, P., and Fernandes, C. 2007. Intelligence and educational achievement. *Intelligence* 35:13–21.

———, Whiteman, M. C., Starr, J. M., Whalley, L. J., and Fox, H. C. 2004. The impact of childhood intelligence on later life: Following up the Scottish Mental Surveys of 1932 and 1947. *Journal of Personality and Social Psychology* 86:130–47.

Eibl-Eibesfeldt, I. 1989. *Human ethology.* New York: Aldine.

Freedman, D. G. 1979. *Human sociobiology.* New York: Free Press.

Gladwell, M. 2005. *Blink: The power of thinking without thinking.* New York: Little, Brown.

Gottfredson, L. S. 2004. Life, death, and intelligence. *Journal of Cognitive Education and Psychology* 4:23–46.

———. 1997. Mainstream science on intelligence: An editorial with 52 signatories, history, and bibliography. 1997. *Intelligence* 24:13–23.

———. 2003. The challenge and promise of cognitive career assessment. *Journal of Career Assessment* 11:115–35.

———, and Deary, I. J. 2004. Intelligence predicts health and longevity, but why? *Current Directions in Psychological Science* 13:1–4.

Griffin, A. W. 2007. Women and weight-based employment discrimination. *Cardozo Journal of Law and Gender* 13:631–62.

Hamer, D. 2004. *The God gene.* New York: Random House.

Hansson, R. O., Hogan, R., Johnson, J. A., and Schroeder, D. J. 1983. Disentangling Type A behavior: The roles of ambition, insensitivity, and anxiety. *Journal of Research in Personality* 17:186–97.

Harper, B. 2000. Beauty, stature and the labour market: A British cohort study. *Oxford Bulletin of Economics and Statistics* 62: 771–800.

Harrison, A. A., and Saeed, L. 1977. Let's make a deal: An analysis of revelations and stipulations in lonely hearts advertisements. *Journal of Personality and Social Psychology* 35:257–64.

Harter, S. 1993. The causes and consequences of low self-esteem in children and adolescents. In *Self-esteem: The puzzle of low self-regard*, ed. R. F. Baumeister, 87–116. New York: Plenum Press.

Harter, J. K., Schmidt, F. L., and Hayes, T. L. 2002. Business-unit-level relationship between employee satisfaction, employee engagement, and business outcomes: A meta-analysis. *Journal of Applied Psychology* 87 (2): 268–79.

Herzberg, F. 1959. *The motivation to work.* New York: Wiley.

Higham, P. A., and Carment, D. W. 1992. The rise and fall of politicians: The judged heights of Broadbent, Mulroney and Turner before and after the 1988 Canadian federal-election. *Canadian Journal of Behavioural Science* 24:404–9.

Hill, S. E., and Buss, D. M. 2008. The mere presence of opposite-sex others on judgments of sexual and romantic desirability: Opposite effects for men and women. *Personality and Social Psychology Bulletin* 34:635–47.

Hogan, J., and Hogan R. 2010. *Motives, values, preferences inventory manual.* Tulsa, OK: Hogan Assessment Systems.

———, and Holland, B. 2003. Using theory to evaluate personality and job-performance relations: A socioanalytic perspective. *Journal of Applied Psychology* 88:100–12.

Hogan, R. 1969. Development of an empathy scale. *Journal of Consulting and Clinical Psychology* 33:307–16.

———. 2006. *Personality and the fate of organizations*. Mahwah, NJ: Earlbaum.

———, and Blickle, G. In press. Socioanalytic theory. In *Handbook of personality at work*, ed. N. D. Christiansen and R. P. Tett, New York: Routledge.

———, and Chamorro-Premuzic, T. 2011. Personality and the laws of history. In *The Wiley-Blackwell handbook of individual differences*, ed. Tomas Chamorro-Premuzic, Sophie von Stumm, and Adrian Furnham, 491–511. Hoboken, NJ: Wiley-Blackwell.

———, and Grief, E. 1973. Theory and measurement of empathy. *Journal of Counseling Psychology* 20:280–84.

———, and Henley, N. 1970. Nomotics: The study of human rule systems. *Law and Society Review* 5:13.

———, and Hogan, J. 2007. *Hogan Personality Inventory Manual*. 3rd ed. Tulsa, OK: Hogan Assessment Systems.

Hosoda, M., Stone-Romero, E. F., and Coats, G. 2003. The effects of physical attractiveness on job-related outcomes: A meta-analysis of experimental studies. *Personnel Psychology* 56:431–62.

Ilies, R., Arvey, R. D., and Bouchard, T. J., Jr. 2006. Darwinism, behavioral genetics and organizational behavior: A review and agenda for future research. *Journal of Organizational Behavior* 27:121–41.

Jackson, L. A., Hunter, J. E., and Hodge, C. N. 1995. Physical attractiveness and intellectual competence: A meta-analytic review. *Social Psychology Quarterly* 58:108–22.

Jansen, P. G. W., and Vinkenburg, C. J. 2006. Predicting management career success from assessment center data: A longitudinal study. *Journal of Vocational Behavior* 68:253–66.

Joseph, D. L., and Newman, D. A. 2010. Emotional intelligence: An integrative meta-analysis and cascading model. *Journal of Applied Psychology* 95:54–78.

Judge, T. A., and Cable, D. M. 2004. The effect of physical height on workplace success and income. *Journal of Applied Psychology* 89:428–41.

———, and Cable, D. M. 2011. When it comes to pay, do the thin win? The effect of weight on pay for men and women. *Journal of Applied Psychology* 96:95–112.

———, Hurst, C., and Simon, L. N. 2009. Does it pay to be smart, attractive, or confident (or all three)? Relationships among general mental ability, physical attractiveness, core self-evaluations, and income. *Journal of Applied Psychology* 94:742–55.

———, Klinger, R. L., and Simon, L. S. 2010. Time is on my side: Time, general mental ability, human capital, and extrinsic career success. *Journal of Applied Psychology* 95:92–107.

———, Livingston, B. A., and Hurst, C. 2012. Do nice guys—and gals—really finish last? The joint effects of sex and agreeableness on income. *Journal of Personality and Social Psychology* 102:390–407.

———, Locke, E. A., and Durham, C. C. 1997. The dispositional causes of job satisfaction: A core evaluation approach. *Research in Organizational Behavior* 19:151–88.

Kaiser, R. B., Hogan, R., and Craig, S. B. 2008. Leadership and the fate of organizations. *American Psychologist* 63:96–110.

Keeley, L. H. 1996. *Wars before civilization*. Oxford: Oxford University Press.

Keller, L. M., Arvey, R. D., Dawis, R. V., Bouchard, T. J., and Segal, N. L. 1992. Work values: Genetic and environmental influences. *Journal of Applied Psychology* 77:79–88.

Kuncel, N. R., Hezlett, S. A., and Ones, D. S. 2004. Academic performance, career potential, creativity, and job performance: Can one construct predict them all? 2004. *Journal of Personality and Social Psychology* 86:148–61.

Lang, J. W. B., Kersting, M., Hülsheger, U. R., and Lang, J. 2010. General mental ability, narrower cognitive abilities, and job performance: The perspective of the nested-factors model of cognitive abilities. *Personnel Psychology* 63:595–640.

Langlois, J. H., Kalakanis, L., Rubenstein, A. J., Larson, A., Hallam, M., and Smoot, M. 2000. Maxims or myths of beauty? A meta-analytic and theoretical review. *Psychological Bulletin* 126:390–423.

Lerner, R. M., and Moore, T. 1974. Sex and status effects on perception of physical attractiveness. *Psychological Reports* 34:1047–50.

Lord, R. G., Foti, R. J., and DeVader, C. L. 1984. A test of leadership categorization theory. *Organizational Behavior and Human Performance* 34:343–78.

Lubinski, D. 2004. Introduction to the special section on cognitive abilities: 100 years after Spearman's (1904) "'General intelligence,' objectively determined and measured." *Journal of Personality and Social Psychology* 86:96–111.

———. 2009. Exceptional cognitive ability: The phenotype. *Behavior Genetics* 39:350–58.

MacKinnon, D. W. 1944. The structure of personality. In *Personality and the behavior disorders*, vol. 1, ed. J. Hunt, 4–43. New York: Ronald Press.

Marmot, M. 2004. *The status syndrome*. New York: Henry Holt.

McCall, B. P., Cavanaugh, M. A., Arvey, R. D., and Taubman, P. 1997. Genetic influences on job and occupational switching. *Journal of Vocational Behavior* 50:60–77.

McEvoy, G. M., and Cascio, W. F. 1989. Cumulative evidence of the relationship between age and job performance. *Journal of Applied Psychology* 74:11–17.

McGregor, D. 1960. *The human side of enterprise*. New York: McGraw-Hill.

McNeill, W. H. 1982. *The pursuit of power*. Chicago: University of Chicago Press.

Mead, G. H. 1934. *Mind, self, and society*. Chicago: University of Chicago Press.

Mulford, M., Orbell, J., Shatto, C., and Stockard, J. 1998. Physical attractiveness, opportunity, and success in everyday exchange. *American Journal of Sociology* 103:1565–92.

Olea, M. M., and Ree, M. J. 1994. Predicting pilot and navigator criteria: Not much more than *g*. *Journal of Applied Psychology* 79:845–51.

Pawlowski, B., Dunbar, R. I. M., and Lipowicz, A. 2000. Tall men have more reproductive success. *Nature* 403:156.

Pinker, S. 2010. *The better angels of our nature: Why violence has declined*. New York: Penguin Group USA.

Puhl, R., and Brownell, K. D. 2003. Psychosocial origins of obesity stigma: Toward changing a powerful and pervasive bias. *Obesity Reviews* 4:213–27.

Ramachandran, V.S. 2006. Mirror neurons and imitation learning as the driving force behind "the great leap forward" in human evolution [original essay post]. Re-

trieved from http://www.edge.org/conversation/mirror-neurons-and-imitation
-learning-as-the-driving-force-behind-the-great-leap-forward-in-human-evolution.

Ree, M. J., and Earles, J. A. 1991. Predicting training success: Not much more than *g*.
Personnel Psychology 44:321–32.

———, Earles, J. A., and Teachout, M. S. 1994. Predicting job performance: Not much
more than *g. Journal of Applied Psychology* 79:518–24.

Rhodes, S. R. 1983. Age-related differences in work attitudes and behavior: A review
and conceptual analysis. *Psychological Bulletin* 93:328–67.

Rizzolatti, G., and Craighero, L. 2004. The mirror-neuron system. *Annual Review of
Neuroscience* 27:169–92.

Roberts, J. V., and Herman, C. P. 1986. The psychology of height: An empirical review.
In *Physical appearance, stigma, and social behavior*, ed. C. P. Herman, M. P. Zanna,
and E. T. Higgins, 113–40. Hillsdale, NJ: Lawrence Erlbaum.

Roberts, B. R., Kuncel, N. R., Shiner, R. L., Caspi, A., and Goldberg, L. R. 2007. The
power of personality: The comparative validity of personality traits, socioeconomic status, and cognitive ability for predicting important life outcomes.
Perspectives on Psychological Science 2:313–45.

Roehling, M. V. 1999. Weight-based discrimination in employment: Psychological
and legal aspects. *Personnel Psychology* 52:969–1016.

———, Roehling, P. V., and Odland, L. M. 2008. Investigating the validity of stereotypes about overweight employees: The relationship between body weight and
normal personality traits. *Group and Organization Management* 33:392–424.

Rule, N. O., and Ambady, N. 2008. The face of success: Inferences from chief executive officers' appearance predict company profits. *Psychological Science* 19:109–11.

Schmidt, F. L., and Hunter, J. 2004. General mental ability in the world of work:
Occupational attainment and job performance. *Journal of Personality and Social
Psychology* 86:162–73.

Shepperd, J. A., and Strathman, A. J. 1989. Attractiveness and height: The role of stature in dating preference, frequency of dating, and perceptions of attractiveness.
Personality and Social Psychology Bulletin 15:617–27.

Sigelman, L. 1981. Is ignorance bliss? A reconsideration of the folk wisdom. *Human
Relations* 34:965–74.

Spisak, B. R., Nicholson, N., and Van Vugt, M. 2011. Leadership in organizations:
An evolutionary perspective. In *Evolutionary psychology in the business sciences*, ed.
G. Saad, Berlin: Springer-Verlag.

Steinberg, J. 2010. *Bismarck: A life*. Oxford: Oxford University Press.

Stirrat, M., and Perrett, D. I. 2012. Face structure predicts cooperation: Men with
wider faces are more generous to their in-group when out-group competition is
salient. *Psychological Science* 23:718–22.

Stogdill, R. M. 1948. Personal factors associated with leadership: A survey of the literature. *Journal of Psychology* 25:35–71.

Taylor, F. W. 1911. *The principles of scientific management*. Retrieved from http://www
.marxists.org/reference/subject/economics/taylor/index.htm

Todorov, A., Mandisodza, A. N., Goren, A., and Hall, C. C. 2005. Inferences of competence from faces predict election outcomes. *Science* 308:1623–26.

Turkheimer, E. 2000. Three laws of behavior genetics and what they mean. *Current Directions in Psychological Science* 9:160–64.

Van Vugt, M., Hogan, R., and Kaiser, R. B. 2008. Leadership, followership, and evolution. *American Psychologist* 63:182–96.

Wade, N. 2006. *Before the dawn*. New York: Penguin Books.

Waldman, D. A., and Avolio, B. J. 1986. A meta-analysis of age differences in job performance. *Journal of Applied Psychology* 71:33–38.

Whetton, D., and Cameron, K. 1994. Organizational effectiveness: Old models and new constructs. In *Organizational behavior: The state of the science*, ed. J. Greenberg, Northvale, NJ: Lawrence Erlbaum.

Wiggins, J. S. Ed.. 1996. *The five-factor model of personality*. New York: Guilford.

Wilhelm, O., Herzmann, G., Kunina, O., Danthiir, V., Schacht, A., and Sommer, W. 2010. Individual differences in perceiving and recognizing faces—One element of social cognition. *Journal of Personality and Social Psychology* 99:530–48.

Wilson, D. S., and Sober, E. 1994. Reintroducing group selection to the human behavioral sciences. *Behavioral and Brain Sciences* 17:585–654.

——, Van Vugt, M., O'Gorman, R. 2008. Multilevel selection theory and major evolutionary transitions: Implications for psychological science. *Current Directions in Psychological Science* 17:6–9.

Wong, E. M., Ormiston, M. E., and Haselhuhn, M. P. 2011. A face only an investor could love: CEOs' facial structure predicts their firms' financial performance. *Psychological Science* 22:1478–83.

Woolley, A. W., Chabris, C. F., Pentland, A., Hashmi, N. and Malone, T. W. 2010. Evidence for a collective intelligence factor in the performance of human groups. *Science* 330:686–88.

Young, T. J., and French, L. A. 1996. Height and perceived competence of US presidents. *Perceptual and Motor Skills* 82:1002.

Zebrowitz, L. A., Collins, M. A., and Dutta, R. 1998. The relationship between appearance and personality across the life span. *Personality and Social Psychology Bulletin* 24:736–49.

Zhang, Z., Zyphur, M. J., Narayanan, J., Arvey, R. D., Chaturvedi, S., Avolio, B. J. et al. 2009. The genetic basis of entrepreneurship: Effects of gender and personality. *Organizational Behavior and Human Decision Processes* 110:93–107.

SIX

Neurobiological Systems:
Implications for Organizational Behavior

Jayanth Narayanan and Smrithi Prasad

INTRODUCTION

Organizational contexts are characterized by change and the need for rapid decision-making (Eisenhardt 1989). In the face of this ever-changing environment, our actions are driven by our primitive brain, which evolved to survive in an ancestral environment (Tooby and Cosmides 1992). In our understanding of the complexities of dealing with such an environment, we need to be mindful of the implications that our primitive brains hold. Despite the secure yet complex nature of the current work environment, it tends to bring out our fundamental nature. As Nicholson (2000) points out in his book for managers, we have to learn to manage our "stone age minds in the information age." Our brains and biology drive our social behaviors. The last few decades have seen a tremendous growth in studies that examine how our biology affects our social behaviors. Three decades of cognitive neuroscience research have systematically uncovered the neural underpinnings of social behaviors in humans and other animals (see Gazzaniga 2010 for a comprehensive review). The application of this research in allied disciplines such as economics has been rampant (Camerer, Loewenstein, and Prelec 2005; Camerer 2008), while organizational behavior has yet to fully embrace these changes (see Heaphy and Dutton 2008; Akinola 2010; Becker, Cropanzano, and Sanfey 2011 for exceptions). This presents an opportunity for organizational scholars to adopt a strong paradigm such as neurobiology as a basis for theorizing. This chapter seeks to provide a preliminary framework that can not only help with the interpretation and application of findings in these domains of interdisciplinary research but can also provide us with directions for the generation of novel research questions. In order to understand the underpinnings of the social behaviors driven by our evolutionary heritage, we identify three basic motivations for behavior that are similar to those of our hunter-gatherer ancestors. These are the motivations to protect ourselves from threats, to seek rewards, and to forge affiliative bonds[1]. Threats can affect our survival in any environment, whether on the treacherous terrain of the savannah or on Wall Street. Humans have evolved and adapted to cope with threats across the spectrum, from a venomous snake to an abusive boss. Beyond this primal survival instinct of protecting ourselves, we are also motivated to seek objects that satiate our needs, such as food, shelter, and money, and we have also learned to forge bonds. Even though we are still adapting to and coping with new environments, our brains remain hard-wired to solve the same problems that our hunter-gatherer ancestors faced. Therefore, despite the differences of environmental triggers and behavioral responses, the underpinnings and biological apparatus of these behaviors for coping with threats, seeking rewards, and building affliatory bonds have remained the same.

We focus on two core biological methodologies—endocrinology and neuroscience.[2] Specifically, we consider four hormones/neurotransmitters—testosterone, cortisol, oxytocin, and serotonin—and neuroscience research on brain regions that have been functionally localized to predict social behaviors. The link between biology and social behaviors then provides an opportunity to apply these findings to organizational settings using the three motivational categories. Further, we argue that these fundamental motivational systems are useful not only in interpreting current research but also as a theoretical basis for generating new research within the organizational behavior domain.

OVERVIEW OF THE THREE MOTIVATIONAL SYSTEMS

The *threat system* motivates the evolutionary need for humans to thrive in difficult circumstances and thereby sanctions a set of complex machinery and biochemical changes to cope with the threat. The threat system is primarily driven by the hormone cortisol, in addition to others like epinephrine and norepinephrine. The endocrine systems (consisting of the cortisol, adrenalin, and epinephrine responses) work in tandem with the amygdala, thalamus, and other cortical regions in the brain to respond to threats while also generating a cardiovascular response. Within the organizational context, stress is a common phenomena that confronts and threatens individuals. Stressors can be either chronic or acute, and they are both known to have an impact on endocrine and cardiovascular functioning.

The second neurobiological system motivates us to seek objects, people, and situations that are rewarding. Early humans were motivated to satiate basic desires, such as food and sex. As we evolved, however, the nature of rewards has changed to include more complex social needs like status, morality, and fairness. This reward system is governed by three hormones—dopamine, serotonin, and testosterone. These hormones work in tandem with executive control regions—those responsible for cognitive control and processing in the brain when a person must choose between two conflicting needs.

The need to belong to a social group is also a fundamental human motivation (Baumeister and Leary 1995). An important function of our neurobiological system is to forge and maintain these social bonds, and the primary reason humans have such a large brain is so that we can manage all our social relationships in groups (Dunbar 1992). At the core of organizational life is the ability to coordinate with social actors. Accompanying this imperative is the necessity of trust and cooperation. The *affiliation system* performs this important function of social connection at the neurobiological level. The research in this domain has focused mainly on the role of oxytocin.

In the sections that follow, we provide a more detailed examination of these three motivational systems. For each motivational system, we examine the fundamental biological processes that drive it, and we also describe how the system under consideration operates to give rise to social behaviors. We then examine the resulting implications for organizational behavior (OB) scholars and the challenges and the limitations inherent in integrating this approach for OB researchers.

THREAT SYSTEM

Although the world we live in is not as hostile as that of our hunter-gatherer ancestors, we are still faced with situations that threaten our well-being. While the threats that our ancestors faced were physically challenging, at work we encounter situations that are psychologically threatening. The most common threats at work could be an abusive su-

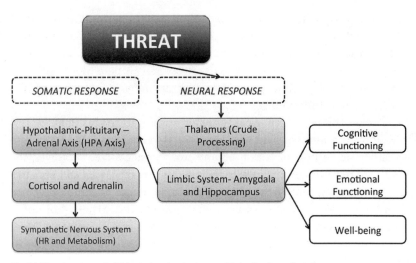

Fig. 6.1 Threat system—its biological underpinnings and behavioral manifestations

pervisor, an unfair compensation system, or even an approaching dead-line that requires overtime. These threats manifest themselves as stressors that could be temporary (episodic, like a deadline) or sustained (chronic, like a bad relationship with one's supervisor). Stressors compromise our functioning by diminishing the value we place on work or the quality of our performance. In the face of physical danger, the human body has evolved to produce an involuntary response, called the fight-or-flight response (Cannon 1932). We need not consciously perceive a threat in order for it to be processed and responded to. The presence of a threat or even anything that looks like one (for example, a hose that looks like a snake) can be enough to generate the fight-or-flight response. Similarly, while dealing with threats in the work environment, our bodies are designed to produce a similar response. The biological mechanisms that ensue are complex and evoke several physiological systems at once.

Biological Mechanism

Our reactions to threats are involuntary and almost seem reflexive. When the eyes perceive the presence of a threat, a signal is sent to a brain region called the *thalamus*. The thalamus sends the information to the *amygdala*, a pea-shaped brain region associated with fear processing. The thalamus simultaneously sends a message to the *cerebral cortex*. The cortex includes several brain regions that cognitively analyze information and attribute value. When the cortex receives the message of the threat, it facilitates the recognition and comprehension of the magnitude of the threat and calibrates a proportionate response.

The brain is the control center for the entire body, and the activation of the threat areas in the brain facilitates a somatic (bodily) response. The activation of the brain results in a chain of biochemical reactions, which are channeled by a combination of hormone-producing glands called the HPA (hypothalamic-pituitary-adrenal) axis. The main by-product of this axis is the production of the stress hormone called cortisol. This hormone is responsible for enabling the body to cope with the threat through several other biochemical changes. The activation of the HPA axis produces changes that include an increased heart-rate, slower digestion, and increased blood-flow to the muscles (by means of the *sympathetic nervous system*). After the body responds to the threat, a complementary mechanism helps to restore its original state of homeostasis after the upheaval (by means of the *parasympathetic nervous system*).

Behavioral Manifestation

The biological response to threats results in compromised cognitive and emotional functioning (Häusser, Mojzisch, and Schulz-Hardt, in press; Fox, Dwyer, and Ganster 1993; Takahashi 2005). In this section, we describe how both these modules are affected. Takahashi (2005) exposed participants to a social stressor (the Trier social stress task; see Kirschbaum, Pirke, and Hellhammer 1993) targeted to experimentally manipulate cortisol levels. When exposed to the stressor, participants experienced an increase in cortisol that was accompanied with a decrement in memory function. The cortisol produced as a result of stress compromised the brain's cognitive ability to process and store information. It is also not uncommon that when faced with threatening stimuli, we are motivated to express negative emotions. For example, when working with an abusive supervisor, we might have an outburst of anger after being treated badly. Like other threat-system responses, anger is also accompanied by increases in cortisol, heart-rate, and blood pressure. When anger is experienced, it also translates into other negative behaviors. For example, Pillutla and Murnighan (1996) found that when participants experienced anger and spite, they tended to engage in emotional reactions of unfairness in an ultimatum game. Similarly when individuals are treated unfairly and some are given an opportunity to ruminate over the act, they behave in more punishing ways (Wang et al. 2011) than those who were made to cognitively reappraise the situation. Both studies emphasized that anger manifests itself through an up-regulation of emotional expression along with compromised cognitive functioning.

Implications for Organizational Behavior

While the nature of threats has changed over time, the human mind and body adapt by producing a similar set of neurobiological responses to more complex and subjective threats. In an organizational context, the fight-or-flight response is usually a reaction to threats in the form of stressors. Stressors at work could be job-related (i.e., a rapidly approaching deadline) or organizational (i.e., a rude supervisor). In addition to this, the spill-over of non-work-related stressors (e.g., from the family) has also become a common phenomenon. Although we must deal with many threats that are different from those confronted by our ancestors, our biological reactions to any form of stress are similar. Several studies in organizational behavior have examined the biological implications of organizational stressors. In a study of nurses, Fox, Dwyer, and Ganster (1993) found that higher job demands resulted in greater cortisol responses. Much like threats faced in the environment, job demands also generate a neural and somatic reaction to cope with the situation. Job strain was also found to produce a heightened cortisol morning or awakening response and a subsequent demonstration of anger in the workplace (Steptoe et al. 2000). Higher workload and its associated stress also result in more affective distress and increased blood pressure, which have a bearing on our daily well-being (Ilies, Dimotakis, and Pater 2010). Individuals who experience high work stress face a 50% higher risk of cardiovascular heart diseases (Kivimäki et al. 2006). Therefore, threats in the form of stressors not only have a detrimental impact on our cognitive functioning and emotional expression, but in the context of organizations, they directly affect our well-being through lowered cardiovascular health and greater cortisol reactivity to stress.

REWARD SYSTEM

Rewards in modern society go beyond the basic needs that our ancestors had. The nature of what we perceive as being rewarding has also undergone tremendous change. In an organization, rewards could be purely monetary, yet also have social implications regarding, for example, reputation and status. The complex processing of these socially constructed

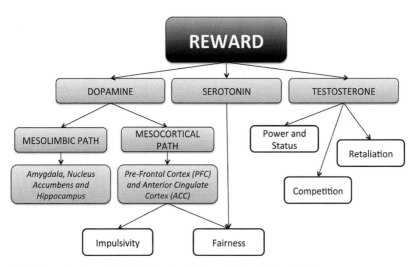

Fig. 6.2 Reward system—its biological underpinnings and behavioral manifestations

rewards involves more than one biological system. We highlight the role played by the biochemicals dopamine, serotonin, and testosterone in understanding the motives behind reward-seeking behaviors today.

Dopamine and Its Associated Brain Regions

Biological Mechanism

The presence or even the anticipation of a reward results in the release of dopamine and the activation of dopamine-rich reward centers in the brain—the *substantia niagra* and the *ventral tegmental area*. Through the two main dopamine-rich pathways—the *meso-limbic* pathway, connected to the emotional regions of the brain (the *amygdala* and *hippocampus*), and the *meso-cortical* pathway, connected to the cognitive centers of the brain (the *pre-frontal cortex* [PFC] and *anterior cingulate cortex* [ACC])—rewarding stimuli are processed emotionally and cognitively.

Behavioral Manifestation

Conflicts often arise when individuals are presented with two rewards and must choose between them. When faced with the conflict between choosing economic gains and evolutionarily adaptive and socially constructed rewards like fairness and morality, individuals' vary in what they subjectively perceive as having more value. Research has explored the nature of this conflict and the biological factors driving individual choice between utilitarian gains or social norms and conduct. Usually the dopaminergic system through its meso-cortical pathway and its associated areas, the PFC and ACC, help in resolving these conflicts. The ultimatum game has been used as an economic paradigm to test the conflict that arises in a choice between economic benefits and fairness. The rejection of unfair offers in an ultimatum game indicates that more weight and value are placed on fairness as compared to utility. The act of rejecting these unfair offers is accompanied by greater activation in the insula, a brain region associated with disgust, which indicates the emotionally aversive nature of unfairness. On the other hand, the acceptance of unfair offers is marked by activation of the PFC (Sanfey et. al. 2003; Tabibnia, Satpute, and Lieberman 2008). The activation of this executive region highlights the brain's need to down-regulate the intuitive response of rejecting these offers and, instead, to cognitively process the information and choose monetary benefits over the fairness. Similarly, moral dilemmas pose a conflict between utility and morality in our decision making. These dilemmas also produce greater activation in the executive regions of the PFC and ACC when the individual chooses utility over morality (Greene et al. 2006). These findings, though counterintuitive with regard to our rational and utilitarian stance in decision making, highlight how fairness and morality have tremendous value and salience in our rather primitive decision-making process. The degree of executive control required to curb our instinctive desires to act fairly or morally indicates the evolutionary value of these rewards today.

Serotonin

Biological Mechanism

Serotonin is a neurotransmitter that also facilitates the drive to seek rewards and also affects regions associated with moral judgments, such as the ventromedial prefrontal cortex, the insula, and the amygdala (Crockett et al. 2010).

Behavioral Manifestation

Like dopamine, serotonin plays an important role in conflict resolution between fairness and economic gains. Crockett and colleagues (2008) modulated the levels of serotonin in the brain and measured reactions to unfairness in an ultimatum game. The findings indicated that individuals with depleted levels of serotonin tended to value fairness less and accepted unfair offers, thereby making economic gains. Individuals in the control condition (with normal levels of serotonin), however, tended to view fairness as more salient and rejected unfair offers, thereby sacrificing economic benefits (Crockett et al. 2008). Serotonin, therefore, also plays a role in governing how we value economic rewards and those that are socially constructed, such as fairness.

Testosterone

Biological Mechanism

From an evolutionary standpoint, in a situation of limited resources, the presence of rewards drives individuals to compete with one another. The acquisition of these resources then guarantees higher status. The need to acquire rewarding resources and increased status is driven by the hormone testosterone. Though this hormone is known primarily for the role it plays in male sexual development, it also affects our social behaviors (Archer 2006; Mazur and Booth 1998; Dabbs et al. 1988; Grant and France 2001).

Behavioral Manifestation

Testosterone facilitates the need to compete for access to limited resources. The anticipation of competition and victory is accompanied by an increase in testosterone levels (Booth et al. 1989). Although it was generally believed that a loss reduces testosterone and a win increases testosterone, research has shown that this effect is not uniform (Mehta and Josephs 2006). Following a loss in a competition, some people show an increase in testosterone. These people then strive to restore their lost status and reputation by seeking to compete again (Mehta and Josephs 2006). Testosterone is implicated in seeking and competing for limited resources, and the motivation to do so may be governed by the need to maintain and restore status. Testosterone is also well known for its role in promoting aggressive and confrontational behaviors when rewards are denied or have been unfairly distributed (Burnham 2007; Ronay and Galinsky 2010; Mehta and Beer 2010). As noted earlier, unfair offers in the ultimatum game are usually rejected. Higher levels of testosterone prompted more retaliatory behaviors along with the rejection of unfair monetary offers, so that both parties stood to lose. These findings further illustrate that high testosterone levels motivate individuals to seek fairness in order to maintain their reputations (Burnham 2007) at the cost of economic gain.

Organizational Behavior Implications

Organizations utilize rewards to motivate employees to meet performance standards and goals. While monetary rewards primarily drive performance, these come with the condition of having to be fair within the social exchange context, or else they possess little or no value. Reputation within an organization has today attained the status of being rewarding. Zyphur and colleagues (2009) measured the testosterone levels of a group of individuals and matched them to the status of individuals within the group. They found that when there was a match between the testosterone levels and the status of the individuals, the group enjoyed greater collective efficacy. However, a mismatch between the two resulted in lower levels of collective efficacy. This study interestingly indicates how testosterone-motivated status-seeking results in collective efficacy within a group context.

AFFILIATION SYSTEM

Affiliation is a fundamental social need that has promoted the survival of the human race, which might otherwise have succumbed to chaos

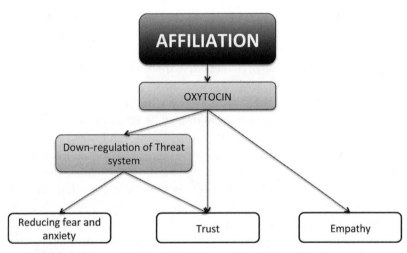

Fig. 6.3 Affiliation system—its biological underpinnings and behavioral manifestations

and anarchy in the fight for limited resources. The development of social bonds and relationships has also provided us with a buffer against stressors and threats.

Biological Underpinnings

Oxytocin, a neuropeptide, which is instrumental in childbirth and lactation, also forms the biological basis for social relationships.

Behavioral Manifestation

Social psychologists and neuroeconomists have studied oxytocin's role in facilitating social bonds through trust, empathy, and altruism (Kosfeld et al. 2005; Zak, Kurzban, and Matzner 2005). The social implications of oxytocin were first studied in the domain of trust. Individuals to whom it was administered demonstrated a higher degree of trust in a complete stranger in a trust game (Kosfeld et al. 2005). Conversely, the presence of a trusting relationship also results in an increase in oxytocin (Zak, Kurzban, and Matzner 2005), demonstrating that oxytocin acts as both an antecedent and an outcome of affiliative bonds. Affiliation can be demonstrated in a variety of ways, one being through touch. The early experiments on touch found that momentarily being touched by a waitress or librarian prompted positive appraisal of the individual (Crusco and Wetzel 1984; Fisher, Rytting, and Heslin 1976). Though these studies did not uncover the biological basis of touch then, today we know that physical contact is accompanied with the release of oxytocin, which in turn predicts the positive evaluation of the individual making the contact (Zak et. al. 2005; Carter 2006; Odendaal and Meintjes 2003). In another study, Morhenn and colleagues (2008) increased oxytocin levels through massages, where higher levels of oxytocin resulted in more trusting behaviors toward anonymous counterparts. This finding suggests that (appropriate) touch could potentially be used as a trust-building activity within the workplace. Recent evidence also indicates that touching nonhuman objects that have anthropomorphic properties, such as a teddy bear, leads to satisfaction of this fundamental need for affiliation(Tai, Zheng, and Narayanan 2011). Humans also possess a unique ability to imagine and vicariously experience the emotional turmoil inflicted upon another, which is known as empathy. Individuals who received oxytocin had a higher degree of empathic accuracy compared to those who received a placebo (Guastella et al. 2008). Oxytocin-generated empathy is also known to foster more prosocial and altruistic behaviors (Barazza and Zak

2009; Zak, Stanton, and Ahmadi 2007). Evidence also suggests that oxytocin not only facilitates altruistic decision making but also results in parochial or self-sacrificial altruism (i.e., generosity toward one's in-group at a cost to the self). Individuals who were administered oxytocin were willing to undergo personal financial losses in order to promote profitable behavior in their in-group (de Dreu et al. 2010).

Organizational Behavior Implications

The research on oxytocin can be applied within an organization to two broad domains: organizational culture and leadership. Building strong affiliative bonds within the workplace could potentially foster more trust, empathy, compassion, and generosity among employees. The bidirectional association of oxytocin with positive social behaviors highlights their mutually reinforcing nature and indicates the need for strong and trusting social networks within organizations. The research on oxytocin can also be applied to leadership. Leaders in organizations have long been perceived to have transactional relationships with their employees. Recently, we have also come to recognize and acknowledge the fundamental and critical importance of emotions, trust, bonding, and empathy for the successful functioning of a leader. These newer components of leadership are being studied under the umbrella of *transformational leadership*. While no research so far has uncovered the biological basis of such leadership, we imagine that a transformational leader's ability to understand the emotions of employees and to build trust could be enhanced by oxytocin levels.

INTERACTIONS BETWEEN SYSTEMS

The three motivational systems, though comprehensive in nature, are not mutually exclusive. The overlap between these three systems also means that the underlying biological processes interact with one another. Only a few studies have been conducted to examine these interactions, and the following section presents some of them as a starting point for more research in this direction.

Interaction of the Threat and Reward Systems

The interface between the threat and reward systems is especially important in power and status relationships. Being in a position of power is accompanied by an increase in testosterone. However, for those in positions of power, the loss of power is always a looming threat. In these volatile and unstable situations where acquisition of power and fear of its loss act together, the threat and reward systems interact. In his early work on free-range baboons in Africa, Robert Sapolsky (1990) found that when the hierarchy among the baboons was unstable, dominant males showed increased levels of cortisol and testosterone until a stable hierarchy was established. Once there was stability in the hierarchy, these transient increases in hormone levels fell. These findings indicate the overlapping nature of the need for power (with higher testosterone levels) and the reaction to threat (with higher cortisol levels) in unstable hierarchies. Sapolsky (1990) provided us with the first evidence that the reward and threat systems interact with one another. This overlap could be due to the antagonistic effects on each other of the biological systems that produce cortisol (the HPA axis) and testosterone (the hypothalamic–pituitary–gonadal (HPG) axis; see Terburg, Morgan, and van Honk 2009). To explore how both hormonal systems interact, Mehta and Josephs (2010) proposed the *dual hormone hypothesis*, which highlights the combined effort of both hormones to produce dominance behaviors. Their study found that at lower levels of cortisol, testosterone positively predicted dominance. However, at higher levels of cortisol, this effect was blocked. Therefore, dominance behaviors (that can be rewarding) are suppressed by the presence of threats in the environment or were produced when individuals had high testosterone and low cortisol.

Carney, Cuddy, and Yap (2010) also explored the testosterone and cortisol relationship; they made use of nonverbal physical postures to induce changes in hormonal levels. Participants were made to adopt postures of powerfulness and of powerlessness. Those who adopted postures of high power demonstrated an endocrine profile that was accompanied with an increase in testosterone levels and a decrease in cortisol. Those with powerless postures showed a decrease in testosterone levels and an increase in cortisol levels. Those with the power profile showed greater risk-taking behaviors. Taken together, these studies suggest that it might be worthwhile to examine the endocrine profiles of leaders within organizations and their underlying needs for power (high T) and lack of stress (low C) and how those factors affect decision making.

Interaction of the Affiliation and Threat Systems

Evolutionarily speaking, affiliative bonds have served to protect us from threats in the environment. Biologically, oxytocin that is produced as a result of positive social behaviors suppresses our fear of perceived threats (Insel and Young 2001). Oxytocin functions by down-regulating the activity of the limbic-HPA axis system (Kirsch et al. 2005; Winston et al. 2002). Heinrichs and colleagues (2003) found that when participants were administered oxytocin and provided with social support, they showed lowered levels of cortisol reactivity, increased calmness, and low anxiety levels with regard to an experimental social stress. Oxytocin was therefore found to enhance the buffering effect of social support, which independently also resulted in lower reactivity to threat and thereby facilitated a healthier reaction to stress. It has been shown that the mere presence of social support increases levels of oxytocin and results in lower cardiovascular reactivity, marked by low blood pressure and better well-being (Grewen et al. 2005). These studies highlight the positive effects that the affiliative system bears on the well-being and health of individuals under situations of threat or stress. Within organizations, the presence of extensive social-support networks may act as ways to alleviate stronger and unhealthier reactions to stress and threats in the environment.

Interaction of the Reward and Affiliation Systems

We have argued that rewards can span a broad range of things from those that are monetary to those that are socially constructed. Social bonds are rewarding, and it could be argued that they produce a biological response similar to that produced by money, fairness, or status. To elucidate this relationship between rewards and affiliation, in an fMRI study, Singer and colleagues (2004) conducted a Prisoner's Dilemma (PD) experiment in which participants were shown the faces of their opponents after the game and informed if the opponent had cooperated with them intentionally or unintentionally. In essence, intentional cooperation indicated the opponent's desire to foster social ties and bonds. The faces of participants who had cooperated intentionally produced greater activation in the reward regions of the brain than the faces of those who had cooperated unintentionally. This shows that deliberate attempts to foster social connections are more rewarding. Workplaces, in addition to providing incentives to employees, can also create cultures and environments that facilitate social affiliation and bonding that may be equally rewarding.

CHALLENGES FOR ORGANIZATIONAL BEHAVIOR SCHOLARS

This chapter attempts to provide OB scholars with three motivational categories and their underlying biological processes that can be useful in the study of workplace behaviors. The application of this neurobiological research to organizational theory is not without its challenges. We believe that OB scholars can adopt either an interpretive or a generative approach. Many of the current applications that we have discussed are interpretive. This approach uses existing findings in neurobiology to reinterpret OB. Armed with this understanding, organizational scholars can generate fresh hypotheses for examination. An alternative approach would be to use neurobiological methods in actual studies of organizational employees. This approach presents more challenges than the previous one. We do not mean to imply that the two approaches are mutually exclusive, but the challenges faced by a researcher are different with each approach.

The first challenge facing OB scholars is that the discipline has no strong, underlying paradigm that makes assumptions about human behaviors. Economics is one of the few disciplines within the social sciences that makes a set of canonical assumptions about human behavior and then goes on to build predictions of how people "should" behave. While this classical view has been criticized ad nauseam, it is not without benefits. These assumptions allow economists to make clean predictions. These assumptions also allow economists to apply research from neurobiology better than scholars in any other discipline, as they can directly test their assumptions from a neuroscientific point of view. Therefore it is not a surprise that neuroeconomics as a discipline has penetrated the realm of economics. However within the field of OB, scholars are more likely to adopt an interpretative approach rather than a generative one, due to the lack of a clean paradigm to study behaviors in the workplace, although we may be proven wrong.

The other major challenge for OB scholars is the complexity of neurobiology as a field. Many researchers from psychology and neuroscience are now taking positions in business schools, which may alleviate the problem to a certain degree. However, neurobiology is a field replete with methods that are rather difficult to apply to OB research. Our recommendation is that OB scholars should collaborate with neuroscientists, especially if they wish to take a generative approach and use these methodologies to study workplace phenomena. We also predict that neuroendocrine methods involving hormones are more likely to be studied than neuroscience methods because the former can lead to more genera-

tive research than the latter and are less expensive. Challenges notwithstanding, OB researchers are beginning to pay attention to this emerging
field of organizational biology. The purpose of our review is to provide
OB scholars with an understanding of the basic neurobiological systems
that may have implications for research in our field. We certainly believe
that the time is ripe for this work to take off, as the publication of this
volume testifies. We hope that by identifying three basic motivational
components of OB, we have suggested approaches that can be adopted to
generating new research.

Notes

1. We wish to acknowledge that this categorization has been adopted from a talk
given by Tania Singer, of the Max Planck Institute for Human Cognitive and Brain
Sciences, Leipzig, Germany, at a conference in Zurich in April 2010.

2. For a detailed overview of these processes, see, respectively, Taylor et al. 2000,
and Camerer, Loewenstein, and Prele 2005.

References

Akinola, M. 2011. Measuring the pulse of an organization: Integrating physiological measures into the organizational scholar's toolbox. *Research in Organizational
Behavior* 30:203–23.

Archer, J. (2006). Testosterone and human aggression: an evaluation of the challenge
hypothesis. *Neuroscience and Biobehavioral Reviews* 30 (3): 319–45.

Barraza, J., and Zak, P. 2009. Empathy towards strangers triggers oxytocin release and
subsequent generosity. *Annals of the New York Academy of Sciences* 1167:182–89.

Baumeister, R. F., and Leary, M. R. 1995. The need to belong: Desire for interpersonal
attachments as a fundamental human motivation. *Psychological Bulletin* 117 (3):
497–529.

Becker, W. J., Cropanzano, R., and Sanfey, A. G. 2011. Organizational neuroscience:
Taking organizational theory inside the neural block box. *Journal of Management*
37 (4): 933–61.

Booth, A., Shelley, G., Mazur, A., Tharp, G., and Kittock, R. 1989. Testosterone and
winning and losing in human competition. *Hormones and Behavior* 23 (4): 556–71.

Burnham, T. C. 2007. High-testosterone men reject low ultimatum game offers. *Proceedings of the Royal Society of Biology* 274:2327–30.

Camerer C. F. 2008. Neuroeconomics: Opening the gray box. *Neuron* 60 (3): 416–19.

———, Loewenstein, G., and Prelec, D. 2005. Neuroeconomics: How neuroscience can
inform economics, *Journal of Economic Literature* 43:9–64.

Carney, D. R., Cuddy, A. J. C., and Yap, A. J. 2010. Power posing: Brief nonverbal
displays affect neuroendocrine levels and risk tolerance. *Psychological Science*
21:1363–68.

Cannon, W. B. 1932. *The wisdom of the body.* New York: W. W. Norton.

Carter, C. S. 2006. Biological perspectives on social attachment and bonding. In *Attachment and bonding: A new synthesis*, ed. C. S. Carter, et al. 85–100. Cambridge, MA: MIT Press.

Crockett, M. J., Clark, L., Tabibnia, G., Lieberman, M. D., and Robbins, T. W. 2008. Serotonin modulates behavioral reactions to unfairness. *Science* 320:1739.

———, Clark L., Hauser M. D., and Robbins T. W. 2010. Serotonin selectively influences moral judgment and behavior through effects on harm aversion. *Proceedings of the National Academy of Sciences* 107 (40): 17433–38.

Crusco, A., and Wetzel, C. G. 1984. The Midas touch: The effects of interpersonal touch on restaurant tipping. *Personality and Social Psychology Bulletin*, 10 (4): 512–17.

Dabbs, J. M., Jr., Ruback, R. B., Frady, R. L., Hopper, C. H., and Sgoutas, D. S. 1988. Saliva testosterone and criminal violence among women. *Personality and Individual Differences* 9 (2): 269–75.

De Dreu, C. K. W., Greer, L. L., Handgraaf, M. J. J., Shalvi, S., Van Kleef, G. A., Bass, M., et al. 2010. The neuropeptide oxytocin regulates parochial altruism in intergroup conflict among humans. *Nature* 328:1408–11.

Dunbar, R. I. 1992. Neocortex size as a constraint on group size in primates. *Journal of Human Evolution* 22 (6): 469–93.

Eisenhardt, K. M. 1989. Making fast strategic decisions in high-velocity environments. *Academy of Management Journal* 32 (3): 543–76.

Fisher, J. D., Rytting, M., and Heslin, R. 1976. Hands touching hands: Affective and evaluative effects of interpersonal touch. *Sociometry* 39:416–21.

Fox, M., Dwyer, D., and Ganster, D. C. 1993. Effects of stressful job demands and control on physiological and attitudinal outcomes in a hospital setting. *Academy of Management Journal* 36 (2): 289–318.

Gazzaniga, M. S. 2010. *The cognitive neurosciences*. 4th ed. Cambridge, MA: MIT Press.

Grant, V. J., and France, J. T. 2001. Dominance and testosterone in women. *Biological Psychology* 58 (1): 41–47.

Greene, J. D., Nystrom, L. E., Engell, A. D., Darley, J. M., and Cohen, J. D. 2004. The neural bases of cognitive conflict and control in moral judgment. *Neuron* 44 (2): 389–400.

Grewen, K. M., Girdler, S. S., Amico, J., and Light, K. C. 2005. Effects of partner support on resting oxytocin, cortisol, norepinephrine, and blood pressure before and after warm partner contact. Psychosomatic medicine 67 (4): 531–38.

Guastella, A. J., Mitchell, P. B., and Dadds, M. R. 2008. Oxytocin increases gaze to the eye region of human faces. *Biological Psychiatry* 63 (1): 3–5.

Häusser, J. A., Mojzisch, A., and Schulz-Hardt, S. In press. Endocrinological and psychological responses to job stressors: An experimental test of the Job Demand–Control Model, *Psychoneuroendocrinology*.

———, Mojzisch, A., and Schulz-Hardt, S. 2011. Endocrinological and psychological responses to job stressors: An experimental test of the Job Demand–Control Model. *Psychoneuroendocrinology* 36 (7): 1021–31.

Heaphy, E. D., and Dutton, J. E. 2008. Positive social interactions and the human body at work: Linking organizations and physiology. *Academy of Management Review* 33 (1): 137–62.

Heinrichs M., Baumgartner T., Kirschbaum C., and Ehlert U. 2003. Social support and oxytocin interact to suppress cortisol and subjective responses to psychosocial stress. *Biological Psychiatry* 54:1389–98.

Ilies, R., Dimotakis, N., and de Pater, I. E. 2010. Psychological and physiological reactions to high workloads: Implications for well-being. *Personnel Psychology* 63 (2): 407–36.

Insel, T. R., and Young, L. J. 2001. The neurobiology of attachment. *Nature Reviews Neuroscience* 2 (2): 129–36.

Kirsch, P., Esslinger, C., Chen, Q., Mier, D., Lis, S., Siddhanti, S., et al. 2005. Oxytocin modulates neural circuitry for social cognition and fear in humans. *Journal of Neuroscience* 25 (49): 11489 –493.

Kirschbaum, C., Pirke, K.-M., and Hellhammer, D. H. 1993. The Trier Social Stress Test: A tool for investigating psychobiological stress responses in a laboratory setting. *Neuropsychobiology* 28 (1–2): 76–81.

Kivimäki, M., Virtanen, M., Elovainio, M., Kouvonen, A., Väänänen, A., and Vahtera, J. 2006. Work stress in the etiology of coronary heart disease: A meta-analysis. *Scandinavian Journal of Work, Environment and Health* 32 (6): 431–42.

Kosfeld, M., Heinrichs, M., Zak, P., Fischbacher, U., and Fehr, E. 2005. Oxytocin increases trust in humans. *Nature* 435:673–76.

Mazur, A., and Booth, A. 1998. Testosterone and dominance in men. *Behavioral and Brain Sciences* 21 (3): 353–63.

Mehta, P. H., and Beer, J. S. 2010. Neural mechanisms of the testosterone-aggression relation: The role of the orbitofrontal cortex. *Journal of Cognitive Neuroscience* 22:2357–68.

———, and Josephs, R. A. 2006. Testosterone change after losing predicts the decision to compete again. *Hormones and Behavior* 50 (5): 684–92.

———. 2010. Testosterone and cortisol jointly regulate dominance: Evidence for a dual-hormone hypothesis. *Hormones and Behavior* 58 (5): 898–906.

Morhenn, V. B., Park, J. W., Piper, E., and Zak, P. J. 2008. Monetary sacrifice among strangers is mediated by endogenous oxytocin release after physical contact. *Evolution and Human Behavior* 29 (6): 375–83.

Odendaal, J. S. J., and Meintjes, R. A. 2003. Neurophysiological correlates of affiliative behaviour between humans and dogs. *Veterinary Journal* 165 (3): 296–301.

Nicholson, N. 2000. *Managing the Human Animal*. London: Texere.

Pillutla, M. M., and Murnighan, J. K. 1996. Unfairness, anger, and spite: Emotional rejections of ultimatum offers. *Organizational Behavior of Human Decision-making Processes* 68 (3): 208–24.

Ronay, R., and Galinsky, A. D. 2011. *Lex talionis*: Testosterone and the law of retaliation. *Journal of Experimental Social Psychology* 47 (3): 702–5.

Sanfey, A. G., Rilling, J. K., Aronson, J. A., Nystrom, L. E., and Cohen, J. D. 2003. The neural basis of economic decision-making in the ultimatum game, *Science* 300:1755–58.

Sapolsky, R. 1990. Stress in the wild. *Scientific American* 2:106–13.

Singer, T., Kiebel, S. J., Winston, J. S., Dolan, R. J., and Frith, C. D. 2004. Brain responses to the acquired moral status of faces. *Neuron* 41 (4): 653–62.

Steptoe, A., Cropley, M., Griffith, J., and Kirschbaum, C. 2000. Job strain and anger expression predict early morning elevations in salivary cortisol. *Psychosomatic Medicine* 62 (2): 286–92.

Tabibnia, G., Satpute, A. B., and Lieberman, M. D. 2008. The sunny side of fairness: Preference for fairness activates reward circuitry and disregarding unfairness activates self-control circuitry. *Psychological Science* 19 (4): 339–47.

Tai, K., Zheng, X., and Narayanan, J. 2011. Touching a teddy bear mitigates negative effects of social exclusion to increase prosocial behavior. *Social Psychological and Personality Science* 2 (6): 618–26.

Takahashi, T. 2005. Social memory, social stress, and economic behaviours. *Brain Research Bulletin* 67 (5): 398–402.

Terburg, D., Morgan, B., and van Honk, J. 2009. The testosterone-cortisol ratio: A hormonal marker for proneness to social aggression. *International Journal of Law Psychiatry* 32 (4): 216–23.

Tooby, J., and Cosmides, L. 1992. The psychological foundations of culture. In *The adapted mind: Evolutionary psychology and the generation of culture*, ed. J. H. Barkow, L. Cosmides, and J. Tooby, 19– 136. Oxford: Oxford University Press.

Wang, C. S., Sivanathan, N., Narayanan, J., Ganegoda, D. B., Bauer, M., Bodenhausen, G. V., and Murnighan, K. 2011. Retribution and emotional regulation: The effects of time delay in angry economic interactions. *Organizational Behavior and Human Decision Processes* 116 (1): 46–54.

Winston, J. S., Strange, B. A., O'Doherty, J., and Dolan, R. J. 2002. Automatic and intentional brain responses during evaluation of trustworthiness of faces. *Nature Neuroscience* 5 (3): 277–83.

Zak, P. J., Stanton, A. A., and Ahmadi, S. 2007. Oxytocin increases generosity in humans. *PLoS ONE* 2 (11): e1128.

———, Kurzban, R., and Matzner,W. T. 2005. Oxytocin associated with human trustworthiness. *Hormones and Behavior* 48 (5): 522–27.

Zyphur, M. J., Narayanan, J., Koh, G., and Koh, D. 2009. Testosterone–status mismatch lowers collective efficacy in groups: Evidence from a slope-as-predictor multilevel structural equation model. *Organizational Behavior and Human Decision Processes* 110 (2): 70–79.

SEVEN

Physiological Functioning and Employee Health in Organizations

Zhen Zhang and Michael J. Zyphur

The functioning of employees' physiological systems plays a critical role in understanding the dynamic interplay between the work environment and people as these affect organizational outcomes. Examining such functioning is important not only for employees' well-being but also for the bottom line of organizations. For example, Ganster, Fox, and Dwyer (2001) found that elevated levels of salivary cortisol persisting for several hours after employees leave work can explain 25% of the variance in subsequent health-care costs for organizations. This stands in contrast to traditional organizational behavior (OB) research and occupational health psychology, which uses cognitive, affective, and behavioral approaches to examine employee behavior and its antecedents and outcomes in organizations (Mowday and Sutton 1993; O'Reilly 1991). Although OB researchers have long studied physiological measures as they relate to employee well-being and health (e.g., elevated blood pressure as an indicator of job-caused strain; Bruning and Frew 1987), such variables often play a peripheral role in OB research.

Recently, researchers have started to examine employee physiology in light of the positive OB agenda in organizations (e.g., Wright et al. 2009; Xie, Schaubroeck, and Lam 2008). Many have called for a more extensive integration of human physiology in organizational research (e.g., Heaphy and Dutton 2008; White, Thornhill, and Hampson 2006; Wright and Diamond 2006). Within the OB literature, various theories and research streams have strong implications for employee physiological functioning

job stress, organizational justice, work events, and social support). By
:hesizing these research topics, summarizing their current status, and
ntifying future directions, we attempt to contribute to this emerging
:rature on employee physiology. We examine these more proximal an-
:edents of employee physiological processes (i.e., those stemming from
ιe immediate work environment) in the greater context of the more dis-
ιl, evolutionary perspective. In the first section below, we ground our
.hapter in an overarching evolutionary psychological perspective, provid-
ιng a framework for understanding why we function as we do and more
distal causes of physiological functioning, which in turn informs possible
interventions for stress and other outcomes of work environments. We
first highlight the mismatch between modern work environments and
those of our ancestors, pinpointing ways to enhance the physiological
functioning of employees. Second, we offer an organizing framework for
prior research on employees' physiological functioning in organizations,
defining its key constructs and variables. Third, we review OB research
that has investigated the relationship between work environments in organizations and employee physiological functioning and health. Fourth,
we articulate the value of examining physiological variables by reviewing
findings that link them to important work outcomes. We then show how
organizational interventions can change employees' physiological functioning and enhance their health. Lastly, we discuss the implications for
research (i.e., current research gaps, measurement and methodological issues, and directions for future research) and suggest managerial practices
that can promote a better and healthier workplace.

EVOLUTIONARY PSYCHOLOGY AND EMPLOYEES
IN MODERN ORGANIZATIONS

Evolutionary perspectives tell unique stories about employees' physiological responses to their working lives in modern organizations. Generally, our thesis is that the modern working environment presents environmental stressors and social difficulties for which humans have not
yet evolved. Two specific evolutionary theories offer helpful insights into
modern organizations and physiological functioning: environment of
evolutionary adaptedness (EEA) and the mismatch theory (Gaulin and
McBurney 2003; Wright 1995). EEA refers to the environment to which
a particular evolved cognitive or physical mechanism is adapted. During human evolution, the majority of human psychological mechanisms

were adapted to Pleistocene environments. The mismatch theory proposes that humans are mostly adapted to Pleistocene environments, and therefore psychological and physiological mechanisms can exhibit "mismatches"to modern environments. One good example is that people exhibit more fear of spiders and snakes than of a pointed gun, despite the fact that significantly more people are killed every year by guns. According to mismatch theory, this is because spiders and snakes (but not guns) were a threat to human ancestors throughout the Pleistocene environment (Pinker 1999).

The mismatch between the environments in which humans evolved and those in which they find themselves at work creates substantial difficulties. There are many aspects of modern work environments that are absent in the EEA, including stricter organizational hierarchy, larger workloads, relative lack of social support, reduced physical activity, lack of sunshine in office and factory settings, noise in the industrial environment, sleep deprivation due to shift work and work-to-family conflicts. With regard to hierarchy, modern organizations provide a work environment characterized by many hierarchical levels, an unequal distribution of power and decision-making latitude, and high job demands, which is different from that of older, hunter-gatherer societies. As argued by Boehm (1999), hunter-gatherers have a flat structure in their social life, and the level of egalitarianism is far higher than that in modern organizations. This mismatch creates status hierarchies that are difficult to understand and traverse, causing acute and chronic stress. Further, such large status differences create desires for status that lead people to place unreasonable demands on their time and mental energy in order to "get ahead," sacrificing their mental and physiological health in the name of social status and material wealth.

Moreover, one key difference from our EEA is the sheer volume of work and stress that are characteristic features of modern working life and modern life in general. Anthropologists estimate that in earlier periods of human evolution people worked 4–8 hours per week—depending upon environmental pressures—whereas modern humans' 40–80 hour work-week is an order of magnitude greater (Sahlins 1972). This rapid and substantial shift in the amount of work has created a mismatch between the environment and the physiological systems attempting to adapt to the new environment, resulting in chronic stress, the breakdown of traditional familial and other social relationships that buffer stress, and the many stress-related physiological maladies observed today (e.g., high blood pressure, heart disease, etc.).

As noted by Nesse and Williams (1996), stress-related physical and psychological maladies have increased substantially in the recent past. This suggests that our physiological systems, resulting from millions of years of evolution, are mismatched with modern environments, reducing our ability to cope effectively with the more recent, rapidly changing work environment, which is often characterized by low levels of social support and unreasonable degrees of stress. While our ancestors were adapted to deal with occasional acute stress (e.g., fleeing or fighting when encountering an enemy or predator), in modern work settings the stress is chronic, and people need to deal with it every minute of their working lives (even after work, which often produces work-to-family conflict). Such work environment issues (e.g., stricter space confinement and more layers in the hierarchical reporting/monitoring systems) increase the need to examine job stress, justice, and specific events at work.

Employees often work in groups and teams, as did their ancestors. However, although humans evolved with a focus on status and status hierarchies in small groups, the need to collaborate and act while embedded within very large organizations populated by people who hardly know each other presents challenges for cooperation and collaboration in light of evolved desires to wrangle over status. This mismatch brings with it unavoidable social interactions that necessitate investigating the relationship between factors like social support and physiological functioning. More practically, by understanding human evolution and the environments for which we have evolved, it is possible to design interventions to reduce stress by creating a better *match* between old and modern environments. For example, this could be done at work by creating socially supportive cultures, reducing social and other uncertainties, increasing natural lighting, and minimizing physical space constraints, as well as reducing workloads on employees.

Evolutionary psychology offers additional interesting—albeit speculative—hypotheses regarding the development of various adaptive psychological systems that can inform how human physiology is affected by modern working life. Specifically, if we assume that humans evolved in the context of highly social groups with strong ties and support mechanisms, as they do in indigenous cultures around the world, we can see modern working life as presenting substantial challenges. Membership in today's organizations often requires a severe bifurcation of "work" and "life," and where they intersect, terms such as *spillover* are used (Williams and Alliger 1994)—this would have been far less true in the past, where social and familial ties were a natural part of the materiality and work-related activity of hunting and gathering. With a bifurcation between "working" and "living," the social connections and other evolved mechanisms that can act as buffers against stress are remanded to separate spheres, and the self is fragmented to fit with the competing domains of life inherent in modernity (Lifton 1993).

In sum, by attending to the history of human evolution, we can identify the areas of working life that have created the greatest mismatch as well as the highest likelihood of being relevant to the study of human physiology in organizations. Generally, the point of our discussion is that the mismatch between the environments in which we evolved and those that we face in modern organizations presents us with substantial challenges. Levels of hormones such as testosterone that relate to status may be understood as being important for understanding status hierarchies in organizations. Stressors such as social and other uncertainties as well as environmental factors in organizations have implications for levels of cortisol and other correlates of health and well-being outcomes. Below we discuss the elements of modern working life as they relate to various physiological processes, focusing on existing research from within and outside of management science.

AN ORGANIZING FRAMEWORK

Our review of the various research streams in OB and occupational health psychology reveals that the majority of research has been using an input-process-output (I-P-O) model to examine employee physiological functioning. We follow prior research and articulate an I-P-O model to organize this chapter.

Specifically, we expect that the work environment (the input) can have beneficial/detrimental effects on employees' physiological functioning (the process), which in turn can influence various work outcomes (the output). As shown in figure 7.1, individual differences (such as personality traits and values) may alleviate or accentuate the effects of the work environment on employee physiological processes, and organizational interventions can be used to build healthier work environments and more resilient employees.

On the basis of prior research, we first identify the key constructs of physiological functioning and their measurement. The constructs pertaining to employee physiological functioning may include "a broad

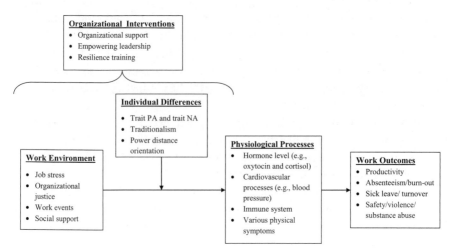

Fig. 7.1 An organizing framework for examining employee physiology functioning at work

range of chronic and acute conditions, ranging from minor viral infections to cancer and heart disease" (Ganster, Fox, and Dwyer 2001, 956). From an evolutionary perspective, the milder forms of physiological responses can be considered as evolved defense mechanisms that alert people and help them to cope with threats and adversities. These responses prompt adaptive behaviors when they are in the normal range. However, extreme levels of change in the work environment can lead to excessive stress and malfunctioning in employee physiology. Thus, physiological systems evolved for life in hunter-gatherer times can be maladaptive in modern organizations (Nesse 1994). Because a comprehensive review of the various conditions underlying this mismatch is beyond the scope of this chapter, we focus on the variables that have been most frequently examined in OB and occupational health psychology research using samples of employees. Interested readers are encouraged to read the review by Miller, Chen, and Cole (2009) for discussion of a broad spectrum of employee physical health outcomes.

Hormone Level (Neuroendocrine System)

Human physiological systems are genetically determined to exist with some baseline levels of a variety of hormones. Interactions with different environments moderate these baselines and can lead to elevated or depressed levels of hormones (such as cortisol, testosterone, and oxytocin), which have been examined as critical physiological responses to work-related stress (e.g., Fox, Dwyer, and Ganster 1993; Ganster, Fox, and

Dwyer 2001)—potentially caused by the evolutionary mismatch we discussed above. Changes in hormone levels are related to cardiovascular processes and changes in immune-system functioning. Epidemiological research shows that exposure to job-related stress activates both an adrenomedullary response and an adrenocortical response. The former involves the release of hormones into the blood, such as cortisol, which does not dissipate quickly. The latter involves the release of hormones such as epinephrine and norepinephrine, which dissipate quickly. These two responses can both increase heart rate and blood pressure, thus enabling individuals to cope rapidly with any threat they face. Because cortisol remains in the blood for a relatively longer period of time, it results in a sustained increase in heart rate and blood pressure, which have negative health consequences (Cohen and Herbert 1996).

Additionally, person-environment interactions abound in the domain of endocrine responses. For example, research shows that testosterone and status contests have a dynamic interplay: winning a status contest temporarily increases testosterone levels, while losing a status contest leads to a temporary decrease (Booth et al. 1989). When examining the endocrine system, therefore, it is important to take its dynamic nature into account. Hormone levels change over the course of a day, week, and predictably throughout the year and lifespan, and are strongly influenced by environmental and experiential factors, such as social interactions and exercise.

Cardiovascular Processes

Blood Pressure (BP)

Elevated blood pressure has been shown to relate to symptoms of varying severity such as fatigue, headaches, and coronary heart diseases (Kannel, Dawber, and McGee 1980; Khattar, Senior, and Lahiri 1998; Steptoe and Willemsen 2004; Theorell and Karasek 1996). There are two measures of blood pressure: diastolic blood pressure (DBP; the minimum pressure between heart contractions) and systolic blood pressure (SBP; the maximum pressure while the heart contracts). According to Theorell and Karasek (1996), DBP seems to be less reliable than SBP when comparing self-monitored and fully automatic blood-pressure measures. In addition, medical research (e.g., Benetos et al. 2001; Pini et al. 2002) also suggests that SBP is a better predictor of health than DBP. Consequently, OB studies have been focusing on SBP as a primary measure of cardiovascular processes (e.g., Ilies, Dimotakis, and De Pater 2010).

Heart Rate

Increased heart rate is considered an indicator of ill health—healthier hearts need to beat less often to circulate equivalent levels of oxygen, and acute stress is associated with higher heart rates. Employee heart rate has typically been measured along with BP. For example, consistent with the notion of mismatch and our evolutionary past being associated with more prosocial environments, Evans and Steptoe (2001) found that co-workers' social support and group cohesion can improve employee health because they decrease employee heart rate during the day and evening of work days. These findings affirm our argument that social support can reduce the mismatch between the modern work environment and that of early humans.

Coronary Heart Disease

Coronary heart disease is the most frequently studied disease associated with job stress in the literature (Melamed et al. 2006). Researchers have examined various measures of diseases, including employees' first myocardial infarction (e.g., Theorell et al. 1998), and the occurrence of angina, chest pain, and doctor-diagnosed ischemia (e.g., Marmot et al. 1997), which are associated with levels of work stress. Given the implication for heart attacks and similarly serious health problems associated with heart disease, this is an important variable when evaluating employee health and potential employee health-care costs.

Immune System

Medical research has long posited that work-related stress affects employees' immune systems (Cohen 1996). Prior studies (e.g., Schaubroeck, Jones, and Xie 2001; Theorell, Orth-Gomér, and Eneroth 1990; Xie, Schaubroeck, and Lam 2008) have examined three key immunoglobulins: immunoglobulin A (IgA), immunoglobulin M (IgM), and immunoglobulin G (IgG), which are antibodies that attack diseased cells (Delves and Roitt 2000). Chronic stress and associated changes in cortisol lead to depressed levels of these antibodies.

Physical Symptoms

As intermediary outcomes of poor physiological functioning, researchers have also examined various physical symptoms, such as musculoskeletal pain (e.g., Armon et al. 2010; Greiner and Krause 2006; Lillefjell and Jakobsen 2007), upper respiratory infections (e.g., Schaubroeck, Jones, and Xie 2001; Xie, Schaubroeck, and Lam 2008), fatigue (e.g., Sonnentag and Zijlstra 2006), headaches, gastrointestinal problems, and interrupted sleep (Kinicki, McKee, and Wade 1996). These symptoms are more easily observable than hormone levels and immune system changes, and can directly relate to organizational outcomes.

ANTECEDENTS OF EMPLOYEE PHYSIOLOGICAL FUNCTIONING

In this section, we review existing research in the OB and occupational health psychology literatures that examined work environmental variables as antecedents of employee physiological functioning. We define work environment broadly to include both physical and social aspects of work. For example, social interactions with coworkers during off-work time are considered as part of the work environment. Although we group the various studies into subcategories, such as job stress, organizational justice, work events, and social support, we should note that all these aspects of the work environment can be organized under the overarching framework of work stress, because all of them are considered stressors. Along the way we highlight how environmental mismatch relates to these important organizational phenomena.

Job Stress and Job Demands

Prior reviews of employee health have all focused on job stress as the key antecedent of poor health (e.g., Danna and Griffin 1999; Zapf, Dormann, and Frese 1996). Although there are different aspects of stress and many types of stressors in the workplace (e.g., organizational politics, situational constraints, hassles, and role ambiguity; Cavanaugh et al. 2000), prior research linking job stress and employee physiological functioning has primarily focused on job demands (sometimes labeled as workload).

Karasek's (1979) job demands–decision latitude model has been the dominant theoretical framework for examining employee physical reactions to stress. This theory posits that jobs with high demands and low control are the most harmful to psychological and physiological health. This prediction is not surprising from the perspective of evolutionary theory, because early humans can be assumed to have had low-demand jobs and relatively high control and autonomy in terms of their pace of work. It is safe to assume, and indeed research shows, that our physiological systems function better under such conditions, pointing the way to environmental interventions that increase control and reduce demands.

Job demands refer to the amount of physical and mental effort required by a job. Decision latitude, or job control, refers to the ability of employees to determine the manner in which they organize and complete their work. Researchers have also differentiated quantitative workload and qualitative workload, the former referring to the (more objectively measured) amount of work employees need to finish within a time unit and the latter referring to the overall complexity of the job. Karasek's theory has been subsequently expanded to include social support as another aspect of job features (i.e., the demands-control-support model; Karasek and Theorell 1990). We discuss social support in a later section.

Large-scale epidemiological studies (e.g., Karasek 1979; Karasek et al. 1981) have confirmed the main effects of job demands and job control on employee physiological functioning and health. Many focus on cardiovascular processes as the outcome (Kamarck et al. 1998 and 2005; Kivimäki et al. 2002; Marmot et al. 1997; Rau and Triemer 2004; Riese et al. 2004). For example, Theorell et al. (1985) found a main effect of job demand on SBP but not DBP. Kamarck et al. (1998) found a significant relationship between job demands and ambulatory blood pressure. Theorell et al. (1998), in a case-control study, found that employees' decreases in job control (measured from occupational histories) were associated with increased risk of myocardial infarction. Marmot et al. (1997) found that employees' perceptions of job control explain the occupational inequalities of coronary heart disease (including angina, chest pain, and doctor-diagnosed ischemia). Using a sample from the Pittsburgh Healthy Heart Project, Kamarck et al. (2005) reported that job demands along with other psychosocial variables are significantly related to within-person change in BP. Moreover, Syme and Balfour (1997) found that job control can reduce risks of coronary heart disease and mortality. In terms of other physiological responses to job stress, it has been well documented that stress is associated with cortisol output (Dickerson and Kemeny 2004), and a high level of cortisol is "the starting point for a complex and tightly regulated chain of events" that occur in physiological systems (Miller, Chen, and Cole 2009, 510), which have important health implications.

The most frequently investigated hypothesis in Karasek's (1979) model is job control's buffer (i.e., moderating) effect on the negative influence of job demands on employee health. From an evolutionary perspective, higher job control reduces the mismatch between employees' physiological systems and the work environment, thus alleviating the arousal and negative physiological consequences that result from high job demands. OB researchers have found support for this buffer effect using within-person (e.g., Ilies, Dimotakis, and De Pater 2010) and between-person designs (Fox, Dwyer, and Ganster 1993). For example, Fox and colleagues found job control's buffering effect on the relationship between job demands and SBP. Ilies, Dimotakis, and De Pater (2010) used an experience-sampling method on a sample of sixty-four middle-aged employees and found that job control (as well as perceived organizational support) moderates the within-person relationship between job demands and SBP.

Recent studies have also examined the moderators or boundary conditions on the buffer effect of job control. For example, Xie, Schaubroeck, and Lam (2008) questioned the universality of the beneficial effects of job control by examining a cultural moderator—Chinese traditionalism, which is characterized by high respect for authority, fatalism, and a sense of powerlessness. Xie et al. found that higher job control can reduce the negative effect of job demands on upper respiratory infections only for employees who are low in traditionalism, while higher control can actually exacerbate the negative effect for employees high in traditionalism. This is an interesting finding, given the assumed desire for autonomy and job control.

Other boundary conditions on the job demands–decision latitude model exist. Examining employees' self-determination as another boundary condition, Fernet, Guay, and Senecal (2004) found that job control moderated the unhealthy effects of job demands only for employees with high levels of work self-determination. Occupation may also be a boundary condition, because Xie's (1996) study in mainland China found that job control reduced the detrimental effects of job demands on health among Chinese white-collar workers but not among blue-collar workers.

Based on the job demands–decision latitude model, Schaubroeck and Ganster (1993) have proposed an "untoughening" hypothesis regarding the relationship among job demands, job control, employee hormones, and physical health. They contend that chronic exposure to work conditions characterized by high job demands and low job control can result in reduced capacity for adrenomedullary response and increased adrenocortical response for employees. Thus, when these employees later face acute job demands, they cannot have effective coping responses (from the adrenomedullary system); rather, they have higher adrenocortical responses, which can result in health problems. Schaubroeck and Ganster's (1993) study and those by Fox, Dwyer, and Ganster (1993) and Ganster, Fox, and Dwyer (2001) have provided support for this hypothesis.

Organizational Justice

The study of organizational justice focuses on perceptions of fairness in organizations (Colquitt et al. 2001). Distributive justice and procedural justice have been most frequently examined as antecedents of employee physiological functioning and wellbeing (e.g., Tepper 2001). Distributive justice refers to equality in outcomes, or whether or not distributed rewards are equal across employees. Procedural justice is defined as the extent to which procedures or decision-making processes are fair. As argued by Greenberg (2010, 205) in his recent review on the injustice-health relationship, the lack of justice can "lead to negative emotional reactions and to unhealthy behaviors (e.g., being sedentary, smoking, and drinking excessively), both of which trigger various negative bodily reactions (e.g., elevated serum lipids)." This phenomenon is aligned with our evolutionary psychological arguments, such that mismatches between the relatively egalitarian social structures in our hunter-gatherer past (Boehm 1999) and the hierarchies in modern organizations can devastate physiological functioning. Additionally, the targets of procedural justice perceptions are social in nature, such as perceptions of fairness in performance-evaluation procedures, reflecting the fact that humans seem to have a natural desire for the type of social order for which they have evolved.

Xie, Schaubroeck, and Lam's (2008) study has shown that organizational justice can affect health and physiological functioning through both main effects and moderating (i.e., buffer) effects. They examined the relationship among job demands, job control, distributive justice, and employee health (including upper respiratory infections, blood pressure, and immune functions). In addition to the main effect of justice, they found that higher distributive justice mitigates the negative effect of job demands on the level of immunoglobulin A (IgA) for employees high in traditionalism (but not for those low in traditionalism). Using a large-scale prospective study, Kivimäki and colleagues (2005) found that justice is associated with reduced risk of coronary heart disease.

More recently, Robbins, Ford, and Tetrick (2012) meta-analytically reviewed prior research on the injustice-employee health relationship, and found that perceptions of unfairness are related to various indicators of health problems (unreliability-corrected correlations range from .10 to .35, with all the 95% confidence intervals excluding zero). More importantly, these authors place special emphasis on psychological contract breach, which refers to the violation of the perceived terms and conditions of a reciprocal-exchange relationship that an individual has with her organization in an informal manner (Rousseau 1990). They argue that the nature of the psychological contract is broader than the various forms of organizational injustice, and that psychological contract breach should therefore affect strain and health above and beyond the effect of injustice alone. Their meta-analytic results supported these propositions.

Although prior studies have not focused on boundary conditions on the relationship between justice and physiological response, we expect that individual differences may affect employees' reactions to injustice (as suggested by Xie, Schaubroeck, and Lam 2008). Employees who have higher power-distance orientations may be more tolerant of injustice, and those who have higher trait negative affect (NA) maybe more susceptible to the negative effect of injustice (Ilies, Dimotakis, and Watson, 2010). Power-distance orientations refer to the extent to which a person accepts that power in the society and organizations is distributed unequally (Hofstede 2001).

Work Events

A solid theoretical foundation supports the effect of work events on employee physiological functioning. Research reveals how people react to events in the modern workplace that are more severe and numerous than they have evolved to handle. To frame our discussion, affective events theory (AET; Weiss and Cropanzano 1996) suggests that work events can affect employee affective responses (mood, or state positive affect [PA] and negative affect). Moreover, prior research has shown that employee's PA enhances physical health (e.g., state PA decreased symptoms and pain; Pressman and Cohen 2005). Ilies, Dimotakis, and Watson (2010) examined momentary PA and NA and found that both PA and NA were related to heart rate, using within-individual analysis. Momentary NA (but not PA) was found to be significantly related to SBP. Although much of prior research has focused on employees' general perceptions of workplace interactions, there is an emerging research stream investigating discrete events at work and their effects on employee health.

General Perceptions of Work Events

Consistent with our focus on social structure and relationships as defining our evolutionary past, researchers typically rely upon self-reported measures of social interactions at work to predict physiological outcomes. For example, Brondolo et al. (2003) found that positive social interaction with colleagues (e.g., pleasant, friendly, agreeable interactions) can reduce DBP, whereas negative social interactions (e.g., anger, upset, tension) increase both DBP and SBP. Brondolo and colleagues (2009) found a strong association between stressful social interactions and blood pressure. Adam and Gunnar (2001) examined the relationship between positive social interaction and salivary cortisol, and found that such interactions predict higher morning cortisol levels, with steeper declines in cortisol level during the workday.

Discrete Work Events

Given the numerous types of specific work events, the few studies on discrete work events focus on one or two particular types. For example, Brondolo et al. (1999) linked communication (i.e., talking) with increased SBP for employees. Future research may look at other discrete events, such as receiving praise or criticism, peer aggression, injury, isolation, and personal conflicts. In addition to these workplace events, off-work events may also be highly relevant to employee health. For example, family conflicts over work and socializing with coworkers after work may have spillover effects on employee's physiological reactions and health.

Coworker and Supervisor Support

As we discussed above, in line with the evolutionary perspective, the demands-control-support model (Karasek and Theorell 1990) emphasizes that job control and social support can enable employees to engage in effective coping when faced with job stress. Existing studies have examined both the main effect and the moderating effect of social support (including coworker, supervisor, and organizational support) on employee physiological functioning.

Regarding main effects, studies on social support and cardiovascular processes have produced mixed results. Some have found beneficial effects of social support. For example, examining 148 employees of various occupations, Undén, Orth-Gomér, and Elofsson (1991) found that coworker support reduced heart rate and SBP. In contrast, others failed to find a significant relationship. For example, Evans and Steptoe (2001) found that coworker support can significantly reduce heart rate, but was not related to SBP or DBP. Rau et al. (2001) used an age-matched control group and found that socializing with coworkers and high social support can reduce heart rate but was not related to SBP or DBP. Regarding the main effect of social support on other physiological responses, Schnorpfeil et al. (2003) found that coworker and supervisor support significantly reduce overnight urinary cortisol.

Regarding moderating effects, Ilies, Dimotakis, and De Pater (2010) have shown that perceived organizational support serves as a moderator on the job-demands/physiological-health relationship. Moreover, Theorell, Orth-Gomér, and Eneroth (1990) examined social support's moderating effect on the relationship between job demands and IgG (which is expected to change as a result of long-term stress but not of short-term stress). Social support was found to moderate the job-demands/IgG relationship such that in low support conditions, the job demands increase IgG, whereas in high support conditions there was no relationship. In three studies, Byrne and Hochwarter (2006) found that high levels of organizational support reduced the adverse effects of chronic pain on employee performance, work intensity, and citizenship behavior.

OUTCOMES OF PHYSIOLOGICAL FUNCTIONING

Employees' physiological reactions to the work environment have been argued to result in various work outcomes, such as reduced productivity and fewer helping behaviors (e.g., Byrne and Hochwarter 2006), increased risk of burnout, and higher health-care cost (e.g., Ganster, Fox, and Dwyer 2001).

Increased Health Care Cost

Using a prospective design, Ganster, Fox, and Dwyer (2001) examined the five-year cumulative health-care costs incurred by employees and found that employees' elevated levels of salivary cortisol after work explained 25% of the variance in subsequent health-care costs to the organizations. Moreover, cortisol level was a significant mediator of the relationship between job demands and health-care costs. In another study, Manning, Jackson, and Fusilier (1996) found that work strain was a significant predictor of several types of employees' health-care costs measured one year after their survey (including doctors' office costs and prescription drug costs).

Decreased Productivity and Absenteeism

Decreased productivity is the result of poor physiological functioning and the associated burn-out, absenteeism, and sick leave. Byrne and

Hochwarter (2006) found that employees' chronic pain is negatively related to self-rated work intensity and supervisor-rated task performance, and this relationship is more pronounced when organizational support is low. When employees have physical symptoms due to poor physiological functioning, their doctors visits and sick leave are both indicators of lost productivity. Given the work cited above on health outcomes, it is reasonable to assume substantial decrements in productivity as a function of absenteeism and illness associated with, for example, chronic and acute stress.

Unsafe Behavior and Substance Abuse

Although we are not aware of any study directly examining employees' impaired physiological functioning and the resulting unsafe behavior and substance abuse, prior research on alcohol abuse has implied such a link. For example, Wang and his colleagues (Wang et al. 2010; Liu et al. 2009) found that daily work stress and daily work-to-family conflict (but not family-to-work conflict) both predicted employees' daily alcohol use. These within-person relationships are shown to be alleviated by coworker support and job involvement. Prior research has shown an evolutionary basis for substance abuse (e.g., Nesse 1994), suggesting that drugs are used to artificially block suffering and distress that are evolved defense mechanisms. Substance use interferes with adaptive behavior at "potentially huge costs of not expressing a defensive response when it is needed" (Nesse 1994, 339). As we note below, by reducing levels of stress and increasing social support, organizations can reduce environmental mismatch and thus reduce some of the underlying causes of substance abuse.

Organizational Interventions

Given the main-effect relationship between job stress, organizational justice, and social support and employee physiological functioning, organizations can change the contents of jobs and policies as well as provide higher support at work in order to increase the fit between the modern work environment and those of our ancient past, thereby mitigating poor physiological functioning. If employees are able to delegate tasks, to effectively prioritize work goals and tasks, or to take time to recover, such enhanced job control could protect them from the negative effects of high workloads. Job control, fair policies, and social support are all structural work-environment factors that organizations can change.

When organizations cannot change existing jobs or policies, they can still to some extent reduce negative effects by enhancing coworker and supervisor support. Specifically, perceived organizational support (POS; Rhoades and Eisenberger 2002) can help to alleviate the negative influences of injustice. As Rhoades and Eisenberger contend "POS is expected to reduce aversive psychological and psychosomatic reactions (i.e., strains) to stressors by indicating the availability of material aid and emotional support when needed to face high demands of work" (413). In fact, Ilies, Dimotakis, and De Pater (2010) have shown the buffering role of POS and job control on the relationship between daily workload and physiological strain: high workload is more positively related to affective distress and increased blood pressure for employees with lower perceived organizational support and job control.

Furthermore, given the established relationship between employees' moods (state PA and NA) and physiological reactions (e.g., Jorgensen et al. 1996; Steptoe, Dockray, and Wardle 2009), organizations can use simple interventions to promote a healthier workplace by enhancing positive moods among employees. Research has shown that simple techniques such as work breaks can help employee recovery from stressful work (e.g., Fritz and Sonnentag 2005; Trougakos et al. 2008). Positive psychology research has also identified methods that can positively affect mood (Lyubomirsky 2008). Particularly, being instructed to focus on positive events (e.g., Seligman, Rashid, and Parks 2006) and helping coworkers (e.g., Glomb et al. 2011; Steger, Kashdan, and Oishi 2008) have been shown to positively influence employee mood and thus potentially reduce poor physiological functioning. Moreover, Fredrickson et al. (2008) showed that loving-kindness mediation has prolonged positive effects on well-being. This is in contrast with the transitory effects induced by, for example, pay raises. In addition, with an experimental intervention, Bono et al. (2013) showed that not only do naturally occurring positive work events matter to employee health, but also positive-reflection interventions can have a meaningful impact. Their findings suggest that organizations need to promote positive work events (and not merely reduce negative ones, because their effects are independent). For employees, even brief, end-of-workday positive reflections can effectively reduce stress and improve health throughout the evening.

Organizations can also train managers to use their leadership styles to increase employees' perceived and actual job control. In a randomized control study, Theorell, Arnetz, and Weingarten (2001) found that management training on coping with work stress can effectively reduce employee cortisol levels. In addition, Berkman et al. (2010) found that managers' practices that promote work-family balance are related to reduced risks of employee cardiovascular disease and longer sleep duration. Furthermore, authentic leadership (i.e., a leader who is aware of her true self, aware of her values and beliefs, and who acts on them when leading people) has been argued to positively influence employee health (Macik-Frey, Quick, and Cooper 2009).

Training employees to focus on the positive recourses available to them is also an effective approach to increasing their psychological capital (e.g., Avey, Luthans, and Jensen 2009; Avey et al. 2010) and their level of resilience to adversities at work (Tugade and Fredrickson 2004). With a randomly assigned field experimental study on 718 employees, Vuori, Toppinen-Tanner, and Mutanen (2012) showed that a group intervention oriented to build resources for career management can decrease depressive symptoms and intentions to retire early, and can increase mental resources up to seven months later. Additionally, organizations need to do more to fulfill their obligations to maintain good physiological and psychological functioning of their employees. Given the seeming lack of voluntary action on the part of many organizations—which are more and more often demanding more stressful work from employees—governments should consider instituting employment regulations that force organizations to do this.

IMPLICATIONS FOR RESEARCH AND PRACTICE

In this section, we discuss the potential gaps in the research on employees' physiological functioning and highlight future research topics in these areas, with the aim of building a better workplace for employees.

Implications for Research

Theoretical Frameworks

Above we discussed various OB topics/frameworks that represent integral parts of the examination of employee physiological functioning. Moving beyond these, we expect that many other OB research streams can be enriched by taking a physiological perspective. For example, person-environment (P-E) fit research can benefit from taking a physiological perspective on the outcomes of misfit. Such physiological outcomes of misfit can be thought of as evidence supporting the mismatch argument presented above that compares modern organizations and humans' early experiences. As predicted by French, Caplan, and Van Harrison (1982), the experience of P-E misfit is likely to lead to psychological and physical poor health. Moreover, there are two unique insights that P-E fit theory can provide to the research on employee physiological functioning. First, P-E fit theory suggests that it is the fit between person and environment, rather than the work environment alone, that influences the physiological processes and outcomes. Thus, a given level of job demands may produce strain for some employees but not others. Prior research on individual differences as the moderators on the job-demands/ outcome relationship has supported this fit perspective. Second, P-E fit theory may offer support for a curvilinear relationship between the work environment and employee health. Specifically, because both undersupply and oversupply of work characteristics (e.g., job control) can result in misfit for a focal employee, we might expect that an employee's level of health would be maximized at a certain level of job control. Future research could explore such curvilinearity (e.g., U-shaped or inverted U-shaped relationships) and identify work and individual difference variables that may affect the location of the inflection point on these curves.

In addition, research on ethical leadership and ethical decision making can be informed by taking into consideration human physiology. Particularly, physiological factors such as hormone levels and blood pressure can be both antecedents and outcomes of unethical decision making or other unethical behaviors. Other types of employee behaviors (e.g., counterproductive, creative, proactive, and prosocial behaviors) may also have specific physiological antecedents and outcomes. For example, neuroscience research shows that oxytocin is related to affiliating behavior, altruism, and trust (Bartz and Hollander 2006; Baumgartner et al. 2008; De Dreu et al. 2010; Kosfeld et al. 2005). Thus, it seems to be logical to argue that oxytocin may be related to helping behaviors at work, given exchange-related expectations that may surround helping behaviors, such as reciprocity.

In addition to the above topics/frameworks, there are many aspects of job stress that have not been thoroughly investigated from a physiological perspective. As we discussed above, research on job stress has often focused on job demands and job control when researchers examine physiological functioning. Future research may examine other aspects of jobs, including shift work, virtual work environment, social isolation, coworker aggression, and intra-organizational politics.

Within-Individual Analysis

Recent organizational research has shown a clear trend from being between-individual, cross-sectionally designed to being within-individual, longitudinally designed. Within-person relationships between work events and employee physiological reactions can, to some extent, partial out innate individual differences and thus offer additional insights above and beyond between-individual relationships. As an example, Ilies, Dimotakis, and De Pater (2010) utilized an experience-sampling methodology to measure daily workload, distress, and blood pressure for ten consecutive days, and found that employee-perceived job control and organizational support can buffer the detrimental effects of workload on affective distress and blood pressure, implying that interventions in this domain can have substantial and positive effects. Slatcher et al. (2010) examined the positive relationship between momentary work worries and salivary cortisol. This methodology is important, because momentary experiences of working life represent a pivotal component of employee well-being (Diener, Oishi, and Lucas 2003).

Experience sampling allows researchers to examine discrete events at work and the associated changes in physiological reactions, while partialing out individual difference variables such as trait negative affectivity and neuroticism. In fact, trait NA (Brief et al. 1988; Schaubroeck, Ganster, and Fox 1992) has been shown to inflate observed relationships by affecting respondents' reporting of both job demands and stress symptoms. Moreover, a within-individual approach can help to reduce concerns regarding alternative causal directions that are associated with between-individual approaches (see Ilies, Dimotakis, and De Pater 2010, 410). For example, physically stressed employees may be more likely to use high workload to explain their strain.

Group-Level Analysis

Another fruitful avenue for research is to take the physiological perspective to the group level. For example, Zyphur et al. (2009) have shown that the mismatch between testosterone and status in a group (as measured by the correlation of testosterone and status within a group) is associated with lower collective-efficacy of the group. Unlike our description above, mismatch in this case is indicated by high testosterone and low status, or low testosterone and high status. The theoretical argument proposed by the authors is that mismatch results in higher levels of felt stress and cognitive preoccupation, which takes individuals' minds away from the focal task and causes difficulties in interpersonal communication, thus lowering levels of collective efficacy. Future research could examine the antecedents that result in the harmony or synchronicity of group members' various physiological measures and relate this group property to topics such as emotion contagion, group collective efficacy, and group performance.

Measurement Issues

In the occupational health psychology literature, although subjective self-evaluations of well-being have been the most important indicator of employee psychological health, researchers who are interested in physiological functioning have to rely upon more objectively-measured indicators. Quite often this represents a challenge to researchers. For example, it may be difficult to accurately measure blood pressure and heart rate using the experience sampling method, especially considering the cumbersomeness of the equipment. Ilies, Dimotakis, and De Pater (2010), as an example, have deleted 12% of their measurements because they were considered to be erroneous or otherwise artifactual. Whatever the variable being measured, attending to measurement issues and assuring valid measurement is a requisite for drawing valid scientific conclusions; it is therefore critical for legitimizing biological study in management and organizations more generally.

Practical Implications

In our discussion above on organizational interventions, we have identified various ways in which organizations can promote a healthy work environment, including job redesign, improving justice, and providing support, among others. We believe that job redesign, which addresses the root of job stress, can help increase job control in order to alleviate the negative impact of high job demands. In addition, support and resources need to be made available to employees. In terms of enhancing justice, as Ferrie and colleagues (2006) argued, in addition to various policies to increase justice, management training should be used to "train supervisory staff in interpersonal skills and good practice" (449).

We recommend that managers take a systematic view of the work environment and policies when designing and implementing these positive changes/interventions. Because various aspects of the work environment are dynamically interrelated, it is difficult for organizations to implement one intervention without changing (often negatively) other aspects of work. To ensure success, organizations could use the help of professional services to set up employee assistance programs and counseling in the workplace (see Berridge, Cooper, and Highley 1997).

CONCLUSIONS

As argued by Heaphy and Dutton (2008), "bringing the body back into accounts of social life" (138) has become a common theme in sociology, economics, and organizational research. From an evolutionary perspective, this chapter reviews the antecedents and outcomes of employee physiological processes in the workplace and identifies the practices of and future research agendas for bettering employees' work life by taking a physiological perspective. In conclusion, we note that in many areas of more traditional organizational behavior research, taking a physiological approach to understanding employee behavior can advance our understanding of the underlying physiology of behavior in organizations. We hope this chapter (as well as the evolutionary perspective and mismatch theory) can help provide a foundation for future integrative research of multiple disciplines (e.g., sociology and neuroeconomics; see Fitzhugh and Leckie 2001; Platt and Glimcher 1999) that will yield a more complete account of human physiology in organizations and in society.

References

Adam, E., and Gunnar, M. 2001. Relationship functioning and home and work demands predict individual differences in diurnal cortisol patterns in women. *Psychoneuroendocrinology* 26:189–208.

Armon, G., Melamed, S., Shirom, A., and Shapira, I. 2010. Elevated burnout predicts the onset of musculoskeletal pain among apparently healthy employees. *Journal of Occupational Health Psychology* 15:399–408.

Avey, J. B., Luthans, F., and Jensen, S. M. 2009. Psychological capital: A positive resource for combating employee stress and turnover. *Human Resource Management* 48:677–93.

———, Luthans, F., Smith, R. M., and Palmer, N. F. 2010. Impact of positive psychological capital on employee well-being over time. *Journal of Occupational Health Psychology* 15:17–28.

Bartz, J. A., and Hollander, E. 2006. The neuroscience of affiliation: Forging links between basic and clinical research on neuropeptides and social behavior. *Hormones and Behavior* 50:518–28.

Baumgartner, T., Heinrichs, M., Vonlanthen, A., Fischbacher, U., and Fehr, E. 2008.

Oxytocin shapes the neural circuitry of trust and trust adaptation in humans. *Neuron* 58:639–50.

Benetos, A., Thomas, F., Safar, M., Bean, K. E., and Guize, L. 2001. Should diastolic and systolic blood pressure be considered for cardiovascular risk evaluation? A study in middle-aged men and women. *Journal of the American College of Cardiology*, 37:163–68.

Berkman, L. F., Buxton, O., Ertel, K., and Okechukwu, C. 2010. Managers' practices related to work-family balance predict employee cardiovascular risk and sleep duration in extended care settings. *Journal of Occupational Health Psychology* 15:316–29.

Berridge, J., Cooper, C., and Highley, C. 1997. *Employee assistance programmes and workplace counseling.* Chichester, UK: John Wiley.

Boehm, C. 1999. *Hierarchy in the forest.* Cambridge, MA: Harvard University Press.

Bono, J. E., Glomb, T. M., Shen, W., Kim, E., and Koch, A. J. 2013. Building positive resources: Effects of positive events and positive reflection on work-stress and health. *Academy of Management Journal*, 56:1601–27.

Booth, A., Shelley, G., Mazur, A., Tharp, G., and Kittock, R. 1989. Testosterone and winning and losing in human competition. *Hormones and Behavior* 23:556–71.

Brief, A., Burke, M., George, J., Robinson, B., and Webster, J. 1988. Should negative affectivity remain an unmeasured variable in the study of job stress? *Journal of Applied Psychology*, 73:193–98.

Brondolo, E., Grantham, K. I., Karlin, W., Taravella, J., Mencia-Ripley, A., Schwartz, J. E., et al. 2009. Trait hostility and ambulatory blood pressure among traffic enforcement agents: The effects of stressful social interactions. *Journal of Occupational Health Psychology* 14:110–21.

———, Karlin, W., Alexander, K., Bobrow, A., and Schwartz, J. 1999. Workday communication and ambulatory blood pressure: Implications for the reactivity hypothesis. *Psychophysiology* 36:86–94.

———, Rieppi, R., Erickson, S. A., Bagiella, E., Shapiro, P. A., McKinley, P., and Sloan, R. P. 2003. Hostility, interpersonal interactions, and ambulatory blood pressure. *Psychosomatic Medicine* 65:1003–11.

Bruning, N. S., and Frew, D. R. 1987. Effects of exercise, relaxation, and management skills training on physiological stress indicators: A field experiment. *Journal of Applied Psychology* 72:515–21.

Byrne, Z. S., and Hochwarter, W. A. 2006. "I get by with a little help from my friends": The interaction of chronic pain and organizational support on performance. *Journal of Occupational Health Psychology* 11:215–27.

Cavanaugh, M. A., Boswell, W. R., Roehling, M. V., and Boudreau, J. W. 2000. An empirical examination of self-reported work stress among US managers. *Journal of Applied Psychology* 85:65–74.

Cohen, S. 1996. Psychological stress, immunocompetence, and upper respiratory infections. *Current Directions in Psychological Science* 5:86–90.

———, and Herbert, T. 1996. Health psychology: Psychological factors and physical disease from the perspective of human psychoneuroimmunology. *Annual Review of Psychology* 47:113–42.

Colquitt, J. A., Conlon, D. E., Wesson, M. J., Porter, C. O. L. H., and Ng, K. Y. 2001.

Justice at the millennium: A meta-analytic review of 25 years of organizational justice research. *Journal of Applied Psychology* 86:425–45.

Danna, K., and Griffin, R. W. 1999. Health and well-being in the workplace: A review and synthesis of the literature. *Journal of Management* 25:357–84.

De Dreu, C. K. W., Greer, L. L., Handgraaf, M., Shalvi, S., van Kleef, G. A., Baas et al. 2010. The neuropeptide oxytocin regulates parochial altruism in intergroup conflict among humans. *Science* 328:1408–11.

Delves, P., and Roitt, I. M. 2000. The immune system: First of two parts. *New England Journal of Medicine* 343:37–49.

Dickerson, S. S., and Kemeny, M. E. 2004. Acute stressors and cortisol responses: A theoretical integration and synthesis of laboratory research. *Psychological Bulletin* 130:355–91.

Diener, E., Oishi, S., and Lucas, R. E. 2003. Personality, culture, and subjective well-being: Emotional and cognitive evaluations of life. *Annual Review of Psychology* 54:403–25.

Evans, O., and Steptoe, A. 2001. Social support at work, heart rate, and cortisol: A self-monitoring study. *Journal of Occupational Health Psychology* 6:361–70.

Fernet, C., Guay, F., and Senecal, C. 2004. Adjusting to job demands: The role of work self-determination and job control in predicting burnout. *Journal of Vocational Behavior* 65:39–56.

Ferrie, J. E., Head, J., Shipley, M. J., Vahtera, J., Marmot, M. G., and Kivimäki, M. 2006. Injustice at work and incidence of psychiatric morbidity: The Whitehall II study. *Occupational and Environmental Medicine* 63:443–50.

Fitzhugh, M. L., and Leckie, W. H. 2001. Agency, postmodernism and the causes of change. *History and Theory* 40 (4): 59–81.

Fox, M. L., Dwyer, D. J., and Ganster, D. C. 1993. Effects of stressful job demands and control on physiological and attitudinal outcomes in a hospital setting. *Academy of Management Journal* 36:289–318.

Fredrickson, B. L., Cohn, M. A., Coffey, K. A., Pek, J., and Finkel, S. M. 2008. Open hearts build lives: Positive emotions, induced through loving-kindness meditation, build consequential personal resources. *Journal of Personality and Social Psychology* 95:1045–62.

French, J. R. P., Jr., Caplan, R. D., and Van Harrison, R. 1982. *The mechanisms of job stress and strain.* Chichester, England: John Wiley.

Fritz, C., and Sonnentag, S. 2005. Recovery, health, and job performance: Effects of weekend experiences. *Journal of Occupational Health Psychology* 10:187–99.

Ganster, D. C., Fox, M. L., and Dwyer, D. J. 2001. Explaining employees' health-care costs: A prospective examination of stressful job demands, personal control, and physiological reactivity. *Journal of Applied Psychology* 86:954–64.

Gaulin, S. J. C., and McBurney, D. H. 2003. *Evolutionary psychology.* Upper Saddle River, NJ: Prentice Hall.

Glomb, T. M., Bhave, D. P., Miner, A. G., and Wall, M. 2011. Doing good, feeling good: Examining the role of organizational citizenship behaviors in changing mood. *Personnel Psychology* 64:191–223.

Greenberg, J. 2010. Organizational injustice as an occupational health risk. *Academy of Management Annals* 4:205–43.

Greiner, B. A., and Krause, N. 2006. Observational stress factors and musculoskeletal disorders in urban transit operators. *Journal of Occupational Health Psychology*
11:38–51.

Heaphy, E. D., and Dutton, J. E. 2008. Positive social interactions and the human
body at work: Linking organizations and physiology. *Academy of Management
Review* 33:137–62.

Hofstede, G. 2001. Culture's consequences: Comparing values, behaviors,
institutions, and organizations across nations. 2nd ed. Thousand Oaks,
CA: Sage.

Ilies, R., Dimotakis, N., and De Pater, I. E. 2010. Psychological and physiological
reactions to high workloads: Implications for well-being. *Personnel Psychology*
63:407–36.

———, Dimotakis, N., and Watson, D. 2010. Mood, blood pressure, and heart rate at
work: An experience-sampling study. *Journal of Occupational Health Psychology*
15:120–30.

Jorgensen, R. S., Johnson, B. T., Kolodziej, M. E., and Schreer, G. E. 1996. Elevated
blood pressure and personality: A meta-analytic review. *Psychological Bulletin*,
120:293–320.

Kamarck, T. W., Shiffman, S. M., Smithline, L., Goodie, J. L., Paty, J. A., Gnys, M., and
Jong, J.Y. K. 1998. Effects of task strain, social conflict, and emotional activation
on ambulatory cardiovascular activity: Daily life consequences of recurring stress
in a multiethnic adult sample. *Health Psychology* 17:17–29.

———, Schwartz, J. E., Shiffman, S., Muldoon, M. F., Sutton-Tyrrell, K., Janicki, D. L.
2005. Psychosocial stress and cardiovascular risk: What is the role of daily experience? *Journal of Personality* 73:1749–74.

Kannel, W. B., Dawber, T. R., and McGee, D. L. 1980. Perspectives on systolic hypertension: The Framingham study. *Circulation* 61:1179–82.

Karasek, R. A. 1979. Job demands, job decision latitude, and mental strain: Implications for job redesign. *Administrative Science Quarterly* 24:285–308.

———, Baker, D., Marxer, E., Ahlbom, A., and Theorell, T. 1981. Job decision latitude,
job demands, and cardiovascular disease: A prospective study of Swedish men.
American Journal of Public Health 75:694–705.

———, and Theorell, T. 1990. *Healthy work.* New York: Basic Books.

Khattar, R. S., Senior, R., and Lahiri, A. 1998. Cardiovascular outcome in white
coat versus sustained mild hypertension: A 10-year follow-up study. *Circulation*
98:1892–97.

Kinicki, A., McKee, F., and Wade, K. 1996. Annual Review 1991–1995: Occupational
Health. *Journal of Vocational Behavior* 49:190–220.

Kivimäki, M., Ferrie, J. E., Brunner, E., Head, J., Shipley, M. J., Vahtera, J., et al. 2005.
Justice at work and reduced risk of coronary heart disease among employees: The
Whitehall II study. *Archives of Internal Medicine* 165:2245–51.

———, Leino-Arjas, P., Luukkonen, R., Riihimäki, H., Vahtera, J., and Kirjonen, J.
2002. Work stress and risk of cardiovascular mortality: Prospective cohort study
of industrial employees. *British Medical Journal* 325:857–67.

Kosfeld, M., Heinrichs, M., Zak, P. J., Fischbacher, U., and Fehr, E. 2005. Oxytocin
increases trust in humans. *Nature* 435:673–76.

Lifton, R. J. 1993. *The protean self: Human resilience in an age of fragmentation*. New York: Basic Books.

Lillefjell, M., and Jakobsen, K. 2007. Sense of coherence as a predictor of work reentry following multidisciplinary rehabilitation for individuals with chronic musculoskeletal pain. *Journal of Occupational Health Psychology* 12:222–31.

Liu, S. Q., Wang, M., Zhan, Y. J., and Shi, J. Q. 2009. Daily work stress and alcohol use: Testing the cross-level moderation effects of neuroticism and job involvement. *Personnel Psychology* 62:575–97.

Lyubomirsky, S. 2008. *The how of happiness: A scientific approach to getting the life you want*. New York: Penguin Press.

Macik-Frey, M., Quick, J. C., and Cooper, C. L. 2009. Authentic leadership as a pathway to positive health. *Journal of Organizational Behavior* 30 (3): 453–58.

Manning, M. R., Jackson, C. N., and Fusilier, M. R. 1996. Occupational stress, social support, and the costs of health care. *Academy of Management Journal* 39: 738–50.

Marmot, M., Bosma, H., Hemingway, H., Brunner, E., and Stansfeld, S. 1997. Contribution of job control and other risk factors to social variations in coronary heart disease incidence. *Lancet* 350 (9073): 235–39.

Melamed, S., Shirom, A., Toker, S., Berliner, S., and Shapira, I. 2006. Burnout and risk of cardiovascular disease: Evidence, possible causal paths, and promising research directions. *Psychological Bulletin* 132:327–53.

Miller, G., Chen, E., and Cole, S. W. 2009. Health psychology: Developing biologically plausible models linking the social world and physical health. *Annual Review of Psychology* 60:501–24.

Mowday, R. T., and Sutton, R. I. 1993. Organizational behavior: Linking individuals and groups to organizational contexts. *Annual Review of Psychology* 44:195–229.

Nesse, R. M. 1994. An evolutionary perspective on substance abuse. *Ethology and Sociobiology* 15:339–48.

———, and Williams, G. C. 1996. *Why we get sick: The new science of Darwinian medicine*. New York: Vintage.

O'Reilly, C. 1991. Organizational behavior: Where we've been, where we're going. *Annual Review of Psychology* 42:427–58.

Pini, R., Cavallini, M. C., Bencini, F., Silvestrini, G., Tonon, E., De Alfieri, W., et al. 2002. Cardiovascular remodeling is greater in isolated systolic hypertension than in diastolic hypertension in older adults. *Journal of the American College of Cardiology* 40:1283–89.

Pinker, S. 1999. *How the mind works*. New York: W. W. Norton.

Platt, M. L., and Glimcher, P. W. 1999. Neural correlates of decision variables in the parietal cortex. *Nature* 400:233–38.

Pressman, S. D., and Cohen, S. 2005. Does positive affect influence health? *Psychological Bulletin* 131:925–71.

Rau, R., Georgiades, A., Fredrikson, M., Lemne, C., and deFaire, U. 2001. Psychosocial work characteristics and perceived control in relation to cardiovascular rewind at night. *Journal of Occupational Health Psychology* 6:171–81.

———, and Triemer, A. 2004. Overtime work in relation to blood pressure and mood. *Social Indicators Research* 67:51–73.

Rhoades, L., and Eisenberger, R. 2002. POS: A review of the literature. *Journal of Applied Psychology* 87:698–714.

Riese, H., Van Doornen, L. J. P., Houtman, I. L. D., and De Geus, E. J. C. 2004. Job strain in relation to ambulatory blood pressure, heart rate, and heart rate variability among female nurses. *Scandinavian Journal of Work Environment and Health* 30:477–85.

Robbins, J. M., Ford, M. T., and Tetrick, L. E. 2012. Perceived unfairness and employee health: A meta-analytic integration. *Journal of Applied Psychology* 97:235–72.

Rousseau, D. M. 1990. New hire perceptions of their own and their employer's obligations: A study of psychological contracts. *Journal of Organizational Behavior* 11:389–400.

Sahlins, M. 1972. *Stone age economics*. London: Tavistock Publications.

Schaubroeck, J., and Ganster, D. 1993. Chronic stress and responsivity to demands. *Journal of Applied Psychology* 78:73–85.

———, Ganster, D., and Fox, M. 1992. Dispositional affect and work-related stress. *Journal of Applied Psychology* 77:322–35.

———, Jones, J. R., and Xie, J. L. 2001. Individual differences in utilizing control to cope with job demands: Effects on susceptibility to infectious disease. *Journal of Applied Psychology* 86:265–78.

Schnorpfeil, P., Noll, A., Schulze, R., Ehlert, V., Frey, K., and Fischer, J. 2003. Allostatic load and work conditions. *Social Science and Medicine* 57:647–56.

Seligman, M. E. P., Rashid, T., and Parks, A. C. 2006. Positive Psychotherapy. *American Psychologist* 61:774–88.

Slatcher, R. B., Robles, T. F., Repetti, R. L., and Fellows, M. D. 2010. Momentary work worries, marital disclosure, and salivary cortisol among parents of young children. *Psychosomatic Medicine* 72:887–96.

Sonnentag, S., and Zijlstra, F. R. H. 2006. Job characteristics and off-job activities as predictors of need for recovery, well-being, and fatigue. *Journal of Applied Psychology* 91:330–50.

Steger, M. F., Kashdan, T. B., and Oishi, S. 2008. Being good by doing good: Daily eudaimonic activity and well-being. *Journal of Research in Personality* 42:22–42.

Steptoe, A., Dockray, S., and Wardle, J. 2009. Positive affect and psychobiological processes relevant to health. *Journal of Personality* 77:1747–76.

———, and Willemsen, G. 2004. The influence of low job control on ambulatory blood pressure and perceived stress over the working day in men and women from the Withehall II cohort. *Journal of Hypertension* 22:915–20.

Syme, S. L., and Balfour, J. L. 1997. Explaining inequalities in coronary heart disease. *Lancet* 350 (9073): 231–32.

Tepper, B. J. 2001. Health consequences of organizational injustice: Tests of main and interactive effects. *Organizational Behavior and Human Decision Processes* 86:197–215.

Theorell, T., Arnetz, B., and Weingarten, A.-M. 2001. Employee effects of an educational program for managers at an insurance company. *Psychosomatic Medicine* 63:724–33.

———, and Karasek, R. A. 1996. Current issues relating to psychosocial job strain and cardiovascular disease research. *Journal of Occupational Health Psychology* 1:9–26.

————, Knox, S., Svensson, J., and Waller, D. 1985. Blood pressure variations during a working day at age 28: Effects of different types of work and blood pressure level at age 18. *Journal Human Stress* 11:36–41.

————, Orth-Gomér, K., and Eneroth, P. 1990. Slow-reacting immunoglobin in relation to social support and changes in job strain: A preliminary note. *Psychosomatic Medicine* 52:511–16.

————, Tsutsumi, A., Hallquist, J., Reuterwall, C., Hogstedt, C., Fredlund, P., et al. 1998. Decision latitude, job strain, and myocardial infarction: A study of working men in Stockholm. *American Journal of Public Health* 88:382–88.

Trougakos, J. P., Beal, D. J., Green, S. G., and Weiss, H. M. 2008. Making the break count: An episodic examination of recovery activities, emotional experiences, and affective delivery. *Academy of Management Journal* 51:131–46.

Tugade, M. M., and Fredrickson, B. L. 2004. Resilient individuals use positive emotions to bounce back from negative emotional experiences. *Journal of Personality and Social Psychology* 86:320–33.

Undén, A.-L., Orth-Gomér, K., and Elofsson, S. 1991. Cardiovascular effects of social support in the workplace: Twenty-four-hour ECG monitoring of men and women. *Psychosomatic Medicine* 53:50–60.

Vuori, J., Toppinen-Tanner, S., and Mutanen, P. 2012. Effects of resource-building group intervention on career management and mental health in work organizations: Randomized controlled field trial. *Journal of Applied Psychology* 97:273–86.

Wang, M., Liu, S. Q., Zhan, Y. J., and Shi, J. Q. 2010. Daily work-family conflict and alcohol use: Testing the cross-level moderation effects of peer drinking norms and social support. *Journal of Applied Psychology* 95:377–86.

Weiss, H., and Cropanzano, R. 1996. Affective events theory: A theoretical discussion of the structure, causes, and consequences of affective experiences at work. *Research in Organizational Behavior* 18:1–74.

White, R. E., Thornhill, S., and Hampson, E. 2006. Entrepreneurs and evolutionary biology: The relationship between testosterone and new venture creation. *Organizational Behavior and Human Decision Processes* 100:21–34.

Williams, K. J., and Alliger, G. M. 1994. Role stressors, mood spillover, and perceptions of work-family conflict in employed parents. *Academy of Management Journal* 37:837–68.

Wright, T. A., Cropanzano, R., Bonett, D. G., and Diamond, W. J. 2009. The role of employee psychological well-being in cardiovascular health: When the twain shall meet. *Journal of Organizational Behavior* 30:193–208.

————, and Diamond, W. J. 2006. Getting the pulse of our employees: The use of cardiovascular research in better understanding behavior in organizations. *Journal of Organizational Behavior* 27:395–401.

Wright, R. C. M. 1995. *The moral animal: Evolutionary psychology and everyday life.* New York: Vintage Books.

Xie, J. L. 1996. Karasek's model in the People's Republic of China: Effects of job demands, control, and individual differences. *Academy of Management Journal* 39 (6): 1594–1618.

————, Schaubroeck, J., and Lam, S. S. K. 2008. Theories of job stress and the role of traditional values: A longitudinal study in china. *Journal of Applied Psychology* 93:831–48.

Zapf, D., Dormann, C., and Frese, M. 1996. Longitudinal studies in organizational stress research: A review of the literature with references to methodological issues. *Journal of Occupational Health Psychology* 1:145–69.

Zyphur, M. J., Narayanan, J., Koh, G., and Koh, D. 2009. Testosterone-status mismatch lowers collective efficacy in groups: Evidence from a slope-as-predictor multilevel structural equation model. *Organizational Behavior and Human Decision Processes* 110:70–79.

EIGHT

The Service-for-Prestige Theory of Leader-Follower Relations: A Review of the Evolutionary Psychology and Anthropology Literatures

Michael E. Price and Mark Van Vugt

In this chapter we examine leader-follower interaction from the perspective of evolutionary psychology, with the goal of identifying the evolved psychological adaptations that enable humans to be and to follow leaders. We argue that adaptations for leadership and followership both evolved to enable individuals to pursue their own evolved interests in ancestral environments; in other words, leadership and followership are equally genetically "selfish" strategies that ancestral humans pursued in order to survive and reproduce. However, leader-follower relationships vary in the extent to which they promote the interests of the followers versus those of the leader. We suggest that the optimal form of leader-follower relationship is one that balances the interests of leaders and followers, in an elaborated form of what biologists call "reciprocal altruism" (Trivers 1971). In this mutually beneficial arrangement, leaders provide services to followers in the form of expertise and group organizational skills, and in exchange, followers provide leaders with social prestige. This reciprocity-based form of leadership prevails when leaders and followers possess relatively equal social bargaining power, and when leaders have low power to exploit followers. However, when leaders' exploitative power increases—due, for example, to followers' poor exit options—leader-follower relationships are more likely to become based on the leader's ability to inflict harm on (rather than provide benefits to) followers. The theory we present here, then, focuses both on the situations that give rise to the optimal form of reciprocity-based leadership and on the risk factors that cause reciprocity-based leadership to degenerate into coercive leadership. We refer to this theory as the "service-for-prestige" theory of leader-follower relations.

Service-for-prestige shares some predictions with existing evolutionary theories of leadership (Price 2003; Van Vugt, Hogan, and Kaiser 2008; Van Vugt et al. 2008), including the overarching "evolutionary leadership theory" presented by Van Vugt and Ahuja (2010). However, service-for-prestige maintains a uniquely strong focus on the optimal leader-follower relationship as a form of reciprocity, in which leader and followers each incur costs in order to provide benefits for one another, and in which the allocation of prestige to leaders constitutes a collective-action problem for followers. This focus allows service-for-prestige to make some novel predictions, which we discuss throughout the chapter, especially in section 3.

1. EVOLUTIONARY PSYCHOLOGY, RECIPROCITY, AND LEADERSHIP: CORE ASSUMPTIONS

Evolutionary psychology assumes that the brain/mind is composed of a large number of genetically encoded mechanisms that evolved because they helped the individual organism's ancestors to solve adaptive problems (Cosmides and Tooby 2005; Tooby and Cosmides 1992). By *adaptive problem*, we mean any recurring obstacle to the individual's success in the competition to survive and reproduce (that is, any challenge to the individual's *fitness*) that existed in the organism's ancestral environments. Evolution solves adaptive problems by endowing individuals with domain-specific, functionally specialized adaptations that are good at solving a particular problem or set of problems but useless for most other tasks. Thus, the pancreas is good at producing insulin but bad at digesting food or filtering blood; opposable thumbs are useful for grasping but not for lactation or sight. A growing body of evidence suggests that this evolutionary design principle of functionally specialized modularity applies to minds as well, including the human mind. For example, people have specialized mate-selection adaptations that are helpful for selecting an appropriate reproductive partner (Buss 1992; Sugiyama 2005) but useless for escaping predators, reading others' emotional states, selecting nutritious food, or avoiding falls from high places.

The large varieties of functionally specialized mental mechanisms that compose our minds were selected because they solved adaptive problems that were chronic and recurrent in human ancestral environments for an evolutionarily relevant length of time (Cosmides and Tooby 2005). We could possess mechanisms that are specialized for leadership and followership, therefore, only if these behaviors solved problems that were present in the types of hunter-gatherer environments in which the vast proportion of human evolution has occurred. The problems that leadership and followership solved for ancestral humans were most likely related to group organization (e.g., solving coordination and collective-action problems) and the sharing of expertise; from a cross-species perspective, leader-follower relationships generally evolve as solutions to these problems (King, Johnson, and Van Vugt 2009; Van Vugt and Ahuja 2010). For example, waggle-dancing honeybees share their knowledge about nest site locations in order to guide their followers to a suitable new site; many varieties of fish follow leaders in order to form shoals, which are useful for foraging and protection from predators; in many species (e.g., ravens, elephants), individuals who know the location of food or water lead their groups to these resources; and in primate species such as chimpanzees, alpha males coordinate their group's cooperative actions against predators and rival groups (Boehm 1999; King, Johnson, and Van Vugt 2009; Krause and Ruxton 2002).

Because leadership has evolved to facilitate the sharing of expertise and cooperative group action in so many species, and because humans are adapted for complex cooperative behaviors that require high levels of expertise and coordination (e.g., in coalitions and collective actions; Tooby, Cosmides, and Price 2006), it would not be surprising if humans had evolved adaptations for leadership and followership behaviors. Indeed, the available evidence suggests that the propensity to engage in these behaviors is a universal aspect of human nature: all societies evidence some form of leadership, including the hunter-gatherer and tribal societies that most resemble those of the human evolutionary past (Bass 1990; Brown 1991). In these small-scale, ancestral-type societies, leadership emerges most often to facilitate cooperation in group activities such as hunting, warfare, and moving camp (Service 1966). These were evolutionarily important activities in ancestral environments, because problems of how to acquire sufficient meat, how to prevail in war, and how to camp in a safe and resource-rich location were highly relevant to individual evolutionary fitness (that is, to the individual's ability to survive and reproduce). Selection could therefore have favored leadership and followership behaviors that enabled people to enhance their chances of success in these domains. Throughout this chapter, we make frequent reference to ancestral-type hunter-gatherer societies, because in order to understand how the mind is adapted for leadership and followership, we need to understand the kinds of environments in which these adaptations evolved.

Note that we have so far been considering how leadership and followership benefited the survival and reproduction of *individuals*. This individual-level perspective on adaptation was popularized by Darwin in the *Origin of Species* (1859) and remains the standard in behavioral biology.[1] Still, because leaders and followers interact in groups, it might seem reasonable to seek instead a "group selectionist" explanation for the evolution of leadership (or a "multilevel selectionist" explanation, which combines individual, group, and possibly other levels, such as intragenomic and species). In other words, one might propose that psychological adaptations for leadership/followership evolved at least in part because these behaviors produced benefits at the group level (e.g., groups with leaders outcompete groups without leaders [Hogan, 2006]). However, while leadership often does produce group-level benefits, we maintain a focus on ordinary, individual-level adaptations (Williams, 1966). Consideration of all possible selective levels is beyond the scope of this chapter, and we believe that an individual-level focus is an especially productive way of generating insights about the evolution of leadership.

Because our focus is on the individual level, and because human leader-follower relationships are cooperative interactions that occur between individuals who are not necessarily close genetic kin, our main theoretical tool is a modified version of the leading individual-level evolutionary theory of non-kin cooperation: Trivers's (1971) reciprocal altruism.[2] In devising reciprocal altruism theory, Trivers realized that if an individual "altruistically" delivers a benefit to a nonrelative (i.e., if the individual incurs a fitness cost in order to benefit the fitness of a nonrelative), then that altruist will be evolutionarily disadvantaged, unless he or she can somehow recoup this fitness cost. Reciprocal altruism theory predicts that altruists will deliver benefits to recipients only for as long as they receive return benefits that compensate them for this altruism. Mutually beneficial exchange can evolve as long as altruists can interact with other altruists (who reciprocate the benefits that they are given), and can avoid interacting with cheaters who fail to reciprocate. If altruists interact too frequently with cheaters instead of with other altruists, cheaters will exploit them to extinction (Henrich 2004).

Traditionally, reciprocal altruism theory has most often been used to explain mutually beneficial exchange that occurs between two individuals. Leader-follower interactions, however, are group interactions, involving exchange between one leader and more than one follower. Efforts have been made, with varying degrees of success, to extend reciprocal altruism to group interactions (Boyd and Richerson 1988; Price 2003 and 2006a; Takezawa and Price 2010; Tooby, Cosmides, and Price 2006). We acknowledge that important theoretical details about how reciprocal altruism evolves in groups remain to be worked out. In order to clarify that we are using a substantially modified version of Trivers's dyadic reciprocal altruism theory, we use the more general term *reciprocity*, as opposed to *reciprocal altruism*, to describe the kind of leader-follower interaction we have in mind. By *leader-follower reciprocity*, we simply mean that leaders and followers are involved in a mutually beneficial transaction, with each side paying costs in exchange for benefits.

Despite unresolved theoretical issues about the evolution of reciprocity in groups, we propose that reciprocity theory does provide a suitable framework for understanding voluntary, noncoercive leader-follower interactions, that is, interactions in which followers voluntarily follow and leaders voluntarily lead because they feel that they can benefit from doing so. We also believe that by testing some of the predictions made by the theory that voluntary leader-follower interaction is a form of reciprocity, we may make progress toward resolving some lingering theoretical questions about how reciprocity evolves in groups. We say more about these theoretical questions and the predictions that could help to resolve them later in the chapter.

Note that our reciprocity theory bears similarities to existing leadership theories, such as social exchange (Hollander 1992), leader-member exchange (Graen and Uhl-Bein 1995), social identity (Hogg 2001), and charismatic, transactional, and transformational perspectives (Bass 1998; Burns 1978), as they all stress the importance of leader-follower interactions. A notable difference, however, with these theories is that they offer proximate explanations for leadership, such as predictions about whether people will decide to follow a transactional or a transformational leader. In contrast, reciprocity theory deals with the question of why humans have evolved to be attracted to leaders who provide different kinds of services to the group, from tangible rewards such as income and material goods to symbolic rewards such as self-esteem and a positive social identity.

As noted above, leader-follower interactions are not always voluntary; they may also be coercive: followers may comply with a leader's wishes in order to avoid reprisal for noncompliance (French and Raven 1959). The service-for-prestige theory focuses on both voluntary and coercive leader-follower interactions, especially on the conditions that cause leader-follower interactions to change from being voluntary to coercive. However, we do believe that the voluntary kind are more effective for balancing the interests of leaders and followers, and we focus on this kind first.

2. VOLUNTARY LEADER-FOLLOWER INTERACTION AS SERVICE-FOR-PRESTIGE EXCHANGE

We regard the voluntary leader-follower interaction as a kind of reciprocity in which leaders incur costs in order to provide followers with expertise and solutions to social coordination and collective-action problems, and followers incur costs in order to provide leaders with social status (Price 2003). Social status can result from two general social abilities: the ability to confer benefits on others, which is prestige, and the ability to inflict harm on others, which is dominance (Cheng, Tracy, and Henrich 2010; Henrich and Gil-White 2001; Sell, Tooby, and Cosmides 2009). The voluntary leader-follower interaction can be characterized as a service-for-prestige transaction because followers willingly agree to allocate status to the leader in exchange for the services the leader provides (see Hollander 1992). Again, we stress that these services may vary from instrumental rewards, such as a good salary, to symbolic rewards, such as feeling pride in your group.

If leader-follower interaction is to be seen as reciprocity, then the services provided by leaders and the prestige provided by followers must both be contributions that are costly to provide. The costs of providing leadership seem relatively clear; they could include, for example, making the effort to share one's expertise, risking one's own safety to lead a hunting or war party, investing time and energy in planning company strategy, or incurring the stress of making high-level decisions. The costs of providing prestige ("paying respect") may seem more obscure, because some superficial prestige indicators seem cheap to produce—for example, calling a higher-raking person "sir" and laughing at his jokes. However, allocating prestige is ultimately a costly process because it involves deferring to the interests of prestigious people and taking pains to ensure their well-being, and because it results in a relatively large share of a group's social, material, and reproductive resources being acquired by or flowing to prestigious people. Prestigious people are prestigious because they possess attributes that others value—for example, physical attractiveness, or skill at generating resources, or reliability as a source of useful information—so they are sought after as social partners, and others treat them well in order to retain them as friends and allies. The flow of shared social and material resources in small-scale societies thus tends to move toward high-prestige individuals; therefore, they become relatively more able to attract mates and provision offspring (Betzig 1986; Hagen, Barrett, and Price 2006). The allocation of prestige in these social groups is costly, then, because it ultimately results in prestigious people having superior access to all kinds of resources that could otherwise be consumed by other group members. An analogous situation occurs in modern societies, in which higher-prestige employees are compensated with larger shares of an organization's resources (Day and Antonakis 2011).

In order to elaborate further on the service-for-prestige theory and to specify the predictions that it makes about effective leadership in modern organizations, it is useful to focus more closely on service-for-prestige exchange in the context of the small-scale, ancestral social environments in which it evolved. In section 3, we consider the evolution of leadership in these environments and discuss how this evolutionary history should influence our understanding of leadership and followership in modern contexts.

3. LEADER-FOLLOWER RELATIONS IN ANCESTRAL ENVIRONMENTS AND IMPLICATIONS FOR MODERN ORGANIZATIONS

In order to understand the nature of the cognitive mechanisms that generate leader and follower behaviors in modern environments, we need to understand what adaptive problems these mechanisms evolved to solve in ancestral environments. Although these environments cannot be observed directly, anthropological studies of small-scale societies provide a reasonable approximation of what they were like. This section, therefore, draws heavily on anthropological observations of such societies.

In considering the kinds of environments in which leadership and followership evolved, it is important to keep in mind that although an adaptation must, by definition, successfully solve some adaptive problem in the environments in which it evolves, it may fail to function adaptively in different, novel environments. In other words, an adaptation's adaptiveness in past environments is no guarantee of its adaptiveness in new environments; there may be a *mismatch* between that adaptation and its new environment. Common examples of mismatch are the human tastes for fat, salt, and sugar (Nesse and Williams 1994). In ancestral environments, these substances were nutritionally essential, yet scarce and difficult to obtain, so our ancestors needed to crave them strongly in order to be motivated to acquire them in sufficient quantities. In modern environments, however, these substances are cheap and easily obtained; as a result, we suffer from maladaptive health consequences, such as obesity, hypertension, and tooth decay. Below we discuss several examples of adaptations for leadership and followership that seem better suited for ancestral conditions than for modern ones (see also Van Vugt et al. 2008).

We also want to emphasize that human psychological adaptations for leadership and followership did not evolve in just one static type of ancestral environment; they evolved across a range of environmental conditions. Under some conditions, leader-follower relations would have been more likely to be based on prestige and reciprocity; under other conditions, they would have been more likely to be based on dominance and coercion. In section 3.1, we discuss implications of the theory that some leader and follower behaviors evolved in the context of reciprocity, and in section 3.2, we consider how variation in ancestral environments would have allowed for leader-follower relations to become more coercive.

3.1. Leader-Follower Relations as a Service-for-Prestige Transaction

3.1.1. In Nomadic Foraging Societies, Followers Decide Whom They Want to Follow

Nomadic foraging (hunter-gatherer) societies are particularly relevant to an understanding of evolved leadership preferences, because these societies approximate the most relevant selective environments for the mental mechanisms that compose the minds of modern humans (Tooby and Cosmides 1992). The most commonly noted aspect of leadership in these societies is that it tends to be informal and based on achievement; any group members can become influential and gain prestige if they happen to have expertise that makes them useful to other people (Fried 1967; Kelly 1995). Leaders in these societies have little coercive power to force others to do what they say; instead, they tend to lead by persuasion and by demonstrating their own expertise to others (Johnson and Earle 1987; Service 1966). Here are a couple of representative anthropological observations: "Nobody ever tells an Eskimo what to do. But some people are smarter than others and can give good advice. They are the leaders" (Chance 1966, 73). An Australian aboriginal man "attracted social prestige only as long as he could validate his status by actual performance" (Meggitt 1960, 250). Because leaders in these societies have relatively little coercive power, the high regard in which followers hold them appears to be voluntarily conferred prestige (Henrich and Gil-White 2001), which followers grant the leader because they perceive that they benefit from the leaders' shared expertise and organizational abilities (Van Vugt and Ahuja 2010). This prestige in turn benefits the leader: prestigious individuals are highly valued by other people as friends, allies, and mates, and therefore social, material, and reproductive resources tend to flow their way (Sell, Tooby, and Cosmides 2009; Von Rueden, Gurven, and Kaplan 2008).

The observation that leaders in foraging societies achieve their position via public displays of competence can be explained in terms of service-for-prestige theory. Followers provide leaders with prestige in exchange for the group-beneficial expertise and social organization services that leaders provide. A number of studies, conducted in both small-scale and industrialized societies, also support the view that in groups where status can be freely allocated by members, it is allocated to those who have demonstrated their ability to provide benefits to the group (Willer 2009; Anderson and Kilduff 2009). Among the hunter-horticultural Shuar of the Ecuadorian Amazon, for example, people who are perceived as doing the most to help their social group—whether that group be the entire village or a smaller, within-village association—receive the most social status and are preferred as leaders within that group (Price 2003, 2006a, and 2006b). Similar relationships between altruism and social status have been found in industrialized societies in both experimental studies of university students (Hardy and Van Vugt 2006) and field studies of business employees (Flynn 2003). This process of acquiring status via engagement in group-beneficial tasks has been described as "competitive altruism" (Barclay 2004; Hardy and Van Vugt 2006; Roberts 1998), because members compete with one another in order to determine who is most able to benefit the group and therefore most deserving of high social status.

The above evidence suggests that this process of competitive altruism—of followers choosing their own leaders by awarding social status to those who outcompete others in demonstrating leadership ability—occurs spontaneously in groups, in all kinds of cultures, whenever followers are allowed to make decisions about whom they want to follow. This process is also, of course, how leaders are supposed to be elected in democratic governments. It appears that, cross-culturally, when given a choice, people prefer to follow leaders whom they have chosen. In contrast, people are less willing to follow leaders who have been imposed on them by some external force (Van Vugt et al. 2004). Results from experimental cooperative groups, for example, show that group members cooperate less when their leaders are selected by experimenters as opposed to when their leaders have volunteered to lead (Rivas and Sutter 2011).

Unfortunately, however, in the vast majority of modern businesses, leaders are imposed on rather than chosen by their followers. The key dynamic of leader-follower reciprocity—of followers freely conferring prestige on leaders in exchange for the services that leaders offer—is thus largely absent in most organizations, which probably results in followers losing motivation to cooperate voluntarily with leaders. Some successful organizations are, however, exceptions to this rule. The best example is W. L. Gore and Associates, which selects its CEO by opening the post up to anyone and allowing employees to nominate candidates (Van Vugt and Ahuja 2010). The philosophy behind this process—"if you attract followers, then you're a leader"—is highly consistent with the notion that people prefer to follow leaders whom they have chosen.

3.1.2. The Preference for Physically Formidable Males as Leaders

The hunter-gatherer activities that most require leadership, especially hunting and warfare, generally require athletic ability, physical strength, aggressive formidability, and skill with weapons. Because of processes in sexual selection (Darwin 1871; Trivers 1972), men are on average better-adapted for such activities. As a result, leaders in small-scale societies tend to be physically formidable males (Van Vugt and Ahuja 2010).

This ancestral need for physically formidable leaders is probably the major reason why a variety of studies have suggested that people tend to prefer male leaders who display cues of health, strength, and height (Judge and Cable 2004; Van Vugt and Ahuja 2010). For females, in contrast, height is not a predictor of leadership emergence (Blaker et al. 2013). Further, a study of West Point graduates revealed that male cadets with more masculine facial appearance—a cue to high testosterone levels and physical formidability—went on to achieve higher-status positions later in their military careers (Mueller and Mazur 1996). Physically attractive leaders are also preferred (Anderson et al. 2001; Van Vugt and Ahuja 2010); the physical traits that people perceive as attractive in others are generally those that would have indicated health and genetic quality in ancestral environments (Grammer et al. 2003).

However, although maleness, height, formidability, and attractiveness probably were important aspects of leader performance in the ancestral past, and although these traits are preferred in modern leaders, not all of them are necessarily associated with better leadership in the present. Could there be a mismatch between any of these traits and modern organizational environments? As noted, these traits were particularly useful in the context of male-dominated coalitional activities such as hunting and warfare—activities that were extraordinarily important matters of life and death in the ancestral past. Hunter-gatherers can acquire high quality protein and other essential nutrients only if their hunters are successful (Tooby and DeVore 1987), and average total mortality rates due to warfare are probably at least twenty times higher in small-scale societies than they were in twentieth-century Western society (Keeley 1996; Bowles 2009). Our modern bias in favor of physically impressive male leaders may be a legacy of our ancestors' need for expertise and coordinated group action in these domains, but this need is reduced in modern business contexts. As a consequence of this bias, followers in modern environments may often overlook qualified female leaders, as well as qualified (but physically unimpressive) male leaders, for reasons that have become largely obsolete (Van Vugt et al. 2008). This mismatch might also be one explanation for why there are persistent negative stereotypes about women leaders.

3.1.3. The Preference for Leaders Who Are Intelligent and Good Communicators

As with traits indicating physical formidability, intelligence and communication skills are also universally valued traits in leaders (Den Hartog et al. 1999; Judge, Colbert, and Ilies 2004), and these preferences make sense in light of the benefits that leaders would have provided followers in the ancestral past (Tooby, Cosmides, and Price 2006; Van Vugt, Hogan and Kaiser 2008). Good communication and oratory skills are essential for social coordination (e.g., communicating plans for a division of labor or for sequences of events in a collective action), and intelligence is related to, for example, good decision making, identifying follower interests and how to achieve them, and effectively communicating plans for group action.

In contrast with traits indicating physical formidability, however, there is probably less of a mismatch between intelligence and communication skills and the job requirements of modern leadership roles. For instance, leadership competence in modern organizations generally does not depend on the ability to wield a spear or physically intimidate your rivals, but it continues to be enhanced by the ability to form a brilliant strategy and communicate it effectively to followers.

3.1.4. Sex Differences in Status Striving and in Using Status to Acquire Sex

Sexual selection and parental investment theory (Trivers 1972) predicts differences in status striving, across all species, based on levels of obligatory parental investment. Because men do not bear the burdens of gestation and lactation, they can reproduce much faster than women can, and they benefit reproductively more than women do from having multiple mates. Thus, to a greater extent than women, men are selected to strive to attract multiple mates, and an important way in which men can acquire mates is by acquiring social status. Status leads to reproductive success for men in small-scale societies, both because it is attractive to women (Ellis 1992), and also because parents in these societies are particularly likely to betroth their daughters to men whom they would like to have as allies, that is, to high-status men (Hart and Pilling 1960; Kelly 1995). As a result, high-status men in these societies have increased mating opportunities, more wives, wives who are more fertile, and more surviving offspring (Betzig 1986; Chagnon 1979 and 1988; Levi-Strauss 1967; review in Von Rueden, Gurven, and Kaplan 2008).

Because men had more to gain reproductively than women did from having high status in ancestral environments (as noted above), they tend to compete more aggressively for status and to desire leadership positions more (Geary 2002; Browne 2006; Croson and Gneezy 2009). It is likely that men emerge more often as leaders in modern organizations not just because followers are biased against women, but also because men (on average) compete for leadership positions more aggressively than do women. However, the fact that men are relatively obsessed with increasing their own status does not necessarily make them better leaders, and could sometimes make them worse ones, if it caused them to focus too much on maintaining their own status at any cost, regardless of whether they are actually leading effectively.

There is one additional aspect of male status-striving and its connection to attracting mates that bears mentioning. Cross-culturally, social status indicates access to social and economic resources, which is much more important as an aspect of male mate-value than as an aspect of female mate-value. In other words, men use status, much more than women do, in order to attract new mates (Ellis 1992; Zeitzen 2008). In contrast, the most important aspects of female attractiveness cross-culturally are fertility indicators such as cues to youth, health, and hormonal status. These sex differences in mate-value make sense from an evolutionary perspective, because they relate to the most important kinds of mating and parental investment that each sex can provide the other: males benefit more from a mate's fertility, and females benefit more from a mate's access to resources (Buss 1992).

These sex differences also have important implications for leadership. They suggest that male leaders will be more likely than female leaders to use their positions in order to attract new mates (particularly, relatively young and attractive mates), and that women will be more likely than men to be attracted to and desire sexual relationships with opposite-sex leaders. These predictions seem consistent with patterns that are now routinely reported in media accounts of political sex scandals, and they probably apply equally well to the sexual behavior of business leaders, although business leaders' behavior is less exposed to public scrutiny than that of politicians. A good business case study is provided by the former CEO of GE, Jack Welch (Stephen Colarelli, personal communication). Welch co-authored *Winning* (Welch and Welch 2005)—an account of the enormous success and prestige he achieved as a leader—with a woman twenty-four years his junior named Suzy Welch (née Wetlaufer). They began their affair a few years before the book's publication, while Welch was still married to his second wife, who was merely seventeen years his junior (Jones 2002). Thus the title *Winning* could be seen as something of a double entendre: a high-prestige male leading an organization to victory, while simultaneously "winning" a new, younger wife.

3.1.5. Different Leaders for Different Roles

Because leadership often depends on expertise, and because different people often have expertise in different activities, the best provider of leadership services in one domain is not necessarily the best leader in another domain: for instance, the leader in a hunting expedition might be different than the leader in a political negotiation (Service 1966). That is why leadership is often shared in successful organizations (Wassenaar and Pearce 2011). A particularly vivid anthropological illustration of this principle is the traditional authority system of the Navajo, which included war chiefs who organized war parties, peace chiefs who led nonviolent political interactions, hunt leaders, diviners who diagnosed illnesses, and singers who led ceremonial chants (Shepardson 1963).

Just as the Navajo (and other North American Plains Indians groups) distinguished among several kinds of leaders, members of modern societies prefer different kinds of leaders for different kinds of roles. For example, experimental studies have found that leaders with more masculine male facial appearance (like John McCain) are preferred to lead during wartime, while more feminine-faced leaders (like Barack Obama) have the edge during peacetime (Little et al. 2006; Spisak et al. 2012); and male leaders are preferred to lead under conditions of intergroup conflict, whereas female leaders are preferred for the resolution of within-group disputes (Van Vugt and Spisak 2008).

Followers' preference for leaders who have shown expertise in a particular activity can sometimes lead them astray in modern environments—another example of a mismatch. In a relatively simple hunter-gatherer collective action, there is probably little difference between being a skilled participant and being a skilled leader; the task of hunting giraffe, for example, is probably not so different from the task of leading a giraffe-hunting expedition. In the more complex organizations of modern societies, however, the distance between participation and leadership is often more vast. In professional sports such as football (soccer), for example, talented former players are often favored for managerial roles, despite the lack of evidence that better players make better managers (Van Vugt and Ahuja 2010). Managing a football team probably involves skills that are quite different than those required to excel in a particular position on a football team, and the apparently unjustified preference for players as managers may represent a mismatch between our evolved leadership preferences and the demands of leadership roles in complex modern organizations. We should be skeptical of our impulse to assume that someone who has demonstrated superior ability in a particular organizational role is necessarily well-qualified to lead in a different role. Good jockeys don't make good race horses!

3.1.6. Concerns about In-Group Advantage

Due to the coalitional, political nature of vital leadership tasks in the ancestral past, followers are biased in favor of leaders who belong to their in-group and best represent their in-group interests (Hogg 2001). This orientation emerges most strongly when the in-group is threatened by some external enemy (Van Vugt, Hogan, and Kaiser 2008); at these times followers benefit most from effective leadership and offer the most support and respect for their leader (the "rally effect"). Experimental results suggest that leaders are more likely to start intergroup conflicts when they are more concerned about how their followers assess their leadership ability (Van Vugt and Ahuja 2010). So the rally effect is probably a two-way street: followers gain security from giving their leaders increased support under conditions of intergroup threat, whereas leaders can boost their own status by provoking such conditions or by at least encouraging the impression that such conditions exist (Van Vugt and

Ahuja 2010). There is thus the potential for abuse of the rally effect; unscrupulous leaders may exaggerate the extent of an external threat and lead their group into an unnecessary conflict simply because they want to consolidate their power.

On the other hand, there are also relatively innocuous and group-beneficial ways in which the rally effect could be used in organizations. By emphasizing the competitive aspects of an organization's aspirations—for example, by identifying outperformance of a rival group as a key organizational goal—a leader can elicit enhanced cooperation from followers, not just in terms of improved compliance, but in terms of greater overall productivity. Experimental evidence suggests that group members cooperate more and are more productive overall when they perceive that their group is competing with an external group (Van Vugt, De Cremer, and Janssen 2007; McDonald, Navarrete, and Van Vugt 2012). It is important to note, however, that this effect has been observed only among male group members, which suggests that it is an adaptation to conditions of male coalitional violence.

3.1.7. The Preference for "Fair" Leaders

As just noted, conditions of coalitional competition can affect followers' perceptions of leaders. However, such competition does not just occur between two external groups; it can also occur within one group, in the form of within-group factionalization (Hart and Van Vugt 2006). Different factions of a group tend to have different political interests and thus vary in terms of the specific leadership services they require. The result may be a failure of reciprocity, if a leader cannot engage in reciprocity equally effectively with everyone in a group simultaneously because the group is split up into different interest groups. Such factionalization often occurs along kinship lines in small-scale societies (Chagnon 1997), but it can be caused by virtually any kind of coalitional conflict of interest (Hogg 2001), and conflicts between different interest groups (department vs. department, management vs. labor, etc.) can occur in any kinds of organization.

A particularly interesting kind of factionalization occurs when interest groups espouse different fairness norms. An important aspect of leadership in cooperative groups, in both ancestral and modern environments, is overseeing the distribution of resources in ways that seem fair to followers (Den Hartog et al. 1999). Leaders of Northwest Coast communities, for example, were responsible for ensuring that group resources were redistributed in a manner that their followers would perceive as fair (Fried 1967; Johnson and Earle 1987). Organizational researchers in modern societies have long recognized that employees are deeply concerned about the fairness of such distributive processes (Adams 1963; Ambrose and Arnaud 2005), and studies about leadership preferences suggest that there is a widespread, cross-cultural preference for fair leaders (De Cremer and Van Knippenberg 2004). However, *fair* is a highly ambiguous term. Many different definitions exist, and an evolutionary perspective suggests that different types of people prefer different kinds of fairness. When different factions have different standards of fairness, a leader will have difficulty achieving successful reciprocity with all factions simultaneously.

In terms of distributive justice alone, for example (ignoring other types of organizational justice, such as procedural, interactional, and retributive justice), fairness in groups is often variously defined in terms of equality (all members get the same amount), equity (higher contributors receive more), or need (the needier receive more; see Ambrose and Arnaud 2005). Each of these distribution systems benefits some members more than others. A comparison of equity versus equality, for example, suggests that equity advantages members who are most capable of contributing highly, but disadvantages members who can contribute the least; equality, on the other hand, is good for low contributors who would otherwise be out-competed by high contributors, but is advantage-reducing for higher contributors.

From this perspective, then, a follower's assessment of a leader's fairness should depend on the type of fairness practiced by the leader as well as the characteristics of the follower. Evidence suggests that this perspective is correct: Increased preferences for meritocratic versus equality-based distribution systems, for example, are expressed by individuals in better positions to benefit from meritocracy, such as the highly educated and wealthy (Kunovich and Slomczynski 2007; Ritzman and Tomaskovic-Devey 1992). Further, people who are wealthier or members of ethnic majorities tend to approve more of social inequality, that is, to be relatively high in "social dominance orientation" (Pratto, Sidanius, and Levin 2006). This "condition-dependence" of fairness preferences may often be more comprehensible in terms of ancestral environments than modern ones; for example, men with more muscular upper bodies tend to be more supportive of social inequality (Price et al. 2011) and policies of political aggression (Price et al. 2012; Sell, Tooby, and Cosmides 2009). These preferences were probably adaptive in ancestral environments in which muscularity was an important component of success in resource competition and war, but they seem less useful in modern industrialized societies, in which access to resources and success in war has much more to do with educational and technological attainment than with physical strength.

3.1.8. The Collective Action Problem of Providing Prestige

The most significant theoretical obstacle to regarding voluntary leader-follower interaction as a service-for-prestige reciprocal transaction is the problem of collective action (Olson 1965). The benefits provided by the leader constitute a kind of public good, as does the leader's motivation to continue to provide them. If increased prestige is what motivates the leader to provide this public good, then the allocation of this prestige is a collective-action problem for the followers (Price 2003). For example, consider a leader who benefits his followers by leading a raid against an enemy tribe or, in a more modern context, leading a hostile takeover of a rival company. The prestige allocated to him in exchange is costly for his followers to provide, because it obligates them to cater to his well-being in a manner that ultimately affords him a relatively large share of the group's social, material, and reproductive resources. In order for the followers to maintain the leader's motivation to provide his services, they must collectively pay these costs of respect. Followers could free ride, and thus gain a fitness advantage over the other followers, if they continued to accept the leader's services while refusing to pay respect (e.g., by not deferring to the leader's interests or by failing to share resources with the leader). Because each individual has the incentive to free ride, the group might not provide enough resources to the leader. Free riders could lose their advantage if they were punished by other followers (Ostrom 1990; Price, Cosmides and Tooby 2002; Price 2005; Yamagishi 1986), but if these punishers were not compensated for their action, they would fall victim to the "second-order free-rider problem" (Boyd and Richerson 1992): their punishment would be altruistic because it would generate benefits for the group, but as only they would pay the costs of punishing, they would be disadvantaged relative to second-order free riders (i.e., relative to followers who paid respect but failed to punish disrespectful followers).

Collective-action dilemmas of this kind are classic problems in social and psychological science (Ostrom 1990; Yamagishi 1986) as well as in biology (Boyd and Richerson 1988 and 1992; Takezawa and Price 2010), and there is no consensus about the specific nature of the evolutionary processes that may solve them. However, there are a variety of plausible ways in which evolution could overcome first- and second-order free-rider problems in the context of leader-follower reciprocity (Price 2003). For example, leaders might take it upon themselves to ostracize or punish disrespectful followers (O'Gorman, Henrich, and Van Vugt 2009; Price 2003) or might selectively favor (and thus compensate) followers who paid the costs of ostracizing or punishing the disrespectful member.

We want to avoid becoming overly distracted by this issue of precisely how evolution may have solved collective-action problems in the context of leader-follower reciprocity. However, service-for-prestige theory does make a general, novel prediction on this issue: because a free-rider problem emerges when some followers accept the benefits of leadership without sharing in the costs of paying respect to the leader, it predicts that those who fail to provide respect to a widely respected leader will suffer social consequences. Punishments in small-scale societies typically take the form of informal social sanctions, such as exclusion from reciprocal exchange interactions (Fried 1967), and in both ancestral-type and modern environments, such sanctions may be imposed on disrespectful followers. Among the hunter-horticultural Shuar, for example, the more a follower is perceived as being respectful of a generally well-respected community leader, the more that follower is respected within the community (Price 2003); less respectful followers are themselves respected less. In modern organizations, it is likely that members who disrespect popular leaders are sanctioned by other members through processes of social exclusion, facilitated by gossip (Barkow 1992; Williams 2007), or they may also be punished directly (e.g., fired) by leaders whom they have treated disrespectfully.

It is also worth noting that whereas co-members will regard a member who disrespects a generally popular leader as a kind of free rider, they will regard a member who disrespects a generally *un*popular leader as a kind of hero. A leader who fails to provide the group with valuable leadership services in exchange for prestige will be unpopular, and with such a leader, followers face the problem not of how to allocate prestige collectively, but of how to collectively strip that leader of prestige. A member who disrespects an unpopular leader will usually be making a personal sacrifice by risking retaliation from the leader, and so will be seen by co-members as an altruistic contributor to the public good. If you brave the wrath of an unpopular king, for example, by throwing his tea into the Boston harbor, you become a hero in the eyes of your fellow colonists. Thus, another novel prediction of service-for-prestige is that followers need to solve collective-action problems not just to supply prestige to a good leader but also to deny prestige to a bad one.

3.2. Coercive Leadership May Emerge in Large Groups with Few Exit Options

The power of leaders is positively correlated with the extent to which their followers depend on their leadership (Emerson 1962), and the ethnographic record suggests that followers depend on their leaders more in some kinds of small-scale societies than in others. In order to understand human adaptations for leader and follower behavior, it is important to consider in some detail the range of environments in which these adaptations probably evolved and how different environmental conditions would have influenced the likelihood that leadership would be based on dominance and coercion as opposed to prestige and reciprocity.

In general, leadership in small-scale societies is least important in hunter-gatherer societies where residential groups are small (about 20–60 people), population density is low, and nomadic foraging is the way of life (Fried 1967; Johnson and Earle 1987; Marlowe 2011). Nomadic foragers depend on wild resources that usually become depleted locally before residential groups exceed this size. Further, most highly coordinated social activities (e.g., collective actions for hunting or raiding) in these societies involve not the entire residential group but only a few members, usually of a particular sex and age class (Kelly 1995; Price and Johnson 2011). Because social groups in these societies remain relatively small, coordination and collective action problems are fairly simple—group members can relatively easily, for example, organize divisions of labor, plan group tasks, monitor co-member contributions, and sanction low contributors—and therefore strong leadership is less necessary (Tooby, Cosmides, and Price 2006; Hooper, Kaplan, and Boone 2010). Moreover, because of low population density and the ease of moving camp, it is relatively easy for nomadic foragers to leave one group to form a smaller group or join another group. Residential group composition is therefore often in flux, and a "fission-fusion" style of social organization generally prevails, with smaller groups coming together and larger groups breaking apart, depending on local resource availability and the quality of within-group social relationships (Kelly 1995; Turnbull 1968). Thus, if a leader in this kind of society tries to become too dominant, his power will be limited by the relative ease with which his followers can simply leave his group (cf. Van Vugt et al. 2004). In such societies, then, followers' dependence on leaders is relatively low: they rely less on leaders for the coordination of collective action, and they are relatively free to escape leaders who would seek to exploit them. Not coincidentally, members of small nomadic foraging groups express relatively strong distaste for domineering leaders, are particularly wary of letting talented individuals become too full of themselves, and are unlikely to recognize anyone in their group as a formal leader (Lee 1993; Service 1966; Turnbull 1968).

Not all small-scale societies, however, exist in environments that are so conducive to low-power leadership. Leaders become more powerful in hunter-gatherer and tribal societies that have larger residential group sizes, higher population density, and a more sedentary rather than no-madic way of life (Johnson and Earle 1987). Under these conditions, peo-ple must cooperate in larger groups, and, as discussed above, coordination and collective-action problems become more difficult in larger groups. Members of larger groups therefore become more reliant on leaders who can solve these problems (Tooby, Cosmides, and Price 2006; Hooper, Ka-plan, and Boone 2010). Moreover, because these people have more seden-tary lifestyles and live in environments that are more densely populated and hence "socially circumscribed" (i.e., communities are more closely surrounded by neighboring communities [Chagnon 1997]), it becomes more difficult for them to pack up and move to an unoccupied site if their leader becomes too dominant.

Because domesticated food sources allow for increases in residential group sizes, sedentism, and population density, leaders become more important, and leadership becomes more formalized after societies be-gin practicing agriculture. For example, in hunter-horticultural societies such as the Yanomamö in Venezuela and the Mae Enga in New Guinea, residential groups typically include 100–400 people, population density is high compared to nomadic foraging societies, and leaders are especially valued for their leadership abilities in politics and war. In contrast to the informality of leadership in nomadic foraging societies, these leaders are formally recognized by everyone in the community as headmen (or "big men"; see Chagnon 1997; Johnson and Earle 1987; Meggitt 1977) and are endowed with an enduring political authority. However, the conditions that are conducive to powerful leadership are ultimately related more to resource concentration and the sedentism that it allows than to agricul-ture per se (Fried 1967). Although Indians in the American Pacific North-west were non-agricultural, for example, they could maintain villages of 500–800 people and population densities of one or two people per square mile by residing near salmon-rich rivers. Both of these figures are unusu-ally high for hunter-gatherers (Johnson and Earle 1987). Leadership in these societies was much stronger than in nomadic foraging societies, with clearly identified chiefs who advertised their wealth and status in potlatch ceremonies involving the giving away or destruction of material goods. Strong leaders were needed in these societies because it is relatively challenging to organize cooperative labor, intervillage ceremonies, and other kinds of collective action in groups of this size. The military operations of the Nootka, for example, were relatively sophisticated compared to those in smaller-scale band and tribal societies and involved a commander-in-chief and other specialized roles. Processes of resource redistribution also become more complex and formalized in larger groups (Fried 1967; Johnson and Earle 1987).

The dark side of the increased power acquired by leaders in larger and more socially circumscribed communities is that their status can become less based on their ability to help and more on their ability to threaten or hurt their followers (Padilla, Hogan, and Kaiser 2007). In a mutually beneficial, reciprocal relationship between equally powerful partners, a main incentive to pay the costs of treating one's partner well is to avoid motivating him to exit the relationship. As followers become more dependent on leaders for the organization of collective action and less capable of leaving their residential group, they become less powerful relative to their leaders. Leaders thus lose their incentive to behave altruistically toward their followers and gain more ability to harm them by excluding them from the benefits of group membership. Thus, with increases in group size and population density, leader-follower relationships become more likely to be based on dominance than on reciprocity and prestige, and more likely to be coercive instead of voluntary. For example, the practice of slavery is rare in the ethnographic record of band and tribal societies, but it was widespread among the relatively large and socially circumscribed Pacific Northwest Coast communities mentioned above. The enslavement of war captives was practiced all along the Northwest Coast, and slaves probably constituted 7–15% of the population in a typical community (Kelly 1995).

3.2.1. Low Tolerance for Unnecessary Leaders

According to the service-for-prestige theory, when leadership is based on reciprocity, followers receive the benefits of the leader's expertise and group organizational skills; when leadership is based on coercion, however, these benefits need not be present. The theory predicts, therefore, that the human mind has evolved to desire and actively seek out leadership only when the benefits that leadership offers—the leader's expertise and group organizational skills—are actually required by group members. In group situations where strong leadership is not really necessary, members tend be unenthusiastic and mistrustful of those who try to lead (Haslam and Platow 2001). People understand intuitively that leaders benefit personally from the prestige that being a leader entails, so people who attempt to claim this prestige without offering any real services in return are rightfully regarded with suspicion.

As a result of this low tolerance for superfluous, self-serving leadership, we would expect people to be less enthusiastic about leaders when they are members of smaller groups, because the lack of challenging social coordination problems in small groups tends to render leaders unnecessary. The presence of leaders will thus more likely be resented and undermine group performance in smaller groups (Van Vugt, Hogan, and Kaiser 2008). Similarly, aspiring leaders who have no beneficial expertise but act as though they do will be resented by potential followers as self-serving and arrogant. Kerr and Jermier (1978), in their "substitutes for leadership" theory, have identified a number of additional factors that may render leadership unnecessary in order for work to get done within an organization. For example, leaders are less required by employees who have a high degree of professional expertise; for tasks that are unambiguous, routine, or intrinsically satisfying; and in situations where the allocation of organizational rewards is not under the control of the leader.

But whereas aspiring leaders will be relatively disliked in groups where they are superfluous, leaders will be sought and embraced in groups where they can really offer benefits to followers. The lesson here for managers is that, although leadership often is a vital aspect of group success, it can undermine success in groups where it is not really needed. Managers should therefore avoid appointing leaders in groups unless it is clear that the other members of the group perceive that the services of that particular leader would contribute significantly to group performance.

3.2.2. The Preference for Leaders with Personality Traits Associated with Altruistic, Pro-group Orientation Rather Than Dominance and Selfishness

The service-for-prestige theory suggests that followers benefited more in ancestral environments from reciprocal leadership as opposed to coercive leadership. Therefore, the minds of followers should be sensitive to cues indicating that a leader is likely to behave in a reciprocal, pro-group manner as opposed to being dominant and narrowly self-serving. Cross-cultural data suggests that followers universally do prefer leaders who are altruistic and competent enough to act in ways that benefit followers

(Van Vugt, Hogan, and Kaiser 2008). The GLOBE list of universally valued leadership traits (Den Hartog et al. 1999) suggests that across sixty-one cultures, people prefer leaders who show signs of being *willing* and *able* to provide altruistic benefits to followers. This willingness takes the form of an altruistic disposition (e.g., trustworthiness, fairness), and this ability takes the form of possessing group-beneficial skills (e.g., intelligence, competence). By the same token, followers express universal aversion to traits associated with coercive, self-serving leadership (e.g., dominance, selfishness).

Along similar lines, in a review of the literature on leadership and personality, Hogan and Kaiser (2005) mention modesty, humility, integrity, decisiveness, competence, and vision as the most important traits of successful leaders. Integrity is described as "keeping one's word, fulfilling one's promises, not playing favorites, and not taking advantage of one's situation" (173). In other words, integrity is essentially trustworthiness, which is a key characteristic that one should seek in a reciprocal partner. Modesty and humility are also cues to a prosocial personality that is oriented toward consideration of others and not just of one's self. Decisiveness, competence, and vision are all involved with the benefits that good leaders provide to followers. Taken together, then, all of these traits have to do with a leader's willingness (modesty, humility, integrity) and ability (decisiveness, competence, vision) to act as a reliable and valuable reciprocal partner.

Leaders are reviled for being selfish (or in the language of reciprocity, for "cheating") if they control group actions or resources in a manner that benefits themselves while injuring followers (Tooby, Cosmides, and Price 2006). The salary of a typical modern business leader is astronomically high compared to that of the average worker, and economic inequality in these organizations is far more severe than could ever occur in a hunter-gatherer society (Smith et al. 2010). Workers in these organizations may perceive their leaders to be hoarding the group's resources for their own selfish interests—a behavior that followers are probably adapted to distrust and resent (Van Vugt, Hogan, and Kaiser 2008).

To some extent, service-for-prestige theory is similar to servant leadership theory (Gillet, Cartwright, and Van Vugt 2011; Greenleaf 2002) in terms of the predictions it makes about which leader characteristics followers will prefer. Both theories emphasize that followers prefer leaders whose personal traits orient them toward promoting the welfare and interests of their followers, often at a large personal cost to themselves. Service-for prestige differs from servant leadership theory, however (as we discuss in more detail below), in that it sees this concern with follower welfare as one side of a mutually beneficial leader-follower transaction, in which the costs borne by each side are reciprocated by the other.

3.2.3. Leaders Are More Likely to Exploit Followers Who Lack Exit Options

According to service-for-prestige, leaders may benefit (at the expense of followers) by adopting a more coercive leadership style when they can get away with it, because leading via coercion saves them the costs of having to deliver benefits to followers. In small-scale societies, leadership tends to become less reciprocal and more coercive in environments in which, because of high population density and resource concentration, followers are less able to exit groups in which coercive leaders have gained control. Similarly, it has long been suggested that in modern organizations and states, when members have fewer exit options, leadership tends to be less responsive and more autocratic (Hirschman 1970). If, on the other hand, leaders attempt to adopt a coercive leadership style when their followers *do* possess good exit options, then their leadership days will likely be numbered. In experimental research by Van Vugt et al. (2004), members were more likely to flee from groups led by autocratic leaders than from groups led by democratic leaders.

In business contexts, the temptations of leaders to resort to a leadership style based on dominance rather than reciprocity should increase when employees are less able or willing to leave their jobs because, for instance, the labor market is bad, or because they will not consider relocating geographically in order to work somewhere else. This prediction of a positive relationship between the quality of leadership and the availability of follower exit options has apparently not been tested explicitly in a business setting. There is evidence, however, that employees with better exit options tend to receive a greater share of organizational rewards, a phenomenon known as "rational selective exploitation" [Rusbult et al. 1988]). Nevertheless, the logic behind the prediction is compelling enough to send a clear message to members of modern organizations: when exit options are few, workers and management ought to be more vigilant to ensure that leadership does not become based on coercion as opposed to reciprocity.

The lack of exit options also makes followers more vulnerable to exploitation by leaders with truly antisocial personalities. When followers have no bargaining power to demand a leader-follower relationship based on reciprocity, it creates a niche for leaders who feel no real responsibility to provide benefits to followers and are motivated to lead by the benefits they can obtain through selfish exploitation of the position. Such toxic leadership may be exhibited by people who score highly on one or more of the "dark triad" traits of Machiavellianism, narcissism, and psychopathy (Paulhus and Williams 2002; Van Vugt and Ahuja 2010).

4. DISCUSSION AND CONCLUSION

The service-for-prestige theory, as presented in sections 3.1 and 3.2, suggests that from an evolutionary psychological perspective, followers and leaders would have faced different kinds of adaptive problems in ancestral environments. In the range of ecological and social environments experienced by our hunter-gatherer ancestors, follower fitness would have benefited more when leader-follower interactions were based on reciprocity as opposed to coercion. Therefore, followers' leadership preferences should be seen as solutions to the adaptive problems of how to encourage leadership services from those who display essential expertise and group organizational skills, and how to avoid leaders who lack these skills or whose interactions with followers more resemble exploitation than exchange. Leaders, on the other hand, would have faced the primary adaptive problem of how to acquire social status in the least costly manner. In small, nomadic foraging groups, the relatively equally powerful negotiating positions of followers and leaders meant that prestige, freely conferred by followers in exchange for leadership services, was the form of status that leaders could most efficiently acquire. In environments in which followers were more dependent on leaders, however, dominance-based status—status based on a leader's ability to harm followers—would often have been cheaper for leaders than prestige, because it would have saved them the costs of producing benefits for followers.

The service-for-prestige theory does not capture all aspects of leader-follower interaction that are relevant from an evolutionary perspective. For one thing, as noted, service-for-prestige focuses on only one level (the individual level) in a selective process that may also involve other levels (Wilson, Van Vugt, and O'Gorman 2008). Further, it may not satisfactorily account for the process by which leadership emerges evolutionarily in the first place, which could have more to do with leadership's role in solving coordination problems between organisms (Van Vugt and Kurzban 2007; Van Vugt, Hogan, and Kaiser 2008) than with its role in being one side of a service-for-prestige transaction.

There are also existing, well-known, non-evolutionary theories of leadership that have important attributes in common with service-for-prestige. For example, leader-member exchange theory (LMX; Graen and Uhl-Bien 1995) suggests that the quality of leadership is heavily influenced by the quality of the exchange relationship between the leader and individual subordinates, and servant leadership theory (Gillet, Cartwright, and Van Vugt 2011; Greenleaf 2002) emphasizes that good leaders are altruistic, compassionate people whose influence rests on their moral authority and ability to provide benefits to followers rather than their dominance. While service-for-prestige shares some predictions with these theories, it also makes some novel predictions, because it sees both leadership and followership as individually adaptive strategies, and because it sees the leader's altruism and the follower's delivery of prestige as two kinds of costly contributions in an exchange transaction. Thus, unlike servant leadership theory, service-for-prestige sees leadership as "altruism" that ultimately profits leaders (as well as followers), and unlike LMX, service-for-prestige focuses not on general aspects of relationship quality but on how evolution designed both leaders and followers to maximize their own fitness benefits and minimize their own fitness costs in their interactions with one another. Unlike either servant leadership theory or LMX, service-for-prestige focuses not just on the conditions under which leaders will be most likely to provide benefits for followers, but also on the conditions under which leaders will be most likely to exploit and coerce followers. Finally, service-for-prestige focuses not just on the material rewards flowing from leaders to followers but also on the symbolic benefits of leadership—for instance, cohesion and identity benefits. In that respect, service-for-prestige has as much in common with transformational leadership models as with transactional models of leadership (Bass 1998). Service-for-prestige is mute about the nature of the service offered to followers, as long as the service ultimately contributed to follower fitness in the ancestral past. For instance, charisma may be an indicator of the prestige awarded to a leader who makes costly contributions to help the group.

In conclusion, the service-for-prestige theory does not claim that either kind of leader-follower relationship—reciprocity or coercion—is more "natural" or more consistent with evolutionary design. People are adapted for both reciprocal and coercive leader-follower interactions. However, it is clear that of the two kinds of relationships, reciprocity involves the greater degree of mutual benefit between leaders and followers. Unlike coercion, reciprocity allows followers to act on their leader preferences and award prestige to group members who, via their ability to benefit the group, are worthy of leadership roles. Reciprocity is also the relationship that is more closely associated with what most would consider to be "good" leadership, that is, leadership that genuinely helps followers achieve their shared goals, as opposed to leadership that primarily serves the leader's narrow self-interest. Coercion is more likely to result in corrupt and exploitative leadership by leaders who strive to maintain their status via their ability to harm instead of to help.

Notes

1. Although Darwin usually focused on individual-level adaptation, he does speculate in *The Descent of Man, and Selection in Relation to Sex* (1871) about how human morality may have evolved as a group-level adaptation. While there has been considerable controversy about the importance of biological adaptation at levels above the individual, such as the group or species (Williams 1966), most adaptationist analyses continue to maintain an individual-level focus. However, our focus on individual fitness should be not interpreted as a rejection of multilevel selection theory (Wilson and Wilson 2007). We acknowledge that selection can operate simultaneously on multiple levels, including intragenomic, individual, and group levels; indeed, one of us has suggested that multilevel selection may explain some important aspects of leadership (Wilson, Van Vugt, and O'Gorman 2008).

2. A distinct theory, Hamilton's (1964) kin selection, is the leading explanation for cooperation among close genetic kin. According to this theory, a gene situated in one individual can cause its own replication, and thus gain an evolutionary advantage, if it can somehow benefit exact copies of itself that exist in other individuals. The gene accomplishes this goal by causing the individual in whom it is situated to behave altruistically toward other individuals who are likely to carry the same gene, that is, toward close genetic kin. This theory thus predicts that altruism will be relatively likely to evolve between genetic kin, especially very close kin (e.g., siblings). Kin-selection theory has been tested and supported in a vast variety of species and was popularized by Dawkins (1976) in his best-selling book *The Selfish Gene*.

References

Adams, J. S. 1963. Toward an understanding of inequity. *Journal of Abnormal and Social Inequity* 67 (5): 422–36.

Ambrose, M. L., and Arnaud, A. 2005. Are procedural justice and distributive justice conceptually distinct? In *Handbook of organizational justice*, ed. J. Greenberg and J. A. Colquitt, 59–84. Mahwah, NJ: Lawrence Erlbaum.

Anderson, C., John, O. P., Keltner, D., and Kring, A. M. 2001. Who attains social status? Effects of personality and physical attractiveness in social groups. *Journal of Personality and Social Psychology* 81 (1):116–32.

———, and Kilduff, G. J. 2009. Why do dominant personalities attain influence in face-to-face groups? The competence-signaling effects of trait dominance. *Journal of Personality and Social Psychology* 96 (2): 491–503.

Barclay, P. 2004. Trustworthiness and competitive altruism can also solve the "tragedy of the commons." *Evolution and Human Behavior* 25 (4): 209–20.

Barkow, J. H. 1992. Beneath new culture is old psychology: Gossip and social stratification. In Barkow, Cosmides, and Tooby 1992, 627–38.

Barkow, J. H., Cosmides, L., and Tooby, J., eds. 1992. *The adapted mind: Evolutionary psychology and the generation of culture*. New York: Oxford University Press.

Bass, B. M. 1990. *Bass and Stogdill's handbook of leadership: Theory, research, and managerial applications*. 3rd ed. New York: Free Press.

———. 1998. *Transformational leadership: Industrial, military, and educational impact.* Mahwah, NJ: Lawrence Erlbaum.

Betzig, L. L. 1986. *Despotism and differential reproduction*. New York: Aldine.

Blaker, N. M., Rompa, I., Dessing, I. H., Vriend, A. F., Herschberg, C., and van Vugt, M. 2013. The height leadership advantage in men and women: Testing evolutionary psychology predictions about the perceptions of tall leaders. *Group Processes & Intergroup Relations* 16 (1): 17–27.

Boehm, C. 1999. *Hierarchy in the forest: The evolution of egalitarian behavior*. Cambridge, MA: Harvard University Press.

Bowles, S. 2009. Did warfare among ancestral hunter-gatherers affect the evolution of human social behaviors? *Science* 324:1293–98.

Boyd, R., and Richerson, P. J. 1988. The evolution of reciprocity in sizable groups. *Journal of Theoretical Biology* 132 (3): 337–56.

Boyd, R., and Richerson, P. J. 1992. Punishment allows the evolution of cooperation (or anything else) in sizable groups. *Ethology and Sociobiology* 13 (3): 171–95.

Brown, D. E. 1991. *Human universals*. New York: McGraw-Hill.

Browne, K. R. 2006. Evolved sex differences and occupational segregation. *Journal of Organizational Behavior* 27 (2): 143–62.

Burns, J. M. 1978. *Leadership*. New York. Harper and Row.

Buss, D. M. 1992. Mate preference mechanisms: Consequences of partner choice and intrasexual competition. In Barkow, Cosmides, and Tooby 1992, 249–66.

Chagnon, N. A. 1979. Is reproductive success equal in egalitarian societies? In *Evolutionary biology and human social behavior: An anthropological perspective*, ed. N. A. Chagnon, and W. Irons, 374–401. North Scituate, MA: Duxbury Press.

———. 1988. Life histories, blood revenge, and warfare in a tribal population. *Science* 239:985–92.

———. 1997. *Yanomamö*. Fort Worth: Harcourt Brace.

Chance, N. 1966. *The Eskimo of north Alaska*. New York: Holt, Rinehart and Winston.

Cheng, J. T., Tracy, J. L., and Henrich, J. 2010. Pride, personality, and the evolutionary foundations of human social status. *Evolution and Human Behavior* 31 (5): 334–47.

Cosmides, L., and Tooby, J. 2005. Neurocognitive adaptations designed for social exchange. In *The handbook of evolutionary psychology*, ed. D. M. Buss, 584–627. Hoboken, NJ: Wiley.

Croson, R., and Gneezy, U. 2009. Gender differences in preferences. *Journal of Economic Literature* 47 (2): 448–74.

Darwin, C. 1859. *On the origin of species*. London: John Murray.

———. 1871. *The Descent of man, and selection in relation to sex*. London: John Murray.

Dawkins, R. 1976. *The selfish gene*. Oxford: Oxford University Press.

Day, D., and Antonakis, J. 2011. *The nature of leadership*. London: Sage.

De Cremer, D., and van Knippenberg, D. 2004. Leader self-sacrifice and leadership effectiveness: The moderating role of leader self-confidence. *Organizational Behavior and Human Decision Processes* 95 (2): 140–55.

Den Hartog, D. N., House, R. J., Hanges, P. J., Ruiz-Quintanilla, S. A., Dorfman, P. W., and GLOBE Associates. 1999. Culture specific and cross-culturally generalizable implicit leadership theories: Are attributes of charismatic/transformational leadership universally endorsed? *Leadership Quarterly* 10 (2): 219–56.

Ellis, B. J. 1992. The evolution of sexual attraction: Evaluative mechanisms in women. In Barkow, Cosmides, and Tooby 1992, 267–88.

Emerson, R. 1962. Power-dependence relations. *American Sociological Review* 27 (1): 31–40.

Flynn, F. J. 2003. How much should I give and how often? The effects of generosity and frequency of favor exchange on social status and productivity. *Academy of Management Journal* 46 (5): 539–53.

French, J. R. P., and Raven, B. 1959. The bases of social power. In *Studies in social power*, ed. D. Cartwright, 150–67. Ann Arbor: University of Michigan Press.

Fried, M. H. 1967. *The evolution of political society.* New York: Random House.

Geary, D. C. 2002. Sexual selection and sex differences in social cognition. In *Biology, society, and behavior: The development of sex differences in cognition*, ed. A. V. McGillicuddy-DeLisi and R. De Lisi, 23–53. Greenwich: Ablex/Greenwood.

Gillet, J., Cartwright, E., and Van Vugt, M. 2011. Selfish or servant leadership? Evolutionary predictions on leadership personalities in coordination games. *Personality and Individual Differences* 51 (3): 231–36.

Graen, G. B., and Uhl-Bien, M. 1995. Relationship-based approach to leadership: Development of LMX theory of leadership over 25 years: Applying a multi-level, multi-domain perspective. *Leadership Quarterly* 6 (2): 219–47.

Grammer, K., Fink, B., Møller, A. P., and Thornhill, R. 2003. Darwinian aesthetics: Sexual selection and the biology of beauty. *Biological Reviews* 78 (3): 385–407.

Greenleaf, R. K. 2002. *Servant leadership: A journey into the nature of legitimate power and greatness.* 25th anniversary ed. New York: Paulist Press.

Hagen E. H., Barrett H. C., and Price M. E. 2006. Do human parents face a quantity/ quality tradeoff? Evidence from a Shuar community. *American Journal of Physical Anthropology* 130 (3): 405–18.

Hamilton, W. D. 1964. The genetical evolution of social behavior, I–II. *Journal of Theoretical Biology* 7 (1): 1–52.

Hardy, C., and Van Vugt, M. 2006. Nice guys finish first: The competitive altruism hypothesis. *Personality and Social Psychology Bulletin*, 32 (10):1402–13.

Hart, C. W. M., and Pilling, A. R. 1960. *The Tiwi of north Australia.* New York: Holt.

Hart, C. M., and Van Vugt, M. 2006. From fault line to group fission: Understanding transformations in small groups. *Personality and Social Psychology Bulletin*, 32 (3): 392–404.

Haslam, S. A., and Platow, M. J. 2001. The link between leadership and followership: How affirming social identity translates vision into action. *Personality and Social Psychology Bulletin* 27 (11): 1469–79.

Henrich, J. 2004. Cultural group selection, coevolutionary processes and large-scale cooperation. *Journal of Economic Behavior and Organization* 53 (1): 3–35.

———, and Gil-White, F. J. 2001. The evolution of prestige: Freely conferred status as a mechanism for enhancing the benefits of cultural transmission. *Evolution and Human Behavior* 22 (3): 165–96.

Hirschman, A. O. 1970. *Exit, voice, and loyalty: Responses to decline in firms, organizations, and states*. Cambridge, MA: Harvard University Press.

Hogan, R. 2006. *Personality and the fate of organizations*. Hillsdale, NJ: Lawrence Erlbaum Associates.

———, and Kaiser, R. B. 2005. What we know about leadership. *Review of General Psychology*, 9 (2): 169–80.

Hogg, M. A. 2001. A social identity theory of leadership. *Personality and Social Psychology Review* 5 (3):184–200.

Hollander, E. P. 1992. The essential interdependence of leadership and followership. *Current Directions in Psychological Science* 1 (2): 71–75.

Hooper, P. L., Kaplan, H. S., and Boone, J. L. 2010. A theory of leadership in human cooperative groups. *Journal of Theoretical Biology*, 265 (4): 633–46.

Johnson, A. W., and Earle, T. 1987. *The evolution of human societies*. Stanford, CA: Stanford University Press.

Jones, D. 2002. Jane Welch seeks half of couple's $1 billion fortune. *USA Today*, March 18. Retrieved from http://www.usatoday.com/money/general/2002/03/19/jane-welch.htm.

Judge, T. A., and Cable, D. M. 2004. The effect of physical height on workplace success and income. *Journal of Applied Psychology*, 89 (3): 428–41.

———, Colbert, A. E., and Ilies, R. 2004. Intelligence and leadership: A quantitative review and test of theoretical propositions. *Journal of Applied Psychology*, 89 (3): 542–52.

Keeley, L. H. 1996. *War before civilization: The myth of the peaceful savage*. Oxford: Oxford University Press.

Kelly, R. L. 1995. *The foraging spectrum: Diversity in hunter-gatherer lifeways*. Washington, DC: Smithsonian.

Kerr, S., and Jermier, J. M. 1978. Substitutes for leadership: Their meaning and measurement. *Organizational Behavior and Human Performance* 22 (3): 375–403.

King, A., Johnson, D. D. P., and Van Vugt, M. 2009. The origins and evolution of leadership. *Current Biology* 19 (19): R911–R916.

Krause, J., and Ruxton, G. 2002. *Living in Groups*. Oxford: Oxford University Press.

Kunovich, S., and Slomczynski, K. M. 2007. Systems of distribution and a sense of equity: A multilevel analysis of meritocratic attitudes in post-industrial societies. *European Sociological Review* 23 (5): 649–63.

Lee, R. B. 1993. *The Dobe Ju/'hoansi*. New York: Harcourt Brace.

Levi-Strauss, C. 1967. The social and psychological aspects of chieftainship in a primitive tribe: The Nambikuara of northwestern Mato Grosso. In *Comparative political systems: Studies in the politics of pre-industrial societies*, ed. R. Cohen and J. Middleton, 45–62. New York: American Museum of Natural History.

Little, A. C., Burris, R. P., Jones, B. C., and Roberts, S. C. 2006. Facial appearance affects voting decisions. *Evolution and Human Behavior* 28 (1): 18–27.

Marlowe, F. 2011. *The Hadza: Hunter-gatherer people of Tanzania*. Berkeley and Los Angeles: University of California Press.

McDonald, M. M., Navarrete, C. D., and Van Vugt, M. 2012. Evolution and the psychology of intergroup conflict: The male warrior hypothesis. *Philosophical Transactions of the Royal Society B: Biological Sciences* 367 (1589): 670–79.

Meggitt, M. J. 1960. *Desert people*. Chicago: University of Chicago Press.

———. 1977. *Blood is their argument*. Palo Alto, CA: Mayfield.

Mueller, U., and Mazur, A. 1996. Facial dominance of West Point cadets as a predictor of later military rank. *Social forces* 74 (3): 823–50.

Nesse, R. M., and Williams, G. C. 1994. *Why we get sick*. New York: New York Times Books.

O'Gorman, R., Henrich, J., and Van Vugt, M. 2009. Constraining free riding in public goods games: Designated solitary punishers can sustain human cooperation. *Proceedings of the Royal Society B: Biological Sciences* 276 (1655): 323–29.

Olson, M. 1965. *The logic of collective action: Public goods and the theory of groups*. Cambridge, MA: Harvard University Press.

Ostrom, E. 1990. *Governing the commons: The evolution of institutions for collective action*. New York: Cambridge University Press.

Padilla, A., Hogan, R., and Kaiser, R. B. 2007. The toxic triangle: Destructive leaders, vulnerable followers, and conducive environments. *Leadership Quarterly* 18 (3): 176–94.

Paulhus, D. L., and Williams, K. M. 2002. The Dark Triad of personality: Narcissism, Machiavellianism, and psychopathy. *Journal of Research in Personality* 36 (6): 556–63.

Pratto, F., Sidanius, J., and Levin, S. 2006. Social dominance theory and the dynamics of intergroup relations: Taking stock and looking forward. *European Review of Social Psychology* 17 (1): 271–320.

Price M. E. 2003. Pro-community altruism and social status in a Shuar village. *Human Nature* 14 (2): 191–208.

———. 2005. Punitive sentiment among the Shuar and in industrialized societies: Cross-cultural similarities. *Evolution and Human Behavior* 26 (3): 279–87.

———. 2006a. Monitoring, reputation and "greenbeard" reciprocity in a Shuar work team. *Journal of Organizational Behavior* 27 (2): 201–19.

———. 2006b. Judgments about cooperators and freeriders on a Shuar work team: An evolutionary psychological perspective. *Organizational Behavior and Human Decision Processes* 101 (1): 20–35.

———, Cosmides L., and Tooby J. (2002). Punitive sentiment as an anti-free rider psychological device. *Evolution and Human Behavior* 23 (3): 203–31.

———, Dunn J., Hopkins S., and Kang J. (2012). Anthropometric correlates of human anger. *Evolution and Human Behavior* 33 (3): 174–81.

———, and Johnson, D. D. P. 2011. The adaptationist theory of cooperation in groups: Evolutionary predictions for organizational cooperation. In *Evolutionary psychology in the business sciences*, ed. G. Saad, 95–134. Berlin: Springer.

———, Kang J., Dunn J., and Hopkins S. 2011. Muscularity and attractiveness as predictors of human egalitarianism. *Personality and Individual Differences* 50 (5): 636–40.

Ritzman, R. L., and Tomaskovic-Devey, D. 1992. Life chances and support for equality and equity as normative and counternormative distribution rules. *Social Forces* 70 (3): 745–63.

Rivas, M. F., and Sutter, M. 2011. The benefits of voluntary leadership in experimental public goods games. *Economics Letters* 112 (2): 176–78.

Roberts, G. 1998. Competitive altruism: From reciprocity to the handicap principle. *Proceedings of the Royal Society B* 265 (1394): 427–31.

Rusbult, C. E., Farrell, D. L., Rogers, O., and Mainous, A. O., III. 1988. The impact of exchange variables on exit, voice, loyalty, and neglect: An integrative model of responses to declining job satisfaction. *Academy of Management Journal* 31 (3): 599–627.

Sell, A., Tooby, J., and Cosmides, L. 2009. Formidability and the logic of human anger. *Proceedings of the National Academy of Sciences USA*, 106 (35): 15073–78.

Service, E. R. 1966. *The hunters*. Englewood Cliffs, NJ: Prentice-Hall.

Shepardson, M. 1963. The traditional authority system of the Navajos. In *Comparative political systems: Studies in the politics of pre-industrial societies* , ed. R. Cohen and J. Middleton, 143–54. New York: American Museum of Natural History.

Smith, E. A., Hill, K., Marlowe, F. W., Nolin, D., Wiessner, P., Gurven, M., et al. 2010. Wealth transmission and inequality among hunter-gatherers. *Current Anthropology* 51 (1): 19–34.

Spisak, B. R., Homan, A. C., Grabo, A., and Van Vugt, M. 2012. Facing the situation: Testing a biosocial contingency model of leadership in intergroup relations using masculine and feminine faces. *Leadership Quarterly* 23 (2): 273–80.

Sugiyama, L. Physical attractiveness in adaptationist perspective. In *The Handbook of evolutionary psychology*, ed. D. M. Buss, 292–343. Hoboken, NJ: Wiley.

Takezawa M., and Price M. E. 2010. Revisiting "The evolution of reciprocity in sizable groups": Continuous reciprocity in the repeated *N*-Person prisoner's dilemma. *Journal of Theoretical Biology* 264 (2): 188–96.

Tooby, J., and Cosmides, L. 1992. The psychological foundations of culture. In Barkow, Cosmides, and Tooby 1992, 19–136.

———, Cosmides, L., and Price, M. E. 2006. Cognitive adaptations for *n*-person exchange: The evolutionary roots of organizational behavior. *Managerial and Decision Economics* 27 (2–3):103–29.

Tooby J., and DeVore, I. 1987. The reconstruction of hominid behavioral evolution through strategic modeling. In *Primate models of hominid behavior*, ed. W. Kinzey, 183–237. New York: State University of New York Press.

Trivers, R. L. 1971. The evolution of reciprocal altruism. *Quarterly Review of Biology* 46 (1): 35–57.

———. 1972. Parental investment and sexual selection. In *Sexual selection and the descent of man, 1871–1971*, ed. B. Campbell, 136–79. Chicago: Aldine.

Turnbull, C. M. 1968. The importance of flux in two hunting societies. In *Man the hunter*, ed. R. B. Lee and I. DeVore, 132–37. New York: Aldine de Gruyter.

Van Vugt, M., and Ahuja, A. 2010. *Selected: Why some people lead, why others follow, and why it matters*. London: Profile Books.

———, De Cremer, D., and Janssen, D. 2007. Gender differences in competition and cooperation: The male warrior hypothesis. *Psychological Science* 18 (1): 19–23.

———, Hogan, R., and Kaiser, R. 2008. Leadership, followership, and evolution: Some lessons from the past. *American Psychologist* 63 (3): 182–96.

———, Jepson, S., Hart, C., and De Cremer, D. 2004. Autocratic leadership in social dilemmas: A threat to group stability. *Journal of Experimental Social Psychology* 40 (1): 1–13.

——, Johnson, D., Kaiser, R., and O'Gorman, R. 2008. Evolution and the social psychology of leadership: The mismatch hypothesis. In *Leadership at the crossroads: Psychology and leadership*, vol. 1, ed. C. L. Hoyt, G. R. Goethals, and D. R. Forsyth, 262–82. Westport, CT: Praeger.

——, and Kurzban, R. K. 2007. Cognitive and social adaptations for leadership and followership: Evolutionary game theory and group dynamics. In *Sydney symposium of social psychology*, vol. 9, *The evolution of the social mind: Evolutionary psychology and social cognition*, ed. J. Forgas, W. von Hippel, and M. Haselton, 229–44. London: Psychology Press.

——, and Spisak, B. R. 2008. Sex differences in leadership emergence during competitions within and between groups. *Psychological Science* 19 (9): 854–58.

Von Rueden, C., Gurven, M., and Kaplan, H. 2008. The multiple dimensions of male social status in an Amazonian society. *Evolution and Human Behavior* 29 (6): 402–15.

Wassenaar, C. L., and Pearce, C. L. 2011. The nature of shared leadership. In *The nature of leadership*, ed. D. V. Day and J. Antonakis, 363–89. Los Angeles: Sage.

Welch J., and Welch, S. 2005. *Winning*. New York: Harper Business.

Willer, R. 2009. Groups reward individual sacrifice: The status solution to the collective action problem. *American Sociological Review* 74 (1): 23–43.

Williams, G. C. 1966. *Adaptation and natural selection: A critique of some current evolutionary thought*. Princeton, NJ: Princeton University Press.

Williams, K. 2007. Ostracism. *Annual Review of Psychology* 58:425–52.

Wilson, D. S., Van Vugt, M., and O'Gorman, R. 2008. Multilevel selection and major evolutionary transitions: Implications for psychological science. *Current Directions in Psychological Science* 17 (1): 6–9.

——, and Wilson, E. O. 2007. Rethinking the theoretical foundation of sociobiology. *Quarterly Review of Biology* 82 (4): 327–48.

Yamagishi, T. 1986. The provision of a sanctioning system as a public good. *Journal of Personality and Social Psychology* 51 (1): 110–16.

Zeitzen, M. K. 2008. *Polygamy: A Cross-Cultural Analysis*. Oxford: Berg.

NINE

Evolved Decision Makers in Organizations

Peter DeScioli, Robert Kurzban, and Peter M. Todd

1. INTRODUCTION

Managers and leaders in organizations seek to influence people's behavior to achieve the organization's objectives. How can they accomplish this goal? A traditional economic approach focuses attention on people's incentives. For example, managers can offer financial rewards to promote desirable behavior and set financial penalties to inhibit undesirable behavior. This intuitive idea can help managers to align individuals' incentives with organizational goals. Nonetheless, we argue that, even if it is sometimes useful, the traditional economic approach to people's behavior is deeply flawed. It ignores fundamental insights from evolutionary biology, experimental psychology, and cognitive science. People are much more than simple incentive-chasers who pursue carrots and avoid sticks; they are computational problem-solvers.

To solve a problem, one needs to use the right tool for the job. The mind has a variety of computational programs so that it can solve a variety of problems (Pinker 1997). Like a carpenter choosing from a box of tools, the human mind uses cues to select which computational program best fits the job. The cognitive mechanisms that are selected to process incoming information determine how people represent their circumstances, how they understand the current situation, and ultimately how they behave. This implies that it is not incentives per se that shape behavior, but people's representations of their environment. These representations can, to be sure, be influenced by incentives, but sometimes in unpredictable ways. For example, people might represent the imposition of a financial penalty not only as a cost, but also as an act of attempted coercion. Modeling the situation as coercion, people might respond with defiance and seek rather than avoid the penalty, causing incentives to backfire. Similarly, the threat of a penalty might be viewed as moral license to perform the act in question, as long as the actor is willing to endure the cost, thereby increasing, rather than decreasing, the undesired behavior (Gneezy and Rustichini 2000). Indeed, a wealth of experimental evidence shows that both positive and negative incentives can have the opposite of the desired effect (Bowles 2008).

With a better understanding of the human mind's toolkit, managers can seek to modify the organizational environment to trigger particular tools and cue sets in people that will lead to behavior in line with the organization's goals. The organization can be understood as an environment that people seek to comprehend and interact with in functional ways by applying evolved cognitive mechanisms. Importantly, each of these cognitive mechanisms is specialized for a distinct type of problem, and understanding this menu of programs is critical for understanding and managing behavior.

Moreover, at the same time that managers (and organizations) seek to influence other people, those people are also trying to influence the managers' understanding of the situation (and the organization's shaping of that situation). How can managers influence a network of people who are trying to influence them? This is also a common problem in human social life more generally, and people use evolved cognitive mechanisms for handling these strategic situations, which we explore in depth below.

1.1. Evolution and Specialization

Biological approaches to cognition posit that the mind consists of a large number of specialized information-processing devices designed to compute solutions to the range of problems faced by our ancestors (Gigerenzer and Selton 2001; Tooby and Cosmides 1992). The logic behind this is no different from Adam Smith's (1776) observations: specialization yields efficiency gains. The process of evolution by natural selection propagates mechanisms that effectively and efficiently facilitate survival and reproduction (Darwin 1859; Dawkins 1976). Because of the relationship between specialization and efficiency, and the adaptive advantages conferred by efficiency, mechanisms—whether physiological (the body) or computational (the mind)—tend to be narrowly specialized.

Specialization, though beneficial, also typically results in a large number of different devices, giving rise to a problem of tool selection. Like computer users selecting from hierarchical menus of functions, human minds have to choose which specialized device to use in any given context (Gigerenzer, Todd, and the ABC Research Group 1999). This makes an important area of study the question of how different choice contexts—including those in organizations—trigger the use of different computational devices.

This idea has clear and direct connections to important issues in organizational behavior. Most transparently, if contexts influence which computational devices are activated, then the details of the cues in organizations might have non-obvious effects on behavior. Consider, for instance, a study by Bateson, Nettle, and Roberts (2006) that varied whether or not a depiction of a pair of eyes was placed on a notice reminding people using a break room to leave money to pay for their coffee. The presence of eyes, a seemingly small cue, increased compliance. More generally, people's decision-making processes can be influenced by how they construe their interactions with their environment, including their relationships with one another and with their organizations more broadly.

1.2. Alternative Views: Mind as Incentive Seeker or Strategy Selector?

In order to achieve goals more often than chance, individuals must make good *choices*. How does one make good choices? The traditional idea from economics is that people seek incentives, a view that is formalized in subjective expected utility theory (SEU). This model predicts that decisions should not vary depending on how the problem is described to the agent, sometimes referred to as "description invariance" (Tversky and Kahneman 1986). Decision makers should reason about "0.2" exactly the same way they reason about "one out of five." Similarly, people should not be influenced by discursive cues surrounding the decision-making problem, such as the words used to describe the interaction. Faced with a choice about how to allocate resources, for instance, this theory says that decision makers should choose an allocation on the basis of their preferences regarding the distribution of the resources, not based on whether the choice is described as part of a "game" or an "interaction."

The commitment to the idea that behavior ought to depend narrowly on the incentive structure of the decision is evident in the way that deviations from this prediction are understood. When two superficially different ways of describing a decision yield different choices, this is referred to as a "framing effect" (Tversky and Kahneman 1981). Probably the best-known such effect is the "Asian Disease Problem," in which two options are presented slightly differently to subjects, which alters the pattern of choice. Framing effects are seen as potentially important challenges to SEU (Tversky and Kahneman 1986)

A modular, or "tool box," perspective views the issue differently. Carpenters facing some task first formulate a goal and then decide which tool to use to achieve this goal. The mind, too, must decide which tool to use to solve the problems it confronts. How does it accomplish this task? It does so by using cues extracted from sense data to identify the problem type and then selects the most relevant cognitive program to run on incoming data. These cues can include information about the payoff structure of the problem, but they may also include a wide range of other information. From this perspective, the mind is expected to respond differently to different descriptions, even if they are intended to have the "same" incentive structure, as defined by the experimenter or theorist. The incentives facing an organism are usually not directly observable (aside from specially constructed situations such as economics experiments), so evolved decision makers must make inferences about them based on contentful descriptions generated from sense data. A sophisticated computational decision mechanism will be closely attuned to the content of the problem at hand.

Two related views of the mind's toolbox have been proposed within an evolutionary perspective: the adaptive toolbox of simple heuristics (Gigerenzer and Todd 1999), and the Swiss-army knife of adaptive modules (Tooby and Cosmides1992). The two views have implications for how tools are selected using cues from the environment, and researchers adopting each view have explored a number of tools that may play important roles in behavior in organizations.

2. THE ADAPTIVE TOOLBOX OF SIMPLE HEURISTICS

Humans (and other animals) must often make decisions within rather severe bounds that our minds and the world impose on us. These bounds include the limited time that we have to make decisions before an opportunity may be gone, the limited and uncertain information we can access within that time, and the limited ability we have to process that information, owing to neural constraints of processing power and memory. To make reasonable choices within these bounds, the mind can resort to a collection of multiple simple tools rather than one complex power tool. Such simple tools have been dubbed "fast and frugal" heuristics (Gigerenzer and Goldstein 1996; Gigerenzer, Todd, and the ABC Research Group 1999)—decision rules that use a small amount of time, information, and processing to come up with what are usually good choices. A heuristic is an information-processing mechanism that ignores much of the available information and instead focuses on just a few key pieces of data to make its decisions. The root of the word *heuristic* refers to guided search, which is just what a heuristic does, guiding the search for crucial information and the good decisions it can lead to.

Consider the computationally fast and information-frugal *recognition heuristic* (Goldstein and Gigerenzer 2002), which can be used to decide which of two companies to invest in based solely on whether the decision maker has heard of one and not the other. It ignores all information other than whether each company is recognized or not, and yet, like other heuristics, it can make very effective decisions when used in appropriate settings (even making significant money on the stock market— see Borges et al. 1999). This use of appropriate heuristics in appropriate environments is key to the heuristics' successful application. Each simple heuristic is built to handle a particular type of decision (rather than the full range of decisions covered by traditional rational approaches), meaning that an appropriate heuristic must be applied in any given setting for good decisions to be reached.

Using simple heuristics in environments to which they are suited can enable decision-making agents to achieve what Herbert Simon (1990) called *bounded rationality*. In contrast to the impossible dream of unbounded rationality, which assumes optimal processing of all available information without concern for computational or informational costs, Simon saw humans as exhibiting a bounded form of rationality emerging from the interaction of two forces: the cognitive capabilities of the agent and the structure of the task environment. These two components should fit together like the two blades of a pair of scissors for adaptive, or boundedly rational, behavior to be produced—that is, mind and environment should be closely matched if decision outcomes are to be useful. This perspective aligns with that of evolutionary psychology, which specifically postulates that the close mind-environment fit has been achieved by evolution honing the former to match the latter. Furthermore, minds can shape their own environments, particularly in social domains, creating institutions and organizations that better fit the decision mechanisms that people bring to bear within them, meaning that the adaptive forces flow in both directions between the organisms and their world.

The research program of *ecological rationality* aims to identify the particular decision mechanisms that can produce bounded rationality in the presence of particular structures of information in the environment (Gigerenzer, Todd, and the ABC Research Group 1999; Todd and Gigerenzer 2007; Todd, Gigerenzer, and the ABC Research Group 2012). The relevant environment can be made up of patterns among physical objects, such as mountains defining a landscape; among biological entities, as in patches of food being sought by a forager; among people, such as social partners or extended family members; and among institutions, such as companies and other organizations. (The application of appropriate heuristics in environments of people and institutions can be more specifically termed *social rationality*; see Hertwig, Hoffrage, and the ABC Research Group 2013.) Ecological rationality emphasizes the importance of considering both environmental information structure and psychological information-processing mechanisms, and how the former enables and constrains the latter to yield adaptive decisions. Ecological rationality is thus a binary relationship—a particular decision mechanism cannot be said to be ecologically rational (or not) in itself, nor to perform well or poorly on its own; rather, it can only be assessed relative to a particular environment. This means that external correspondence criteria are what matter for judging ecological rationality—the extent to which the mechanism leads to adaptive behavior in a specific environment. This is in contrast to the internal coherence criteria used in other definitions of rationality, such as making logically consistent choices, which do not take the environment into consideration. (This does not mean that outcomes of ecologically rational mechanisms are never appropriately described in terms of the rules of logic—just that minds did not evolve specifically to implement those rules.)

When simple heuristics are applied in the environments for which they are fit, they are able to exploit the fact that information in the world is typically structured in useful ways. For example, the reason the recognition heuristic is adaptive in investment is that the individuals, companies, and products that are more widely recognized in society also tend to have higher yearly income, profit margins, and prevalence (Goldstein and Gigerenzer 2002; Pachur et al. 2012). An individual decision maker can capitalize on this structure, which he or she picks up through media and social interactions (learning about, and hence recognizing, what others mention), by using simple heuristics that use recognition as a cue in making choices. Thus, when deciding what company to invest in or what brand to buy, people can use the recognition heuristic to select options they recognize from past experiences. By counting on certain information structures to be present in the environment, decision heuristics can be correspondingly simpler, effectively letting the world do some of the work for them.

Thus, according to this perspective of ecological rationality, rather than relying on a single decision-making power tool, humans use a collection of simple heuristics that together make up the mind's *adaptive toolbox* (Gigerenzer and Todd 1999). These heuristics are composed of even simpler building blocks that guide the search for information or options, stop that search in a frugal manner, and then decide on the basis of the search's results. Building blocks themselves draw on an organism's evolved abilities. For instance, "search for recognition knowledge" is a building block of the recognition heuristic that employs the ability to recognize objects encountered in the past.

The building blocks for guiding search, whether across alternatives or information, are what give search its direction (if it has one). For instance, search for informative cues can be simply random, or in order of some measure related to their usefulness, or based on memory for which cues worked previously when making a similar decision. Next, to operate within the temporal constraints imposed by the environment, search for alternatives or information must be terminated at some point. And to operate within the computational limitations of organisms, the method for determining when to stop search should not be overly complicated. For example, one simple stopping rule is to cease searching for information and make a decision as soon as the first cue or reason that favors one alternative is found—a building block that underlies one-reason decision making (Gigerenzer, Dieckmann, and Gaissmaier 2012). This and other related stopping rules do not need to compute an optimal cost/benefit trade-off for how long to search; in fact, they need not compute any costs or benefits at all. Finally, once search has been guided to find the appropriate information or alternatives and then been stopped, another building block can be called upon to make an inference (or choice) based on the results of the search. These decision rules can also be very simple and computationally bounded—for instance, using only one cue or reason, whatever the total number of cues found during search. Such single-cue decision making does not need to weight or combine cues, and so no common currency among cues need be determined.

The strategy for studying the ecological rationality of particular decision mechanisms in the adaptive toolbox begins with identifying important decision tasks (e.g., in the form of important psychological processes like categorization, or evolutionarily crucial goals like choosing a mate or finding resources) and specifying the structure of information in the environment that can be exploited in making decisions. Next, computational models of candidate heuristics can be proposed that are psychologically plausible, based on what we know about human mental abilities; these algorithmic models must specify the precise steps of information gathering and processing that are involved in generating a decision, allowing the heuristic to be instantiated as a computer program. The heuristics can then be tested via mathematical analysis and computer simulation in various artificially constructed environments to see when they work, and then via experimentation in the lab or observation in field studies to see whether and when people actually use the proposed heuristics. This research program differs from the heuristics-and-biases program (Kahneman, Slovic, and Tversky 1982), in emphasizing the adaptive use of explicit computational models of heuristics.

Many types of heuristics in the adaptive toolbox have been studied from an ecological rationality perspective, and considerable evidence shows that people use these heuristics to make good decisions in appropriate environments (Todd and Gigerenzer 2007, and 2012). In one important class of heuristics, decision rules facilitate choice by limiting the amount of information they seek about each alternative. The recognition heuristic mentioned earlier (Goldstein and Gigerenzer 2002), which chooses options solely on the basis of whether or not the decision maker recognizes them, is one such mechanism. A second important type of heuristic searches for options themselves, rather than information about currently available options, in a fast and frugal way. For example, a *satisficing* heuristic (Simon 1990) uses a predetermined aspiration level—the minimum value that the searcher will settle for—to search through a sequence of options (say, apartments to rent, visited one after another) until one is found that exceeds that aspiration level. We next discuss examples of both types of heuristics with applications to business and organizational behavior.

2.1. Heuristics for Choosing among Options

An ecologically rational decision maker selects a heuristic from the adaptive toolbox that limits information search and processing to fit with the demands of the environment, using a stopping rule that terminates the search for information as soon as enough has been gathered to make a good decision. (Though what counts as a good decision can vary from setting to setting, and as decision importance rises, information use can also rise.) One such approach is to rely on "one-reason decision making" (Gigerenzer and Goldstein 1999): stop looking for cues as soon as one is found that differentiates between the options being considered. The *take-the-best* heuristic combines this search-stopping building block with a search-guiding building block that searches through cues in order of their validity (accuracy), comparing options first on the highest-validity cue and proceeding as needed to lower-validity cues, but stopping search at the first cue that discriminates between the options under consideration, and finally selecting the option with the highest value on that cue. (The particular cues and their ordering, along with the search, stopping, and decision rules, all are ultimately influenced by evolution, either directly or indirectly, through learning processes; see Todd 2000.) Lexicographic (ordered-cue) heuristics like take-the-best are found in the decision making of humans (Payne, Bettman, and Johnson 1993; Bröder 2012) and other animals (Hutchinson and Gigerenzer 2005), particularly when there are costs to information search and quick decisions are at a premium. People appear to rely on such heuristics in situations of consumer choice, making quick judgments about people to interact with, health-care questions, and even rapid business decisions. In these situations, less can be more—for instance, Wübben and Wangenheim (2008) found that managers in airline and apparel industries rely on a simple *hiatus heuristic* to determine if customers are still active (based on a single cue, whether or not the customer has purchased something within the past nine months), which works better than a considerably more complex model that incorporates different distributions for purchase timing, customer lifetimes, and dropout rates.

Other types of decisions call not for choosing a single option but for making an allocation across a number of options. Parents with multiple offspring to care for simultaneously face just such a situation, deciding how to divide up their resources, including time, attention, and food, across their brood (Trivers 1972). Evolved heuristics for this problem of parental investment could direct parents to give resources first to their smallest offspring, or their hungriest, or their strongest (Davis, Todd, and Bullock 1999); human parents also sometimes apply an even simpler *equity heuristic*, dividing up resources equally among all the children living with them (Hertwig, Davis, and Sulloway 2002).[1] These types of evolved allocation heuristics could now be triggered for use in other modern kinds of investment decisions that have analogous structure and so invoke the same decision mechanisms. For instance, when deciding how to invest one's retirement savings across a selection of N assets, roughly half of ordinary people are reported to rely on the so-called *1/N rule*, which says to allocate money equally to each of the N funds (Huberman and Jiang 2006). This heuristic is extremely simple in that it ignores all information about the previous performance of the funds, making it fast and frugal. And yet it outperforms a variety of optimizing asset-allocation policies, including the mean-variance model developed by Nobel prize winner Harry Markowitz, on two standard financial measures (DeMiguel, Garlappi, and Uppal 2009). In environments of rampant uncertainty, simple heuristics that ignore most of the available information can be more robust and perform better than complex mechanisms that try to squeeze all they can out of the data—doing so can result in treating noise in the data as meaningful, a problem termed *overfitting* (Brighton and Gigerenzer 2012).

Allocation across multiple options is also required when one must compete against an opponent on different "battlegrounds," or arenas of competition. Two rivals vying for the attention of a potential mate, for instance, may have to decide whether to best the other in terms of strength, or cunning, or stamina—how should these competitors allocate their efforts to develop each trait? (The same kind of decision is faced by two businesses competing for customers—should they allocate their development efforts to make their product lighter, or cheaper, or more stylish?) Such allocation decisions have been formalized in the Colonel Blotto game (Borel 1921), in which two players with armies of possibly different sizes are to meet on a number of battlefields and must first decide how many army units to assign to each field. Then one of the fields is chosen at random, the size of the two players' forces on that field are revealed, and the player with more units assigned there wins the battle. The game-theoretic solution to this problem is for stronger players to allocate all of their units to all of the fields randomly according to a uniform distribution—a simple heuristic similar to equity, not requiring any information about the battlefield options. Weaker players should give up entirely on a proportion of the fields, depending on their relative strength, and they should use a random, uniform distribution of forces on the remaining fields. And these are essentially the strategies that people follow, both in abstract and business-content settings (Avrahami et al. 2011), producing near-optimal outcomes with simple allocation heuristics from the adaptive toolbox.

2.2. Heuristics for Finding Resources

The heuristics just described can make good choices among available options by searching for and using little information about each alternative. In many decision situations, however, the options are not currently available but must be discovered, as when looking for employees, or jobs, or new business opportunities. The traditional rational approach prescribed by economists in such cases is to look for more alternatives until the cost of further search outweighs any potential benefits (Stigler 1961) and then take the best alternative seen so far. But real-world searches typically do not allow such an approach, as the costs of searching for further options may be largely unknown, their potential benefits may be uncertain, and it might not be possible to return to a previously seen option. Given the prevalence and adaptive importance of sequential search problems that our ancestors had to face, including mate choice (pursue this person now, or wait for a better possibility later?), habitat selection (stop my migration here, or keep moving and look some more?), and hunting (is this antelope as good as I can get, or should I hold out for a bigger one?), we can hypothesize the presence of simple heuristics in the adaptive toolbox for making good sequential decisions.

The challenge of these ubiquitous sequential search problems is that, whatever the option you currently have available—for instance, the job offer you are considering right now—another, possibly better option could become available in the future. Even worse, if you decide not to take this option now, it may be gone if you change your mind and wish to return to it later—someone else may have taken that job. Given these challenges, how can you decide when to stop searching and pursue the current option?

We can begin to get a sense of what kind of heuristic approach is appropriate for such sequential searches by considering a problem of this form that has been well-studied in probability theory, known as the secretary problem or the dowry problem (Ferguson 1989). As the secretary problem, it goes like this: A firm wishes to hire a secretary with the highest available typing speed. The human resources (HR) department collects a pool of one hundred available applicants with an unknown distribution of typing speeds, and arranges to interview each person in succession, in each case asking the applicant's typing speed.. However, because the secretary market is competitive, HR must decide at each interview whether the current applicant is the one out of one hundred with the highest typing speed and hire that person on the spot, or to let them go and not be able to recall them later (because they will be hired elsewhere).

In a search situation like this, where the distribution of available alternatives is unknown, and there is no recall and no switching between alternatives (only one final choice can be made), then searching with an aspiration level can be appropriate—what Simon (1990) called satisficing heuristics. In particular, search can be divided into two phases. In the first phase, alternatives are just looked at without selecting any of them, so that the searcher can gather information about the available options. This information is used to set an aspiration level at the minimum value that the searcher will accept in further search. The second phase consists of looking at additional alternatives until one is found that exceeds the aspiration level set in phase 1. Search is stopped at that point, and that alternative is chosen. (In the case of the secretary problem, where the searcher is trying to maximize the chance of picking the single best alternative, the phase 1 search should go through 37% of the available alternatives; see Ferguson 1989; Todd and Miller 1999.) And indeed, Seale and Rapoport (1997) experimentally investigated sequential search behavior in this simplified setting, and found that most people used a satisficing *cutoff rule* as predicted (though their search was typically shorter than optimal).

But this simple secretary search problem leaves out common complications seen in the real world. There are often competitors who are searching through the same set of options simultaneously, hiring away secretaries before we can even interview them and thus forcing us to speed up our search (Todd 2007). Even more constraining, many important search decisions are two-sided, which means the searchers are being searched in turn at the same time, and choice must therefore be mutual. Secretaries and other job applicants not only seek offers but also decide about those offers themselves, selecting their employers and being selected by them. This added challenge of mutual search can be solved by the searchers on both sides learning about *themselves*—their own relative position within their pool of fellow searchers. Such learning can be based on events such as having one's application or job offer rejected or accepted. Searchers can then use this self-knowledge to determine how high they should aim in their search aspirations (Todd and Miller 1999), rather than merely setting an aspiration level based on the values of a small sample of available options, as in one-sided search.

A simple heuristic learning mechanism that all the searchers can use to solve this problem is to start with very high aspirations and then lower them over time if they fail to find a match that they like and who likes them in return (Kalick and Hamilton 1986). Such a simple strategy can work to get all parties involved in the search matched up with a partner of roughly equal standing to themselves (that is, there is high within-pair correlation in terms of standing or value)—but this matching process can take a long time, as frustrated low-standing searchers have to repeatedly lower their aspirations until they find an acceptable and willing partner. Another heuristic approach can result in faster matching: actively learning one's relative standing among searchers based on feedback received during the first phases of search and setting one's aspiration level near one's own standing (Todd and Miller 1999). This assumes that individual searchers do not know their own standing in the market ahead of time, but must learn it through the interactions they have with others. For instance, a new company hoping to hire a secretary may not know how attractive its jobs are to people in this town, so the more interest it gets (the more serious applications, say), the higher it can raise its self-appraisal and its aspirations for an acceptable secretary; and the more surprising rejections it gets (e.g., the more applications withdrawn after an applicant visits their office), the lower it should set its aspirations. The job-hunting secretaries can do the same, based on the offers and rejections they receive. Over time, both sides will adaptively adjust their aspirations, with the result that mutually acceptable offers between matched employers and employees will emerge.

Such aspiration-adjustment search heuristics have been tested extensively in simulation to find versions that work well to enable a population to pair up quickly in good matches (Todd and Miller 1999). Because they model the mutual sequential mate-search process that humans often engage in, they have also been tested empirically in the mate-search domain and have been found to account for the patterns of choices that people make when searching for long-term marriage partners (Todd, Billari, and Simão 2005) or for relationships in speed dating (Beckage et al. 2009). Given that the job-search process and the hunt for business partners for new ventures has roughly the same mutual sequential choice structure as searching for a mate, these kinds of search heuristics may be triggered and used in these situations as well, guiding useful learning of one's own bargaining position rather than blind attempts to make offers to or rejections of potential partners. Research on how and when such heuristics may be used should thus be an important topic of study for organizational behavior.

For both one-sided and two-sided (mutual) search, the process of exploration before choosing an option is followed by a period of exploiting (making use of) that option. But many search problems also require switching back from exploitation to exploration again at some point—for instance, after the product has been used up or the job has become unrewarding. This is akin to *patch-leaving* decisions in animal foraging behavior—as a food patch becomes depleted, the animal must decide at some point that it will get more reward on average if it leaves this patch and explores to find a new one. Humans and other animals use simple heuristics to decide when to leave a patch and switch from exploiting to exploring, based for instance on the time spent in a patch so far or how long it has been since the last reward was found in this patch (Wilke, Todd, and Hutchinson 2009; Hutchinson, Wilke, and Todd 2008). Whether similar heuristics are also triggered and used in business search settings that call for adaptive switching between exploration and exploitation remains to be explored in further research as well.

2.3. Selecting Appropriate Heuristics

How does the mind choose which cues to use in a given situation, and, equally important, which strategy to process them with? In both cases, evolution could have given us tendencies (or certainties) to use particular cues and strategies, if past decision environments were stable for long enough. In situations that are more evolutionarily novel or variable, our cue and strategy choices may be based on simple learning mechanisms that keep track of the frequency of co-occurrence of cues and outcomes or that adjust the likelihood of using different strategies based on reinforcement received after past use (Rieskamp and Otto 2006). Finally, when more than one decision strategy can be called on, we may use a higher-level strategy-choice heuristic, which itself should be fast and frugal for the same reasons that apply to the individual strategies. All of these possibilities, and when they hold, must be explored further.

3. THE TOOLKIT OF EVOLUTIONARY PSYCHOLOGY

Evolutionary psychology offers a framework for understanding how the mind solves the problem of tool selection. One area in which this issue has been addressed is the emotions. Tooby and Cosmides (2008) argue that emotions can be thought of as a coherent set of computations that are specialized for confronting particular constellations of adaptive problems. Because the mind consists of many different specialized systems, those mechanisms designed for the relevant problem need to be recruited and the other mechanisms suppressed.

Consider fear, for instance. When there is something dangerous in the environment—perhaps a predator, or an enemy—appropriate measures might include the activation of the sympathetic nervous system, the suppression of the digestive system, increasing attention to possible escape routes, and so on. These responses are, obviously, very different from what the mind should do when a very different prospect is faced, such as the appearance of a highly desirable mate. In that case, a very different set of mechanisms should be activated and deactivated.

Crucially, some means is needed to determine which emotional response should be set in motion. The front end of the system that Tooby and Cosmides (2008) propose, therefore, is a set of mechanisms designed to detect which fitness-relevant problem or opportunity is currently being faced (i.e., problems or opportunities related to survival and reproduction). For example, to the extent that there are reliable cues of danger, such as snakes or predatory mammals, these cues should activate the most useful emotional response, allowing the individual to deploy appropriate attention and behavior, given the pending threat.

This idea can be applied to decision making. Problems faced by individuals might have cues that differentially activate or deactivate different elements of the "toolbox," allowing the individual to apply procedures most suited to the problem at hand. This suggests that many aspects of the decision problem that are not relevant under standard economic theories might still be expected to influence behavior. To take one simple example, consider a public goods game (PGG). In the PGG, several subjects are given an endowment and have the opportunity to allocate this money to two different accounts, a private account and a public account. Money placed in the private account is theirs to keep, and money placed in the public account is increased in value and shared equally among players. These two accounts allow an assessment of cooperation or prosociality; players maximize earnings (within a round) by keeping money in their private account, but aggregate wealth is maximized by putting money in the public account.

Kurzban (2001) ran this game, but with modifications that, according to traditional models, should have no effect. In particular, he had participants exchange brief, oblique glances with one another. The idea was to activate psychological mechanisms associated with social coordination, and thereby increase one's motive to benefit others. This minimal manipulation caused an increase in contributions to the group account, though there were sex differences—the effect occurred in males but not females. We next review several other examples from the experimental economics literature in which the observed pattern of results can be explained by viewing minds as program selectors rather than incentive chasers.

3.1. The Double Auction

If it is true that different decision-making contexts recruit different modular systems, then it should be possible to predict behavior once one knows the relevant environmental cues that give rise to different sets of computations. Crucially, the argument that we are making here is not one of "subtraction," as though one can remove all of the cues from an experiment, leaving "only" the structural features in place. Instead, our approach here is one that is better represented by the notion of mapping, in which properties of the experiment—the physical setting, the language used, pragmatic elements, and so on—activate different computational mechanisms.

Under some conditions, the cues in experimental settings can evoke behaviors that correspond to the prediction of economic models. Arguably one of the best examples of this is the double auction, used by Vernon Smith and colleagues during the early years of experimental economics. In the canonical double auction, subjects are assigned roles of buyers and sellers of an abstract commodity. Each participant is assigned a value for the commodity. So, for instance, a buyer might have a value of $1.00 for the first item they buy, and their payoff from that item is simply $1.00 minus the price the buyer pays. The same applies symmetrically for sellers, who earn the price the buyer pays minus their assigned cost for that item. Experiments occur over a series of rounds in which buyers place bids and sellers place asks. In early work in this area, these studies were run by hand, with experimenters recording bids, asks, and—if a price was accepted after a bid or ask was made—transactions. Now these studies are often run electronically, allowing the efficient gathering of a large amount of data.

Strikingly, across a substantial number of variations of this basic design, subjects' aggregate behavior is extremely well predicted by standard rational choice models, even though key assumptions required by the model do not hold. Specifically, buyers and sellers in these experiments typically have access only to their private information; they do not know the values that other buyers and sellers have for the items. With this limited information, prices converge quickly to the predicted equilibrium.

From the point of view of any particular participant, the task is relatively straightforward. They have a very limited range of actions—making bids and accepting offers—and making profitable trades requires only making offers less than the value and bids less than the cost. Further, the setting is one that Smith (1998) refers to as "impersonal exchange," with few cues that might give rise to the sense that one is a part of a cooperative group. Rather, the ambiance evokes—not accidentally—a stock exchange, in which agents are competing with one another to get the best deals and make the most money, even if doing so comes at the expense of other agents. Thus the cues in this setting invoke the selection and use of simple money-increasing trade choice mechanisms from the mind's toolbox.

3.2. Public Goods

In contrast to double auctions, public goods games, described above, seem to recruit mechanisms designed not just for maximizing net benefits for the self, but rather for social relationships. Because contributing nothing to the public good maximizes individuals' financial payoff, economists considering public goods games have entertained the idea that contributions to the public good might be mistakes (Andreoni 1995; Kurzban and Houser 2001; Muller et al. 2008), which would explain the frequently-replicated result that contributions decline over time because subjects learn the incentives of the game.

However, contributions might be thought of as intentional and motivated rather than the result of confusion. The structure of the game makes the trade-offs between one's own outcomes and those of the group obvious, as does the typical language used in such games, which might include reference to a "group account" or a "public account," though terminology differs. It seems likely, then, that such games might be thought of as not only involving systems that can compute costs and benefits, but also other systems designed to deal with social problems, perhaps including reciprocal altruism systems (Trivers 1971), alliance-building systems (DeScioli and Kurzban 2009b), coalitional systems (Kurzban, Tooby, and Cosmides 2001), and systems designed around conforming to moral norms (DeScioli and Kurzban 2009a and 2013).

There is considerable evidence that computations associated with social rather than only material considerations are being applied in these settings. In addition to the findings alluded to above, a number of results point to a role for social computations. For instance, individual differences in dispositions to be altruistic positively predict cooperativeness (Kramer, McClintock, and Messick 1986). Further, manipulations that create "group identity" (such as decreasing group size) increase contributions to the public good (Brewer and Kramer 1986; Kramer and Brewer 1984). An additional body of work with public goods contexts shows that contribution decisions depend on others' contributions, suggesting an important role for reciprocal psychology (Bornstein and Ben-Yossef 1994; Kurzban et al. 2001; Kurzban and DeScioli 2008).

Finally, one reason that people contribute in public goods games might have to do with avoiding punishment for not contributing. There is evidence that not contributing to public goods—or, its functional equivalent, consuming a common pool resource—is viewed as a moral wrong (Cubitt, Drouvelis, and Gächter 2011). In public goods games that have a punishment round, people tend to punish low contributors (Fehr and Gächter 2002; Yamagishi 1986), which in turn seems to increase cooperation (see also Carpenter and Matthews 2004; Ostrom, Walker, and Gardner 1992; Yamagishi 1988).

Taken together, these results imply that in addition to cost/benefit computation systems, public goods games might recruit mechanisms from the mind's toolbox that are associated with prosociality, reciprocity, and the avoidance of social censure. These factors might explain why, in contrast to double auction experiments, public goods experiments do not yield results consistent with self-interest theories.

3.3. Dictator Games

Finally, as a third illustrative example, consider the Dictator Game (DG), in which one person, the Dictator, has an allotment of experimenter-provided money to allocate between themselves and another subject, the Recipient. In contrast to the prediction one would make if people simply money-maximized, instead of keeping the entire stake, subjects routinely give a third to a half of the money away (Camerer 2003, 57–58). More relevant to our focus here, however, is that the DG is sensitive to framing effects (e.g., Branas-Garza 2007). That is, keeping the structural features of the decision constant—the subject is always faced with a decision to allocate resources to self and another entity—behavior can change considerably depending on the details of how the game is presented.

Hoffman, McCabe, and Smith (1996), for example, varied "social distance," the anonymity of decisions, and found that this factor matters a great deal. Dictators who are completely anonymous give less than those who are not (see also Bohnet and Frey 1999). Indeed, even the sense that one is being observed—the presence of eye spots on a computer screen—can give rise to larger transfers than when eye spots are absent (Haley and Fessler 2005). Further, Cherry, Frykblom, and Shogren (2002) showed that when subjects earn the role of Dictator by virtue of their performance on a quiz, they keep a substantially greater fraction of the endowment. Indeed, when the money is earned and the double-blind conditions that Hoffman, McCabe, and Smith (1996) used are combined, Dictators keep nearly all the money.

3.4. Summary

Economic analyses frequently take divergence from the predictions of classical models as the phenomenon to be explained, as if money-maximizing behavior were the default. To be sure, in some contexts, as in the double auction research discussed above, people conform reasonably well to the predictions of classical models. These studies make subjects look like they are both capable of computing the money-maximizing choice and also interested in making that choice. The mechanisms that give rise to these choices are, we note, no less the product of evolution than other mechanisms. Rational behavior should not be seen as the default, as though no further explanation is required, but as behavior that also must be explained (Cosmides and Tooby 1994). That is, we reject the notion that behavior is *either* rational *or* psychological (as in Gigerenzer 2000, vii). Behavior that conforms to neoclassical predictions—rationality—is itself a psychological phenomenon and hence the outcome of evolved mechanisms.

As the examples above show, different contexts recruit other systems, including those that give rise to behavior that has been dubbed "other-regarding" or "prosocial." Public goods games are one example in which altruism mechanisms are activated to a greater or lesser extent. Dictator games are wide open to framing effects. These results suggest that in addition to cost/benefit computations, other computations, specifically social computations, influence decisions.

This last point bears some expansion. Recently, there has been a substantial effort to conduct behavioral economics experiments cross-culturally (Henrich et al. 2001). In this line of work, common games such as the Dictator Game, Ultimatum Game, and Public Goods Game are implemented in anthropological field sites, keeping the instructions and methods as similar to one another as possible (Henrich et al. 2005). The results of these studies show substantial cross-cultural variation. Recently, Henrich et al. (2010) suggested that the best predictor of results across cultures is "market integration," which they define as the fraction of calories in local diets that are purchased (as opposed to hunted or gathered). They suggest that this finding is driven by the fact that fairness norms are required to facilitate trust in societies with transactions among strangers.

This explanation is plausible, but it also seems plausible that other factors are at work. If, as some have argued, the cues present in experiments of this type leave ambiguity about the most relevant cognitive mechanisms, then it is possible that subjects look for properties of the game as described and map its features onto something richly culturally elaborated. For instance, Jean Ensminger, working with the Orma in Kenya, reported that when the research assistants learned the structure of the public goods game, they spontaneously linked it to *harambe* the practice of producing public goods in a community, such as public schools. Ensminger (2004, 376) specifically locates the explanation for behavior in the PGG with the familiarity with *harambe*: "Orma were more willing to trust their fellow villagers not to free ride in the public goods game because they associated it with a learned and predictable institution."

As Hagen and Hammerstein (2006) put it, "Little is currently known about the frames players are using to interpret the experimental economics games" (346). Experimental games, as they are typically constructed, remove, by design, features that might influence how the game is construed by subjects. This allows the subject wide latitude in how they construe the game. Future work should be aimed at understanding how the cues that subjects encounter in these games—or the lack of cues—influence which information-processing mechanisms are recruited when playing them.

4. COORDINATING DECISION MECHANISMS WITH OTHER AGENTS

Organizations consist of a complex mixture of distinct types of relationships. Organizations often have a formal organizational chart that specifies the authority relationships between individuals in the group—who makes which decisions and who reports to whom. There are also exchange relationships, specified in contracts, that describe individuals' obligations to provide each other with goods, services, and monetary compensation. These explicit representations of authority and exchange relationships are, of course, only part of the social landscape. A strong-willed employee might end up bossing around a manager more often than vice versa (like the title character in the television series *House*). An employer might have various side deals set up with workers not specified in the formal contract. In addition, there are other types of relationships such as family, friends, or romantic partners. Two coworkers might be having an affair, likely affecting how they operate together as a team. An executive might feel protective of a nephew, helping him rise through the organizational ranks, which could provoke animosity among the nephew's peers. In sum, people's relationships within organizations have many layers of complexity. To operate successfully in this social context, individuals need to map the relationships in their environment and to dexterously navigate those relationships.

In this regard, organizations do not differ from other human groups, including the groups that our human ancestors long inhabited over evolutionary history. Just as camels are exquisitely well-designed for life in the desert, and polar bears are outfitted with mechanisms for life in the arctic, so too humans have evolved specialized adaptations for living in complex social groups. These include cognitive mechanisms that map and track one's own and others' social relationships, forming an internal model of the social environment that guides behavior adaptively. Humans interact with other humans to accomplish a variety of goals, and these different goals give rise to fundamentally different types of relationships, including family, friends, mates, trade partners, leader-follower, teacher-student, and so forth. People have a "toolkit" of specialized social decision mechanisms for solving problems that are distinct to each type of relationship.

Researchers have begun to specify the different types of relationships that people form, which can serve as a guide to the tools we expect to find in the mind's toolkit for working on social tasks. Fiske's Relational Models Theory holds that people's social interactions are shaped by distinct cognitive models, including communal sharing, equality matching, and authority ranking (Fiske 1992). Communal sharing relationships involve helping others according to their needs and can include close family relationships and in-group relationships. Equality matching relationships involve exchanging goods and favors, as in trade relations or business partnerships. Authority ranking relationships involve asymmetries in power, such as a general's relationship to a soldier or a manager's relationship to an employee. Similarly, Bugental (2000) identified five domains of social relationships: attachment, coalitions, mating, reciprocity, and hierarchical power. Kenrick, Li, and Butner (2003) offered a framework of six distinct goals that people pursue in their social interactions: coalition formation, status-seeking, self-protection (against out-groups), courtship, maintaining romantic relationships, and parent-child relationships. There is also evidence for an important distinction between power relationships based on coercion versus authority based on prestige, ability, and willingness to teach others (Henrich and Gil-White 2001). Finally, there is research indicating that close friendships function as alliances (DeScioli and Kurzban 2009b, 2011; DeScioli et al. 2011).

In sum, converging evidence from a number of sources and literatures indicates that people's social relationships are governed by specialized mental models of distinct relationship types—a social toolkit. Although there is no consensus on the precise composition of the social toolkit, it is likely to include familiar relationship types such as family, parent-child, siblings, mates, trade partners, close friends, enemy, leader-follower, teacher-student, and in-group–out-group. This social alphabet allows the human mind to parse the social world into distinct types of relationships and to apply the most relevant information-processing algorithms and behavioral routines to a particular social interaction. It is generally not functional to kiss your enemy and punch your spouse, or bow to your student and chastise your boss. Cognitive models of the social world fine-tune the mind's computations and behavioral outputs to the distinct adaptive problems associated with different kinds of relationships.

4.1. Matching and Mismatching Social Models

As discussed above, having a diverse toolkit gives rise to the problem of choosing the best tool for a particular job. This problem is especially difficult in the social realm, because the best tool for the job often *depends on the tool that someone else chooses*. Consider a man who meets an attractive female and represents the interaction in a courtship frame in which he flirts and makes sexual advances toward the woman. The woman may represent the situation in the same way, in which case mutual courtship may ensue; or she may instead represent the man as a coworker with whom she has a business-oriented monetary relationship. If the man fails to perceive or to acknowledge which decision frame the woman is applying, he risks ending up with charges of unwanted attention. That is, the costs and benefits for the man applying a mating model to his interaction *depend on which model the woman applies*. It is similarly true of this hypothetical woman that her best course of action often requires a correct assessment of how the man models their interactions, for instance, so she can avoid inadvertently encouraging his subtle advances.

It is worth stepping back for a moment to see how new and different this problem is, compared to choosing tools in nonsocial circumstances. When you choose the best screwdriver for a screw, you do not have to worry about what the screw is going to do. When an organism chooses the best algorithm for navigating a landscape, it does not have to worry that the landscape might choose a new geometry for dealing with the navigator. In social interactions, however, there are multiple decision-making mechanisms tuning each person's behavior to the other's. It is like navigating a moving landscape that can move specifically *in anticipation of your moves*.

How do you anticipate the moves of a system that is anticipating your own moves? This readily leads to an infinite regress in which I anticipate you anticipating me anticipating you . . . and so on. To a computational system like the mind, this recursion could be deadly, spurring a loop that could freeze information-processing and essentially disable the organism. Clearly, the mind needs to avoid these disasters, and it is well designed to do so. Nonetheless, we have all experienced a taste of this brimming chaos as we sweat over the myriad possible meanings of some glance, or a turn of phrase, or a veiled insult in the context of uncertain relationships.

Game theory can offer some insight into how to solve problems in which the best course of action depends on others' decisions (Schelling 1960). For instance, one approach to the problem of infinite recursion is to compute recursively *only until recursive computations converge on the same solution*. When additional recursive processing keeps returning the same best solution, then computation ceases. This is an "equilibrium" concept in the sense that the best move becomes stable against additional recursive processing. It is one example of a decision rule that could help alleviate the problem of coordinating decision mechanisms between agents. One could imagine that adding tens or hundreds more similar rules could create a system that is robust against infinite loops of recursive anticipations.

Fortunately, however, humans have more than the bare logic of game theory to help them coordinate relationships. Humans have content-rich evolved cognitive mechanisms that use many cues to identify appropriate models of their social interactions. Moreover, these cues are enhanced by culturally transmitted inventions that further help demarcate the lines between different types of relationships. A man and a woman who meet in a nightclub can be more confident that the other person models them as a potential mate than if they meet in a bank, simply by virtue of their location. A boxer can be fairly confident that his opponent models him as an adversary, by virtue of the preexisting context of the sport, without specific computations about the particular opponent's mindset.

Another way that people tune their cognitive devices to others' mental models is to enforce the distinctions between different types of relationships. People do this by regarding behavior that blurs the boundary between different relationship types as taboo (Fiske and Tetlock 1997). Selling your car to a friend blurs the line between communal friendship, characterized by caring for the others' needs, and a trade relationship, in which self-interested bargaining is appropriate. Within organizations, managers and workers must choose whether to interact as equal peers or as authorities and subordinates. Crude jokes, for example, might be appropriate with peers but deemed taboo with one's boss. Similarly, sexually enticing dress might be appropriate at a nightclub but viewed as taboo in the office because it blurs the lines between sexual and nonsexual relationships. There can even be conflicts between workplace-appropriate models, such as authority and exchange. An employee might demand a raise from the boss while viewing this as appropriate bargaining behavior within an exchange framework. The boss, however, might view this behavior as insubordination within an authority framework, leading to conflict between them.

4.2. Friendship versus Exchange

One relationship distinction that seems particularly relevant for organizations is the difference between exchange relationships and friendships. Most modern organizations depend heavily on exchange, specifically on the exchange of goods and services for monetary compensation. This is true of interactions both within and between organizations. As a result, people often apply a cognitive model of exchange (e.g., "equality-matching," Fiske 1992; "reciprocity," Bugental 2000) to their organizational relationships, seeing these relationships in terms of costs, benefits, and obligations for repayment. At the same time, however, organizations also create a social world in which people are likely to form close friendships. Coworkers might become best friends, or business partners might develop mutual concern that goes beyond caring only about profits and the bottom line.

The overlap of relationships raises the issue that exchange relationships and friendships are understood via different cognitive models and, moreover, these models have important conflicts. This is why, for example, folk wisdom holds that you should not sell your car to a good friend. In Fiske's relational models theory, exchange relationships operate according to equality matching and reciprocity, in which people share resources with others only to the extent that reciprocation is expected; that is, giving is accompanied by an obligation to repay. In contrast, friendship is a communal relationship in which individuals are primarily concerned with meeting their partner's needs (see also Clark and Mills 1979). (This is not to deny that good management style can also include building personal relationships within an organization that work well because of mutual trust and understanding, sharing many features with friendship.) Experimental research supports this distinction, showing that people keep careful accounting of their acquaintance relationships but not their close friendships (reviewed in DeScioli and Kurzban 2009b).

What then is the functional logic of friendship? Why are people concerned with their friend's well-being, over and above the friend's ability to repay favors? A recent theory explains human friendship in terms of alliances (DeScioli and Kurzban 2009b and 2011; DeScioli et al. 2011). The theory holds that friendship is caused by evolved cognitive mechanisms that function to assemble a support group of allies for potential conflicts. When humans get into disputes, they tend to recruit help from others—a strategic element that is markedly different from fighting behavior in most other animals. To perform well in human conflict, individuals need others who will take their side. Friendships appear to perform this function. Given an alliance function, it is not difficult to see why friends are genuinely concerned about each other's needs. By helping their friends, people are improving the capabilities of their allies and so strengthening their own alliance support. This logic of alliances is particularly apparent on the international stage, in which nations often help each other in disputes without expectation of specific repayment, as when the United States gave resources to Britain during WWII in the Lend-Lease program, which Churchill famously described as the "most unselfish and unsordid financial act of any country in all history."

DeScioli and Kurzban (2009b) tested the alliance hypothesis for friendship by looking at people's perceptions of their ten closest friends. Participants answered questions about each friend, including questions about the benefits received from the friendship, similarity, frequency of contact, duration, age, sex, and traits such as intelligence and attractiveness. For the key alliance measure, participants were asked how they thought each friend would rank the participant among other friends. This variable of relative rank is critical for alliances because friends are unlikely to support you if they have a closer relationship with your adversary. Hence, the reliability of an ally depends how many stronger alliances they have with others. The alliance hypothesis therefore predicts that people will most value friends who rank them above others. This prediction was confirmed by the data. Relative rank was the best predictor out of a dozen variables, outperforming traditional variables such as benefits received, similarly, and frequency of contact. In short, the alliance hypothesis turned up a new key variable, perceived relative rank, which was previously overlooked in decades of relationship research.

In a second study, DeScioli and colleagues (2011) tested the alliance hypothesis by using web crawlers to gather a massive dataset of best friendships ($n = 3,445,329$) on the social network MySpace. MySpace has a Top Friends feature in which users rank their friends, allowing a test of the predictive power of perceived rank among other variables. Consistent with alliance models, an individual's choice of best friend was strongly predicted by how candidate partners rank that individual. The key alliance variable, relative rank, outperformed more traditional variables, including geographic proximity and popularity, by a substantial margin.

The crucial distinction between exchange and friendship raises cautions for individuals in organizational settings. It is important to determine whether a person views a relationship primarily as an exchange based on profits or as a friendship based on loyalty and concern for others' needs. This will determine which tools are used for each interaction and what the reaction may be. For example, a company might switch to a new supplier who offers a lower price. If the old supplier views this decision in the context of exchange, then the switch will be understandable, because a company is expected to maximize profit. However, if the old supplier viewed the company as a friend and ally, the switch could be viewed as a severe betrayal and might cause the old supplier to reject all future transactions, even trades that maximize profit on both sides.

5. CONCLUSIONS

Humans in organizations, like all organisms, are goal-seeking and therefore must make decisions to reach their goals. Good decisions are made not by knowing everything but by using a small number of the most useful available cues, even a single cue in some cases, processed by appropriate, boundedly rational cognitive tools. A primary challenge is then choosing the best cognitive tool for the job. How do decision makers know what tools to use for a given situation? This knowledge is supplied by the evolutionary process both directly and via evolved learning algorithms for selecting or constructing tools for particular problems. To choose the right tool, the mind needs additional cognitive mechanisms that use cues to identify adaptive problems and then activate the most relevant programs from the cognitive toolkit.

Using this approach, we can understand social behavior in economic games that is not well explained by previous theories. People's behavior is shaped by the set of cognitive tools activated in particular environments, and these tools can be subtly manipulated by modifying the cues used by the tool-choosing mechanisms. Further, interpersonal relationships in organizations can be understood as strategic problems. In these situations, the best tool depends on what tool other people choose. This leads to complex tool-selection systems and phenomena such as boundary-setting between different types of relationships.

Managers and leaders can apply this perspective by considering how the organizational and institutional environment triggers particular tools and cue sets in people. Environmental structures created to influence the behavior of individuals are sometimes felicitous, as when governments figure out how to get citizens to donate organs by default or how to design traffic laws for intersection right-of-way in a hierarchical manner that matches our one-reason decision mechanisms (Bennis et al. 2012). In other cases, institutions create environmental structures that do not fit well with people's decision mechanisms, and instead cloud minds and lead to poor choices. For instance, information about medical treatments is often represented in misleading ways (Kurzenhäuser and Hoffrage 2012), casinos make people think the chance of winning is much greater than it really is (Bennis et al. 2012), and store displays and shopping websites crowded with lists of features of different products can lead people to experience information overload and possibly avoid making any choice (Fasolo, McClelland, and Todd 2007). But it might be possible to fix such poor designs and make new ones that are more user-friendly by using research from evolutionary psychology and ecological rationality to design environments that better fit the human mind. Rather than using only rewards and punishments to change people's behavior, an appropriately designed environment can fit with the decision mechanisms available in the mind's adaptive toolbox to solve problems quickly and efficiently. With better knowledge of that tool set and the problems for which it is suitable, we can more appropriately shape the organizational environment to include cues that trigger the decision mechanisms that are most productive in a given situation (e.g., cues for sensible levels of risk-seeking in investment, cooperation with coworkers, competition with rival firms, loyalty with partners, etc.).

Moreover, organizations themselves, like individual organisms, can be understood as goal-seeking machines. The evolved human cognitive toolbox for collaboration is diverse enough to generate an endless variety of human organizations, ranging from small bands of hunters to huge modern corporations. And these infinite variations are themselves subject to selection, allowing cultural evolution to fine-tune, even further, organizational structures for competition against other organizations. By virtue of sharing the special property of goal-seeking behavior, organizations and organisms have more in common than it might seem—in particular, to pursue goals effectively, they both must make good choices. Thus it might be profitable to apply the perspective of evolved decision-making mechanisms presented in this chapter to the question of how organizations themselves—as distinct from the individuals in them—make the choices that determine their fate. This is an open area for further exploration.

The evolutionary perspective on decision making described in this chapter offers a new and profitable way to explore the relationship between cues and choice behavior in organizational contexts. This framing helps to explain why and how some cues in organizational settings activate mechanisms designed for choices based on recognition, allocation of resources, search for opportunities or partners, individual selfishness, status-striving, signaling one's value as a friend or mate, and so on. Considering the mind's evolved decision mechanisms also enables us to see how organizational environments can be modified so that the cues they embody lead to the use of decision procedures that advance, rather than undermine, the goals of the organization.

Notes

1. The term *equity* here would typically be replaced by *equality* in organizational behavior.

References

Andreoni, J. 1995. Warm glow versus cold pickle: The effects of positive and negative framing on cooperation in experiments. *Quarterly Journal of Economics* 110:1–22.

Avrahami, J., Kareev, Y., Todd, P. M., and Silverman, B. 2011. Allocation of resources in competition: The effects of meaningfulness. Manuscript.

Bateson, M., Nettle, D., and Roberts, G. 2006. Cues of being watched enhance cooperation in a real-world setting. *Biology Letters* 12:412–14.

Beckage, N., Todd, P. M., Penke, L., and Asendorpf, J. B. 2009. Testing sequential patterns in human mate choice using speed dating. In *Proceedings of the 2009 Cognitive Science Conference*, ed. Niels Taatgen and Hedderik van Rijn, 2365–70.

Bennis, W. M., Katsikopoulos, K.V., Goldstein, D. G., Dieckmann, A., and Berg, N. 2012. Designed to fit minds: Institutions and ecological rationality. In Todd, Gigerenzer, and the ABC Research Group 2012, 409–27.

Bohnet, I., and Frey, B. S. 1999. The sound of silence in prisoner's dilemma and dictator games. *Journal of Economic Behavior and Organization* 38:43–57.

Borel, E. 1921. La théorie du jeu et les équations intégrales á noyau symétrique. *Comptes Rendus de l'Académie des Sciences* 173:1304–8. Reprinted in English, 1953, as The theory of play and integral equations with skew symmetric kernels. *Econometrica* 21:97–100.

Borges, B., Goldstein, D. G., Ortmann, A., and Gigerenzer, G. 1999. Can ignorance beat the stock market? In Gigerenzer, Todd, and the ABC Research Group 1999, 59–72.

Bornstein, G., and Ben-Yossef, M. 1994. Cooperation in intergroup and single-group social dilemmas. *Journal of Experimental Social Psychology* 30:52–67.

Bowles, S. 2008. Policies designed for self-interested citizens may undermine "the moral sentiments": Evidence from economics experiments. *Science* 320:1605–9.

Branas-Garza, P. 2007. Promoting helping behavior with framing in dictator games. *Journal of Economic Psychology* 28:477–86.

Brewer, M. B., and Kramer, R. M. 1986. Choice behavior in social dilemmas: Effects of social identity, group size, and decision framing. *Journal of Personality and Social Psychology* 50:543–49.

Brighton, H., and Gigerenzer, G. 2012. How simple heuristics exploit uncertainty. In Todd, Gigerenzer, and the ABC Research Group 2012, 33–60.

Bröder, A. 2012. The quest for take-the-best: Insights and outlooks from experimental research. In Todd, Gigerenzer, and the ABC Research Group 2012, 216–40.

Bugental, D. B. 2000. Acquisition of the algorithms of social life: A domain-based approach. *Psychological Bulletin* 126:187–219.

Camerer, C. 2003. *Behavioral game theory: Experiments in strategic interaction.* Princeton, NJ: Princeton University Press.

Carpenter, J. P., and Matthews, P. H. 2004. Why punish? Social reciprocity and the enforcement of prosocial norms. *Journal of Evolutionary Economics* 14:407–29.

Cherry, T. L., Frykblom, P., and Shogren, J. F. 2002. Hardnose the dictator. *American Economic Review* 92:1218–21.

Clark M. S., and Mills J. 1979. Interpersonal attraction in exchange and communal relationships. *Journal of Personality and Social Psychology* 37:12–24.

Cosmides, L., and Tooby, J. 1994. Better than rational: Evolutionary psychology and the invisible hand. *American Economic Review* 84:327–32.

Cubitt, R. P., Drouvelis, M., and Gächter, S. 2011. Framing and free riding: Emotional responses and punishment in social dilemma games. *Experimental Economics* 14: 254–72.

Darwin, C. 1859. *The origin of species.* London: Murray.

Davis, J. N., Todd, P. M., and Bullock, S. 1999. Environment quality predicts parental provisioning decisions. *Proceedings of the Royal Society of London B: Biological Sciences* 266:1791–97.

Dawkins, R. 1976. *The selfish gene.* Oxford: Oxford University Press.

DeMiguel, V., Garlappi, L., and Uppal, R. 2009. Optimal versus naive diversification: How inefficient is the 1/N portfolio strategy? *Review of Financial Studies* 22:1915–53.

DeScioli, P., and Kurzban, R. 2009a. Mysteries of morality. *Cognition* 112, 281–99.

———, and Kurzban, R. 2009b. The alliance hypothesis for human friendship. *PLoS ONE* 4:e5802.

———, and Kurzban, R. 2011. The company you keep: Friendship decisions from a functional perspective. In *Social Judgment and Decision Making,* ed. J. I. Krueger, 209–25. New York: Psychology Press.

———, and Kurzban, R. 2013. A solution to the mysteries of morality. *Psychological Bulletin* 139:477–96.

———, Kurzban, R., Koch, E. N., and Liben-Nowell, D. 2011. Best friends: Alliances, friend ranking, and the MySpace social network. *Perspectives on Psychological Science* 6, 6–8.

Ensminger, J. E. 2004. Market integration and fairness: Evidence from ultimatum, dictator, and public goods experiments in East Africa. In *Foundations of Human Sociality: Economic Experiments and Ethnographic Evidence from Fifteen Small-Scale Societies*, ed. J. Henrich, R. Boyd, S. Bowles, C. Camerer, E. Fehr, and H. Gintis, 356–81. Oxford: Oxford University Press.

Fasolo, B., McClelland, G. H., and Todd, P. M. 2007. Escaping the tyranny of choice: When fewer attributes make choice easier. *Marketing Theory* 7 (1): 13–26.

Fehr, E., and Gächter, S. 2002. Altruistic punishment in humans. *Nature* 415:137–40.

Ferguson, T. S. 1989. Who solved the secretary problem? *Statistical Science* 4:282–96.

Fiske, A. P. 1992. The four elementary forms of sociality: Framework for a unified theory of social relations. *Psychological Review* 99:689–723.

———, and Tetlock, P. E. 1997. Taboo trade-offs: Reactions to transactions that transgress the spheres of justice. *Political Psychology* 18:256–60.

Gigerenzer, G. 2000. *Adaptive thinking: Rationality in the real world*. New York: Oxford University Press.

———, Dieckmann, A., and Gaissmaier, W. 2012. Efficient cognition through limited search. In Todd, Gigerenzer, and the ABC Research Group 2012, 241–74.

———, and Goldstein, D. G. 1996. Reasoning the fast and frugal way: Models of bounded rationality. *Psychological Review* 103:650–69.

———, and Goldstein, D. G. 1999. Betting on one good reason: The take the best heuristic. In Gigerenzer, Todd, and the ABC Research Group 1999, 75–95.

———, and Selten, R., eds. 2001. *Bounded rationality: The adaptive toolbox*. Cambridge, MA: MIT Press.

———, and Todd, P. M. 1999. Fast and frugal heuristics: The adaptive toolbox. In Gigerenzer, Todd, and the ABC Research Group 1999, 3–34.

———, Todd, P. M., and the ABC Research Group. 1999. *Simple heuristics that make us smart*. New York: Oxford University Press.

Gneezy, U., and Rustichini, A. 2000. A fine is a price. *Journal of Legal Studies* 29:1–18.

Goldstein, D. G., and Gigerenzer, G. 2002. Models of ecological rationality: The recognition heuristic. *Psychological Review* 109:75–90.

Hagen, E. H., and Hammerstein, P. 2006. Game theory and human evolution: A critique of some recent interpretations of experimental games. *Theoretical Population Biology* 69, 339–48.

Haley, K. J., and Fessler, D. M. T. 2005. Nobody's watching? Subtle cues affect generosity in an anonymous economic game. *Evolution and Human Behavior* 26: 245–56.

Henrich, J., Boyd, R., Bowles, S., Camerer, C., Fehr, E., Gintis, H., and McElreath, R. 2001. In search of *Homo economicus*: Behavioral experiments in 15 small-scale societies. *American Economic Review* 91:73–78.

———, Boyd, R., Bowles, S., Gintis, H., Fehr, E., Camerer, C., et al. 2005. 'Economic Man' in cross-cultural perspective: Ethnography and experiments from 15 small-scale societies. *Behavioral and Brain Sciences* 28:795–855.

———, Ensminger, J., McElreath, R., Barr, A., Barrett, C., Bolyanatz, A., et al. 2010.

Markets, religion, community size, and the evolution of fairness and punishment. *Science* 327:1480–84.

———, and Gil-White, F. J. 2001. The evolution of prestige. *Evolution and Human Behavior* 22:165–96.

Hertwig, R., Davis, J. R., and Sulloway, F. J. 2002. Parental investment: How an equity motive can produce inequality. *Psychological Bulletin* 128:728–45.

———, Hoffrage, U., and the ABC Research Group. (2013). *Simple heuristics in a social world*. New York: Oxford University Press.

Hoffman, E., McCabe, K., and Smith, V. L. 1996. Social distance and other-regarding behavior in dictator games. *American Economic Review* 86:653–60.

Huberman, G., and Jiang, W. 2006. Offering vs. choice in 401(k) plans: Equity exposure and number of funds. *Journal of Finance* 61:763–801.

Hutchinson, J. M. C., and Gigerenzer, G. 2005. Simple heuristics and rules of thumb: Where psychologists and behavioural biologists might meet. *Behavioural Processes*, 69:97–124.

Hutchinson, J. M. C., Wilke, A., and Todd, P. M. 2008. Patch leaving in humans: Can a generalist adapt its rules to dispersal of items across patches? *Animal Behaviour* 75:1331–49.

Kahneman, D., Slovic, P., and Tversky, A., eds.. 1982. *Judgment under uncertainty: Heuristics and biases*. Cambridge: Cambridge University Press.

Kalick, S. M., and Hamilton, T. E. 1986. The matching hypothesis reexamined. *Journal of Personality and Social Psychology* 51:673–82.

Kenrick, D. T., Li, N. P., and Butner, J. 2003. Dynamical evolutionary psychology: Individual decision rules and emergent social norms. *Psychological Review* 110:3–28.

Kramer, R. M., and Brewer, M. B. 1984. Effects of group identity on resource use in a simulated commons dilemma. *Journal of Personality and Social Psychology* 46:1044–57.

———, McClintock, C. G., and Messick, D. M. 1986. Social values and cooperative response to a simulated resource conservation crisis. *Journal of Personality* 54:101–17.

Kurzban, R. 2001. The social psychophysics of cooperation: Nonverbal communication in a public goods game. *Journal of Nonverbal Behavior* 25:241–59.

———, and DeScioli, P. 2008. Reciprocity in groups: Information-seeking in a public goods game. *European Journal of Social Psychology* 38:139–58.

———, and Houser, D. 2001. Individual differences and cooperation in a circular public goods game. *European Journal of Personality* 15:S37–S52.

———, McCabe, K., Smith, V. L., and Wilson, B. J. 2001. Incremental commitment and reciprocity in a real time public goods game. *Personality and Social Psychology Bulletin* 27:1662–73.

———, Tooby, J., and Cosmides, L. 2001. Can race be erased? Coalitional computation and social categorization. *Proceedings of the National Academy of Sciences* 98:15387–92.

Kurzenhäuser, S., and Hoffrage, U. 2012. Designing risk communication in health. In Todd, Gigerenzer, and the ABC Research Group 2012, 428–53.

Muller, L., Sefton, M., Steinberg, R., and Vesterlund, L. 2008. Strategic behavior and learning in repeated voluntary contribution experiments. *Journal of Economic Behavior and Organization* 67:782–93.

Ostrom, E., Walker, J., and Gardner, R. 1992. Covenants with and without a sword: Self-governance is possible. *American Political Science Review* 86:404–17.

Pachur, T., Todd, P. M., Gigerenzer, G., Schooler, L. J., and Goldstein, D. G. 2012. When is the recognition heuristic an adaptive tool? In Todd, Gigerenzer, and the ABC Research Group 2012, 113–43.

Payne, J. W., Bettman, J. R., and Johnson, E. J. 1993. *The adaptive decision maker.* Cambridge: Cambridge University Press.

Pinker, S. 1997. *How the mind works.* New York: W. W. Norton.

Rieskamp, J., and Otto, P. E. 2006. SSL: A theory of how people learn to select strategies. *Journal of Experimental Psychology: General* 135:207–36.

Schelling, T. C. 1960. *The strategy of conflict.* Cambridge, MA: Harvard University Press.

Seale, D. A., and Rapoport, A. 1997. Sequential decision making with relative ranks: An experimental investigation of the "secretary problem." *Organizational Behavior and Human Decision Processes* 69:221–36.

Simon, H. A. 1990. Invariants of human behavior. *Annual Review of Psychology* 41:1–19.

Smith, A. 1776. *Wealth of nations.* London: W. Strahan and T. Cadell.

Smith, V. L. 1998. The two faces of Adam Smith. *Southern Economic Journal* 65:1–19.

Stigler, G. J. 1961. The economics of information. *Journal of Political Economy* 69: 213–25.

Todd, P. M. 2000. The ecological rationality of mechanisms evolved to make up minds. *American Behavioral Scientist* 43:940–56.

———. 2007. Coevolved cognitive mechanisms in mate search: Making decisions in a decision-shaped world. In *Evolution and the social mind: Evolutionary psychology and social cognition,* ed. J. P. Forgas, M. G. Haselton, and W. von Hippel, 145–59. Sydney Symposium of Social Psychology Series. New York: Psychology Press.

———, Billari, F. C., and Simão, J. 2005. Aggregate age-at-marriage patterns from individual mate-search heuristics. *Demography* 42:559–74.

———, and Gigerenzer, G. 2007. Environments that make us smart: Ecological rationality. *Current Directions in Psychological Science* 16:167–71.

———, and Gigerenzer, G. 2012. What is ecological rationality? In Todd, Gigerenzer, and the ABC Research Group 2012, 3–30.

———, Gigerenzer, G., and the ABC Research Group. 2012. *Ecological rationality: Intelligence in the world.* New York: Oxford University Press.

———, and Miller, G. F. 1999. From pride and prejudice to persuasion: Satisficing in mate search. In Gigerenzer, Todd, and the ABC Research Group 1999, 287–308.

Tooby, J., and Cosmides, L. 1992. Psychological foundations of culture. In *The adapted mind,* ed. J. Barkow, L. Cosmides, and J. Tooby, 19–136. New York: Oxford University Press.

———, and Cosmides, L. 2008. The evolutionary psychology of the emotions and their relationship to internal regulatory variables. In *Handbook of emotions,* 3rd ed., ed. M. Lewis, J. M. Haviland-Jones, and L. F. Barrett, 114–37. New York: Guilford.

Trivers, R. L. 1971. The evolution of reciprocal altruism. *Quarterly Review of Biology* 46:35–57.

———. 1972. Parental investment and sexual selection. In *Sexual selection and the descent of man, 1871–1971* ed. B. Campbell. Aldine-Atherton.

Tversky, A., and Kahneman, D. 1981. The framing of decisions and the psychology of choice. *Science* 211:453–58.

———, and Kahneman, D. 1986. Rational choice and the framing of decisions. *Journal of Business* 59:S251–S278.

Wilke, A., Todd, P. M., and Hutchinson, J. M. C. 2009. Fishing for the right words: Decision rules for human foraging behavior in external and internal search tasks. *Cognitive Science* 33:497–529.

Wübben, M., and Wangenheim, F. V. 2008. Instant customer base analysis: Managerial heuristics often "get it right." *Journal of Marketing* 72:82–93.

Yamagishi, T. 1986. The provision of a sanctioning system as a public good. *Journal of Personality and Social Psychology* 51:110–16.

Yamagishi, T. 1988. Seriousness of social dilemmas and the provision of a sanctioning system. *Social Psychology Quarterly* 51:32–42.

TEN

Primal Business: Evolution, Kinship, and the Family Firm

Nigel Nicholson

OVERVIEW: THE FITNESS OF FAMILY FIRMS

In 2011, one of the world's leading, publicly traded family businesses—News Corporation International, headed by Australian media tycoon, Rupert Murdoch—was enveloped in scandal around allegations of illegal phone-hacking, collusion with the police, and invasions of privacy. This was clearly a turning point in the history of one of the world's leading family firms, compounded more recently by the quite public breakup of Murdoch's third marriage, raising fresh questions about ownership and inheritance. Without making comment on the political and ethical arguments swirling around this case, it is possible to look more dispassionately at it as a human drama, consistently explicable within the framework of evolutionary science.

One can see this thoroughly modern business as a contemporary manifestation of a primal business model of families working together on an enterprise to benefit their kin and their surrounding community. It is not unknown for this model to fail in the contemporary context—there are numerous recent examples (Gordon and Nicholson 2008)—through excessive nepotism, insularity, corruption, blinkered decision making, excessive attachment to relationships or products, succession disasters, or internecine warfare among kin or between kin and non-kin. At the same time, there are many exemplary family firms that stand the test of time and outperform their competitors (Dyer 2006; Miller and Le-Breton

Miller 2005). They do so through their capacity for fast and flexible decision making, indelible high-trust relationships with all their stakeholder groups, and powerful, positive family bonds and values suffused throughout the business—in short their ability to command an inimitable, sustainable, competitive advantage through their familial culture (Nicholson 2008). NewsCorp has shown both sides of this bivalence (Tagiuri and Davis 1996).

In this chapter I aim to show how family business is both a key topic in its own right that benefits greatly from evolutionary analysis, but I also use it as an exemplar to demonstrate the integrative capacity of evolutionary theory. In particular, I intend to show how one of the leading edges of evolutionary thought is about historical change: how coevolutionary forces shape our social institutions and the fate of business forms.

My argument proceeds through the following steps. First, I discuss the role of kinship in evolutionary theory and then the nature and status of the family as a vehicle for adaptive fitness. Then I discuss the intersection of work and kinship that family businesses embody and how their bivalent patterns of failure and success can be explained by evolutionary theory. This develops into a discussion in more detail of interior family dynamics of cooperation and conflict and how they are manifest in family firms, as well as what determines their differential patterns of adaptive and maladaptive form and function. I conclude with consideration of another leading edge of evolutionary theory—its treatment of the self, and how this may relate to the key topic of leadership.

BIOLOGY AND KINSHIP

The family is a fundamental biological entity. It can be defined as members of a species who interact and often co-reside for the purposes of procreation and the nurturing of offspring (Davis and Daly 1997). In many species this is a highly transient association, but in others—many birds, mammals, and some reptiles—the care of the young and mutual provisioning require more prolonged co-residence (Emlen 1997). Among primates, the family assumes even greater significance as a building block in complex social organization, reaching its most refined form in the clan, whose structure comprises interlocking family groups (Harcourt and Stewart 2007; Meder 2007). Families take many different forms. In some species pairs bond to provide exclusive and interchangeable care for their offspring. In others one finds haremic systems, where a single male corrals several females and their shared offspring. Among primates, one finds highly communal forms, with collective and reciprocal care for offspring and interbreeding among both related and unrelated group members (Imanishi 1960).

These kinship systems are closely coupled with the environmental niches and challenges that species face; that is, they are adaptive to contexts and the cycles of change that recur predictably within them, thereby constituting solutions to the problem of maximizing reproductive fitness over a range of recurrent circumstances (Megarry 1995). Kinship systems are born of multilevel selection processes. At the individual level, sexual selection, natural selection, and kin selection (the latter meaning design features and dispositions that aid the bearers of shared genes) direct the drives and orientations of individuals toward specific social forms, including mating preferences, nurturance of the young, competition, status seeking, display, and social preferences (Cummins 2005; Tudge 1998).

COEVOLUTION AND THE HUMAN FAMILY

The historical development of kinship forms follows the logic of coevolution: human preferences shape social structure, including familial forms, which are simultaneously units of selection and socialization (Keesing 1975); that is, they are at the heart of the recursive processes of coevolution (Boyd and Richerson 1985). At the widest level of the breeding community, one finds among some species, especially the Great Apes, manifestations of what amounts to culture (Ghufran 2009; Sommer and Parish 2010). These are socially evolved customs in such elements as tool use, grooming, and forms of display (McGrue 1992). They have arisen to facilitate provisioning and social organization. These vary in ways that meet and master the selective pressures of their ambient environments, such as river, mountain, or forest habitats. Species and subsets of species adapt to the ecology of their environments, including such inputs as the presence of pathogens, predators, climate variation, and symbiotic relations with other life forms.

Relations within and between species—for example, between predators and prey—play a part in coevolutionary development, whereby changes in context act as filters for phenotypic fitness; that is, characteristics that confer advantage at one time can become liabilities at others (Darwin and Carroll 2003). This coevolutionary reasoning applied to humans has become known as dual inheritance theory, according to which cultures and genes coevolve. Cultures form critical aspects of the context within which the expression of genes results in successful or unsuccessful phenotypes (Henrich 2004; McElreath and Henrich 2007; Richerson and Boyd 2005; Sober and Wilson 1998). The ability of most adults to absorb lactated milk is an early example, arising during the millennia that witnessed the first agrarians and pastoralists.

So intense is human sociality that it is no exaggeration to say that other humans have always been a central focus of the context to which we must adapt. For something like a hundred and seventy thousand years, our species foraged and hunted in nomadic clans across savanna and tundra plains, bonded together by a loose, fluid, and largely egalitarian, clan-based social organization (Erdal and Whiten 1996; Whiten 1998). With the advent of agriculture and fixed settlements about ten thousand years ago, our adaptive focus shifted toward our cultural creations and social institutions (Klein and Edgar 2002). Religions, customs, social rules, and structures of authority historically altered the rules of the genetic inheritance game by shifting the criteria for selection. Sexual selection is especially open to this kind of moving bias—for example, tough fighters may be preferred in times of conflict, while intelligent and inventive partners are preferred in times of peace and plenty (Van Vugt, Hogan, and Kaiser 2008). The dual inheritance process is recursive, of course, which implies that humans can shape their own evolution via the adoption of norms and creation of cultures, a cultural form of what evolutionary theory terms "niche construction" (Laland 2007). Interestingly, these are not always adaptive, and, as history has shown us, some cultural forms prove unsustainable (Betzig 1993; Harris 1979). The story of family business is a microcosm of social experimentation: an intersection of culture, market and business environment, and kinship.

Humanity embodies many features that reflect our primate ancestry plus some distinctive aspects. All are social, but we humans have a particularly intense sociality—necessitated by the prolonged vulnerability of the neonate and facilitated by such factors as concealed female ovulation (Strassmann 1981). Alloparenting (parenting by non-kin) and adoptive relationships are common (Hrdy 2009) in our species. These factors favor complexity and fluidity in the human group, including the acceptance of adoptive and affinal (non-kin) relationships. We are inclined to give relatedness the benefit of the doubt. This is important, for adoptive relationships, though generally successful, are also risky and one of the chief causal factors implicated in violence against children (Daly and Wilson 1985).

The genius of the human design, and the source of our capacity for global domination as a species, is highly adaptive and multiformed social organization. This arises partly from the factors identified above—namely, a propensity for group living and great flexibility in ways of living—as well as from special features of the human design (Barrett, Dunbar, and Lycett 2002). Principal among these are (1) tool use of great sophistication; (2) language facility of remarkable complexity; and (3) reflexive self-consciousness. Together these facilitate the power to imagine, create, and inhabit institutions and cultures.

THE CULTURAL EVOLUTION OF KINSHIP

Cultures frame and are regulated by systems of rules that govern how people work and live together, in the form of marriage laws, moral codes, inheritance rules, courtship customs, and various taboos. These forms differ widely, and contemporary evolutionary anthropologists identify both the selective pressures that give rise to these variations and their residue in human culture and history (Cronk and Gerkey 2007). Peoples of the desert, mountains, and rivers have evolved distinctive conventions of kinship and sociality that reflect the constraints of their environments—natural hazards, food supply, resources, competition, threat, warfare, and the like (Low 2007). Religions are examples as cultural schema that guide people by codes that match the needs of their times—for example the simultaneous rise of industrialization and Protestantism.

Although the contingent link between environments and cultures is strong (Sperber 1996; Wilson 1998), it is not determining. As Richerson and Boyd (2005) show, there is a degree of arbitrariness, or rather willed choice, in the systems we adopt. The authors present examples of tribes living under identical conditions who, having adopted different marriage, inheritance, and property laws reap quite different outcomes, to the degree that the more successful colonize the less successful. Such assimilation is a major engine of cultural evolution. Richerson and Boyd argue that the norms of former cultures persist as residues in conditions where they no longer have relevance. They cite research identifying the roots of the culture of honor that persists in the southern United States, from their European pastoralist origins, where reputation is part of one's defense against marauding thieves, in contrast to the more confident, easygoing, and law-abiding agrarians of neighboring regions (Nisbett and Cohen 1996). One may reflect that such cultural echoes play a part in the cross-cultural variation to be found in family firms around the globe and even within polyglot economies.

This raises an important point. All forms of social organization are successful to the degree that they are able to serve simultaneously the contingencies and challenges of ambient environments, on the one hand, and the dispositions, needs, and interests of the people who inhabit them on the other (Foley and Lahr 2011; Sperber 1996). The former are apt to change faster than the latter, many of which are species-general. The imperfections in this coevolutionary lock-step are what lead organizations, institutions, and indeed entire social systems to fail, as did communism, for example, by not meeting either requirement. In that case the ideology came into fundamental conflict with human instincts, partly because it deliberately incorporated the Lamarckian fallacy of the inheritance of acquired characteristics. It also failed to deliver economic outcomes that could satisfy the people's interests in consumption (Brenner 1993).

ADAPTATION AND DYSFUNCTION IN FAMILIES

The reasoning discussed above applies to the family. In many areas of the developed world, families are under great stress as divorce, poverty, lone parenting, homelessness, drug dependency, and crime afflict communities (Brandwein, Brown, and Fox 1974; Seccombe 2000). It has been suggested that widening wealth inequalities are responsible for weakening the bonds of cohesion and community that have hitherto marked our success as a species (Wilkinson 1996). In other words the untethering of market forces under capitalist economic systems is proving problematic for our communal human nature. To put it another way, economics has trumped our psychology: short-term incentives of consumption have damaged our long-term interests. This is fundamentally a problem of self-regulation—the psychological processes by which we defer gratification and plan for the long term (Carver and Scheier 1998; Karoly 1993).

Yet despite current dire prognostications about the breakdown of the family, it persists as an institution because of its unique capacity for efficient adaptation and need fulfillment (Becker 1981). However, cultural evolution is changing the shape, structure, and functioning of the family in ways that make it more fragile, coincidentally with increased complexity of demand. As societies develop economically, the strategy of maximizing fitness by maximizing one's family size (spreading the risk and sharing the labor) shifts decisively to concentrating parental investment in fewer offspring (due to reasonably assured longevity and increased resource competition). Thus one sees the amorphous, large family clan being supplanted by the "beanpole" family structure—"tall" from increasing numbers of generations co-locating, and narrow from the reduced number of offspring (Markson 2003). This structural change has profound implications for the shape of family business. First, there is reduced choice in role adoption/allocation for family members and, by implication, greater risk to performance. A corollary is the shift, already occurring in areas of fallen birth rate, to greater emphasis on "responsible ownership" than on executive leadership, which is becoming increasingly professionalized (Family Business Network 2007).

FAMILIES AND WORK

The account just provided is also the story of family business. Among hunter-gatherers there is no concept of institutionalized work, nor of leisure; there are merely tasks that must be shared and executed if the community is to survive, supported by voluntary activities conducted for pleasure, such as adornment, education, and entertainment (Boehm 1999; Chagnon 1997; Coon 1979; Sahlins 1972; Whiten 1998). The division of labor is highly gendered. Males hunt, especially at long distance; females forage closer to the natal home range, yet many activities are shared between the sexes, including the making and use of tools for everyday living. The advent of agriculture brought increased structure to both time and place (Diamond 1997). Work now took place around fixed settlements, with the rhythm of life dictated by the seasons. Long periods of simple self-maintenance were punctuated by periods of intense activity. Crafts grew in importance, along with a host of activities associated with fixed settlements, but work and family were closely intertwined as units of both production and consumption. Innovations in transportation provided the basis for division of labor and the first industries (Landes 1998). The rest is history, as they say, as we have galloped into a world of commerce, trade, industrialized production, and financing.

Family businesses were among the first business organizations, and have persisted in markets. The oldest family business still in existence is a Japanese construction firm founded in 578, and multigenerational family firms have figured in every society up to the present day (O'Hara 2004), except where private ownership has been prohibited. But even in such systems, families often work together in the same factories as well as living together (Grieco 1988). Kinship bonds are compelling, offering security, belonging, and developmental opportunities. Family members generally help each other, as we discuss shortly (Stewart 2003).

Around the world, family businesses persist as a form, arguably because they represent one of the prime remaining examples of how work and love—two fundamental needs according to Freud and evolutionary theory—can be reconciled (Babcock 1998). Expressions of positive sentiments and shared, goal-directed activity are central to the continuing appeal of family firms. From an economic standpoint, they also solve an important agency problem: uniting accountability with ownership (Jensen and Meckling 1976). They raise other issues, which we explore below, but it does appear from an evolutionary perspective that they are the form of business that is closest to our nature, satisfying our preference for high trust exchange within a communal structure, with permeable and flexible boundaries between economic and social interests (Stewart 2003).

The popularity of the form is evidenced by its endurance, prevalence, and strength. Endurance is measured by age—and in addition to the Japanese construction company, many family firms have endured for well beyond double figures of generations of existence, giving the lie to the adage "clogs to clogs in three generations" ("shirtsleeves to shirtsleeves" in modern parlance), a maxim that occurs in many languages and cultures, capturing the belief that in family business the first generation founds the enterprise, the second develops it, and the third wastes the assets (Ward 2004). There is clearly no inevitability to this life cycle, though it does express the critical challenge that family firms face at key junctures of intergenerational transition (Kepner 1991), about which we say more later. We should also note that all small firms have a rising "death curve," called "the liability of newness" in entrepreneurship (Freeman, Carroll, and Hannan 1983). Part of the association with intergenerational succession is spurious—firms of all kinds at around the time a family business reaches its third generation may sell out or dissipate their assets, for a variety of reasons.

Indeed, one may observe that, far from weakening ties to the firm over generations, succeeding generations may feel a stronger attachment and obligation to keeping the firm going as part of its legacy and bloodline. However, what truth there is in the adage does stem from intergenerational discontinuities, which I discuss shortly.

The prevalence of family firms is universal. In every country with established market economies, family businesses make up a large proportion of total firms, in most between 60% and 90% (Colli 2003; Gersick et al. 1997). This calculation needs to be qualified by the observation that family firms are concentrated in the smaller, private, and unlisted sectors of business and hence account for a lower proportion of total employment—around 27% in the United States, for example (Shanker and Astrachan 1996; Astrachan and Shanker 2006). As in many other economies, a large proportion of total US employment is accounted for by workers in big listed corporations or in the public sector. How you count the numbers also depends on how you define a family business (Rothausen 1999). This is not a simple matter—high estimates are arrived at by including first-generation, founder-owned and run businesses, which may be justified on the grounds that many will continue to develop into multigenerational businesses. At the other end of the spectrum are large public corporations in which families retain a substantial interest, such as Ford or Wal-Mart. We need not dwell on the issue, but note that family businesses are found in every economy for the reasons we have discussed—they are attractive as a "primal" form of organization.

THE UNIQUENESS OF FAMILY FIRMS

The strength of family firms comes from their unique characteristics. Much controversy is visible in the literature about the advantages and disadvantages of family firms. Some agency theorists assert that families are vulnerable to various kinds of moral hazards, especially altruism (e.g., nepotistic bias in resource allocation) (Schulze et al. 2001; Schulze, Lubatkin, and Dino 2003). Their argument runs that the sentiments and self-interest of family members lead them to make decisions and take actions that run counter to the economic interests of the firm. There is some truth in their argument, so the question is whether the countervailing advantages of family outweigh these risks, or whether the agency hazards can be easily overcome. The answer is that they can, to a degree. The strength (and vulnerability) of family firms comes from four sources, shown in figure 10.1.

1. Co-ownership by a kin-related group
2. Intergenerational transmission of ownership
3. Teamwork between kin and non-kin
4. Genetic wildcard inheritance

This also illustrates the risks associated with family firms. The point here is that the advantages of the primal origins of family firms are also points of weakness in the hyperrational world of market economies.

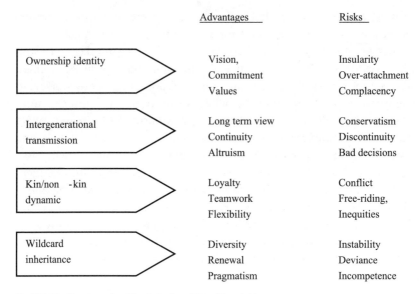

	Advantages	Risks
Ownership identity	Vision, Commitment Values	Insularity Over-attachment Complacency
Intergenerational transmission	Long term view Continuity Altruism	Conservatism Discontinuity Bad decisions
Kin/non-kin dynamic	Loyalty Teamwork Flexibility	Conflict Free-riding, Inequities
Wildcard inheritance	Diversity Renewal Pragmatism	Instability Deviance Incompetence

Fig. 10.1 What's unique about family business? Benefits and risks

Ownership Identity

Family co-ownership is the "genetic shareholding" that lends a business a grounded identity and a sense of purpose. This biological common interest enables the owners to generate an unusual degree of attachment to, and involvement with, what they own and produce—as one observer put it, there is great significance in having the "family name above the door" (Brokaw 1992). The benefits are high attention to quality, service, customer and supplier relations, and ethical conduct, plus access to extended and durable network structures (Aldrich and Cliff 2003).

The risks, in the world of changing markets and complex, high-speed decision-making, are over-attachment, insularity, complacency, and failures to seek advice (Gordon and Nicholson 2008).

Intergenerational Transmission

Intergenerational transmission transforms the nature of the firm's assets into a source of value that is inextricably linked with the fitness of the founder's bloodline stretching into the future. The mere possibility of the title and ownership of the business being handed through generations of a family completely alters the dynamic of the enterprise, making even first-generation owners of family firms inclined to take a view beyond their own life span. As Anderson and Reeb (2003) put it in their study of the performance advantage of quoted family firms, "Founding families view their firms as an asset to pass on to their descendants rather than wealth to consume during their lifetimes" (1305). The family is the primary mechanism for the transmission of identity beyond one's life span (Emlen 1982), which gives family firms a special power to imbue their family owners and managers with meaning, self-sacrifice, and altruism. By-products include long-term strategic and financial perspectives (Aronoff, Ward, and Visscher 1995), "patient capital" to go with their extended time horizons (Donckels and Frohlich 1991), and a preference for financial strategies that will not put the firm at risk (Dreux 1990).

The dark side of these advantages is discontinuity at points of intergenerational transition, and overly conservative and risk-averse approaches to strategic and financial decisions, through their concern for preservation (Lyagoubi 2006). The agency hazard of altruism also arises from this factor.

Teamwork between Kin and Non-kin

Teamwork between kin and non-kin is essential for any family business to grow beyond the dimensions of a mom-and-pop store. Humans can be hostile to strangers, but are also more inclined to trade with them than fight (Ridley 1996), for cooperation and coalition with non-kin is much more essential to our success as a species than is "tooth and claw" conflict (Richerson and Boyd 1999). Kinship, rather than dividing groups, can be the glue that holds unrelated people together by providing a cultural nucleus than embraces non-kin in an inclusive clan-like spirit. As I have analyzed elsewhere, a chief source of advantage to family firms is their culture (Nicholson 2008). It is the ability of a firm to contribute "family capital" to the culture—the added value conferred by family identity with a business—that generates competitive advantage through social capital (Habbershon and Williams 1999; Nahapiet and Ghoshal 1988; Tokarczyk et al. 2007). This is achieved typically by value-driven leadership, often with a stewardship orientation that is coupled with effective partnership between kin and non-kin (Gomez-Mejia, Nunez-Nickel, and Gutierrez 2001; Miller and Le-Breton Miller 2006).

The risks include conflicting goals between owning and non-owning executives, family members free-riding, and inequitable treatment across the family/nonfamily divide (Ainsworth and Cox 2003; Gomez-Mejia, Larraza-Kintana, and Makri 2003).

Wildcard Inheritance

Wildcard inheritance refers to the behavioral genetics of families. Family members resemble each other much less than we might expect from a simple view of inheritance. Although many of the individual differences most associated with voluntary behavior—values, interests, personality, and abilities—are highly heritable (40–90% by most estimates from twin studies), most are encoded in non-additive gene combinations (Ilies, Arvey, and Bouchard 2006). Other factors coming to light in genetics, such as genomic imprinting, epigenesis, horizontal gene transfer, and gene regulatory networks also show how the genotype is not determined solely by the forces of selection (Fodor and Piatelli-Palmarini 2010). The net result is a low correlation on psychological attributes between parents and children and between siblings, with the exception of identical twins (Lykken et al. 1992). This has potential advantages, such as the dynamics of naturally occurring diversity and renewal from the infusion of new perspectives. One can also reason—as I have heard family business owners and leaders state—that knowing they are secure in their position gives family leaders an incentive to be "servant" leaders (Greenleaf 1991)—surrounding themselves with talent, making pragmatic decisions, and avoiding self-interested and ego-defensive posturing. The risks of this randomness are the various negative consequences that come from defects of will and character that might befall family executives and owners, brought about by failures to assess the fit between individual characteristics and the demands of roles in the business (Gordon and Nicholson 2008; Judge, Piccolo and Kosalka 2009).

The overall challenge for family firms is to capture their primal advantage in their culture and operations. One way of looking at this is that they experience more extreme centrifugal and centripetal forces than other kinds of organizations. The centrifugal forces are the scope for disagreements among people who did not choose each other as associates; and the centripetal are the bonds of genetic relatedness that give them an overriding, shared genetic interest. In other words, they can tolerate more conflict than other kinds of firms because they have stronger bonds of affiliation to rescue them. But this is a risky game, and interpersonal conflicts prove to be most destructive of family firms.

THE DARWINIAN DYNAMICS OF THE FAMILY FIRM

This logic of the preceding discussion explains away any empirical controversy about the pros and cons of family firms. This amounts to a recognition that family capital, principally embodied in the inclusive ethos of the culture and the high-trust relationships among stakeholders (Nicholson 2008), has attendant risks through its dependence on the existence of a healthy family dynamic. The survivors who get it right have tangible advantages and enjoy a performance premium, yet it is a challenge to get to that point (Dyer 2006). Family firms have liabilities beyond "newness" in the shape of their emotional configurations. "Two sides of the same coin" is a well-worn cliché, but it does apply here—the bonds that create family capital are liable to interfere with the rational order of the firm, bias outcomes, and create irreparable fracture lines (Tagiuri and Davis 1992). The apparent controversies around whether family firms perform better or worse than nonfamily firms is not only a methodological or empirical problem but also a theoretical and operational one. Conventional measures of performance do not recognize the intangible value created by family firms—such as social capital, longevity, and philanthropy.

At root the problem is that merging these two orders—the emotional and the rational; work and nonwork—works well in the fluid communal context of tribal living, though even here family disputes can be a source of disruption, but in the segmented domains of modern living, they require strong discipline to be reconciled. Let us look at this on two levels: the potential areas of conflict that are species universals and those that are specific and unique to families.

Four Kinship-Conflict Dynamics

There are four forms of universal tensions in family firms that are biogenetic in origin, and they are common sources of derailment: nepotism, parent-offspring conflict, affinal bonds, and sibling rivalry.

Nepotism

Nepotism, the principle of favoring kin over non-kin, as we have said, is the glue that holds families and their enterprises together (Neyer and Lang 2003). Elsewhere I have written about what I call the "as if principle" (Nicholson 2000)—the idea that in the EEA (the environment of evolutionary adaptedness; the context in which humans evolved) dealing with a "stranger" was an exceptional occurrence—we mostly co-acted within communities of familiars, entering at birth and exiting at death. This means that now when we interact with people who are new to us, we quickly give them our trust, making an instinctive, implicit (favorable) assumption that we "know" them (unless they markedly differ from us in appearance and custom). This is one of the most important and least discussed features of modern life—how we cooperate in large-scale social entities with numerous bonds of trusting interdependence. Moments of betrayal by strangers are thus extremely painful and disappointing to us, often creating a lasting disposition to suspicion. The homophily phenomenon is underpinned by the "as if" principle (McPherson, Smith-Lovin, and Cook 2001), as is its converse, the tendency for stereotyping, low-trust dispositions toward people who are manifestly and physically different from us—implicitly not of our tribe—which is a prime cause of racism and other forms of discrimination (McVeigh and Sikkink 2005).

Family firms, like other businesses, have homophilic tendencies, drawing their staff from familiar constituencies. Mostly they are embraced by the family culture, but with the implicit understanding as to whose tribe it is. The climate of even the most enlightened family firms tends to have a paternalistic ethos, generating among their employees an aura of appreciative deference to the leading family. Nepotism toward the next generation is expected, even welcomed by members of the community, as a mark of commitment and continuity—valued in a world where market uncertainties often weaken loyalties. Loyalty is indeed a prominent value in family firms. This is also accompanied in many of them by secrecy and privacy, for family firms are notoriously impenetrable and autonomous. They run on cash with low debt, and when they do borrow, in many cultures they do so via interlocking networks of connections with banks and other investors. Indeed, successful family firms are often so cash-rich that their family offices operate as de facto private equity providers.

Senior nonfamily professionals are often reluctant to enter this world, and they are not always welcomed. This of course is fatal to growth, and "tissue rejection" by families of incoming executives is a recurrent problem (Gordon and Nicholson 2008). To overcome it, firms need to take special steps in terms of a prolonged and careful courtship process of mutual selection. This has to set clear boundaries of powers, accountabilities, and expectations, as well as governance structures that bring clarity and confidence to decision making. Such careful steps to achieving integration are increasingly needed, for the demography of the family makes it ever more imperative to integrate non-family leadership successfully. As commentators are apt to note, the future of the family firm is one of "responsible ownership," with the bulk of executive decision making devolved to the professionals.

The second universal source of tension is parent-offspring conflict. Nepotism arises because of genetically shared interests—family is favored over nonfamily, according to the kin-selection principle. One may expect parents and offspring to have substantial shared interests, alongside their 50% shared genes. They do, and the harmony of many family firms is born of the love between generations. Yet, as Trivers (1974) pointed out, the potential for conflict lies in the 50% that is not shared. Parents have a powerful interest in seeing their genetic investment come to best fruition (as they see it) and will be concerned that their 50% material investment is wisely deployed by their offspring. Children, on the other hand are conscious that their 100% self-interest is self-directed. The scene is set for a battle for control—well-meaning parents seeking to shape their children's destiny to ensure the continued prosperity of the genes they carry, and children seeking to wrest control and resources from their parents to achieve power and autonomy.

In many family firms, parent-offspring conflicts are visible as battles of will through various proxies, such as the strategic direction of the firm, which, of course, is the repository of the entire family's wealth and resources—the embodiment of its genetic shareholding. Parent-offspring conflict occurs in four combinations—compounded by gender. The two same-sex combinations—father-son and mother-daughter—are infused with parents' consciousness of knowing what is best from their own experience and the children's desire to differentiate themselves from same-sex role models. In the case of father-son relations, there is another potential amplifier of conflict: competitive egos (Davis and Tagiuri 1989). Sons are apt to assert and test their growing confidence and competence, and fathers apt to defend theirs against the weakening of age. Old stag and young buck lock horns in trials of proof. Nor are mothers and daughters immune from competition.

Historically documented conflicts between fathers and sons have periodically risen to extreme levels. Shakespeare dramatized many examples, including those where mothers ally themselves conspiratorially with a son's interests. This makes perfect sense in gene politics, for the bond with their offspring is much superior to the non-genetic, affinal bond they have with their mate—even in history to the point of patricide. In family wars, wives and mothers have often taken an important but largely hidden role in seeking to advance the interests of their children over those of their partners (Gordon and Nicholson 2008).

The third source of potential conflict is the affinal bond—the union between unrelated adults. There is an extensive literature on the biology of human mating and the biochemistry of love, and how it engineers bonds of passion that last long enough to give the best chance for more material commitments (offspring) to form the basis of a more lasting union (Fischer 2004; Kelly and Dunbar 2001). Thereafter the shared genetic investment in the young provides a platform for the endurance of family life. Assortative mating—young adults freely engaging in mate choice spurred by shared interests—is the foundation of the platform (Luo and Klohnen 2005), though in many cultures and traditions the interests of parents for political alliances between family clans directs more engineered partnerships. Arranged marriages, dowries, and the bride-price are part of the economic architecture of parental power.

Potential conflicts of interest are averted by the structure of rules and exchange (Harris 1977). In the context of family firms, these play a part by cementing business interests together via marriage and also ensuring that status—a key value in the dynamics of mate choice—is not compromised (Kaye 1999). It is in such dynamics that one often witnesses the cross-combinations of father-daughter and mother-son relations played out, with opposite-sex parents often taking a special interest in mate choice.

Divorce is the most obvious manifestation of the vulnerability of the affinal bond and represents a substantial threat to family firms at two levels (Dodd 2011). The first is the nascent business founded by marriage partners—the copreneurial enterprise (Marshack 1993). These are delicate arrangements and widely subject to recurrent difficulties caused by failures to realize and execute the mechanisms that sustain the achievement of common interests. Breakdown occurs through perceived inequities of inputs, problems of coordination through divergences of style and preference, and the intrusion of emotional conflicts into the operational space. As we explore later, these matters are highly individualized. In-law relationships are also potentially areas of tension in family firms through misaligned concepts of rights and belonging (Kets de Vries 1993; Marotz-Baden and Mattheis 1994).

The second level of vulnerability comes from more mature, multigenerational family business arrangements, in which family branches are sewn into more complex configurations, such as what is called the "cousin consortium" or, in more mature businesses, the "networked family business clan." At relatively early stages of the family firm life cycle, breaches between families united by marriage can threaten the integrity of the business, and also at later stages if unprotected by their corporate governance (Carlock and Ward 2001). In cultures that practice polygamy, one can expect competition among wives seeking to advance the interests of their children. Analogous problems arise where the interests of children from a patriarch's successive marriages are pitted against one another.

Sibling Rivalry

This brings us to one of the prime and often most public of conflicts that afflict family firms—sibling rivalry. In evolutionary biology, the fight for survival among siblings is an extremely common phenomenon (Mock 2004). Take, for example, the great egret, a bird found in temperate areas, often close to water and grazing livestock. The male and female adults pair for life and lay two eggs in succession. The first hatches and is nurtured. When the second egg is laid and hatched, the emergent newborn is diligently and deliberately pecked to death by the firstborn, under the indifferent gaze of the parents! The evolutionary logic explaining this callousness is that the second egg is no more nor less than a backup—plan B should the firstborn perish in its fragile infancy. This is a sound insurance strategy for a species that requires intense parental investment to secure a single, healthy offspring; hence the unsentimental stance toward protecting and nurturing that investment (Mock 2004).

How different is the situation for humans? As I have argued, although we are broadly accepting and not rigidly discriminatory in our approach to extended family relationships, we are nonetheless strategic in how we view our investments. Most parents eschew and indeed deny favoritism, but practice it nonetheless (Harris and Morgan 1991). An example is the behavior of parents toward preterm twins, where typically one is born notably weaker than the other. A test of the Darwinian prediction that the mother would devote more care to the stronger than the weaker was born out by observational evidence (Beaulieu and Bugental 2008). However, when children are healthy, parents may seek to equalize their offspring's advantages by lavishing more care on the weaker child. Other bases for favoritism may include parental identification and even the child's ability to elicit favorable responses from the parent, for, as behavior geneticists have shown, parental warmth is a heritable quality *of the child* (Plomin 1994). In other words, some kids are better at switching on parents' love than others.

The Darwinian game of family dynamics is thus a contest for the limited resources of parental investment. As Sulloway (2001) has argued, this is a miniature ecosystem in which the dependent parties, the children, have to develop strategies to maximize their fitness. In this contest the firstborn has an advantage and can quickly calculate which behaviors earn favor with parents. The only child enjoys peculiar advantages that may carry her on to success in life, though with the possible handicap of unrealistic expectations about her claims to advantage—the spoiled-child syndrome. The arrival of the next-born signals the onset of a psychic drama. The firstborn becomes immediately aware of a rival for parental time, affections, and resources and shows scaled-down little egret behavior, metaphorically pecking at his little sibling (Mock 2004). The laterborn for her part will soon enough figure out what game is being played and the need to develop a novel strategy for attracting benefits for herself.

Sulloway insists that for laterborns, rebellion against the established order is the optimal and preferred strategy against the conformist strategy that the firstborns deploy to maintain their dominance. There is mixed support for these predictions (Michalski and Shackelford 2002). It seems that this ecology shapes life "scripts" and behavioral strategies rather than personality, for personality remains firmly under the control of DNA and the genotype. Support for the "strategic" perspective comes from the work of Salmon (1999), who confirmed predictions about middleborns taking a position of relative detachment in this competitive game between the position of attached firstborns and vulnerable, insurgent laterborns.

Given what we know about how pervasive and strong the genetic origins of individual differences are, we need to consider how these constant sources of evolutionary conflict are played out in the unique configuration of each particular family. Sulloway's analysis of the family ecosystem can be broadly accepted, though the outcomes it predicts are highly contingent.

To this analysis we should pause to pay special attention to gender issues, to which other writers in this volume have also alluded. Researchers have been interested in the roles that women play in the family group and the challenges they face. In family firms, wildcard inheritance often brings women to the fore earlier than in other kinds of business. The question of what influence they bring to the conduct of family business has been less explored, but the gender-specific dispositions and preferences of women undoubtedly affect the climate of the family firm and its conduct (Brush 1992; Cole 1997; Danes and Olson 2003).

THE UNIQUE FAMILY

As we have intimated, behavior genetics points toward a more contingent configural conception of the family (Moynihan and Peterson 2001). The literature on friendship, attraction, and marriage suggests that some patterns of interpersonal similarity underlie parents' affinal bonds, but only when they have bonded by preference rather than external imperatives. This family dynamic is shaped by the wildcard genetic inheritance factor—in short, the character of one's children is a gene lottery. The gender of one's children is also a matter of chance, as is, to varying degrees, family size and age-spacing of the children.

All these elements figure in the climate and functioning of the family ecosystem, which confirms our expectation of extreme variation in the form, functioning, and success of family firms. One can infer that some families will be lucky—blessed with cooperative and complementary dispositions among their members. Others are cursed with recalcitrant personalities and implacable enmities that trigger a multitude of dysfunctional outcomes. Two sets of contingencies moderate these effects: cultural norms and intrafamilial processes, the latter sometimes a by-product of the former.

Let us look at culture first. It is said that Japanese mothers talk to their babies to pacify them, and American mothers to stimulate them. This is a nice illustration of dual inheritance theory—cultural expressions that mold consistent personal orientations among families. This coevolutionary viewpoint suggests that we may expect regional variations in the global character of family firms as a function of cultural conditioning and selective processes. For example, in the Far East, Confucianism is a powerful force for social cohesion, especially between generations, and this is reflected in the character of family firms in the region (Wong 1985; Yan and Sorenson 2006). Tribal forms pervade Africa and the Middle East, and complex clan structures predominate in the family firms of the Americas and Europe (Loomis and McKinney 1956). These variations are compounded by local regimes of tax, inheritance, and ownership conventions that affect the enterprise and its family governance. Networks, educational resources, advisory services, and a growing body of scholarly knowledge about the dynamics of family firms have arisen around the world to assist their adjustment to local legal, financial and cultural contingencies.

Much of the thrust of these resources is to help families regulate the pressures and conflicts that arise within their firms (Kellermans and Eddleston 2004). This is the second moderator of family firm climate and outcomes—the processes that families deploy for self-management. There is a degree of circularity here. Families' configural dynamic may make them incapable of solving their own problems, thus rendering them unfit to manage a firm, because family firms, by their nature, are apt to lock family members into collaborations that they would otherwise avoid, were it not for their co-dependence on the business. Many family firms fail after generations of amity by falling into the hands of a generation for whom the gene lottery has disposed that they will find it almost impossible to get along or find any way to regulate their conflicts.

Of course, there are numerous remedies for such situations that involve abandoning any attempt to work together and co-own, yet the ideology of kin selection made manifest in the family firm proves too compelling an obligation, even if it proves to be ultimately destructive.

THE MEDIATING SELF AND LEADERSHIP IN THE FAMILY FIRM

Darwinians have generally viewed notions of the self with suspicion, mainly because they are seen to reinstate such unhelpful and discarded notions as free will and dualism (Dennett 1995; Kurzban and Aktipis 2007). One can agree with the advocates of the modular mind that it is fallacious to embody the self as a homunculus (Kurzban 2010)—a person within a person—yet they may be undervaluing the special kind of consciousness that we humans possess (Donald 2001). Among Darwinians are several—myself included—who would argue that evidence from a wide range of sources supports the idea that reflexive self-consciousness is an evolved capacity that has taken humans far beyond other primates, as well as the hominids that preceded us (Heyes 1998; Tomasello 1999). Perhaps it has even taken us to a new level of development for *Homo sapiens*, since over the first hundred and sixty thousand years of our existence there is no evidence of advanced material culture, until what has been called the Great Leap Forward forty thousand years ago (Diamond 1991). The sudden appearance of a rich array of cultural artifacts has been attributed to the emergence of the self-aware ego (Leary and Buttermore 2003; Mithen 1996), because it enables the kind of reflexive cognition necessary for the notions of possession and reverence that are embodied in these artifacts.

Our advanced self-consciousness facilitates psychological inference (the "reading" of other minds), foresight, planning, empathy, personal reflection, and various quite sophisticated forms of self-regulation (Bandura 1982; Byrne and Whiten 1988; Humphrey 1980). Self-regulation comprises the processes by which humans defer or reschedule goals, deliberate upon their own actions, and select among them in order to achieve desired outcomes, including the control of moods and emotions (Baumeister, Schmeichel, and Vohs 2007; Vohs and Baumeister 2004). Self-regulatory failures are visible in many manifestations, such as failings in impulse control, procrastination, and various addictions (Sayette 2004; Steele 2007; Wiederman 2004). Self-control and the exercise of willpower are seriously weakened when the executive ego is swamped by competing control demands, such as conditions of high cognitive load or emotional stress (Baumeister, Muraven, and Tice 2000; Fischer, Greitemeyer, and Frey 2007).

Self-regulation is highly relevant to leadership, where ego-control plays a major part (Van Knippenberg et al. 2005; Zaccaro, Kemp, and Bader 2004). Leadership, as we have seen elsewhere in this volume, is an adaptive function of social systems and may take different forms according to contextual contingencies, especially the states of mind and needs of followers (Van Vugt, Hogan, and Kaiser 2008; see also Spisak, Nicholson, and Van Vugt 2011). Family firm leadership exemplifies the point, especially when examined at the key generational stages of firm and family. In the owner-founder first stage of development, the model is the patriarchal, or more rarely, matriarchal leadership model. The relationship with followers is one of familial embrace—which often falls foul of the risks we have reviewed, where the embrace is stifling and resistant to outside advice. In the next one or two generations, partnership models become more important. They are vulnerable to the sibling and cousin contests we have considered, yet many family firms exhibit great strength through their sibling and cousin collaborations and divisions of labor. As one moves to the mature family firm, leadership, along with governance, becomes more complex.

Most contemporary leadership in complex organizations can be decomposed into different elements corresponding to the multiple roles a leader may have to face: managing the top team, deal-making with stakeholder groups, being a figurehead to the massed ranks of followers, using diplomacy with the outside world and political skills in the inside world of the business. In family business the additional layer of complication comes with the family role, since multiple branches and generations may have claims on the identity and purposes of the enterprise. Some mature family firms have hundreds of scattered owners and require elaborate governance systems to enable them to act and decide in consort.

Behavior genetics shows us how important heritable individual differences are to role performance (Ilies, Arvey, and Bouchard 2006; Judge et al. 2002) and to the fate of family firms, as we have seen earlier. Individual differences pose a challenge not just to leadership succession, but to the very essence of leadership and organizational effectiveness. The challenge is adaptability and its limits. A sophisticated view of self-regulation recognizes that hard-wired individual differences limit the room for maneuvering in the self-concept; leaders with extreme self-delusions about their limitations are apt to self-destruct or to be neutralized or removed (Hogan, Hogan, and Kaiser 2011; Judge, Piccolo, and Kosalka 2009; McCall and Lombardo 1983).

I lack space in this chapter to analyze the transactional processes of the self that lead to these different outcomes. This I have sought to develop elsewhere (Nicholson 2011). Let us conclude by reflecting on an implication of the self-perspective for family firms that has yet to figure in the literature. This is the idea of collective self-identity concepts (Brewer and Gardner 1996). These seem likely to prove important in the broader context of cultural co-evolutionary processes. Self-reflective space is where notions of social and personal value can be stored and transacted. Pride, honor, reputation, spite, belonging, and the like are sentiments that are intimately connected with the self and are strongly represented in the cultural values that sustain groups, tribes, and families and guide their decisions and choices.

How social groups conceive of themselves and of their members can be seen as a form of group self-regulation, a concept as yet not conceived in the literature. Families are embedded in the norms of their cultural contexts. These vary in strength; the Indian family, for example, is arguably subject to stronger norms of conduct than the British family, yet both will absorb, reject, or modify these normative forces according to how the unique configuration of individual and collective dispositions and goals of family members is enacted. Clearly, in some cultural contexts there is greater scope for novel adaptive strategies versus open conflict than in others. The integration of evolutionary theory with elaborations of the self-concept across levels of analysis—to embrace even the extended self-concepts of peoples, races, and nations—opens up a rich vein for theoretical and empirical innovation in the social sciences and certainly, as we have seen, in the family business field.

CONCLUSION

This volume centers on the application of the new Darwinism to organizational behavior (OB), but it is plain that the former is more developed and unified than the latter. As a psychologist, when I first encountered OB, I naïvely assumed it was a discipline, alongside the other subjects of business schools—economics, finance, marketing, operations management, and accounting. Studying industrial relations, I realized that OB was actually just another field of study on which various disciplines came to bear. Industrial relations strove (and failed) to be interdisciplinary as befits a field of study. Now I have come to doubt whether OB has even that status, since it consists of pockets of disciplinary specialists studying their subtopics with meso- or low-level theories and with ever larger methodological toolkits. This is true of many other business school disciplines except one, economics, which retains a true disciplinary status, albeit with multiple centers of gravity. One may speculate whether the reason that evolutionary economics exists—it even has its own journal—is because economists, largely consistent in their meta-theoretical assumptions and worldview, recognize and take note when challenged by a new paradigm: evolutionary theory. I doubt we will ever see an evolutionary OB, because OB itself lacks coherence, except perhaps as a label for a cluster of business school pedagogy. It is notable that in a recent special issue of *The Academy of Management Review* (Suddaby, Hardy, and Huy 2012) entitled "Where Are the New Theories of Organization?" not a single paper mentions evolutionary theory.

Given the state of OB, it is no surprise that such a volume as this will inevitably consist of a series of applications or demonstrations of how evolutionary theory can make fresh sense of and explain work in the various subfields of the OB cloud. One of these is family business, which assuredly is a genuine field of study; that is, an identifiable business phenomenon whose description and explanation require a synthesis of multiple disciplinary perspectives. This is true of most other topics in this volume, which renders each of them ideally suited to the consilience approach that the evolutionary frame compels (Wilson 1998).

Throughout history families have been a wellhead for the foundation of new businesses, and this continues to be true. Given the compelling advantages for families and economic outcomes, one can predict that they will always occupy a commanding and strategic position within market economies, although colored by local cultural and institutional conditions. This makes an understanding of their underlying dynamic a matter of fundamental importance. Within the family business field, the evolutionary perspective has not yet taken hold, but it clearly has considerable explanatory power, along with the capacity to integrate current theorizing: meso-level accounts from agency, stewardship, and resource-based perspectives.

This review has been intended not just to demonstrate the integrative capacity of evolutionary theory, but also to show how family business is a microcosm through which transcendent issues about the co-evolution of social forms and processes can be viewed afresh. The relevance of self-identity processes has also been highlighted as a new domain for the extension of evolutionary theory.

References

Ainsworth, S., and Cox, J. W. 2003. Families divided: Culture and control in small family business. *Organization Studies* 24:1463–85.

Aldrich, H. E., and Cliff, J. E. 2003. The pervasive effects of family on entrepreneurship: Toward a family embeddedness perspective. *Journal of Business Venturing* 18:573–96.

Anderson, R. C., and Reeb, D. M. 2003. Founding family ownership and firm performance: Evidence from the S&P 500. *Journal of Finance* 58:301–26.

Aronoff, C. E, Ward, J. L., and de Visscher, F. 1995. *Financing transitions: Managing capital and liquidity in the family business*. Marietta, GA: Business Owner Resources.

Astrachan, J. H., and Shanker, M. C. 2006. Family businesses' contribution to the US economy: A closer look. In *Handbook of research on family business*, ed. P. Z. Poutziouris, K., Smyrnios, X., and Klein, S. B., 56–64. Cheltenham, UK: Edward Elgar.

Babcock, C. R . 1998. PsychoDarwinism: The new synthesis of Darwin and Freud. In *Handbook of evolutionary psychology*, ed. C. Crawford and D. Krebs, 457–583. Mahwah, NJ: Lawrence Erlbaum.

Bandura, A. 1982. Self-efficacy mechanisms in human agency. *American Psychologist* 37:122–47.

Barrett, L., Dunbar, R., and Lycett, J. 2002. *Human evolutionary psychology*. Basingstoke, UK: Palgrave.

Baumeister, R. F., Muraven, M., and Tice, D. M. 2000. Ego depletion: A resource model of volition, self-regulation, and controlled processing. *Social Cognition* 18: 130–50.

———, Schmeichel, B. J., and Vohs, K. D. 2007. Self-regulation and the executive function. In *Social psychology: Handbook of basic principles*, 2nd ed., ed. A. W. Kruglanski and E. T. Higgins, 516–38. New York: Guilford Press.

———, and Vohs, K. D., eds. 2004. *Handbook of self-regulation*. New York: Guilford Press.

Becker, G. S. 1981. *A treatise on the family*. Cambridge, MA: Harvard University Press.

Beaulieu, D. A., and Bugental, D. 2008. Contingent parental investment: An evolutionary framework for understanding early interaction between mothers and children. *Evolution and Human Behavior* 29:249–55.

Betzig, L. 1993. Sex, succession and stratification in the first six civilizations: How powerful men reproduced, passed power on to their sons, and used power to defend their wealth, women and children. In *Social stratification and socioeconomic inequality*, ed. L. Ellis, 1:37–74. 2 vols. Westport, CT: Praeger.

Boehm, C. 1999. *Hierarchy in the forest: The evolution of egalitarian behavior*. Cambridge, MA: Harvard University Press.

Boyd, R., and Richerson, P. J. 1985. *Culture and the evolutionary process*. Chicago: University of Chicago Press.

Brandwein, R. A., Brown, C. A., and Fox, E. M. 1974. Women and children last: The social situation of divorced mothers and their families. *Journal of Marriage and the Family* 36:498–514.

Brenner, Y. S. 1993. What went wrong with communism. *International Journal of Social Economics* 20:103–16.

Brewer, M. B., and Gardner, W. 1996. Who is "we"? Levels of collective identity and self representations. *Journal of Personality and Social Psychology* 71:83–93.

Brokaw, L. 1992. Why family businesses are best. *Inc.* 14 (3): 72–78.

Brush, C. G. 1992. Research on women business owners: Past trends, a new perspective and future directions. *Entrepreneurship Theory and Practice* 16:5–30.

Byrne, R. W., and Whiten, A. 1988. *Machiavellian intelligence: Social expertise and the evolution of intellect in monkeys, apes and humans*. Oxford: Clarendon Press.

Carlock, R. S., and Ward, J. L. 2001. *Strategic planning for the family business: Parallel planning to unify the family and the business*. New York: Palgrave Macmillan.

Carver, C. S., and Scheier, M. F. 1998. *On the self-regulation of behavior*. Cambridge: Cambridge University Press.

Chagnon, N. A. 1997. *Yanomamo*. London: Wadsworth.

Cole, P. M. 1997. Women in family business. *Family Business Review* 10:353–71.

Colli, A. 2003. *The history of family business, 1850–2000*. Cambridge: Cambridge University Press.

Coon, C. S. 1979. *The hunting peoples*. New York: Penguin.

Cronk, L., and Gerkey, D. 2007. Ecological and socio-cultural impacts on mating and marriage systems. In Dunbar and Barrett 2007, 463–78.

Cummins, D. 2005. Dominance, status and social hierarchies. In *The handbook of evolutionary psychology*, ed. D. M. Buss, 676–97. New York: John Wiley.

Daly, M., and Wilson, M. 1985. Child abuse and other risks of not living with both parents. *Ethology and Sociobiology* 6:197–210.

Danes, S. M., and Olson, P. M. 2003. Women's role involvement in family businesses, business tensions, and business success. *Family Business Review* 16:53–68.

Darwin, C., and Carroll, J., eds. 2003. *On the origin of species by means of natural selection*. Peterborough, Ontario: Broadview Press.

Davis J. A., and Tagiuri, R. 1989. The influence of life-stage on father-son work relationship in family companies. *Family Business Review* 2:47–74.

Davis, J. N., and Daly, M. 1997. Evolutionary theory and the human family. *Quarterly Review of Biology* 72:407–25.

Dennett, D. C. 1995. *Darwin's dangerous idea: Evolution and the meanings of life*. New York: Simon and Schuster.

Diamond, J. 1991. *The rise and fall of the third chimpanzee*. London: Radius.

———. 1997. *Guns, germs, and steel*. New York: Random House.

Dodd, S. D. 2011. Mapping work-related stress and health in the context of the family firm. *International Journal of Entrepreneurship and Innovation* 12:29–38.

Donald, M. 2001. *A mind so rare: The evolution of human consciousness.* New York: W. W. Norton.

Donckels, R., and Frohlich, E. 1991. Are family businesses really different? European experiences from STRATOS. *Family Business Review* 4:149–60.

Dreux, D. R. 1990. Financing family business: Alternatives to selling out or going public. *Family Business Review* 3:225–43.

Dunbar, R. I. M., and Barrett, L., eds. 2007. *Oxford handbook of evolutionary anthropology.* Oxford: Oxford University Press.

Dyer, W. G. 2006. Examining the "family effect" on firm performance. *Family Business Review* 19:253–74.

Emlen, S. T. 1997. Predicting family dynamics in social vertebrates. In *Behavioral ecology: An evolutionary approach*, 4th ed., ed. J. R. Krebs and N. B. Davies, 228–53. Oxford: Wiley-Blackwell.

Erdal, D., and Whiten, A. 1996. Egalitarianism and Machiavellian intelligence in human evolution. In *Modelling the early human mind*, ed. P. Mellars and K. Gibson, 139–50. Cambridge: McDonald Institute for Archaeological Research.

Family Business Network. 2007. *Family businesses: Perspectives on responsible ownership.* Lausanne: The Family Business Network.

Fischer, H. 2004. *Why we love: The nature and chemistry of romantic love.* New York: Henry Holt

Fischer, P., Greitemeyer, T., and Frey, D. 2007. Ego depletion and positive illusions: Does the construction of positivity require regulatory resources? *Personality and Social Psychology Bulletin* 33:1306–21.

Fodor, J., and Piatelli-Palmarini, M. 2010. *What Darwin got wrong.* London: Profile Books.

Foley, R. A., and Lahr, M. M. 2011. The evolution of the diversity of cultures. *Philosophical Transactions of the Royal Society* 366:1080–89.

Freeman, J.; Carrol, G.; Hannan, M. T. (1983): The liability of newness: Age dependence in organisational death rates. *American Sociological Review* 48:692–710.

Gersick, K. E., Davis, J. A., Hampton, M. M., and Lansberg, I. 1997. *Generation to generation: Life cycles of the family business.* Cambridge, MA. Harvard Business School Press.

Gomez-Mejia, L. R., Nunez-Nickel, M., and Gutierrez, I. 2001. The role of family ties in agency contracts. *Academy of Management Journal* 44:81–95.

———, Larraza-Kintana, M., and Makri, M. 2003. The determinants of executive compensation in family-controlled public corporations. *Academy of Management Journal* 46:226–37.

Gordon, G., and Nicholson, N. 2008. *Family wars.* London: Kogan Page.

Greenleaf, R. K. 1991. *Servant leadership: A journey into the nature of legitimate power and greatness.* New York: Paulist Press.

Grieco, M. 1988. *Keeping it in the family: Social networks and employment chance.* Cambridge: Cambridge University Press.

Ghufran, A. M. 2009. The roots of leadership and primate heritage. Working paper, INSEAD, France.

Habbershon, T. G., and Williams, M. L. 1999. A resource-based framework for assessing the strategic advantages of family firms. *Family Business Review* 12:1–25.

Harcourt, A. H., and Stewart, K. J. 2007. *Gorilla society: Conflict, compromise, and cooperation.* Chicago: University of Chicago Press.

Harris, K. M., and Morgan, S. P. 1991. Fathers, sons, and daughters: Differential paternal involvement in parenting. *Journal of Marriage and Family* 53:531–44.

Harris, M. 1977. *Cannibals and kings.* Glasgow: William Collins.

Henrich, J. 2004. Cultural group selection, coevolutionary processes and large-scale cooperation. *Journal of Economic Behavior and Organization* 53:3–35.

Heyes, C. M. 1998. Theory of mind in non-human primates. *Behavioral and Brain Sciences* 21:101–48.

Hogan, J., Hogan, R., and Kaiser, R. B. 2010. Management derailment: personal assessment and mitigation. In *American Psychological Association handbook of industrial and organizational psychology,* ed. S. Zedeck, 555–75. Washington, DC: American Psychological Society.

Humphrey, N. 1980. Nature's psychologists. In *Consciousness and the Physical World,* ed. B. D. Josephson and V. S. Ramachandran, 55–75. New York: Pergamon.

Hrdy, S. B. 2009. *Mothers and others: The evolutionary origins of mutual understanding.* Cambridge, MA: Harvard University Press.

Ilies, R., Arvey, R. D., and Bouchard, T. J. 2006. Darwinism, behavioral genetics, and organizational behavior: A review and agenda for future research. *Journal of Organizational Behavior* 27:121–42.

Imanishi, K. 1960. Social organization of subhuman primates in their natural habitat. *Current Anthropology* 1:393–407.

Jensen, M. C., and Meckling, W. H. 1976. Theory of the firm: Managerial behavior, agency costs and ownership structure. *Journal of Financial Economics* 3:303–60.

Judge, T. A., Bono, J. E., Ilies, R., and Gerhardt, M. W. 2002. Personality and leadership: A qualitative and quantitative review. *Journal of Applied Psychology* 87:765–80.

———, Piccolo, R. F., and Kosalka, T. 2009. The bright and the dark sides of leader traits: A review and theoretical extension of the leader trait paradigm. *Leadership Quarterly* 20:855–75.

Karoly, P. 1993. Mechanisms of self-regulation: A systems view. *Annual Review of Psychology* 44:23–52.

Kaye, K. 1999. Mate selection and family business success. *Family Business Review* 12:107–15.

Keesing, R. M. 1975. *Kin groups and social structure.* New York: Holt, Rinehart and Winston.

Kellermans, F. W., and Eddleston, K. A. 2004. Feuding families: When conflict does a family firm good. *Entrepreneurship Theory and Practice* 29:209–28.

Kelly, S., and Dunbar, R. I. M. 2001. Who dares wins: Heroism vs. altruism in women's mate choice. *Human Nature* 12:89–105.

Kepner, E. 1991. The family and the firm: A coevolutionary perspective. *Family Business Review* 4:445–61.

Kets de Vries, M. F. R. 1993. The dynamics of family controlled firms: The good and the bad news. *Organizational Dynamics* 21:59–71.

Klein, R. G., and Edgar, B. 2002. *The dawn of human culture.* New York: John Wiley.

Kurzban, R. 2010. *Why everyone (else) is a hypocrite: Evolution and the modular mind.* Princeton, NJ: Princeton University Press.

————, and Aktipis, C. A. 2007. Modularity and the social mind: Are psychologists too self-ish? *Personality and Social Psychology Review* 11:131–49.

Laland, K. N. 2007. Niche construction, human behavioural ecology and evolutionary psychology. In Dunbar and Barrett 2007, 35–48.

Landes, D. S. 1998. *The wealth and poverty of nations.* New York: W. W. Norton

Leary, M. R., and Buttermore, N. R. 2003. The evolution of the human self: Tracing the natural history of self-awareness. *Journal for the Theory of Social Behavior* 33:365–404.

Loomis, C. P., and McKinney, J. C. 1956. Systemic differences between Latin-American communities of family farms and large estates. *American Journal of Sociology* 61:404–12.

Low, B. S. 2007. Ecological and socio-cultural impacts on mating and marriage systems. In Dunbar and Barrett 2007, 449–62.

Luo, S., and Klohnen, E. C. 2005. Assortative mating and marital quality in newlyweds: A couple-centered approach. *Journal of Personality and Social Psychology* 88:304–26.

Lyagoubi, M. 2006. Family firms and financial behavior: How family shareholder preferences influence firms' financing. In *Handbook of research on family business,* ed. P. Z. Poutziouris, K. X. Smyrnios, and S. B. Klein, 537–51. Cheltenham, UK: Edward Elgar.

Lykken. D. T., McGue, M., Tellegen, A., and Bouchard, T. J. 1992. Emergenesis: Genetic traits that may not run in families. *American Psychologist* 47:1565–77.

Markson, E. W. 2003. *Social gerontology today: An introduction.* Los Angeles: Roxbury.

Marotz-Baden, R., and Mattheis, C. 1994. Daughters-in-law and stress in two-generational farm families. *Family Relations* 43:132–37.

Marshack, K. J. 1993. Coentrepreneurial couples: A literature review on boundaries and transitions among copreneurs. *Family Business Review* 6:355–69.

McCall, M. W., and Lombardo, M. M. 1983. *Off the track: Why and how successful executives get derailed.* Technical Report No. 21: Greensboro, NC: Center for Creative Leadership.

McElreath R., and Henrich, J. 2007. Dual inheritance theory: The evolution of human cultural capacities and cultural evolution. In Dunbar and Barrett 2007, 555–70.

McGrue, W. C. 1992. *Chimpanzee material culture: Implications for human evolution.* Cambridge: Cambridge University Press.

McPherson, M., Smith-Lovin, L., and Cook, J. M. 2001. Birds of a feather: Homophily in social networks. *Annual Review of Sociology* 27:415–44.

McVeigh, R., and Sikkink, D. 2005. Organized racism and the stranger. *Sociological Forum* 20:497–522.

Meder, A. 2007. Great Ape social systems. In *Handbook of paleoanthropology,* ed. W. Henke, I. Tatersall, and T. Hardt, 2:1235–71. 3 vols. New York: Springer-Verlag.

Megarry T. 1995. *Society in prehistory: The origins of human culture.* London: Macmillan

Michalski, R. L., and Shackelford, T. K. 2002. An attempted replication of the relationships between birth order and personality. *Journal of Research in Personality* 36:182–88.

Miller, D., and Le Breton-Miller, I. 2005. Managing for the long run: Lessons in competitive advantage from the great family businesses. Cambridge, MA: Harvard Business School Press.

———, and Le Breton-Miller, I. 2006. Family governance and firm performance: Agency, stewardship, and capabilities. *Family Business Review* 19:73–87.

Mithen, S. 1996. *The prehistory of the mind*. London: Thames and Hudson.

Mock, D. W. 2004. *More than kin and less than kind: The evolution of family conflict*. Boston, MA: Belknap Press of Harvard University Press.

Moynihan, L. M., and Peterson, R. S. 2001. A contingent configuration approach to understanding the role of personality in organizational groups. In *Research in Organizational Behavior*, ed. B. W. Staw and R. Sutton. Greenwich, CT: JAI Press.

Nahapiet, J., and Ghoshal, S. 1988. Social capital, intellectual capital, and the organizational advantage. *Academy of Management Review* 23:242–66.

Neyer F. J., and Lang, F. R. 2003. Blood is thicker than water: Kinship orientation across adulthood. *Journal of Personality and Social Psychology* 84:310–21.

Nicholson, N. 2000. *Managing the human animal*. London: Thomson/Texere.

———. 2008. Evolutionary psychology, corporate culture and family business. *Academy of Management Perspectives* 22:73–84.

———. 2011. The evolved self, co-evolutionary processes and the self-regulation of leadership. *Biological Theory* 6:12–44.

Nisbett, R. E., and Cohen, D. 1996. *Culture of honor: The psychology of violence in the South*. Boulder, CO: Westfield Press.

O'Hara, W. T. 2004. *Centuries of success: Lessons from the world's most enduring family businesses*. Avon, MA: Adams Media.

Plomin, R. 1994. *Genetics and experience: The interplay between nature and nurture*. Thousand Oaks, CA: Sage.

Richerson, P. J., and Boyd, R. 1999. The evolutionary dynamics of a crude super organism. *Human Nature* 10:253–89.

———, and Boyd, R. 2005. *Not by genes alone: How culture transformed human evolution*. Chicago: University of Chicago Press.

Ridley, M. 1996. *The origins of virtue*. New York: Viking.

Rothausen, T. J. 1999. "Family" in organizational research: A review and comparison of definitions and measures. *Journal of Organizational Behavior* 20:817–36.

Sahlins, M. D. 1972. *Stone age economics*. Chicago: Aldine.

Salmon, C. A. 1999. On the impact of sex and birth order on contact with kin. *Human Nature* 10:183–97.

Sayette, M. A. 2004. Self-regulatory failure and addiction. In Baumeister and Vohs 2004, 447–65.

Schulze, W. S., Lubatkin, M. H., and Dino, R. N. 2003. Toward a theory of agency and altruism in family firms. *Journal of Business Venturing* 18:473–90.

———, Lubatkin, M. H., Dino, R. N., and Buchholtz, A. K. 2001. Agency relationships in family firms: Theory and evidence. *Organization Science* 12:9–116.

Seccombe, K. 2000. Families in poverty in the 1990s: Trends, causes, consequences, and lessons learned. *Journal of Marriage and the Family* 62:1094–1113.

Shanker, M. C., and Astrachan, J. H. 1996. Myths and realities: Family businesses' contribution to the U.S. economy: A framework for assessing family business statistics. *Family Business Review* 9:107–24.

Sober, E., and Wilson, D. S. 1998. *Unto others: The evolution and psychology of unselfish behavior.* Cambridge, MA: Harvard University Press.

Sommer, V., and Parish, A. R. 2010. Living differences: The paradigm of animal cultures. In *Homo novus: A human without illusions*, ed. U. J. Frey, C. Störmer, and K. P. Willführ, 19–33. Berlin: Springer-Verlag.

Sperber, D. 1996. *Explaining culture: A naturalistic approach.* Oxford: Blackwell.

Spisak, B. R., Nicholson, N., and Van Vugt, M. 2011. Leadership in organizations: An evolutionary perspective. In *Applications of evolutionary psychology in the business sciences*, ed. G. Saad, 165–90. Heidelberg: Springer.

Steele, P. 2007. The nature of procrastination: A meta-analytic and theoretical review of quintessential self-regulatory failure. *Psychological Bulletin* 133:65–94.

Stewart, A. 2003. Help one another, use one another: Toward an anthropology of family business. *Entrepreneurship Theory and Practice* 27:383–96.

Strassmann, B. I. 1981. Sexual selection, paternal care, and concealed ovulation in humans. *Ethology and Sociobiology* 2:31–40.

Suddaby, R., Hardy, C., and Huy, Q. N., eds. 2012. Where are the new theories of organization? Special issue, *Academy of Management Review* 36 (2).

Sulloway, F. J. 2001. Birth order, sibling competition, and human behavior. In *Conceptual challenges in evolutionary psychology: Innovative research strategies*, ed. H. R. Holcomb III, 39–83. Studies in Cognitive Systems, vol. 27. Dordrecht, the Netherlands: Kluwer.

Tagiuri, R., and Davis, J. A. 1992. On the goals of successful family companies. *Family Business Review* 5:43–62.

———, and Davis, J. A. 1996. Bivalent attributes of the family firm, *Family Business Review* 9:199–208.

Tokarczyk, J., Hansen, E., Green, M., and Down, J. 2007. A resource-based view and market orientation theory examination of the role of "familiness" in family business success. *Family Business Review* 20:17–32.

Tomasello, M. 1999. *The cultural origins of human cognition.* Cambridge, MA: Harvard University Press.

Trivers, R. L. 1974. Parent-offspring conflict. *American Zoologist* 14:249–64.

Tudge, C. 1998. *Neanderthals, bandits and farmers.* London: Wiedenfeld and Nicolson.

Van Knippenberg, B., De Cremer, D., Hogg, M. A., and Van Knippenberg, D. 2005. Leadership, self, and identity: A review and research agenda. *Leadership Quarterly* 15:825–56.

Van Vugt, M., Hogan, R., and Kaiser, R. B. 2008. Leadership, followership, and evolution: Some lessons from the past. *American Psychologist* 63:182–96.

Vohs, K. D., and Baumeister, R. F. 2004. Understanding self-regulation: An introduction. In Baumeister and Vohs 2004, 1–12.

Ward, J. L. 2004. *Perpetuating the family business: 50 lessons learned from long-lasting, successful families in business.* Houndmills, Basingstoke: Palgrave Macmillan.

Whiten, A. 1998. The evolution of deep social mind in humans. In *The Evolution of the hominid mind*, ed. M. Corballis and S. E. G. Lea, 173–93. Oxford: Oxford University Press.

Wiederman, M. W. 2004. Self-control and sexual behavior. In Baumeister and Vohs 2004, 525–36.

Wilkinson, R. G. 1996. *Unhealthy societies: The afflictions of inequality.* London: Routledge.

Wilson, E. O. 1998. *Consilience: The unity of knowledge.* New York: Vintage Books.

Wong, S. 1985. The Chinese family firm: A model. *British Journal of Sociology* 36:58–72.

Yan, J., and Sorenson, R. 2006. The effect of Confucian values on succession in family business. *Family Business Review* 19:235–50.

Zaccaro, S. J., Kemp, C., and Bader, P. 2004. Leader traits and attributes. In *The nature of leadership*, ed. J. Antonakis, A. T. Ciancialo, and R. J. Sternberg, 101–24. Thousand Oaks, CA: Sage.

ELEVEN

Evolution and Cooperation: Implications for Organizational Behavior and Management Theory

Roderick E. White and Barbara Decker Pierce

We live in challenging times threatened by economic crisis, environmental catastrophe, and political instability. Conflict exists over vital resources, and social disorder and reordering increase within our communities. To address these challenges, we hear the call from management and organizational scholars for more insight into individual decision making, stronger and more ethical leadership, as well as for more effective organizations functioning within improved regulatory frameworks, and more effective social institutions. No doubt there is a need to understand these phenomena better, but they have been studied mostly as separate and unconnected, although Darwinian thinking makes it increasingly clear that they are related and interdependent. Evolutionary theory, especially the multilevel selection version, shows how the pieces of this complex puzzle connect and interlink one with another (Wilson 2007).

What is required to address the challenges of organizations in particular, and society more broadly, is a paradigm that illuminates how hierarchically interlinked cooperative systems form, function, and fail to function. The near global economic collapse of 2008–9 and its aftermath demonstrated the cascading failure of interlinked, cooperative systems. It was initiated by a financial crisis that occurred, in large part, because of the inability or unwillingness of the many organizations involved to recognize that the self-interested behaviors of organizational subunits and individual actors within this interlinked system put at risk the survival not just of specific organizations but ultimately of the global financial and economic systems. Fundamentally, this costly episode was a near catastrophic failure of a multilevel cooperative system with interlinked and interdependent parts.

This recent experience has called into question the validity of the dominant paradigm of self-interested rational actors transacting within efficient and largely unregulated markets and organizations. We need a better understanding of how individuals, organizations, and institutions actually act, interact, and interrelate. While the landscape of evolved, cooperative systems is very large, a significant part of it—organizations and how the people in them behave—is the province of organizational behavior and organization and management theory (OB/OMT). Yet OB/OMT remains a largely disparate field of study without a unifying paradigm. The most prevalent paradigm seems to be the Standard Social Science Model (SSSM; see Tooby and Cosmides 1992; Pinker 2002). It shares many basic assumptions about human behavior with neoclassical economics, making a set of implicit and explicit assumptions about the malleability of human nature that are anchored in a simplistic interpretation of behavioral psychology.

We contend in this chapter that Darwinian evolution, particularly multilevel selection theory,[1] as it is now understood, is an intellectual framework more capable of providing the insights needed by behavioral, organizational, and social theorists to coherently address the challenges of ever-increasing interdependencies, which are influenced both by the benefits inherent in expanding the scope of cooperative relationships and by the risks and costs of doing so. Although some OB/OMT theorists have employed an evolutionary perspective (e.g., Weick 1979; Nelson and Winter 1982; Hannan and Freeman 1989; Aldrich and Ruef 2006), their works remain largely separate and distinct, and wholly unconnected to the work of evolutionary biology and evolutionary psychology. We can look to the evolutionary biologists (Maynard Smith and Szathmary 1995; Wilson 2007) and evolutionary anthropologists (Richerson and Boyd 2005) for a deeper and more unified understanding of how evolutionary processes have created layers or levels of increasingly complex and cooperative biological and *social* aggregations. Admittedly this is a very long story, involving more than three billion years of biological and then social evolution that crosses many disciplinary boundaries. But while important questions remain to be answered, the broad outlines of what E. O. Wilson (1998) calls "consilience"—the unification of the biological and social sciences—are increasingly well established. It is imperative for OB/OMT scholars to understand where our work fits within this grand scheme. Indeed, initial efforts by an expanding group of these scholars and scholars in related fields are being made to provide a neo-Darwinian explanation for our understanding of organizational life (Markoczy and Goldberg 1998; White and Pierce 2000; Nicholson and White 2006; Nicholson and de Wall-Andrews 2005; Wilson 2007, chap. 26; Nicholson 2010; Van Vugt and Ahuja 2011).

In this chapter we employ neo-Darwinian theory, returning to the first principles of what an organization is and then discussing how and where organizations and the behaviors that occur in and around them fit into a nested hierarchy of increasingly complex cooperative systems. We do so in the belief that the dynamics involved are best viewed and understood through the lens of evolutionary theory. Dennett (1995) contends that neo-Darwinian theory has the property of a universal acid: the ability to erode all other theories. We prefer Wilson's (2007) more benign metaphor—that of a jigsaw puzzle. Darwin's powerful theory does not necessarily erode all others; rather, it provides a robust paradigm for identifying, organizing, and understanding the fundamental relationships among them.

We begin by establishing the common ground between organizations and organisms, which are both cooperative systems. We go on to explain how Darwin's profound insight—descent with modification—is being extended beyond the purely biological (i.e., genetic) through social cognition and learning processes to groups, organizations, cultures, and societal institutions. We develop and discuss the implications of this paradigm for OB/OMT.

ORGANIZATIONS AS COOPERATIVE SYSTEMS

At its core an organization is a cooperative system. Such systems form when individuals come together to accomplish a valued outcome that they could not achieve independently. This conception is not new to organizational theorists. It was well stated by Chester Barnard (1968) in his seminal work, *The Functions of the Executive*, first published in 1938. He recognized that "cooperation has no reason for being except as it can do what the individual cannot do. Cooperation justifies itself, then, as a means of overcoming the limitations restricting what individuals can do" (1968, 23) The simple act of working together to overcome individual limitations can result in a basic form of cooperation—mutualism. Mutualism occurs when two or more individuals work together—for example, to move a heavy log (Tomasello 2009)—to do what one of them is physically unable to do independently. The self-interest of both parties benefits from combining their efforts. Free-riding, shirking, and other such selfish behaviors are not a problem in this type of simple, self-regulating situation—if one partner shirks, then the desired outcome is not accomplished. Mutualistic cooperation, because it serves the interests of the cooperating individuals, is easily explained. But as more individuals are involved in accomplishing more complex outcomes requiring interdependent, specialized tasks over a longer period of time, the potential for opportunistic, self-interested behavior (e.g., shirking, free riding) arises and can threaten the viability of the cooperative system. In this context a specific form of cooperation is needed to regulate the self-interested behavior of individuals. This type of cooperation—known as altruistic cooperation—has a precise meaning, which we employ in the remainder of this chapter: *Altruistic cooperation occurs when the individuals constituting the group limit (and even sacrifice) their immediate self-interest in order to participate in and promote the interests of the group.*

Temporary cooperative relationships are often based upon mutualism; when the joint purpose is accomplished, these relationships do not survive or endure. However, in some instances what began as mutualism can develop into sustained cooperation, and what emerges can be identified as an organization. This probably occurs relatively infrequently. As Barnard asserts, in a statement worthy of Darwin, "Successful cooperation in or by formal organizations is the abnormal, not the normal condition. What are observed from day to day are the successful survivors among innumerable failures. The organizations commanding sustained attention, almost all of which are short-lived at best, are the exception, not the rule" (5). He goes on to state that "the only measure of the efficiency of a cooperative system is its capacity to survive" (44).

One of the principle benefits of sustaining a cooperative relationship, indeed perhaps the primary raison d'être of any ongoing cooperative system, is the efficiency gained from the specialization of the individual units that make up the group and the advantages for survival that this specialization provides for the group and its members. Cooperation and specialization featured prominently in Barnard's thinking (Barnard 1968). However, the advantages of specialization are only realized if the specialized subunits are coordinated. For Barnard, formal organizations came into existence when there was "a system of *consciously* coordinated activities" (1968, 73; emphasis in original). But Barnard also recognized that formal organizations came from somewhere; they emerged from a bottom-up process. In his view, systems of cooperation emerge when individuals form informal groups, some of which develop into formal organizations.

Barnard had a nuanced understanding of the multilevel character of cooperation and the difficulty of drawing distinct boundaries between levels. He posed the question, "What is an individual?" He recognized the human organism as a distinct biological unit but also noted that "human organisms do not function except in conjunction with other human organisms" (11). Cooperative groupings involve interactions among two or more individuals. In Barnard's view, if the cooperative grouping was sustained, it became "something more or different from the mere sum of the interactions between the individuals composing it. In this sense, the group presents a system of social action which, *as a whole*, interacts with each individual within its scope" (42; emphasis in original). Barnard was among the first writers to clearly conceive of organizations as multilevel cooperative systems. Although he did not explicitly explain his theory of cooperative systems in evolutionary terms, evolved systems do have the inherent potential to generate levels (Maynard Smith and Szathmary 1995).

Barnard's work was foundational for several areas of management scholarship; both OB and OT, as well as organization systems theory. Kozlowski and Klein (2000) identify the multilevel perspective as being reflected in other examples of early organization theory, "including the Hawthorne studies (Roethlisberger and Dickson 1939), Homans's theory of groups (1950), Lewin's field theory (1951) sociotechnical systems theory (Emery and Trist 1960), Likert's theory of organizational effectiveness (1961), Thompson's (1967) theory of organizational rationality and Katz and Kahn's (1966) social organization theory, to name but a few" (3). However, Kozlowski and Klein (2000) conclude that a multilevel perspective, even in more recent applications, has done little to move organizational theorizing forward in a coherent way. We believe evolutionary theory, particularly multilevel selection theory, can provide organizational scholars with clarity and reduce the confusion that Kozlowski and Klein identified. However, established linkages between evolutionary and organizational theorizing are few and far between. Kozlowski and Klein review the state of multilevel theorizing in the organizational sciences by drawing on 136 referenced works. Their chapter makes no reference to multilevel selection theory, evolutionary biology, or its modern extensions into dual inheritance theory, evolutionary economics, and cultural evolution.

Since its inception, evolutionary theorizing has been multilevel. Darwin recognized that evolution could occur not only at the level of the individual but also at the level of the group (i.e., tribe). Since Darwin's time, and especially after pioneering work on genetics beginning with

J. B. S. Haldane in the 1950s, multilevel evolutionary theory and research have been extremely active areas within evolutionary biology, genetics, and related fields. Arguably, this topic has received more attention from these scholars than from those in any other discipline. Over the years, evolution theorists have engaged in heated debate, but the field now appears to be converging around what D. S. Wilson (1997b), E. O. Wilson (2008), and others call multilevel selection theory (MLST). MLST highlights the role cooperation plays in evolution and bridges the biological and the sociological. This raises the possibility that behavioral and organizational theory may be subsumed by neo-Darwinian theory. Alfred Marshall, a founding father of modern economics, stated that economics "is a branch of biology broadly interpreted" (1920, 637). Organization theory and organizational behavior may be another branch of the same tree.

COOPERATION IN EVOLVED SYSTEMS

Until recently, cooperation and the related topics of altruism and group selection have been highly controversial, even among evolutionary biologists. The popular notion is that evolution is much more about competition than it is about cooperation. "Survival of the fittest," a phrase often attributed to Darwin but actually coined by Herbert Spencer after reading *On the Origin of Species*, reflects this perception. Darwin would agree that competition for resources that enable survival and reproductive success is a key aspect of his theory of natural selection. Thomas Malthus's insight—population size is constrained by limited resources and the competition for those resources—was central to Darwin's conception of the forces underpinning the processes of natural selection. This competitive element of the evolutionary process led many to conclude (inaccurately, we argue) that this process is purely a Hobbesian "war of all against all." Many agree with the observation that "individuals who exploit their neighbors would seem to be adaptive according to Darwin's criteria, whereas individuals who help their neighbors should quickly go extinct" (Wilson 1997b, S1) People with this interpretation of natural selection often reject evolutionary theory because of its apparently selfish, competitive character and its inability to explain the level of altruistic cooperation evident in human social groups.

Darwin, like many observers of human nature, appreciated that natural selection operating only at the individual level did not describe the level of within-species cooperation noted in everyday interaction. His proposed explanation and great insight was that selection could operate at more than one level—evolution is a multilevel process. "It must not be forgotten that although a high standard of morality gives but a slight or no advantage to each individual man and his children over the other men of the same tribe, . . . an increase in the number of well-endowed men and an advancement in the standard of morality will certainly give an immense advantage to one tribe over another" (Darwin 1871, 166).

This reasoning affirms that an individual can be an adaptive unit—a unit for selection—but so too can a grouping of individuals. Specifically, natural selection could operate at the level of the group (in Darwin's example the "tribe") as well as at the level of the individual. By applying his theory of natural selection *across levels*, Darwin realized that, while selfish individuals would out-compete less selfish individuals, groups composed of more helpful and cooperative individuals, groups of cooperators, could out-compete groups composed of less cooperative, more selfish individuals.

Darwin's explanation was compelling at first. But during the twentieth century, as we improved our understanding of genetic transmission, group selection was deemed to be exceedingly improbable. Questions arose about how a cooperative group could develop in the first place, or, once constituted, how it could maintain cooperation over time. Dawkins (1976) posed the central evolutionary problem for cooperative groups: "If there is just one selfish rebel, prepared to exploit the altruism of the rest, then he by definition is more likely to survive and have children. Each of these children will tend to inherit his selfish traits. After several generations of this natural selection, the "altruistic group" will become overrun by selfish individuals and will be indistinguishable from the selfish group" (8).

This perspective resonated well with the methodological individualism that Don Campbell identified as dominating "the neighboring fields of economics, much of sociology, and all of psychology's excursions into organizational theory" (1994, 23). At the level of the individual, it would appear that *selfish* beats *altruistic* every time. Without other factors at play, groups with altruistic cooperators should neither develop nor survive. But we believe that they do. In fact, we also know that at the level of the group *altruistic* beats *selfish* every time. The challenge for evolutionary theorists and the topic of the next section is to explain how humankind has developed cooperative groups (and organizations) from the aggregation of genetically self-interested individuals.

Cooperation among Organisms

The conceptual framework grounding any discussion of evolution is that of natural selection. Darwin's dangerous idea begins with the observation that a population comprises a number of organisms, each of which exhibits a set of physiological and behavioral traits that effect its ability to survive and reproduce in a particular environmental niche. Additionally, the population of organisms exhibits *variation* in the distribution of these traits among its members. Some organisms are better able to respond to the challenges to survival and reproduction presented by their environment because they possess certain traits. These individuals are considered to have greater fitness when compared to others in the population. Over time, those individuals with advantageous traits survive and reproduce at a greater rate and are deemed more fit. Thus the fittest have been *selected*. The advantageous traits must be transmittable to other organisms. They must replicate. If the fittest survivors reproduce, and their replicators are passed on to their offspring, the probability is improved that those endowed with these replicators will survive and reproduce. Thus advantageous replicators are *retained* in these organisms, and their frequency increases within the population of organisms—the species.

Evolution is incremental and path-dependent. But in rare situations, this process brings about something very different from the precursor organisms: Individual organisms aggregate and function as parts of an interdependent grouping. If this aggregate is able to survive and reproduce, then a new adaptive unit (or level) emerges. The elements that constitute the aggregate grouping retain some of their individuality but are integrated into a new "whole," a new organism. Grouping into symbiotic aggregates allows for the evolution of specialization and the attendant survival advantages. Through this process, the group evolves to become different from the sum of its constituent, cooperating parts. This shift in frame creates a new adaptive unit that may be recognized as a new level of selection. Groups, like the individual organisms that comprise them, can have traits that vary, creating a new arena for competition. If this is the case, selection pressures take place between groups. Groups better able to fit with their environment—that is, better able to access needed resources—will outcompete other groups. The adaptations enabling group survival will be retained by the group. Multilevel selection theory reminds us, however, that sustained cooperation among the lower-level organisms is required for selection to shift to the higher-level arena. If within-group competition is not constrained, then, as Dawkins and others maintain, cooperative groupings will never emerge. Thus it is essential for groups to develop and employ mechanisms that promote co-operation and regulate or suppress destructive competition among their constituent parts. Such cooperative mechanisms can be considered examples of adaptations at the more aggregated level.

The emergence of a new level of selection in this fashion is described by Maynard Smith and Szathmary (1995) as a "transition." They maintain that the history of life on earth can be understood as a series of major transitions, each introducing a new level of selection, a new level of aggregation or complexity. Through cooperation, evolution has crafted entirely new organisms. This is not just the refinement of existing individual organisms—giraffes with longer necks or peacocks with more colorful tails. Instead, through aggregation and cooperation, evolution has added distinct and novel organisms to the life forms of this planet. For this reason Michod and Roze (n.d.) assert that "cooperation is now seen as the primary creative force behind ever greater levels of complexity and organization in all of biology" (1). An important feature of this process is the emergence of levels or strata, or at least what appear to be levels. It is tempting to assume that the more recently emerged, more complex organisms are of a higher order. The danger in using the word *higher* is that it will be equated with better. In fact these "higher" levels can be described as more complex, more specialized, more recent, perhaps even more evolved; but they are not intrinsically higher or lower, or better or worse than the simpler strata that preceded and underpin them.

The biological mechanisms for maintaining cooperation within the constituent components of a multicellular organism are numerous, varied, and often interlinked. Many have been studied, and some are relatively well understood. But most remain to be identified, and all are worthy of further study. While it is not possible to prespecify what may or may not qualify as an evolved/successful cooperative mechanism, Michod and Roze (n.d.) described what is required in terms of the fitness calculus. "Cooperation creates new levels of fitness by increasing the fitness of the group, and, if costly at the lower level, by trading fitness from the lower level (the costs of cooperation to group members) to a higher level (the benefits to the group)" (4). Thus anything that permits that transfer of fitness between levels can be considered an enabling mechanism.

An important insight of multilevel selection theory is that within-group selection does not completely disappear once a group is formed. Within-group selection and the potential for destructive infighting and self-interested behavior are never entirely suppressed. There is an ongoing dynamic tension between levels of selection. The resulting balance depends on the effectiveness of mechanisms available to promote cooperation among lower-level individuals (i.e., among the constituent parts of the larger cooperative system). Self-interested individuals must experience some form of self-regulation or regulation from the higher level, or both, to sustain cooperation and thereby suppress selection pressure at the lower level (Nowak 2006). If cooperation cannot be achieved among the individuals at the lower level (i.e., less aggregate), higher levels of selection (complexity) will not emerge. Thus all existing complex organisms (and organizations) have evolved mechanisms of within-group cooperation. These group-level adaptations limit the ability of constituent parts to exhibit self-interested behavior, or they change the behavior of individual members from self-interested to other-interested.

Bees group together in hives; termites, in colonies. Humans group together in extended family units, hunting teams, tribes, communities, societies, and nations. At various levels, people belong to a family unit, a community, and usually to an organization that is part of a larger economy that functions within and is regulated by the broader society. We contend that evolutionary processes are at work for groupings of individual organisms, and these processes can be extended to other sociological/cooperative systems, including human organizations. OB/OMT scholars generally have limited professional interest in the biological processes that maintain cooperation within individual organisms. But, as we argued in the introduction to this chapter, they should be very interested in interorganism cooperation, especially in how one particular species—humankind—has developed cooperative groupings from aggregations of self-interested individuals and how these groupings function as adaptive units.

Evolution of the Cognitive Capacity for Cooperation

An obvious and important difference between humans and most other social species, especially in comparison to the social insects, is our enhanced cognitive capacity. Humans in particular have evolved large brains. It is hypothesized that large brains evolved primarily to solve the adaptive problems of group life and the "computational demands of the complex social systems that characterize the (primate) order" (Dunbar 1998, 178). From an evolutionary perspective, big brains and the supporting cognitive, perceptual, and memory apparatus are costly. They require considerable resources and energy; their existence must have offsetting benefits. Some of these benefits may simply be advantageous for individual fitness, but others may enable cooperation among individuals and the related fitness advantages for the group. While cognitive abilities such as memory, language, and emotions enable cooperation; the survival advantages inherent in cooperative behaviors may also have contributed to the evolution of this enhanced cognitive capacity. Because evolution works in a progressive, incremental, fashion, cooperation may explain, at least in part, the evolution of enhanced human cognitive capacity and, conversely, cognitive capacity may also explain much about human cooperation.

Consider a simple kind of cooperative behavior—when one individual helps another individual with the expectation that the other will return the favor in the future. This is known as reciprocal altruism, or direct reciprocity. To be of interest, the helping behavior must be costly to the donor and beneficial to the recipient, and the benefit to the recipient must exceed the cost to the donor. The donor acts in the belief that at some point the recipient will incur a cost in order to benefit the donor, and the debt will be repaid. On the surface, at the time of the initial helping behavior, the act may appear to be altruistic. But if the donor and recipient are likely to interact on an ongoing basis, there are grounds for belief that the donor's generosity will be repaid. For direct reciprocity to function effectively, those involved must have the cognitive ability to recognize and remember one another. Evidence for operation of this mechanism comes from experiments involving the well-known prisoner's dilemma game (Axelrod 1984). Generally, the most successful strategy in situations involving frequently interacting dyads has been demonstrated to be "tit-for-tat."[2] A player employing this strategy begins by cooperating with the other player. For all subsequent exchanges, she mimics the response made by her partner from the last interaction. This strategy works as long as interaction between the two players is ongoing. The dominant strategy for a one-shot game, or end-game (i.e., when the players know they will not encounter each other in the future) is for both players to defect—not to cooperate.

Direct reciprocity is very limiting to the scope of potential cooperation and social exchange. It requires repeated encounters between the same two individuals (dyads). Each of them must be able to provide help and must need help from the other individual, and that help must be more beneficial to the recipient than it is costly to the donor. Outside of small, close-knit groups, such situations are uncommon. However, indirect reciprocity, also called reputation-based cooperation, can originate from direct reciprocity in the presence of an interested audience. It can significantly increase the incidence of cooperative behavior among members of the group since it does not require the repeated interaction of the same individuals. Rather, the decision to help another person is based upon their reputation (for helping others). Nowak (2006) explained the cognitive requirements of this type of cooperation:

"Indirect reciprocity has substantial cognitive demands. Not only must we remember our own interactions, we must also monitor the ever-changing social network of the group. Language is needed to gain information and spread the gossip associated with indirect reciprocity. Presumably, selection for indirect reciprocity and human language has played a decisive role in the evolution of human intelligence" (1561).

In its simplest form, indirect reciprocity does not require language (i.e., when C observes A helping B and subsequently helps A on the basis of this observation), if members of the population can communicate their observations to others, the cooperative network can be greatly expanded. Through social processes like gossip, members of a population acquire reputations, and reputations influence behavior. When members of a group have reliable knowledge of cooperative or uncooperative behavior by other members of their group, they can use this information to decide whether or not to help others. Individuals who are observed helping others or contributing to the public good incur costs, but they acquire good reputations and good reputations can have benefits. Individuals with good reputations are more likely to be sought out as partners and receive help than individuals with no reputation or a poor reputation (Nowak and Sigmund 1998).

Just as good reputations elicit helping behavior from other members of the group, poor reputations can result in punishment. Third-party punishment (or rewarding) occurs when a bystander punishes noncooperators (or rewards cooperators). It is also called "altruistic punishment," because individuals will punish others, even though exacting the punishment has a cost for them and provides them with no direct benefit. While both altruistic punishment and reward are possible, Fehr and Fischbacher (2003) argue, "Evolutionary explanations . . . of altruistic rewarding are likely to be much more difficult than explanations of altruistic punishment because when cooperation is frequent, rewarding causes high costs for the altruists, whereas a credible punishment threat renders actual punishment unnecessary" (790). They also conclude that strong altruistic punishment—the punishment of both noncooperators and nonpunishers—may be critical to the emergence of cooperation within larger groups. However, the difficulty with altruistic punishment is that the punishment of free riders is what economists call a "second-order public good," in which the punisher bears a cost by providing a group incentive for cooperation and thus creates a benefit for everyone in the group but receives little personal benefit, especially in larger groups. If the personal benefit for third-party punishment is small, the cost must be even smaller; otherwise self-interested individuals will not punish, and the emergence of cooperation within larger groups becomes problematic. However, it can be shown that, in the presence of a certain number of altruistic punishers in a group, it is in every member's self-interest to cooperate and avoid punishment. Gintis and colleagues (2003) demonstrate that a small number of strong reciprocators with a predisposition to cooperate with others and punish noncooperators can invade a population of self-interested individuals.

Much of the experimental research done on the question of rewarding and punishing noncooperators investigates peer punishment—when members sanction one another in unstructured groups. The effect of institutional punishment—when a boss "punishes" uncooperative team members—upon cooperative behaviors has been less thoroughly studied. However, Gurek, Irlenbusch, and Rockenbach (2006) demonstrated that the organizations that sanctioned individual behavior outperformed sanction-free institutions, and, when allowed mobility, individuals chose organizations that sanctioned over those that did not. Interestingly, recent work also suggests that a single, designated punisher may be equally effective and more efficient than allowing peer group members to punish one another (O'Gorman, Henrich, and Van Vugt 2009). Fehr and Fischbacher (2003) have argued that punishment should be more effective than reward at promoting cooperation, but more recent work on this topic has challenged this generalized finding. Rand and colleagues (2009) demonstrate that when the identity and reputation of other group members are known, and targeted/selective interactions are possible, then "rewards go further than punishment in both benefitting the public good and in building cooperation, despite the efforts of free riders" (Nowak 2011, 231). As a result, there has been renewed interest in understanding the role that reward and punishment play in evoking cooperation within groups. It may be simply that punishment deters self-interest, and reward elicits cooperation, but more research is needed to determine how these cooperative mechanisms work within established organizations.

The decision by individuals to altruistically punish a free rider or reward a cooperator is not necessarily motivated by a rational cost/benefit calculus. Reciprocal altruism (both direct and indirect) is regulated by a range of emotions, including friendship, sympathy, gratitude, guilt, a sense of justice, and moralistic aggression—the latter being the punishment of cheaters or free riders. Much evidence indicates that altruistic punishment is motivated by emotions, such as anger and annoyance (Frank 1988; Fehr and Gächter 2002; Burton-Chellew, Ross-Gillespie, and West 2010). Other interesting research on the role of emotions in sustaining group cooperation shows that people derive personal satisfaction from punishing norm violators (de Quervain et al. 2004). Even though there is evidence that humans may be more rational and less emotional than our common ancestor and our living primate cousins (Keverne, Martel, and Nevison 1996) evolved human cognition related to cooperation is about more than just (rational) thinking; it has a significant emotional component as well (Trivers 1971; Damasio 1994). Human evolution has fashioned a number of emotional states that help enable and sustain cooperation among members of our species.

Cooperation on a Larger Scale

So far we have been addressing the mechanisms that promote cooperation between individuals and among those in fairly small group settings (for example clans, tribes, and workgroups). It is interesting to note at this point that studies of primate brain size find a fairly consistent positive correlation between relative brain size (neo-cortex to weight ratio) and social group size. Since humans have larger brains than other primates when adjusted for body size, we would expect and do find that humans form larger social groups. Correlation analyses generate estimates of an extended human group size of around a maximum of 150 (Dunbar 1993). This number corresponds well with other evidence. Known nomadic hunter-gatherer bands number around 30 individuals but gather together occasionally in groups of more than 100. In our ancestral environment, hunter-forager groupings may have been larger because they often subsisted in more resource-abundant ecologies than most known contemporary hunter-forager groups. As well, the size of intimate social networks in modern human societies also agrees with the estimate of 150 (Hill and Dunbar 2003).

There are several possible solutions to the conundrum of cooperation on an increasingly larger scale. Cooperation may begin within smallish groups and evolve in scale. But growth in scale brings with it growth in complexity and new challenges to sustaining cooperation. Introducing reputation-based cooperation increases the cognitive load on the cooperators but does allow for larger cooperative networks to develop. Cooperation on an even larger scale can be achieved with altruistic reward and punishment. Nowak (2006) draws on multilevel evolutionary theory to suggest how cooperative groups can evolve in larger populations. He begins his description by proposing a population comprising three types of groups: high-cooperation, low-cooperation, and mixed-cooperation. Low-cooperation groups would quickly become extinct, because internal contestation and free riding severely compromise their survival potential, particularly when in competition with high-cooperation groups. High-cooperation groups would be very successful and would likely produce a large number of cooperative "offspring." Over time there is a tendency for high-cooperation groups to divide because of increasing size, thereby adding to the number of high-cooperation groups in the population. Within the mixed-cooperation groups, the self-interested out-reproduce cooperators because of selection at the individual level. Over time, a mixed-cooperation group becomes a low-cooperation group. As such, it becomes vulnerable when in competition with high-cooperation groups, and, as initially, the low-cooperation group is likely to become extinct. Competition at the group level favors cooperative groups again, increasing their representation in the overall population, and over time the population becomes one composed of highly cooperative groups.

Interestingly, higher levels of intergroup competition appear to increase altruistic cooperation within groups (Bornstein and Ben-Yossef 1994). When facing external threat, individuals regard their group mates more as collaborators and less as competitors (Burton-Chellew, Ross-Gillespie, and West 2010). If so, then intergroup competition could actually amplify the evolution of within-group cooperation.

The most obvious challenge to Nowak's theory, however, is the issue of how a cooperative group might emerge in the first place. Recall Dawkin's daunting scenario—the destructive force and reproductive potential of one selfish rebel in a group of cooperators. One suggestion is that the initial emergence of a highly cooperative group might have been a stochastic event—improbable but still possible. Alternatively, cooperators may deliberately band together through a process known as assortative interactions. As with other cooperative mechanisms, this process has certain cognitive and perceptual requirements. But if cooperators can identify kindred spirits and join together, they could create a group of like-minded individuals. Either or both of these processes could result in groups with higher frequencies of cooperators. As Nowack describes, even if only a few groups in a structured population of multiple groups develop a strong norm or culture for cooperation, then selection pressures at the group level that favor larger, more cooperative groups can increase the frequency of those norms within the overall population.

Human biological/genetic evolution provides the substrate for large-scale cooperation; it is a necessary but not sufficient condition. As suggested in the prior section, there is more at work in human evolution and the achievement of ultrasociality than the transmission of genes alone. Evolution selects for behaviors; it is blind to the mechanisms for transmission and retention. Learned behaviors transmitted and retained across individuals within a population allow for another system of inheritance that can also evolve.[3] Selection for socially learned behaviors is usually called cultural evolution. But it is not limited to cultures; the process is applicable to any defined human social grouping: tribes, teams, departments, organizations, and societies. The human cognitive capacity for social learning and imitation underpins cultural evolution.

Richerson and Boyd and their colleagues are well known for their many studies of cultural evolution. They assert that the human capacity for "high fidelity imitation is one of the most important derived characters distinguishing us from our primate relatives" (Richerson and Boyd 2005, 258). Cognitive capacity enables learning. But Skinnerian trail-and-error, individual learning is costly. There are adaptive solutions to the learning problem other than random trials by each individual entailing many costly errors and infrequent success. Social learning, the cultural transmission of learned or imitated behaviors, is biased by decision rules: "copy the successful," "copy the prestigious," or "copy the majority." These rules (or heuristics) "allow individuals to acquire rapidly and efficiently adaptive behaviors across a wide range of circumstances and play an important role . . . in the origins of cooperative tendencies in human behavior" (258).

A cultural grouping is any stable assembly of unrelated (or distantly related) individuals. Any such assembly provides the opportunity for the group to realize advantages from cooperation. Groups better able to realize these advantages will outperform and outcompete groups less able to do so. Assuming there are limited resources, and selection pressures are present, selection at the level of the group will occur. Group selection for genetically retained characteristics is still controversial (Pinker 2002). But group selection on the basis of culture is less contentious, because while individuals cannot change their genes; they can change their behavior based upon social learning. It is the behaviors of the adaptive unit that are selected. It does not matter if it is genes or social learning and imitation that transmit those behaviors. Genetically dissimilar members of the same group can learn to behave in similar ways. Some kind of conformist social learning and appreciation of the associated heuristics are crucial to cultural group selection and evolution. With these rules in place, new members of the group learn established norms and converge upon similar behaviors. Adoption of these group or cultural norms reduces within-group behavioral variation. The reduction of within-group variation in behaviors allows for the selection of advantageous between-group differences. Over time, this process diminishes behavioral differences within groups and leads to the extinction of less well-adapted groups.

Coevolution and the Cooperative Instinct

Cultures can evolve, and they can also coevolve with genes. This process acknowledges the sequential interdependence of genes and culture (Campbell 1965; Boyd and Richerson 1985; Lumsden and Wilson 1981). Given sufficient time, any cultural innovation may have genetic fitness consequences—including social innovations. Boyd, Richerson, and Henrich (2005) clearly explain how social innovations could interact and co-evolve with genetic changes in our ancestral environment, and we quote them at length below.

> Rudimentary cooperative institutions favored genotypes that were better able to live in more cooperative groups. Those individuals best able to avoid punishment and acquire the locally relevant norms were more likely to survive. At first such populations would have been only slightly more cooperative than typical nonhuman primates. However, genetic change leading to moral emotions, like shame and a capacity to learn and internalize local practices would allow the cultural evolution of more sophisticated institutions that in turn enlarged the scale of cooperation. These successive rounds of co-evolutionary change continued until eventually people were equipped with capacities for cooperation with distantly related people, emotional attachments to symbolically marked groups, and a willingness to punish others for transgression of group rules. . . . Of course, selfish and nepotistic impulses are never entirely suppressed; our genetically transmitted evolved psychology shapes human cultures, and, as a result, cultural adaptations still often serve the ancient imperatives of inclusive genetic fitness. However, cultural evolution also creates new selective environments that *build cultural imperatives into our genes.* (26; emphasis in original)

Christopher Boehm's (1997) description of the egalitarian ethos of our hunter-forager ancestors suggests a coevolutionary contribution to the development of a cooperative instinct. Boehm argues that humans evolved sufficient political intelligence to reverse the male-dominance hierarchy found in most primate groups (Wrangham and Peterson 1996) and established the egalitarian cultural traditions common to human hunter-forager groups. These learned behaviors were in place for thousands of generations—long enough to affect selection mechanisms at the level of the gene. There are many examples of how our modern gene pool was crafted and refined during this prolonged period of social stability (Tiger and Fox 1971). The cultural practices that emerged from an ethos of equal status and power-sharing among members of a group also resulted in self-interested noncooperators being sanctioned through gossip, criticism, and ridicule and more severely punished through ostracism, exile, and, in extreme cases, execution. Obviously such practices would severely curtail the reproductive advantages normally ascribed to status-seeking by self-serving individuals, thereby reducing the frequency of the associated genes in future generations.

This line of thinking leads to the cooperative instinct hypothesis—most people are innately (i.e., genetically) prepared to interact with others in ways that sustain cooperative groups. Experimental research in this stream of inquiry suggests that a high proportion of humans have an instinctive bias toward initial cooperation and helping other group members (Selten and Stoecker 1986; Warneken and Tomasello 2006). Benkler (2011) maintains that 30% of individuals will behave in their own self-interest most of the time. For another 20% of the population, the expression of cooperative behavior is unpredictable—sometimes these individuals cooperate, and sometimes they do not. But Benkler also suggests that a full 50% of the population systematically and predictably behaves cooperatively. Those in this category will greet cooperative overtures with cooperative responses (recall tit-for-tat strategy) or act cooperatively if contextual cues signal cooperation is expected (Kay, Wheeler, Bargh, and Ross 2004). Interestingly, he also identifies the presence of an extreme group of "unconditional cooperators" who will cooperate even at an expected cost to themselves.

We maintain that the success of the human species can be attributed to its ultrasociality (Campbell 1983)—its ability to constrain self-interest and promote cooperation in social interactions. This predisposition has coevolved and is innate; but how it manifests in diverse cultural practices varies widely. For example, the markings used to recognize fellow group members are cultural and learned. Similar logic applies to various approaches to rewarding and sanctioning group members or the treatment of out-group members (Boyd and Richerson 1982). While the evolution of cultural norms and traditions has resulted in much diversity in cooperative practices among human groups (Durham 1991), it is clear that they exist in every human society, which argues for the existence of a human universal—a cooperative instinct embedded in our genes as well as our culture. Genes and culture interacting over millennia of human history (Richerson and Boyd 1978) have forged within our species a frequent preference for cooperation and the mechanisms required to sustain cooperative interaction in larger social groups.

Cooperation: A Multilevel Phenomenon

We began the chapter by comparing organizations to organisms and highlighting the critical role that cooperative behavior plays in the dynamics affecting both. We maintain that biological organisms and human organizations are multilevel, cooperative systems subject to the process of natural selection. We identified the role that evolution played in the development of the cognitive and emotional underpinnings for cooperation in human groups. Recognition, memory, language, and emotions support the development of cooperative mechanisms that effectively constrain destructive intragroup contestation between members pursuing their individual self-interest, and they enable group-level adaptations to emerge. In addition to genetic traits, humans can learn behaviors—cultural norms and routines that can further extend the net of cooperative practices and enfold larger and larger groups of individuals into cooperatively functioning groups. Some of these larger cooperative groups extend beyond groups and teams to the formal organizations referred to by Barnard.

Formal organizations are a significant part of the fabric of any modern society, and they are believed to have the ability to replicate behaviors through routines. This concept of routines was developed by Nelson and Winter (1982). They identified routines as the replicators in their evolutionary process, equivalent to genes in biological evolutionary theory. And they asserted that "the behavior of firms can be explained by the routines they employ" (128). Groups form to take advantage of the principle that the whole is greater than the sum of its parts, and organizations do the same on a larger scale. Indeed, Nelson and Winter focused on organizations that were large and complex because they wanted to theorize about entities "that face a substantial coordination problem; typically because they have many members, performing many distinct roles, who make complementary contributions to the production of a relatively small range of goods and services. In such an organization, most of the working interactions of a large number of the members are primarily with other members" (97).

Organizations can be expected to employ many routines. Some of these routines work with, and work around, the more innate cooperative (and self-interested) tendencies of the members and groups making up the organization. If something like the cooperative instinct hypothesis is correct, then the social predispositions to cooperate forged in our past are still with us today. Indeed these instincts will have affected the form, function, and practices (i.e., the routines) of modern organizations.

If routines are to organizations as genes are to a biological organism, and organizations compete for the resources necessary for their survival, then it follows that populations of organizations will also evolve, similar to the way populations of organisms do. Hannan and Freeman (1989) popularized this approach to understanding the evolution of organizations. They argued that soon after its founding, an organization's basic structure/strategy and routines are established. More controversially, they asserted that these routines do not change—once established, organizations are not adaptable. In this view adaptations occur within a population through the founding (i.e., birth) of many new organizations, a few of which survive and grow, and the failure (i.e., death) of mature organizations that become less able to compete successfully for resources. This logic implies that established organizations cannot imitate the routines of their more successful competitors nor learn new routines and adapt to changing ecological circumstances. As a consequence it has not been popular with many organization and management scholars. However, the adaptation versus adaptability debate should not cloud the basic point that populations of organizations are subject to an evolutionary process and pressures. Those best able to solve the cooperation problem will flourish; those less able to do so will not.

Organizations also exist within an institutional ecology, and since these ecologies differ among countries and cultures, they present the organizations operating within them with different adaptive problems and opportunities. For example, Fukuyama (1995) found that societies differ markedly in how far they have progressed in developing institutional trust (an enabler of large-scale cooperation). He considers trust to be based on shared norms that exist in a stable and cooperative society. Consistent with North (1991), he observed that the members of some societies are confident that their institutions induce trustworthy behavior among most other members of their community. In these situations economic actors confidently deal with unrelated exchange partners, and large, well-capitalized, professionally managed organizations are commonplace; other societies without such institutions restrict trust to familial or tribal linkages and are populated by organizations that, although they may become sizeable under the leadership of a founding entrepreneur, eventually experience problems of scale and continuity typical of family businesses (Gordon and Nicholson 2008).[4] Fukuyama's work (1992 and 1995) illustrates the different ways organizations have adapted to differing institutional ecologies. Fully consistent with MLST, he found that when institutional trust at the societal/country level is underdeveloped, adjustments were made at the next level down—organizations limited their exchange networks, giving preference to kin and tribal relationships. Having explored cooperation as a multilevel phenomenon through an evolutionary lens, we consider next how the evolution of cooperation has begun to influence the development of theory related to human behavior in the workplace, and may continue to do so.

IMPLICATIONS OF MULTILEVEL SELECTION THEORY FOR ORGANIZATIONAL BEHAVIOR AND ORGANIZATION AND MANAGEMENT THEORY

The idea that individual behavioral and social predispositions forged in our ancestral environment affect actions taken in modern corporations and can inform organizational and managerial choices has existed in the popular literature for some time (Jay 1971; Semler 1993). The depth, rigor, and diversity of the thinking and research underpinning this insight have emerged more recently. The burgeoning area of evolutionary psychology (EP) is best known for attempting to explain our evolved behaviors. It has added much to the understanding of how our evolved biology affects behavior and cognition. At the university level, introductory courses are increasingly common, and evolutionary psychology textbooks are now available (Buss 2008). Over the past two decades, evolutionary psychology (and the evolutionary biology underpinning it) has achieved some prominence and is widely accepted within psychology and the cognitive neurosciences. Its insights are being applied, albeit slowly, to better explain established psychological constructs (McCrea and Costa 2008) and to aid in understanding many different types of individual behaviors in and around organizations. For example, in their review article Michalski and Shakelford (2010) assert that "large strides have been and will continue to be made through a union of personality science and evolutionary science" (509).

But our psychology (and sociology) evolved to address a plethora of adaptive problems—mate choice, parental investment, promiscuity, and so forth. Many of these have little to do with the adaptive problem of how to sustain cooperation within groups, and groupings of groups (i.e., larger organizations). And while recognizing that humans evolved in social groups, the focus of evolutionary psychology has been largely on the evolved biology/cognition of the individual. Buss (2011) suggests a way to begin broadening the focus and challenges researchers to ground their investigations in evolutionary processes. "Ultimately, it would be desirable to formulate a comprehensive taxonomy of all key social adaptive problems. This would permit examining each problem through the theoretical lens of difference detecting adaptations and formulating a program of research to test hypotheses about their role in evolved solutions" (32). Buss's challenge to broaden the field remains largely unanswered, since most researchers are attempting to explain how our evolved psychology addresses a subset of adaptive problems (i.e., only those at the individual level); however, some research is beginning to help us understand how social/cooperative groupings come into existence and evolve.

In the remainder of this section we examine how EP and MLST have informed the question of developing and sustaining cooperation within groups and organizations. Because EP can be employed to address almost any area of human behavior, this review is highly selective. We do not provide an exhaustive review; rather, we hope to illustrate how evolutionary thinking can inform our understanding of behaviors relevant to group and organizational settings, as well as suggest the potential for this kind of thinking to provide OB and OMT with a strong and coherent theoretical foundation. We consider work that has employed evolutionary process models at different levels of analysis, as well as the work of evolutionary scholars who have dealt with topics relevant to OB/OMT. As we do this, we also consider how MLST thinking can extend current EP thinking across levels. We urge readers to consider carefully the potential that this type of thinking, when interpreted with a neo-Darwinian perspective, holds for an integrated meta-theory connecting multiple levels.

Application to OB/OMT

OB/OMT scholars should view evolutionary psychology as a field of investigation with enormous potential to contribute to theories that strengthen our understanding of individual behavior as well as workplace behaviors within groups and organizational settings. Simplistic concerns about things such as biological determinism versus free will and relevance to our modern environment are misplaced (Confer et al. 2010). As we learn more and more about the rich fabric of our evolved psychology, it is clear that our evolved biology (and sociology) have provided for considerable variation among individuals within a population, as well as flexibility in how individuals respond to different situations. Moreover, an evolutionary perspective holds tremendous benefits. It provides a paradigm for understanding the basis for our motivation and predicting regularities (or explaining observed regularities) in behavior. The fundamental proposition is that our biology, psychology, and sociology evolved to address domain-specific adaptive problems in our ancestral/historical environment.

Those solutions transmitted to others, either genetically to offspring or through social learning to other members of the same social group, are still with us and affect us today. We describe this as a paradigm (or perhaps a meta-theory) rather than as theory because it cannot be tested in its entirety, just as Darwin's general proposition of descent with modification and natural and sexual selection was not testable. Detailed propositions related to specific adaptive problems, possible solutions, and testable hypotheses must be developed. The "truth" of the paradigm will be judged on the basis of the preponderance of hypotheses tested (with positive results) that flow from theories consistent with this paradigm. Of course, much work remains to be done, but this process is already under way, and in our judgment the accumulation of evidence thus far is supportive.

A new and different paradigm can be threatening to the established order (Kuhn 1962). But a new perspective can also be liberating, allowing us to hypothesize relationships and see connections that we could not previously perceive. We believe adopting an evolutionary perspective holds this potential for OB/OMT. It does not necessarily mean that existing OB/OMT theories/topics are incompatible with an evolutionary explanation; they may be partially or fully consistent. However, those compatibilities and consistencies need to be assessed. In this spirit, what follows is a brief and admittedly incomplete review of OB/OMT topics that have received scrutiny from evolutionary scholars.

Decision Making—Individual, Group, and Organizational

Decision-making is a pervasive topic featured prominently in many different fields. Within the business/management area, deciding is a salient topic not only in OB/OMT (Simon 1957; March and Simon 1958) but also in almost every other business discipline, from marketing (consumer decision-making) to operations research. We focus on how an evolutionary perspective informs decision making at levels most relevant for OB/OMT—individual, group, and organizational.

Individual Decision Making

An evolutionary perspective can affect decision making research in many ways. Most models of decision making require that the preferences (or utility) of the decision maker be known a priori, or at least that they be revealed through the decisions made. Evolution can provide straightforward explanations for the origin of preferences (e.g., cravings for sugar, salt, fatty meats, etc.). Beyond simple preferences, evolutionary psychologists seek to demonstrate that our minds incorporate numerous domain-specific "decision" modules and, when triggered by environmental conditions, combine with cultural inputs to initiate behavior. These modules were created in response to adaptive problems linking this thinking to evolutionary theory. Kenrick , Griskevicius, Sundie, Li, Li and Neuberg (2009) explain in more detail: "A key assumption of the evolutionary perspective is that the human brain contains not one monolithic rational decision-making device, but rather a number of different decision-systems, each operating according to different rules. Which system is currently doing the decision-making depends on adaptively relevant features of the current environment, as well as on the decision-maker's sex, mating strategy, and phase in the life-cycle, among other factors" (765). Of particular interest are those modules related to decisions concerning participation in social exchange and whether or not to do so in a cooperative trustworthy manner.

Tooby and Cosmides (1992) have proposed that natural selection has crafted a cognitive module to improve discrimination between those likely to be trustworthy and those likely to cheat. If cooperators can detect potential cheaters (or fellow cooperators), decisions about engaging in social exchanges become much less precarious. They concluded from their extensive program of research "the human mind includes cognitive procedures that are adaptations for reasoning about social exchange" (Tooby and Cosmides 1992, 206).

Work on a cheater detection module is a noteworthy example of our observation that for the most part evolutionary psychologists have concentrated on the level of the individual. Cheater detection is advantageous to the individual. Individuals with this ability avoid engagement with potential cheaters, and the outcome of this caution benefits that individual. But the ability to detect cheaters, while an individual attribute, also supports more widespread cooperation within a group of individuals endowed with this ability. Groups composed of individuals able to detect cheaters will make cheating (and attempts to cheat) within that group less frequent than within groups made up of individuals not endowed with this ability. It has also been shown that collectively work teams have the ability to identify and sanction shirkers (intentional non-co-operators) (Price 2006). Groups with these abilities have an adaptive advantage and will be able to outperform (and out compete) groups without these abilities. Thus a cognitive ability advantageous for each individual with that ability is also advantageous for groups made up of individuals with this ability. Fitness at both the individual and the group are improved by this cognitive adaptation.

Group Decision Making

Wilson (1997a) has moved the thinking about cognitive adaptations for decision making beyond the individual level and developed the idea of groups as adaptive decision-making units. He proposes two ways that human decision making could have evolved to enhance the fitness of groups. "First individuals might function as independent decision makers whose goal is to benefit the group. This is the way that we usually think about altruism. Second, individuals might cease to function as independent decision makers and become part of a group-level cognitive structure" (358). How altruistic decisions by individual members benefit the group, while controversial, is straightforward. Some individuals are imbued with what we have called the cooperative instinct; when making decisions, they will, at least in some situations, give preference to the fitness of the group over their individual fitness. As discussed earlier, the challenge is to explain how individual altruism evolved, or coevolved. The second possible benefit presupposes an evolved, group-level decision-making process—something akin to a group mind. (McDougall 1973).

When groups form and become units for selection, decisions will be made that affect the fate of the group. The way these decisions are made can evolve if, in some significant circumstances, a particular type of group decision-making process enhances group fitness more than other decision-making alternatives available to the group. Under these conditions, the group's decision-making process could be considered an adaption that could evolve and coevolve. We expect that cognitive modules or biases favoring processes with a greater fitness advantage could have coevolved to become an innate part of the human psyche. An example may help illustrate this possibility.

A hunter-forager band is often confronted with decisions affecting the survival and reproductive success of the group. At regular intervals, the group must move its encampment in search of food and water. These movements raise risks related to encountering potentially hostile bands or dangerous predators, as well as uncertainty as to success in securing needed resources. On the positive side, traveling presents the possibility of encounters with other friendly bands and associated trading and mating opportunities. Now consider two different groups. In one group the nominal leader coordinates the decision process. Without offering his own views, the coordinator solicits input from all qualified members of the band. Members feel they can express their views freely, and indeed they are under a moral obligation to contribute. All clansmen listen to and consider the thoughts and evidence of their fellows. Dialogue ensues. Although unanimity may not be achieved, a consensus emerges, and the coordinator/leader moves to closure, summarizing and announcing the decision reached by the band. The other band is led by a capable and knowledgeable leader. He may seek input from other group members, but in order to sustain the cohesiveness of the group and possibly to avoid retribution, members are reluctant to make suggestions or debate alternative views. Instead they defer to their leader and quickly converge upon the leader's solution.

These two hypothetical cases raise an interesting question. In terms of fitness (survival and reproductive success), which group will, on average, do better—one that engages in collective problem solving, or one that defers to its most able member? This is an empirical question. Anthropological evidence documents hunter-forager bands employing the first decision-making process when the decision affects the fate of the entire group, and time is not a critical element (Meggitt 1977; Boehm 1996). However, contemporary research investigating whether or, more aptly, under what circumstances groups make better decisions than their most able member(s) remains equivocal on this question. Kerr and Tindale (2004) summarize the situation as follows:

> The ubiquitous finding across many decades of research is that groups usually fall short of reasonable potential productivity baselines. . . . Some recent work, though, has sought to identify informative exceptions to this rule—that is, to identify tasks and performance contexts in which groups might reach or even exceed their apparent potential. One such potential productivity baseline is the

performance level of the group's most capable member. A few studies have reported performance groups attaining this criterion (Laughlin et al. 1995; Laughlin, Shupe, and Magley 1998; Laughlin, Gonzalez, and Sommer 2003). And a very few studies (Laughlin, Bonner, and Miner 2002; Michaelson, Watson, and Black 1989; Tindale and Sheffey 2002; Sniezek and Henry 1989) have reported the elusive assembly bonus effect—group performance that is better than the performance of any individual or any combination of individual member efforts. (625)

However, asking if a problem-solving process that engages group members is "superior" to an approach in which one member decides on behalf the entire group (although a prevalent theme in the group decision-making literature) misses the point from a MLST perspective.

Under each scenario, a decision is made either by or for the group that affects the fate of the entire group. In fact, both of these are viable group decision-making processes and either, or both, could have been selected for in our ancestral environment. If the decision being made affects the fate of the entire group, then a process should evolve that better addresses adaptively relevant problems confronting the group. Actually the group's fitness may be better served by having different processes in different decision contexts. For example, a tribe may have sufficient time to involve multiple group members in making a decision to raid another tribe. But during actual hostilities, time is at a premium, and the circumstances may not allow for input and involvement by all group members. From a survival standpoint, in situations requiring quick decisions, members would prefer to have a capable leader make decisions. Again, the anthropological literature provides examples of hunter-forager societies adopting different leaders and different decision-making processes, depending upon the decision context (war chiefs and peace chiefs; see Moore 1990). Facultative adaptations respond to different environments in different ways. We expect that group decision-making processes could have this characteristic.

The group decision-making research done by psychologists, sociologists, and OB scholars is considerable. Although Kerr and Tindale (2004) point to the potential, little of this work has employed "evolutionary principles and models to explore adaptiveness of various forms of group decision making" (642). However, Wilson (1997a) did an extensive review of the group decision-making literature to see if there was evidence supporting (or not) groups as adaptive decision-making units. And while the research he reviewed was not specifically designed to explore the question of groups as adaptive decision-making units, a few studies did report evidence consistent with this hypothesis. One example is particularly interesting. Wilson (1997a, 373) postulates that if an effective decision-making process is generally believed to go through a sequence such as idea/option generation, criteria identification, evaluation, selection, and implementation, then groups should have social norms and expect their members "to be non-conformist" and noncritical "during the idea generation stage, more conformist" and critical "during the idea selection" and implementation stage. He cites one study that manipulated the campsite decision of a Scout troop and found that when one member (a confederate in the research project) of this egalitarian group exhibited behavior "inappropriate" to the current stage of the decision process (but appropriate to another stage), that individual was socially sanctioned by other members of the group (Kruglanski and Webster 1991). This result is expected if there is an evolved cognitive module for a sequenced group-decision process in this context. While it suggests the existence of such an evolved cognitive module, this research is open to other interpretations. Furthermore it was not designed to address whether the alignment of behavior to the stage of the decision process or the sanctioning of misaligned behaviors were learned or innate social behaviors. More generally Wilson, Timmel, and Miller (2004) observe that "theoretically we should expect cognitive cooperation in humans to be richly context-sensitive and protected by social control mechanisms" (17). So far, however, there is little empirical research specifically designed to test a theory of an evolved group mind.

Most of the research on group decision making is carried out using temporary experimental groups; a much smaller proportion examines decision making by semipermanent or intact work groups. Formal organizations, which (as Barnard observed) can be thought of as more formal groupings of groups within an established structure, also make corporate decisions (e.g., resource allocation; Bower 1970) that affect the fate of the entire organization. Engel (2010) asks the question, "Do corporate actors (i.e., organizations) exhibit better judgment and decision making than groups or individuals?" After reviewing the literature, he identifies some difference in preferences, cognition, and decision making across the levels—individual, group, and organizational —but concludes, "In many respects, collective [group] and corporate [organizational] actors suffer from the same biases as individuals. Sometimes they do better, in the sense of being closer to standard rational choice assumptions, sometimes they do worse" (463). This conclusion leaves ambiguous the answer to the important question, "Is there an organizational mind?" Do organizations make better decisions than their most able members (or subunits)?

Organizational Decision Making

But organizations can be more than decision-making units. They may also be a cost-effective way to limit self-interested opportunism within large social groups. Economists argue that larger organizations may be necessary to realize production economies of scale. Simply stated, the production technology needed to achieve lower costs requires the detailed and time-dependent coordination of large numbers of people. This coordination can be more easily and cheaply achieved within an organization than by self-interested individuals (or small groups) transacting across markets. Coase's great insight was that total costs include not only production costs, but also coordination or, in his terms, *transaction costs* (Coase 1937). Williamson (1993) expanded upon this idea, positing that transaction costs are driven by the need to deter self-interested, opportunistic behavior. This is the same problem or trade-off posed by MLST—realizing the benefit of the group requires individual members to moderate their self-interested behavior.

Within economics, opportunism is generally treated as a behavioral constant, although Williamson acknowledges that its frequency can vary depending upon the context (Williamson 1993). Evolutionary biologists and psychologists believe this variability depends upon numerous factors, including group size and affiliation, leader characteristics, and other contextual variables. Cordes et al. (2011) develop this idea and relate it to firm size, theorizing that, other things being equal (1) smaller firms have more intense group-socialization processes that facilitate cooperation and therefore experience less opportunistic behavior; (2) the greater the business leader/entrepreneur's charismatic potential, the larger the group in which a cooperative regime can be maintained; and (3) a more formal managerial control system can keep in check opportunistic behavior in larger organizations. They assert that because of coevolution, human agents are inclined toward cooperative cultural variants and role-model bias in cultural transmission. They suggest that business leaders can use both these dispositions to influence the evolution of cooperative corporate cultures (17). While these authors assume that management-control systems keep opportunism in check, they do not specify the form or detailed functioning of these systems.

There is a vast literature on organizational and management control systems. But many questions remain about how large organizations formally regulate the opportunistic behavior of subunits and individual members. Principal-agent models prescribe aligning incentives so the pursuit of individual self-interest will accomplish the desired organizational outcomes. But for complex organizations confronting dynamic environments, this problem has proven intractable. Indeed much of the relevant OB/OMT research explores the dark side—how formal organizational rewards and incentives encourage self-interested behaviors at odds with desired outcomes (Harris and Bromiley 2007). Akerlof and Kranton (2005) identify multiple concerns with aligning individual monetary incentives with the goals of the enterprise and observe, "Empirical work validates these theoretical concerns. People respond almost too well to monetary incentives. That is, 'firms get what they pay for,' but since the schemes cannot be targeted well, what firms get is often not what they want" (11). They propose instead that organizations align the identity of their individual members with organizational goals; thus individual members "will lose utility—if they fall short of the ideals of" (9) the enterprise. When organizational practices are consciously designed to convert self-interest into group interest—that is, the individual believes that what is best for the group is best for the individual—their interests are aligned. Akerlof and Kranton use West Point's reengineering of the identity of its cadets as an example. The inculcation of West Point norms into their cadet corps is similar to what Selznick (1957) recognized as the "infusion of values." Selznick identified the role of leadership in establishing values in new organizations and representing those values in established organizations.[5] Evidence indicates that organizations in which individual and organizational goals are aligned experience a lower level of organizational politics (Witt 1998) and outperform organizations that lack such alignment (Yearout and Miles 2001).

Leadership and Cooperation

Probably the most popular of all management topics is the exploration of leadership. A great deal has been written in scholarly journals and the popular press about the phenomenon and its influence on organizational performance. How would one approach the topic of leadership using an MLST evolutionary lens? This path of inquiry begins by positioning leadership as an aspect of the group's social structure. Leadership is a feature of the social relationship between leaders and followers and cannot be considered as separated from the form and function of these relations (Van Vugt and Ahuja 2011). From the perspective of a multilevel theory, leadership is not simply a set of personal traits or a repertoire of behaviors exhibited by the leader (the focus of much the extant leadership research). Leadership and followership are structural phenomena, and as such the roles and actions of both leaders and followers depend not as much on the personal characteristics of those assuming these roles as on the function and interaction of these roles in enhancing group survival.

From this perspective, leadership is a process of leader-follower influence (Northouse 2007), but little attention has been given to considering it as a multilevel phenomenon (Kinicki et al. 2011). While volumes of text have been written about leadership and leadership practice, not much of it draws in evolutionary theory or multilevel selection (Kinicki et al. 2010; Lichtenstein and Plowman 2009; Yammarino and Dansereau 2008). Some aspects of leadership, when viewed with an evolutionary lens, may become understandable if we see them as mechanisms developed by our social species to enhance cooperative behavior at the group level while regulating self-interest at the individual level. Multilevel selection theory could be used to explain certain aspects of leader/follower behavior as well as inform our understanding of organizational performance.

For example, by way of position alone, a leader acquires a powerful tool in the quest to influence follower behavior. Followers watch their leaders closely to see what behavior is expected of them. As already noted, evolution has crafted heuristics that support behavioral imitation. By observing the actions of their leaders, followers learn how best to perform as members of the group (Kurtzman 2010). Evidence is accumulating that human brains have evolved specialized neurons (called mirror neurons) that enable us to observe and mimic the actions of others (Keysers 2010). A group's leader is a prime target for imitation. Chun and colleagues (2009) found evidence that the style of the most senior leader in an organization is strongly associated with the leadership style of the next level of executives in the corporation. One way in which leaders can influence followers' behavior is through their observable actions. Others have identified the importance of leader behavior by exhorting leaders to "model the way" (Kouzes and Posner 2002) or "walk the talk" (Peters and Waterman1982). Leaders who display and publicly endorse the value of cooperation over destructive competition and of group interest over self-interest can have a significant impact on the cooperative nature of their group (Lord and Brown 2001). Biology has equipped humans with the cognitive ability to perceive and interpret the behavior of others and to imitate the behavior of leaders.

Leaders have other important functions; the role requires them to be instrumental in the development and communication of the organization's vision. Vision is the idealized future state that those working for the organization aspire to achieve. Vision is a powerful unifying force (Senge 1990), and, as with goal alignment, committing to the organization's vision requires individuals to set aside their immediate self-interest and to act in ways that contribute to the attainment of the organization's greater goals. Leaders who are able to inspire their followers with their organization's vision have common ground for establishing cooperative behavior and thereby enhancing the fitness of their organizational unit.

As multilevel selection theory suggests, to maintain cooperative group relations, the emergence of self-interested behaviors needs to be kept in check for all members of the group, including the group's leader. It is acceptable for the leader to appear dominant if the outcome of his direction benefits the group, but if self-interest replaces group interest, the rise of a despotic or tyrannical leader can threaten the group's well-being. Despotic or tyrannical leaders are seen as self-interested. They direct the group toward accomplishing ends that provide advantages to themselves and often their kin, blatantly exploiting the members of the group for their own benefit. If this opportunistic behavior goes unchecked for long the cooperative nature of the group and the survival advantage resulting from this condition is threatened. To respond to this problem, our hunter-gatherer ancestors found it effective to employ the same cultural practices developed to constrain self-interest among members of the group (Boehm 1999). Followers would form alliances and employ gossip, criticism, ridicule, shunning, ostracism, and exile—even assassination—to control the self-interested behavior of a despotic leader. These techniques are still used in contemporary human groups (and organizations) to control leaders or individual members who are free riding or interfering with the cooperative ethos of the group.

Many popular models of organizational leadership prescribe other-interest over self-interest (Quinn 2004); leaders should enable others to act (Kouzes and Posner 2002) and inspire followers to lead (Bass and Avolio 1994). From an evolutionary perspective, the function of leadership, as with all other aspects of the group's social structure, is to maintain the cooperative character of the group and to enhance its survival. Leaders can do this through aligning individual identity with collective identity, by modeling values and practices of cooperation, by establishing and communicating empowering visions and by approaching their role as an adaptive mechanism that delivers a survival advantage, not as a way to increase personal power and control. Groups whose leadership does not foster cooperative relations among its members will be at a decided disadvantage when competing with groups whose leadership is better able to moderate the inherent self-interest of its members.

SUMMARY AND CONCLUSIONS

Evolution has been employed by a few OB and OMT scholars but largely limited to one level of analysis and most often as a metaphor. We believe it is more than a metaphor. A metaphor is a linguistic means of understanding one thing in terms of another, but it does not imply that the two things are causally related. The enhanced understanding of the biological and cultural evolution processes suggests that organizations are part of a multilevel evolutionary process broadly conceived. Organizations do not stand apart from the ongoing, multilevel evolutionary process; they are part of it. Evolution creates adaptive units at many different levels—both biological and sociological. Just as an individual is an evolved aggregation of many different types of cooperating cells, organizations are aggregates of departments; departments are aggregates of teams and teams are aggregates of individuals. And there are levels of selection above organizations; societies are aggregates of many different types of organizations and institutions.

The ability of the variation/selection/retention process to evolve more aggregated and more cooperative strata makes evolutionary theory intrinsically multilevel. Each stratum or level is based upon and causally linked to the strata preceding it. If evolutionary processes are operative at the newly emerged level, we can anticipate that another stratum may emerge. Although evolutionary systems have this potential, they are not teleological. The system does not have the goal of becoming more complex or more cooperative. This process (V-S-R) holds the potential for explaining the existence of levels and the causal linkages between the levels. By employing evolutionary theory, the biological sciences can now more clearly see the relationship between our simple, single-cell ancestors and more complex, multicellular organisms. But we can also see how biological organisms with evolved cognitive capacities can form groups, learn from one another, and develop organizations and institutions that are also subject to evolutionary forces. By employing this theoretical perspective, the organizational sciences can better understand where they fit into this grand synthesis. Admittedly this synthesis is still a work in progress, but OB/OMT scholars can and should contribute to it. Such a contribution will require a major shift in our thinking.

A recent special issue of the *Academy of Management Review* called for papers addressing the question, "Where are the new theories of organization?" (Suddaby, Hardy, and Huy 2011) We believe there was a long-standing, implicit assumption behind this call (Pfeffer 1997; Hinings 1988)—specifically, that organizational and management research should be a more independent discipline, more distinct from psychology and sociology. It is argued that management researchers should develop their own truly indigenous theories of management and organization. This desire is entirely understandable—it promotes a separate group identity. But we believe it may prove counterproductive. Historically, theory development within psychology and sociology was fragmented, lacking a unifying paradigm. These researchers developed theories to address phenomena specific to their context. The vast majority of organizational and management theories have borrowed from these other disciplines. Such theories are often "awkwardly imported" by organizational scholars "without fully adapting them to the new context." This leads to pleas for de novo and radical theory development by OB/OMT scholars, and a more two-way flow of ideas (Oswick, Fleming, and Hanlon 2011). These are admirable aspirations, but they ignore what we believe will become the theoretical unification of the biological and social sciences under the neo-Darwinian paradigm and multilevel selection theory. There is nothing inappropriate or belittling about adopting this perspective, borrowing from these scholars, and applying MLST to organizational and management questions. OB/OMT scholars can and should do more theorizing, but we would argue those theories should draw upon and be consistent with this emerging paradigm and synthesis. Collectively, the field of OB/OMT will either go its separate way, or—we would hope—it will contribute to this grand synthesis.

Currently the discipline of evolutionary psychology has a small following among OB/OMT scholars. However, for the most part they focus on the biological (i.e., genetic) basis for individual and, occasionally, small-group behaviors. Dual inheritance models and theories of socially transmitted behaviors are only beginning to gain traction. Multilevel theory and research has attracted some more interest among traditional organizational and management researchers (Kozlowski and Klein 2000; Hitt et al. 2007). But this work has dealt more with questions of methods and micro-linkages between levels. It has been agnostic as to the overarching paradigm linking the levels. Along with others (Wilson, Van Vugt, and O'Gorman 2008), we have argued here that multilevel selection theory is that paradigm. However, we acknowledge that OB/OMT researchers employing MLST will confront challenges. A major challenge will be addressing how these ideas affect management practice. A major criticism of management theories generally is how little they seem to directly address management practice (Pfeffer 1997; Mol and Birkinshaw 2007). Indeed, this lack of influence is used to argue for the development of indigenous organizational and management theories. However, influence should not be the only criterion used to guide theory development. A bad theory, or a good theory poorly or simplistically applied, can have negative consequences. Indeed, Alan Greenspan's acceptance of the precepts of efficient market theory may have contributed significantly to the 2008 near meltdown of the global financial system.

The practical value of MLS theory remains to be determined. But it directs the researchers' attention across levels and to the tension between the levels. At its most basic, this tension is between the interests of the aggregate grouping and the self-interests of its constituent parts. This should be a core focal area for OB/OMT. As Barnard (1968) observed, human groups and organizations only emerge and sustain themselves if they have an ongoing adaptive advantage relative to the members or subunits pursuing their self-interest. Thus, how much self-interest individuals bring with them and the social control that group members exert over one another's self-interest affect the viability of the group. Similarly, the time and effort that organizations invest in corporate cultures and management-control systems affect the frequency of self-interested behaviors by their members and subunits. In addition, differential selection pressures across levels also affect the evolution of cooperative groupings. Strong and persistent between-group selection pressures, often brought about by intergroup competition, favor the emergence of stronger and more viable groups—simply put, competition is good for groups. However, if within group (i.e., between self-interested individuals) selection pressures are strong, relative to between-group selection pressures, it will reduce the viability of the group. MLS theory and an evolutionary perspective provide the structure for a cross-level narrative, bridging the biological and sociological, to explain the development of contemporary social groupings. Fukuyama (1995) employs this structure to describe the evolved interrelationship between broad organizational forms and societal institutions. We believe this perspective provides management scholars with a unique opportunity for new insights and understanding that can serve to advance the field of OB/OMT. As well, these insights have the potential to contribute to the resolution of critically important organizational, social, and global problems. Doing so requires the researcher to appreciate fully the potential for individual self-interest at each level and the challenge that poses for the larger social grouping. However, using the insights generated from research employing this perspective should enable us, through enlightened social arrangements and leadership, to avoid deceiving ourselves about false solutions, to better understand and, hopefully, control our innate biases, to perceive and better understand the interrelationships between levels, and to accept the discipline required to reach collective solutions to global problems.

Notes

1. Throughout this chapter, we refer to the contemporary interpretations of evolution as a multilevel process that can extend beyond the genetic to social learning as neo-Darwinian theory.

2. The most successful strategy depends on the mix of strategies at the outset. But tit-for-tat or a similar strategy most often emerges as the winning strategy.

3. Richard Dawkins, in his book *The Selfish Gene*, coined the term *meme* for a unit of culturally transmitted information roughly equivalent to a gene. Thinking of memes as the cultural genes has gained some popularity (Blackmore 2000). Unfortunately, the literal application of the gene metaphor to social learning and cultural evolution has probably caused more confusion than enlightenment.

4. Alternately, they rely on state ownership to organize large-scale enterprises. Arguably, the managers of these organizations are held accountable to the citizen-owners through the political system.

5. Selznick (1957) made a clear distinction between "organizations" and "institutions." Institutions were infused with values; organizations were value-neutral. To avoid confusion with societal institutions, we employ the word *organizations* for both types.

References

Akerlof, G. A., and Kranton, R. E. 2005. Identity and the economics of organizations. *Journal of Economic Perspectives* 19 (1): 9–32.

Aldrich, H. E., and Ruef, M. 2006. *Organizations evolving.* 2nd ed. Thousand Oaks, CA: Sage.

Axelrod, R. M. 1984. *The evolution of cooperation.* New York: Basic Books.

Barnard, C. I. 1968. *The functions of the executive.* Cambridge: Harvard University Press. Orig. pub. 1938.

Bass, B. M., and Avolino, B. J. 1994. *Improving organizational effectiveness through transformational leadership.* Thousand Oaks: Sage.

Benkler, Y. 2011. The unselfish gene. *Harvard Business Review* 89 (7–8): 77–85.

Boehm, C. 1996. Emergency decisions, cultural-selection mechanics, and group selection. *Current Anthropology* 37:763–93.

———. 1997. Impact of the human egalitarian syndrome on Darwinian selection mechanics. *American Naturalist* 150 (S1): S100–S121.

———. 1999. *Hierarchy in the forest: The evolution of egalitarian behavior.* Cambridge, MA: Harvard University Press.

Blackmore, S. The power of memes. *Scientific American*, October 2000, 64–73.

Bornstein, G., and Ben-Yossef, M. 1994. Cooperation in intergroup and single-group social dilemmas. *Journal of Experimental Social Psychology* 30:52 –67.

Bower, J. L. 1970. *Managing the resource allocation process: A study of corporate planning and investment*. Homewood, IL: R. D. Irwin.

Boyd, R., and Richerson, P. J. 1982. Cultural transmission and the evolution of cooperative behavior. *Human Ecology* 10:325–51.

———, and Richerson, P. J. 1985. *Culture and the evolutionary process*. Chicago: University of Chicago Press.

———, Richerson, P. J., and Henrich, J. 2005. Cultural evolution of human cooperation. In *The origin and evolution of cultures*, ed. R. Boyd and P. J. Richerson, 251–81. Oxford: Oxford University Press.

Burton-Chellew, M. N., Ross-Gillespie, A., and West, S. A. 2010. Cooperation in humans: Competition between groups and proximate emotions. *Evolution and Human Behavior* 31:104–8.

Buss, D. M. 2008. *Evolutionary psychology: The new science of the mind*. 3rd ed. Boston: Pearson/Allyn Bacon.

———. 2011. Personality and the adaptive landscape: The role of individual differences in creating and solving social adaptive problems. In *The evolution of personality and individual differences*, ed. D. M. Buss and P. H. Hawley, 29–60. New York: Oxford University Press.

Campbell, D. T. 1965. Variation and selective retention in socio-cultural evolution. In *Social change in developing areas: A reinterpretation of evolutionary theory*, ed. H. Barringer, G. Blanksten, and R. Mack, 19–49. Cambridge, MA: Schenkman.

———. 1983. Two distinct routes beyond kin selection to ultrasociality: Implications for the humanities and social sciences. In *The nature of prosocial development: Interdisciplinary theories and strategies*, ed. D. L. Bridgeman, 11–41. New York: Academic Press.

———. 1994. How individual and face-to-face group selection undermine firm selection in organizational evolution. In *Evolutionary dynamics of organizations*, ed. J. A. C. Baum and J. V. Singh, 23–38. New York: Oxford University Press.

Chun, J. U., Yammarino, F. J., Dionne, S. D., Sosik, J. J., and Moon, H. K. 2009. Leadership across hierarchical levels: Multiple levels of management and multiple levels of analysis. *Leadership Quarterly* 20:689–707.

Coase, R. H. 1937. The nature of the firm. *Economica* 4:386–405.

Confer, J. C., Easton, J. A., Fleischman, D. S., Goetz, C. D., Lewis, D. M. G., Perilloux, C., and Buss D. M. 2010. Evolutionary psychology: Controversies, questions, prospects and limitations. *American Psychologist* 65:110–26.

Cordes, C., Richerson, P., McElreath, R., and Strimling, P. 2011. How does opportunistic behavior influence firm size? An evolutionary approach to organizational behavior. *Journal of Institutional Economics* 7 (1): 1–21.

Damasio, A. R. 1994. *Descartes' error: Emotion, reason, and the human brain*. New York: Putnam.

Darwin, C. 1871. *The descent of man, and selection in relation to sex*. London: John Murray.

Dawkins, R. 1976. *The selfish gene.* New York: Oxford University Press.

Dennett, D. C. 1995. *Darwin's dangerous idea: Evolution and the meanings of life.* New York: Simon and Schuster.

de Quervain, D. J. F., Fischbacher, U., Treyer, V., Schellhammer, M., Schnyder, U., Buck, A., and Fehr E. 2004. The neural basis of altruistic punishment. *Science* 305:1254–58.

Dunbar, R. I. M. 1993. Coevolution of neocortical size, group size and language in humans. *Behavioral and Brain Sciences* 16:681–735.

———. 1998. The social brain hypothesis. *Evolutionary Anthropology* 6 (5): 178–90.

Durham, W. H. 1991. *Coevolution: Genes, culture and human diversity.* Stanford, CA: Stanford University Press.

Emery, F. E., and Trist, E. L. 1960. Socio-technical systems. In *Management science, models and techniques,* vol. 2, ed. C. W. Churchman and M. Verhurst, 2:83–97. London: Pergamon Press.

Engel, C. 2010. The behavior of corporate actors: How much can we learn from the experimental literature? *Journal of Institutional Economics* 6 (4): 445–75.

Fehr, E., and Gächter, S. 2002. Altruistic punishment in humans. *Nature* 415:137–40.

———, and Fischbacher, U. 2003. The nature of human altruism. *Nature* 425:785–91.

Frank, R. H. 1988. *Passions within reason: The strategic role of emotions.* New York: W. W. Norton.

Fukuyama, F. 1992. *The end of history and the last man.* New York: Free Press.

———. 1995. *Trust: The social virtues and the creation of prosperity.* New York: Free Press,

Gintis, H., Bowles, S., Boyd, R., and Fehr, E. 2003. Explaining altruistic behavior in humans. *Evolution and Human Behavior* 24:153–72.

Gordon, G., and Nicholson, N. 2008. *Family wars.* London: Kogan Page.

Gurek, O., Irlenbusch B., and Rockenbach, B. 2006. The competitive advantage of sanctioning institutions. *Science* 312:108–11.

Hannan, M. T., and Freeman J. 1989. *Organizational ecology.* Cambridge, MA: Harvard University Press.

Harris, J., and Bromiley, P. 2007. Incentive to cheat: The influence of executive compensation and firm performance on financial misrepresentation. *Organization Science* 18:350–67.

Hill, R. A., and Dunbar, R. I. M. 2003. Social network size in humans. *Human Nature* 14:53–72.

Hinings, C. R. 1988. Defending organizational theory: A British view from North America. *Organization Studies* 9:2–7.

Hitt, M. A., Beamish, P. W., Jackson, S. E., and Mathieu, J. E. 2007. Building theoretical and empirical bridges across levels: Multilevel research in management. *Academy of Management Journal* 50:1385–89.

Homans, G. S. 1950. *The human group.* New York: Harcourt Brace.

Jay, A. 1971. *Corporation man: Who he is, what he does, why his ancient tribal impulses dominate the life of the modern corporation.* New York: Random House.

Katz, D., and Kahn, R. L. 1966. *The social psychology of organizations.* New York: John Wiley.

Kay, A. C., Wheeler, S. C., Bargh, J. A., and Ross, L. 2004. Material priming: The influ-

ence of mundane physical objects on situational construal and competitive behavioral choices. *Organizational Behavior and Human Decision Processes* 95: 83–96.

Kenrick, D. T., Griskevicius, V., Sundie, J. M., Li, N. P., Li, Y. J., and Neuberg, S. L.
2009. Deep rationality: The evolutionary economics of decision making. *Social
Cognition* 27:764–85.

Kerr, N. L., and Tindale, R. S. 2004. Group performance and decision making. *Annual
Review of Psychology* 55:623–55.

Keverne, E. B., Martel, F. L., and Nevison, C. M. 1996. Primate brain evolution: Genetic and functional considerations. *Proceedings of the Royal Society of London B*
263:689–96.

Keysers, C. 2009. Mirror neurons. *Current Biology* 19:R971–973.

Kinicki, A. J., Jocobson, K. J. L., Galvin, B. M., and Prussia, G. E. 2011. A multilevel systems model of leadership. *Journal of Leadership and Organization Studies*
18:133–49.

Kouzes, J. M., and Posner, B. Z. 2002. *The leadership challenge*. San Francisco: Jossey-
Bass.

Kozlowski, S. W. J., and Klein, K. J. 2000. A Multilevel approach to theory and research in organizations: Contextual, temporal, and emergent processes. In *Multilevel theory, research, and methods in organizations: Foundations, extensions, and
new directions*, ed. K. J. Klein and S. W. J. Kozlowski, 3–90. San Francisco, CA:
Jossey-Bass.

Kruglanski, A. W., and Webster, D. M. 1991. Group member's reactions to opinion
deviates and conformists at varying proximity to decision deadline and of environmental noise. *Journal of Personality and Social Psychology* 61:212–25.

Kuhn, T. 1962. *The structure of scientific revolutions*. Chicago: University of Chicago
Press.

Kurtzman, J. 2010. *Common purpose: How great leaders get organizations to achieve the
extraordinary*. San Francisco, CA: Jossey-Bass.

Laughlin, P. R., Bonner, B. L., and Miner, A. G. 2002. Groups perform better than the
best individuals on Letters-to-Numbers problems. *Organizational Behavior and Human Decision Processes* 88:605–20.

———, Chandler, J. S., Shupe, E. I., Magley, V. J., and Hulbert, L. G. 1995. Generality
of a theory of collective induction: Face-to-face and computer-mediated interaction, amount of potential information, and group versus member choice of evidence. *Organizational Behavior and Human Decision Processes* 63:98–111.

———, Gonzalez, C. M., and Sommer, D. 2003. Quantity estimations by groups and
individuals: Effects of known domain boundaries. *Group Dynamics* 7:55–63.

———, Shupe, E. I., and Magley, V. J. 1998. Effectiveness of positive hypothesis testing for cooperative groups. *Organizational Behavior and Human Decision Processes*
73:27–38.

Lewin, K. 1951. *Field theory in social science: Selected theoretical papers*. New York:
Harper.

Lichtenstein, B. B., and Plowman, D. A. 2009. The leadership of emergence: A complex systems leadership theory of emergence at successive leadership levels.
Leadership Quarterly 4:617–30.

Likert, R. 1961. *New patterns of management.* New York: McGraw-Hill.

Lord, R. G., and Brown, D. T. 2001. Leadership, values and subordinate self-concepts. *Leadership Quarterly* 12:133–52.

Lumsden, C. J., and Wilson, E. O. 1981. *Genes, mind, and culture: The coevolutionary process.* Cambridge, MA: Harvard University Press.

March, J., and Simon, H. 1958. *Organizations.* New York: John Wiley.

Markoczy, L., and Goldberg, J. 1998. Management, organization and human nature: An introduction. *Management and Decision Economics* 19:387–409.

Marshall, A. 1920. *Principles of economics.* 8th ed. London: Macmillan.

Maynard Smith, J., and Szathmary, E. 1995. *The major transitions in evolution.* New York: W. H. Freeman Spektrum.

McCrea, R. R., and Costa, P. T. 2008. The five factor theory of personality. In *Handbook of personality: Theory and research,* ed. O. P. John, R. W. Robins, and L. A. Pervin, 159–81. New York: Guilford Press.

McDougall, W. 1973. *The group mind.* New York: Putnam. Orig. pub. in 1920.

Meggitt, M. 1977. *Blood is their argument.* Palo Alto, CA: Mayfield.

Michaelsen, L. K., Watson, W. E., and Black, R. H. 1989. A realistic test of individual versus group consensus decision making. *Journal of Applied Psychology* 74:834–39.

Michalski, R. L., and Shakelford, T. K. 2010. Evolutionary personality psychology: Reconciling human nature and individual differences. *Personality and Individual Differences* 48:509–16.

Michod, R. E., and Roze, D. n.d. A multi-level selection theory of evolutionary transition in individuality. Retrieved December 19, 2012, from http://www.ugr.es/~jmgreyes/michod_roze.pdf.

Mol, M. J., and Birkinshaw, J. 2007. Giant steps in management: Key management innovations. London: Pearson Education.

Moore, J. H. 1990. The reproductive success of Cheyenne war chiefs: A contrary case to Chagnon's Yanomamö. *Current Anthropology* 13:322–30.

Nelson, R. R., and Winter, S. G. 1982. *An evolutionary theory of economic change.* Cambridge, MA: Harvard University Press.

Nicholson, N. 2010. The design of work—an evolutionary perspective. *Journal of Organizational Behavior* 31:422–31.

———, and de Waal-Andrews, W. 2005. Playing to win: Biological imperatives, self-regulation, and trade-offs in the game of career success. *Journal of Organizational Behavior* 26:137–54.

———, and White, R. E. 2006. Darwinism—A new paradigm for organizational behavior? *Journal of Organizational Behavior* 27:111—19.

North, D. C. 1991. Institutions. *Journal of Economic Perspectives* 5 (1): 97–112.

Northouse, P. 2007. *Leadership: Theory and Practice.* Thousand Oaks, CA: Sage.

Nowak, M. A. 2006. Five rules for the evolution of cooperation. *Science* 314:1560–63.

———. 2011. *Super cooperators.* New York: Free Press.

———, and Sigmund, K. 1998. Evolution of indirect reciprocity by image scoring. *Nature* 393:573–77.

O'Gorman, R., Henrich, J., and Van Vugt, M. 2009. Constraining free riding in public goods games: Designated solitary punishers can sustain human cooperation. *Proceedings of the Royal Society B* 276:323–29.

Oswick, C., Fleming, P., and Hanlon, G. 2011. From borrowing to blending: Rethinking the processes of organizational theory building. *Academy of Management Review* 36:318–37.

Peters, T. J., and Waterman, R. H. 1982. *In search of excellence: Lessons from America's best run companies*. New York: Harper Row.

Pfeffer, J. 1997. *New directions for organization theory: Problems and prospects*. Oxford: Oxford University Press.

Pinker, S. 2002. *The blank slate: The modern denial of human nature*. New York: Viking.

———. n.d. The false allure of group selection. Retrieved December 19, 2012 from http://edge.org/conversation/the-false-allure-of-group-selection.

Price, M. E. 2006. Monitoring, reputation, and "greenbeard" reciprocity in a Shurar work team. *Journal of Organizational Behavior* 27:201–19.

Quinn, R. E. 2004. *Building the bridge as you walk on it: A guide for leading change*. San Francisco: Jossey-Bass.

Rand, D. G., Dreber, A., Ellingsen, T., Fudenberg, D., and. Nowak, M. A. 2009. Positive interactions promote public cooperation. *Science* 325:1272–75.

Richerson, P. J., and Boyd, R. 1978. A dual inheritance model of the human evolutionary process: Basic postulates and a simple model. *Journal of Social and Biological Systems* 1:127–54.

———, and Boyd R. 2005. *Not by genes alone: How culture transformed human evolution*. Chicago: University of Chicago Press.

Roethlisberger, F., and Dickson, H. A. 1939. *Management and the worker: An account of a research program at the Western Electric Company, Hawthorne Works, Chicago*. Cambridge, MA: Harvard University Press.

Selten, R., and Stoecker, R. 1986. End behavior in sequences of finite prisoner's dilemma supergames: A learning theory approach. *Journal of Economic Behavior and Organization* 7:47–70.

Selznick, P. 1957. *Leadership in administration: A sociological interpretation*. White Plains, NY: Row, Peterson.

Semler, R. 1993. *Maverick: The success story behind the world's most unusual workplace*. New York: Warner Books.

Senge, P. 1990. *The fifth discipline: The art and practice of learning organizations*. New York: Doubleday.

Simon, H. A. 1957. *Administrative behavior: A study of decision-making processes in administrative organizations*. New York, NY: Free Press.

Sniezek, J. A., and Henry, R. A. 1989. Accuracy and confidence in group judgment. *Organizational Behavior and Human Decision Processes* 43:1–28.

Suddaby, R., Hardy, C., and Huy, Q. N. 2011. Introduction to special topic forum: Where are the new theories of organization? *Academy of Management Review* 36:236–46.

Thompson, J. D. 1967. *Organizations in action: Social science basis of administration*. New York: McGraw-Hill.

Tiger, L., and Fox, R. 1971. *The imperial animal*. New York: Delta.

Tindale, R. S., and Sheffey, S. 2002. Shared information, cognitive load, and group memory. *Group Processes and Intergroup Relations* 5:5–18.

Tomasello, M. 2009. *Why we cooperate*. Cambridge, MA: MIT Press.

Tooby, J., and Cosmides, L. 1992. The psychological foundations of culture. In *The adapted mind*, ed. J. H. Barkow, L. Cosmides, and J. Tooby, 19–136. Oxford: Oxford University Press.

Trivers, R. L. 1971. The evolution of reciprocal altruism. *Quarterly Review of Biology* 46:35–57.

Van Vugt, M., and. Ahuja, A. 2011. *Naturally selected: The evolutionary science of leadership*. New York: Harper-Collins.

Warneken, F., and Tomasello, M. 2006. Altruistic helping in human infants and young chimpanzees. *Science* 311:1301–3.

Weick, K. 1979. *The social psychology of organizing*. New York: McGraw-Hill.

White, R. E., and Pierce, B. D. 2000. On Maslow, monkeys and evolution. *Academy of Management Review* 10:697–99.

Williamson, O. E. 1993. Calculativeness, trust, and economic structure. *Journal of Law and Economics* 36:453–86.

Wilson, D. S. 1997a. Incorporating group selection into the adaptationist program: A case study involving human decision-making. In *Evolutionary social psychology*, ed. J. A. Simpson and D. T. Kenrick, 345–86. Mahwah, NJ: Lawrence Erlbaum.

———. 1997b. Introduction: Multilevel selection theory comes of age. *American Naturalist* 150 (July): S1–S4.

———. 2007. *Evolution for everyone: How Darwin's theory can change the way we think about our lives*. New York: Delacorte Press.

———, Timmel, J. J., and Miller, R. R. 2004. Cognitive cooperation—When the going gets tough, think as a group. *Human Nature* 15 (3): 1–15.

———, Van Vugt, M., and O'Gorman, R. 2008. Multilevel selection theory and major evolutionary transitions: Implications for psychological science. *Current Directions in Psychological Science* 17:6–9.

Wilson, E. O. 1998. *Consilience: The unity of knowledge*. New York: Knopf.

Witt, L. A. 1998. Enhancing organizational goal congruence: A solution to organizational politics. *Journal of Applied Psychology* 83:666–74.

Wrangham, R. W., and Peterson, D. 1996. *Demonic males: Apes and the origins of human violence*. Boston: Houghton Mifflin.

Yammarino, F. J., and Dansereau, F. 2008. Multi-level nature of and multi-level approaches to leadership. *Leadership Quarterly* 19:135–41.

Yearout, S., and Miles, G. 2001. *Growing leaders*. Alexandria, VA: American Society of Training and Development.

TWELVE

Biology, Evolution, and Organizations: Promises and Challenges in Building the Foundations

Glenn R. Carroll and Kieran O'Connor

INTRODUCTION

At this point in the book, you know very well, dear reader, that the preceding chapters contain many interesting ideas, lots of fascinating facts, and an abundance of intriguing suggestions for future theory, research, and practice. That alone is enough to make a book a successful contribution, and worthy of wide readership. But the editors and many of the authors of this book want more—they tell us that their goal is to generate interest and excitement for a new approach to the venerable old field of organizational behavior, one with a new foundation based in biology. We call this the "Biological Foundations Project."

What would organizational theory and research look like if it were erected on the foundations of biology? What is its promise? Can it be realized? Why or why not? What are the challenges? These are the types of issues that we have been asked to contemplate in this last chapter. Obviously, our thoughts on the matter can be at best suggestive and speculative, but that does not mean that we hold them lightly or that they might not be provocative. Nor do we expect the authors of the book (or even the editors) to endorse them or to even agree with them. Rather, we hope to stimulate discussion and dialogue about how ever more rapid develop-

We appreciate helpful comments by the editors (Stephen Colarelli and Rich Arvey) and David Pervin on an earlier draft.

ments in biology might productively be used to help us understand organizations and behavior within them. In other words, we share the goal of the contributors to this volume: development of a biologically informed field of organizational behavior.

First, we should clarify some things about the field called "organizational behavior." Despite a long history of research and practice, organization studies have never became fully formed or unified as a single field or discipline. As defined by Clegg and Hardy (1996, 3), organization studies are "a set of conversations, in particular those of organization studies researchers who help to constitute organizations through terms derived from paradigms, methods and assumptions, themselves derived from earlier conversations." By no means is this a precise definition, in large part because organization studies evolved from diverse roots, thereby necessitating reference to studies (plural) rather than a paradigmatically coherent field.

In tracing the intellectual lineage of organizational behavior, Scott (1998) points to sociologists Karl Marx and Max Weber in the bureaucratic tradition, while others connect the lineage to psychologist Kurt Lewin or even to social engineer Frederick W. Taylor, both of whom worked on the micro level. These different claims about the field's intellectual origins reflect a major unresolved tension within contemporary organization studies: the simultaneous development of individual-level (or micro-level) theories from industrial and social psychology alongside structural-level (or macro-level) theories from sociology. This bifurcation manifests itself today in a pronounced divide between micro-level organizational studies (often known as organizational behavior, or OB), and macro-level research (known as organizational theory, or OT).

The divide sometimes generates (usually mild) turf battles between the two sides over phenomena commonly regarded as important, such as power, culture, or social networks. But more typically, the divide reveals itself in research programs that appear unconnected and unconcerned with each other's developments (Staw 1984; O'Reilly 1991).[1] Institutionally, the two types of organization studies are organized separately into different divisions of the professional Academy of Management (Organizational Behavior for the micro-level and Organization and Management Theory for the macro-level) and into separate (if occasionally overlapping) specialty journals such as the *Academy of Management Journal* (mainly micro-level) and the *Administrative Science Quarterly* (mainly macro-level). The disciplinary associations—American Sociological Association and the American Psychological Association—and their official journals also serve to keep the two parts of the field distinct.

At the outset, we should also make clear our generic classification of the chapters in the book with regard to the biological foundations of organization studies. Although the title and other orienting statements found here often use the single rubric of "biology," biology is, of course, a very diverse field that encompasses many different and, at times, isolated areas. Thus, it should be no surprise that the book contains more than one basic approach. Indeed, taking a broad view of the chapters (and at the risk of oversimplifying), we see them as reflecting two main themes that contain unique and somewhat separate sets of issues for organization studies. The first theme appears in those studies that tend primarily to consider the *organic basis of behavior*, including genes, DNA, and hormones. Here we include the chapters by Song, Li, and Wang (chapter 2); Ilies and Dimotakis (chapter 3); Shane and Nicolaou (chapter 4); Judge and Hogan (chapter 5); Narayanan and Prasad (chapter 6); and Zhang and Zyphur (chapter 7). The second theme explicitly brings *evolution and evolutionary processes* into the picture and appears in the chapters by Price and van Vugt (chapter 8); DeScioli, Kurzban, and Todd (chapter 9); Nicholson (chapter 10); and White and Pierce (chapter 11).

These two themes—the organic basis of behavior and evolutionary processes—can be discussed in relative isolation because they each raise important, unique issues and challenges for behavioral researchers. We accede to this convention initially in our comments, but we subsequently consider the two themes jointly and simultaneously. We do so not as an afterthought but in full concentration, because we claim (as do many of the authors of these chapters) that it is the promise of combining the two approaches that makes this Biological Foundations Project unique and potentially path-breaking. But we think the combination also makes the project extremely challenging and perhaps daunting. We attempt to articulate some of the reasons behind our view below.

Before embarking on our commentary about the book, we make a slight detour. To give some background to the uninitiated, we provide in the next section a very brief overview of the field of OB and its macrolevel sibling, OT. Following that, we describe broadly organizational ecology, the theoretical perspective in these fields that makes the most explicit and sustained use of evolutionary theory. These discussions extend and elaborate the background of the field sketched by Collarelli and Arvey in chapter 1.

In the spirit of full disclosure, we should perhaps also say something now about ourselves and our backgrounds. We are both organizational analysts, in the mainstream organizational behavior (micro) OB/organizational theory (macro) OT fields. Carroll is a sociologist who works in organizational theory, and has been active in organizational ecology. O'Connor is a social psychologist, who is working on problems of morality and justice. Neither of us is a biologist or is trained formally in biology, beyond a few courses in graduate school. Like most researchers in these fields, both of us are unapologetic followers of what Colarelli and Avery call in Chapter 1 the "standard social science model," borrowing from Tooby and Cosmides (1992). But we both also maintain interest in organizations and evolution, and a curiosity about how developments in biology will affect organizational behavior. We like to think we are open-minded.

Open-mindedness is an essential virtue for social scientists to remember when reading and evaluating this book. While biology excites plenty of social scientists, we sense from colleagues that it scares or angers even more. Why? For many, claims and evidence about the biological foundations of behavior apparently threaten social science's very existence, as fears arise that reductionist explanations will eventually make psychology and sociology obsolete. For others, the concern is that biological markers of behavior will fall into the wrong hands and foster an Orwellian-like age of genetic engineering. We think both views are misguided. In our opinion, bringing biology into the picture actually heightens the demands on, and centralizes the role of, social science theory and research in explaining behavior, as many have noted above and as we articulate again below. Furthermore, we do not think finding genetic or other organic links to behavior should generate any more alarm than finding strong dispositional traits does today. Moreover, we believe that the potential for socially beneficial use of both kinds of knowledge more than outweighs the concerns. In any event, ignoring the issue will not make it go away, and we believe that volumes such as this one do a great service to the social sciences by bringing the topic to center stage, however controversial that might prove to be.

Our goals in this chapter are threefold. First, we seek to explain why, despite the many developments in understanding the biological basis of human behavior, it has had little visible influence on the established fields of organizational behavior and theory. As Colarelli and Arvey say in the introductory chapter, "Modern genetics and the theory of evolution by natural selection have had such a small impact on the study of organizational behavior" (2). Our effort to account for this rarity is by its very nature somewhat speculative. Second, we attempt to develop arguments that support and bolster the view that biology should play a greater role in the study of organizations and associated behavior. Our efforts here may be seen as elaborations on the claims in other chapters about what might be gained. Third, we identify and discuss some of the major challenges facing the establishment and acceptance of a biologically informed field of organizational behavior, and outline generally some of the things that might be needed to overcome these challenges. All in all, we attempt to provide a friendly but frank commentary.

ORGANIZATIONAL STUDIES: A BRIEF FIELD GUIDE

How did organization studies develop as an academic field, and did biological factors play a role in it? Organizational scholars typically trace the roots of organizational studies to early twentieth-century work by administrative and management theorists. With the rapid industrial development in the United States, work processes came into scientific focus. The legendary Frederick W. Taylor made the first mark in this regard by studying individual workers within organizations; he aimed to discover ways to maximize the efficiency of tasks, attempting to maximize output and minimize labor input. Around the same time, early industrial psychologists defined the field in terms of the human aspects of organizational labor, including incentives, training, and selection, and even the influence of the physical environment on workers (Myers 1977). While the present volume focuses on the prospective opportunities to study biological foundations within OB, some early scholars had explored factors that are perhaps still relevant to these chapters. For example, early studies examined physical phenomena such as factory fatigue and the posture of workers (sometimes labeled as "biological" by early scholars). Even Münsterberg's (1913) foundational text, *Psychology and Industrial Efficiency*, discusses various tests with an anthropometric focus, such as finger length, breathing patterns, pulse, vision, and hearing, in addition to the more cognitive features like memory and attention.

Industrial and organizational (I/O) psychology emerged from this scientific management tradition led by Taylor. Marking the beginnings of I/O psychology, Roethlisberger and Dickson (1939) conducted their landmark Hawthorne studies at the Western Electric Company plant outside Chicago. They found that worker productivity increased with increases in lighting; however, they also found, paradoxically, that productivity increased with decreases in lighting, even to the point where visibility was nearly zero. Eventually, it was recognized that productivity increased in both conditions simply because workers were under close observation, producing what have become widely known as "Hawthorne effects." Accordingly, research shifted to look more closely at the internal, and more psychological, processes of production, such as worker morale and the human relations between workers.

As research on efficiency progressed, interest emerged in other phenomena, such as norms and their evolution in workgroups (Blau and Scott 1962). Social psychologists sought to identify inherent traits in individuals and to determine how they interacted with group-based situational contexts, such as leadership style. For instance, Lewin, Lippit, and White (1939) studied the effects of different styles of leadership on group dynamics and the emergence of difference social climates. Specifically, Lewin conceptualized situational forces that acted upon individuals as parallel to forces of physics acting on objects, emphasizing the interaction between the person and situation.

These various origins of organizational studies may partially account for the lingering divide between the subfields of micro OB and macro OT. As Blau and Scott (1962, 12) put it, "A fundamental dilemma is posed for the study of organizations by the double requirement of examining the interdependence between elements in a social structure, on the one hand, and of observing many independent cases to substantiate generalizations, on the other." Organization analysts typically confront this challenge by decoupling research problems into levels of analysis. That is, they commonly believe it is very difficult, if not impossible, to investigate cleanly and simultaneously within the design of a single study all of the following: (1) the independent psychology of each individual, (2) the interrelations among individuals within groups, (3) the various groups within environments, and (4) the environments within larger organizing boundaries, such as nation-states and cultures. It may be possible to study small groups of individuals in highly controlled experimental settings with lots of situational variation. It may also be possible to do something comparable on a larger scale among organizations in a given industry across time. However, researchers working at different levels of analysis often begin to ask different questions, to be driven by different theories from disparate disciplines, and to develop tests with different methodologies. In general, what organizational analysis gains through experimental controls, it often loses in organic reality.[2]

The divide within organizational studies is mirrored by (often contentious) divisions within both OB and OT individually. A long-standing tension in OB occurs between dispositional versus situational effects, a parallel to the tension between personality and social psychology. Early theory and research largely assumed that dispositional factors of individuals resulted in stable, cross-situational consistencies in behavior (Allport 1937). A large body of evidence supported this assumption, especially for certain elements of personality. For instance, intellectual features (e.g., problem-solving strategies) appeared robust across situations, as did self-reports of individuals.

Subsequent researchers began to challenge assumptions about the stability of dispositional traits (Mischel 1968). Behavioral consistency occurred most reliably when individuals were sampled multiple times in very similar situations (see Mischel 1973). As situations varied, sometimes in subtle or seemingly trivial ways, cross-situational behavioral consistency decreased, at times producing no correlation at all and, at others, producing correlations that could not substantiate the assumptions made about the strength of personality and dispositions in determining behavior. Over time, psychologists reached consensus on a distilled set of robust, essential traits (the so-called Big Five), including extraversion, neuroticism, conscientiousness, agreeableness, and openness to experience (McRae and Costa 1987; Digman 1990; Goldberg 1990). Conversely, within I/O psychology, personality dimensions such as IQ and other intelligence measures have reliably predicted job performance across several roles, leading some to suggest that if employers used only this metric, they would do well in selecting potential high performers for virtually any job (see Ree and Earles 1992; but see also Sternberg and Wagner 1993).

Within OB, researchers at various times explored the general idea that individuals possess relatively stable dispositions that can predict effectiveness at work. For example, Stogdill (1974) searched for the traits of an effective leader, Holland (1973) thought personality determined one's career choice, and Staw and Ross (1985) argued that dispositions may affect job satisfaction across different positions and organizations. In fact, job satisfaction may have a biological foundation, such as people's predisposition to interpret positive and negative content in their lives, or their dispositional temperament (Arvey et al. 1989). Further, conscientiousness—one of the Big Five—consistently predicts job performance across several types of occupations, while the evidence for the other dimensions varies as a function of job type (Barrick and Mount 1991).

In reaction, Davis-Blake and Pfeffer (1989) argued that the search for dispositional effects across organizational context constituted merely the pursuit of a "mirage," a view embraced by many social psychologists. They claimed that little evidence explains why individuals would be non-adaptive (e.g., stable) across different positions and organizations. Critics also pointed to much evidence suggesting that individuals' dispositions are shaped by the organizations in which they participate, and they also noted certain measurement problems associated with dispositional research. Many psychologists would consider this position extreme (Kenrick and Funder 1988). Within OB, House, Shane, and Herhold (1996) responded vigorously to this position, countering the critics' arguments by pointing to the genetic origins of dispositions among individuals.

Within both contemporary psychology and OB today, the volume of the general person-situation debate has subsided (Fleeson 2004), and interesting syntheses abound (Roberts and Pomeranz 2004; Fleeson and Noftle 2008). But we believe, nonetheless, that most OB analysts implicitly still endorse (or subscribe to) one position or the other. We speculate that such positions arise from practical considerations—combining dispositional and situational approaches may be too complex and challenging, given contemporary research methods (see Funder 2006; 2009). Moreover, we imagine that the heightened visibility of biological research on what we call the organic basis of behavior could potentially reactivate the debate (much as it did in development studies [Roberts and Caspi 2001], as we elaborate below).

The tension between dispositional and situational effects in OB manifests a fundamental complexity of human behavior. Behavior in organizational settings (as in many other settings) likely contains strong elements of both dispositional and situational effects, as well as interactions between the two (Funder 2009)). The challenge for researchers following the Biological Foundations Project, then, is to extend these relationships into biological theory and evidence. Such research can excite the field because of its potential to advance organizational studies in novel ways, yielding insights that elaborate and deepen our understanding of organizational behavior. Yet, the increased complexity resulting from another type of analysis may compound an already challenging set of research problems. The good news is that adding certain types of biological factors to the analysis of organizational behavior may actually enhance research designs and provide greater leverage in isolating important effects empirically, including situational ones, as we discuss in some detail below.

Organizational Ecology—an Evolutionary Theory

Within the macro field of OT, evolutionary theory has received considerable attention. In particular, the theoretical perspective known as organizational ecology embraces an explicitly evolutionary theory that addresses some of the questions posed in their chapters by authors interested in evolutionary processes. Simply put, organizational ecology aims to explain the emergence, growth, and decline of populations of organizations. Populations are characterized by the relative homogeneity of member organizations.

Organizational ecology generally uses a selection model of organizational evolution. In this model, change over time in an industry occurs through the selective replacement of some organizational forms with others as environmental conditions shift. In a selection model, the environment acts as a sieve or screen that causes organizations less attuned to current conditions to falter and favors better-attuned organizations. The use of environmental selection as the motor of change stands in contrast to most organizational theories, which instead assume that change occurs through the adaptations of individual organizations. Selection requires constraints on the adaptability of individual organizations, otherwise they could change hand-in-hand with environmental change. Selection focuses attention on the vital rates of populations—rates of founding and mortality in particular, although growth and transformation are also of interest. Selection-driven evolution does not always imply a "winnowing" of organizational diversity; such winnowing becomes more likely when limits or constraints exist on new entry, such as regulation or sunk investments.

Within organizational ecology, empirical research programs have developed that follow so-called theory fragments. These are coherent "partial theories stated as universal rules and formalized in predicate logic" (Hannan, Pólos, and Carroll 2007, 7). The fragments have developed through the generation and testing of falsifiable predictions; in many cases, they generate cumulative knowledge in their domain areas.

Two of the major theory fragments are known as *density dependence* and *niche width*. The core density-dependent model assumes associations between density (the number of organizations in a population) and (1) legitimation of the form of organization and (2) competition among the population's members. Increasing initial density enhances the legitimation of a form and increases the capacity of organizations to mobilize resources; however, further increases in density generate intense diffuse competition for scarce resources. The main empirical expectations of the model consist of nonmonotonic relationships between density and population vital rates, which have been largely confirmed in empirical studies (Carroll and Hannan 2000). Research also shows a robust positive effect of density on organizational mortality at the time of founding (Carroll and Hannan 2000).

In the niche width fragment, the niche concept describes an organization's adaptive capacity over the various possible states of its environment. Niche width concerns the span of environmental states in which an organization can operate successfully. According to niche-width theories, a broad niche carries extra cost in a stable, competitive, or institutional environment. But environmental uncertainty and variability affect the trade-off between niche width and viability, making broad niches favorable under many conditions (Dobrev, Kim, and Hannan 2001; Hsu 2006; Negro, Hannan, and Rao 2010).

Empirical research in organizational ecology typically starts with the enumeration of all constituent organizations that ever appeared in a population, including most notably those that failed. The most powerful research designs compile precise life-history data on member organizations (including timing information on founding, transformation, and mortality, as well as updated temporal data on covariates) that date back to the origins of the population. Analysis does not assume temporal equilibrium and often consists of estimating stochastic hazard-rate models of vital events, linking organizational and environmental characteristics to the rates in a regression-like framework. In many observers' eyes, organizational ecology has made rapid, cumulative theoretical progress in the last twenty-five years because of its focused empirical research programs.

Accordingly, we would encourage many of the authors of chapters in this volume, especially those dealing with evolutionary processes, to strengthen connections with organizational ecology. In many instances, we think the two sets of researchers have much to learn from each other. For instance, as we explain below, we think that within an organizational population, analysts might compare the fates of family and non-family firms in various social and economic contexts, thus potentially providing evidence pertinent to Nicholson's arguments in chapter 10.

Organizational Ecology and Biology

An interesting aspect of organizational ecology is that its adherents took pains to distance themselves explicitly from biological analogies or connections; instead they use bioecology mainly as a source of general ideas and models. Consider the stark disclaimer in Hannan and Freeman's (1977, 862) paradigmatic statement of the perspective: "We do not argue 'metaphorically.' That is, we do NOT argue as follows: an empirical regularity is found for certain protozoans; because we hypothesize that populations of organizations are like populations of protozoans in essential ways, we propose that the generalization derived from the latter will hold for organizations as well" (emphasis in original).

Indeed, organizational ecologists have often emphasized several key conceptual differences between organizational and biological evolution, including especially (1) the possibility of dramatic transformation among individual members of a population and (2) the potential immortality of organizations, lessening the need for an explicit generational transmission mechanism (see Carroll and Hannan 2000). Now, some may say that these conceptual shifts mean that organizational ecology is not truly an evolutionary theory, and in the sense in which *evolution* is often used in this volume, that is true. But that view depends, of course, on how you define evolution in the first place (see Sloan 2010); both approaches do retain the same underlying conceptual structure of variation-selection-retention. From our reading of this volume's chapters, it would seem that many of the authors featured here would prefer a stronger connection to some biological aspect of evolution, probably involving descent with modification, certainly not a disclaimer along the lines of Hannan and Freeman's (1977), which implies a broader definition involving change over time. In our view, this is a topic of OB/OT that would benefit from more explicit discussion and research.

THE ORGANIC PROGRAM OF THE BIOLOGICAL FOUNDATIONS PROJECT

What we call the organic program of the Biological Foundations Project comprises research that seeks to connect biological materials—the organic matter of life—to behavior and especially to organizational behavior. Many of the studies in this program are empirical. Generally speaking, these studies document or confirm a relationship between a behavior and an organic component of life, such as DNA, hormone production, brain activation, galvanic skin response, and so forth. Chapters 2 through 5 in this book describe and review much of this research.

Generally speaking, the research in the organic program constitutes very good science by almost any standard. It often uses carefully controlled research designs with large samples and sound measurement techniques. The standard of rigor in these studies is typically higher than it is for many social science areas. And many of the empirical findings have been replicated in subsequent studies by independent research teams. This research program is also highly fecund, producing what seems to be an almost limitless run of new findings, many of which seem to be highly pertinent to social science, since they purportedly explain behavior. Some research of this kind links biological mechanisms to behaviors widely studied throughout the social sciences, such as work linking higher levels of testosterone—collected via saliva samples during a laboratory study—with moral decision making (Carney and Mason 2010).

As the editors and authors of this book aptly point out, despite all the rigor and productivity of the organic program, to date its findings have not had a great impact on the fields of OB and OT. Among others, Bearman (2008) registers a similar complaint about the lack of impact on sociology. Of course, this apparent unresponsiveness may arise from many sources, including those who regard social scientists as unaware of developments in other disciplines, those who consider them closed-minded about biological factors, those who see them as threatened by these developments, or those who regard them as acting primarily politically to exclude this line of inquiry.

Without denying the plausibility of any of these explanations, we find a different interpretation intriguing. Perhaps the issue is that, despite the obvious progress on the biological front, in their current state the organic program's findings may appear in and of themselves to many conventional scholars in OB to offer limited new value to behavioral analyses. Why might this be the case? Consider that (as reviewed above) OB theory and research has long recognized dispositional causes of behavior, linking behavior to a personality characteristic or some other dispositional trait. We would also venture that, given the strong disciplinary connections that many of them have to contemporary social psychology, the majority of contemporary OB scholars favor situational over dispositional explanations. To these analysts, a "new" finding from biology showing that a characteristic has an identifiable organic basis may unfortunately be seen as doing little new—the trait remains dispositional in nature. In this view, all that has apparently changed is that the trait now is linked to some part of the brain, or some DNA sequence, or the like, perhaps confirming its heritability. If, say, a personality characteristic was previously considered immutable, then the fact that it has now been demonstrated to have an organic basis may be seen (by a situationalist) as not changing much of importance from an organizational, behavioral, or managerial viewpoint. That is, just being able to map it to something physical or organic does not necessarily mean that it will be seen as providing a deeper explanation or giving managerial help. For example, Derbyshire (2009, 21) comments on a similar general line of research: "Brain activation (associated with an event or a behavior) does not provide an explanation, only a new level of description for what we already know is happening."

Research Design Advantages

We think that the "nothing-is-really new" position is too quick to dismiss the emerging biological evidence. While we agree that studies that also advance and support theoretical mechanisms would be even better, we also contend that a "new level of description" potentially has great value. Descriptions that measure different features of an entity and highlight previously unknown aspects of a phenomenon can yield insights that spawn new theories or make other established theories seem suddenly relevant. Consider medical diagnostic imaging technologies: the X-ray, ultrasound, and magnetic resonance imaging. Are these not all simply providing new levels of description of many of the same known ailments and diseases? New evidence, especially when coming from a "new level," may radically change our perspective on and understanding of a problem. If so, then the challenge for theorists and theories is to consolidate the old and new evidence in a sharper explanation.

Moreover, the "nothing-is-really-new" position also ignores (or at least strongly underplays) some very attractive possibilities for using biological factors in designing research to isolate effects of specific causes, including social and situational ones. How? In a nutshell, identification of one or more "observable" descriptors may in fact provide strong inferential leverage in empirical research, especially if the descriptor can be considered exogenous. Because genetic endowments are fixed at conception, they are largely immune to the possibly confounding influences of context, social and other—they are strictly exogenous from a behavioral viewpoint.[3] This means that if one can measure and control for the genetic contribution to a behavior, then the social contribution (cause) will be estimated more cleanly and precisely (see Guo, Tong, and Cai 2008).

Accordingly, controlling for exogenous genetic effects would allow social scientists to isolate better the social or situational effects of their primary interest. Guo et al. (2008) give the sociological example of how the effects of social origins might be clarified with such a design. Because the effects of genes and context are often correlated in actual behavioral outcomes, full measure of the genetic component is required to gain this benefit (Guo et al. 2008). Many of these genetic measures remain unknown at the moment, and additional empirical findings from the organic program would bring this possibility closer to reality for many research problems. For example, recent work on fraternal and identical twins documents the percentage of variance explained in leadership roles by shared genetics among twins (Arvey et al. 2007). These studies have isolated shared genetics (32%) from other environmental and developmental predictors, which may open the door for similar developments in this area.

Another general research possibility that may appear more exciting to many social scientists involves exploring those effects commonly referred to as "gene-environment interaction." Basically, "gene-environment interaction refers to the principle [that] an environment may influence how sensitive we are to the effects of a genotype and vice versa" (Guo et al. 2008, S42). Guo et al. give both a biological and sociological example of such interactions. The biological example involves a specific genetic combination that lowers rates of HIV infection and hinders progression of the disease if contracted, even for persons in similar environments. The sociological example comes from a study showing that mistreatment of children was less likely to result in violent behavior for those children with a certain specific genotype (Caspi et al. 2002), even though the presence of the genotype itself apparently shows no direct effect on the tendency toward violence.

In discussing neuroeconomics, the nascent field blending biologically based brain science and economics, Bernheim (2009) also identifies several additional possible ways to use organic information to enhance research design. These include using the information to eliminate omitted variable bias, using it as an instrument in studying peer groups, using it as a condition in forecasts, and using it in applying predictions to new populations. These types of proposals usually require fuller specification of the underlying basic causal model thought to be operant (see Freese 2008).

For the most part, it appears that these potential advantages have yet to be exploited—even partially—in research on OB and OT. The potential value here is enormous and cannot be underemphasized. Moving in this direction would appear to be a wise priority for those wishing to elevate the status of the biological program in organizational studies. However, questions about exactly how to proceed in this context abound. Scientists often start lines of research by using hunches or intuition about what might be going on with respect to some particular phenomenon. They then get serious about specifying a theoretical claim or isolating some effect to produce evidence. The problem here may be that social scientists will not have many good hunches about genes and other organic processes unless they get more involved with the relevant literature. Likewise, the behavioral ideas that come naturally to many geneticists may not connect readily with many social scientists' research programs. The impasse can perhaps be overcome through extended dialogue between the various disparate research communities, but initiating and sustaining such dialogue is easier said than done.

Challenges Ahead

In our view, another important challenge ahead in making the organic program more central to organizational studies involves identifying and developing ideas about the theoretical mechanisms involved in the operation of biological phenomena. This issue has both an empirical and a theoretical side. The empirical side seems fairly straightforward: it involves moving away from findings of effects and attempting to isolate the operative mechanism(s) from among the many plausible ones. To do this likely requires searching for evidence of effects on other outcomes that are plausibly linked to the same mechanism. For instance, if sensation-seeking is the general trait linking certain genes and entrepreneurship (see chapter 4 by Shane and Nicolaou), then it should manifest itself in other behavioral outcomes (such as crime?) as well.

The theoretical side involves specifying the mechanisms and conditions under which the demonstrated organic effects operate. The generic "gene-environment interaction" mechanism discussed above is one very important type of needed theoretical development. Another important one involves aggregating up to the group or organizational level and linking the processes involved to outcomes of major interest to organizational analysts. As discussed above, the problem of aggregating across levels of analysis already exists in organizational studies in the micro-macro (OB-OT) divide; the organic program would add another level of aggregation to this issue.

Entrepreneurship as an Example

Consider again the findings on biology and entrepreneurship reviewed by Shane and Nicolaou in chapter 4. (We use this chapter for illustration because of its strength and clarity as well as the familiarity of its topic to us, not because we want to make it a target per se.) They describe studies that purport to show that the following phenomena are heritable: entrepreneurship (starting a business; being an owner-operator; being self-employed); opportunity recognition; and entrepreneurial performance. They claim that empirical evidence suggests the patterns may be attributed to genetically shaped personality characteristics such as sensation-seeking, extraversion, agreeableness, emotional stability, openness to experience, and conscientiousness. They also review empirical studies suggesting an environmentally moderated effect of testosterone and the DRD4 gene associated with novelty-seeking. They also describe some more preliminary hints in the data about hormones and other personal characteristics, such as attractiveness, ADHD, and dyslexia.

This is a treasure chest of findings, and—even throwing out the weaker, possibly extraneous ones (such as physical attractiveness and ADHD and dyslexia)—we are offered more systematic empirical evidence than exists in some areas of social science. Clearly, a neutral, third-party observer would appear to be reasonable in thinking that these findings would help us explain and understand entrepreneurship. However, Shane and Nicolaou do note that the mechanisms behind these effects are not clear. In chapter 3, Ilies and Dimotakis (64) make a comment motivated by similar concerns: "The greatest contributions at this point may come from researchers who utilize methodological and conceptual advances to outline, develop, and test theoretically grounded models of the pathways (including affective, dispositional, and perceptual processes) by which genetics can influence conceptually linked clusters of organizational variables (such as work-related attitudes [e.g., job satisfaction], behaviors, or performance)."

These observations raise questions about the best approach for analysts to take in moving the research program on entrepreneurship forward. In particular, should it be focused on developing theory, or should it continue to build empirical evidence without worrying excessively about theoretical integration? For the long term, the answer is clear: as the chapters by Ilies and Dimotakis (chapter 3) and by Shane and Nicolau (chapter 4) point out, specification and development of theory to account for the evidence is critical for understanding. And, given the history of the dispositional-situational controversy in OB, this development is likely imperative for widespread acceptance and integration into the larger field.

Indeed, sparse theory is available to explain connections of many individual-level phenomena with actual rates of entrepreneurship (start-up events), unless one adopts a strongly reductionist theoretical approach. As a result, many analysts interested in entrepreneurship may not find adding a biological factor that compelling—or that different from adding another personality trait or dispositional factor thought to be associated with entrepreneurship. But, as discussed above, this view ignores the new leverage that may be gained in looking at something in a different way and in a different research design.

Still, developing the kind of theory advocated will likely prove to be complex. Consider that the rate of founding within an organizational population—its rate of entrepreneurship—can be usefully decomposed into two underlying component rates: the level of organizing attempts and the relative success of these attempts in generating an operating organization (Delacroix and Carroll 1983; Carroll and Khessina 2005). That is, organizational founding consists of two separate processes: a first one about the rate at which individuals initiate attempts to start new organizations, and a second about the success of those attempts in actually opening a firm. Success in this second process is associated with the founding event itself and is to be distinguished from the success or failure of the organization once founded, which is a separate issue associated with the organizational mortality rate. Increases in the factors affecting either attempts or the success of attempts will result in an increased number of entrepreneurial startups.

To illustrate, consider the places where in recent decades we have seen dramatic increases in entrepreneurship: China, Russia, and the old Eastern bloc countries. The high intertemporal variation in entrepreneurship witnessed in these places is likely the result of increases in the conditions producing both attempts at entrepreneurship (positive sanctions and incentives have replaced negative ones, including ostracism and even jail) and the success rate of such attempts (legalization of private enterprise alone produced huge effects). But neither can be plausibly ascribed to biological or organic factors, as the human populations would appear to have changed little in the interim. Accordingly, it would seem that at best one could offer an explanation of cross-sectional differences once institutional and resource differences are controlled. Yet, how much of the variation in the outcome will be explained? And, more importantly, how relevant is that part of the explanation? If one is interested in rates of entrepreneurship, the issue for biology may be whether there is enough organic material in the human stock to generate a sustainable baseline rate of attempts at founding, and that number may be sufficiently high in many human populations.

But even if the long-term goal of theory development is clear, what about the short-term, right now: should analysts continue to build the evidentiary base of effects, or slow down until more theoretical progress has been made? Perhaps surprisingly, our view is that given the progress currently being made empirically, analysts should continue to accumulate evidence before it all must be sorted out. A new study should use what is deemed important and novel for its setting and context, both in terms of explanations and controls. As the program progresses, some avenues that currently appear promising may never develop and live up to their possible promise; yet others may emerge from what seems like nowhere.

Moreover, empirical research may be increasingly designed to take advantage of the properties of biological phenomena, and it enhances the isolation of causal effects through identification, as explained above. And finally, as the evidence accumulates, the payoff for advancing a plausible theoretical account increases considerably, attracting more and better theorists to solve the puzzle. The bigger evidentiary base should also facilitate this task by giving more clues as to what is going on.[4]

In defense of this empirical strategy, we would point to behavioral decision theory as a successful example, an area that has developed as rapidly as any in social science in the last thirty years (see chapter 9 by DeSciolo, Kurzban, and Todd for more on this research area). Recall that early studies in behavioral decision theory, and many studies today, revolve around empirical studies of "effects," often appearing initially as anomalies from strict rationality, for which there is no obvious theoretical explanation (at least initially), even if the empirical pattern is robust. In some instances, however, constructions such as prospect theory subsequently emerged to account for the newly established empirical patterns, and then gained supporters and adherents who took and used the theory generatively in deductive fashion. Lack of patience initially with the inability to explain empirical patterns would have precluded all these future developments. Entrepreneurship researchers should be careful not to fall into that trap when dealing with apparently anomalous, biologically based findings.

Research Design Levers Arising from Biological Data

Given this kind of complexity, it seems unlikely to us that in the near future genetics or any organic compound alone will provide compelling alternative explanations of aggregate social behavior in groups or organizations, and especially in institutions. Social context matters, a fundamental fact that legitimates much of social science in the first place. What may be different now, however, is that the organic program's findings may point to newly identified factors that interact with social context to generate outcomes—what we referred to above as "gene-environment interaction." That is, if one takes these findings as valid, then there is room for, indeed a need for, theory that specifies how and when organic attributes will express themselves most fully. That theory could be about institutions, organizations, work groups, families, or jobs. A common structure of the arguments would likely be that certain social structural arrangements allow (or even induce) an organic disposition to affect behavior, while other arrangements do not (Freese 2008).

Some very promising research already moves in this direction and shows its potential. For instance, Bearman (2008) mentions the well-known argument that obesity occurs only with the joint presence of a genetic predisposition and economic surpluses. Zhang, Ilies, and Arvey (2009) find that genetic influences are weaker for children brought up in families with higher socioeconomic status, higher perceived parental support, and lower perceived conflict with parents, a combination they label "enriched social environments." Nonetheless, we think that more effort is being directed to, and more excitement is arising from, the production of new empirical findings in the organic program rather than the development of theories about context. While we would never call the empirical effort misplaced, we do not think it will yield the influence and impact on OB that similar effort on theory eventually would.

THE EVOLUTIONARY PROGRAM OF THE BIOLOGICAL FOUNDATIONS PROJECT

What we call the evolutionary program of the Biological Foundations Project is the set of research studies that seek to connect changes over (usually long periods of) time in the structure of life to organizational behavior. For the most part, the studies of this program are theoretical. Generally speaking, these studies propose or derive theories about the adaptive value of different distributions of traits or structural arrangements among human groups, organizations, or communities. These theories sometimes use findings from the organic project as the phenomenon to be explained. At other times, the effort focuses on purely behavioral or social arrangements. The field of evolutionary psychology looms large here; it emphasizes the adaptive value of observed psychological traits.

In general, our view is that this research constitutes a very good source of interesting and often innovative ideas. Evolutionary research often starts with established empirical findings and then develops theoretical challenges to existing explanations of them and other phenomena. The approach often forces analysts to think more broadly about established evidence and the implications of known empirical facts than they would otherwise. Newly developed theory then often opens up many additional avenues for inquiry. For instance, this is the way we regard the claim by Cosmides and Tooby (1996) that humans and their brains process information about the frequencies of events better than probabilities because that was the schema most useful in prehistoric eras of man's evolution. Parts of the evolutionary program are highly rigorous, using deductive frameworks to derive and test theories about the precise conditions under which certain arrangements will flourish or perish.

Although its impact may still be limited, generic evolutionary theory has generated some significant interest in organizational behavior. As explained above, much of this impact has been in the macro OT area (especially organizational ecology), and has occurred independently of the more micro developments described in this book. On the micro end of the field, the evolutionary program often uses findings from behavioral decision theory or social psychology, typically drawing on very strong empirical research. Consider behavioral decision theory and its well-established decision heuristics, discussed at several places in this book. Or, more specifically, the research on ecological rationality (see DeScioli, Kurzban and Todd's chapter 9 in this volume), that links environmental information structures to specific heuristics from the mind's toolkit, thereby allowing humans to navigate complex social life in groups. The rich computational system—which receives social information, processes it in light of contextual cues, and selects an appropriate heuristic response—contains an abundance of relevant theoretical predictions relevant to functional behavior. A fair amount of this theory and research is already used by organizational analysts and managers. For instance, decision-making heuristics and cognitive biases (reviewed in chapter 9) are taught in required core OB courses in virtually every major business school. The emphases in these courses are typically twofold—first to make managers aware of biases that might affect their decisions and those of others unknowingly (see Bazerman, Loewenstein, and Moore 2002) and how to overcome them, and secondly, to design environments that align better with known tendencies (see Plassmann et al. 2008).

Yet, in and of itself, this research is not necessarily evolutionary. What sometimes makes it part of the evolutionary program are arguments about the adaptive value of certain observed behavioral patterns or trends, especially as they concern the evolution of a species (or population or group) and its social life. And, even with arguments about adaptiveness, classification of this research as evolutionary may be qualified, depending on one's time horizon. For instance, some analysts would consider the short-run adaptiveness of groups or organizations over different kinds of environments to be classified as evolutionary. However, in our view, the predicted general isomorphism of social structures and environments is a somewhat weak evolutionary claim per se in the sense that it says nothing about how the system got to a particular point or where it is headed, only that certain structures seem better matched to certain environments.

A stronger evolutionary claim, which appears to be advocated by many authors of these chapters, is to link these behaviors and trends to longer term temporal patterns and distributions of phenomena. For instance, the claim that 150 persons is the optimal clan size of humans given our brain size has been linked to life on the savannah plain (Dunbar 1998; Nicholson 1998). In our view, the empirical validity of many of these core theoretical claims about long-term adaptive value would typically be considered by organizational analysts as the weaker part of the evolutionary research program. That is, a claim like the optimality of a 150-person social unit would be regarded as speculative and subject to much dispute, as is drawing an analogy between the heuristic processes evoked by two rivals competing for mates and two businesses competing for customers (chapter 9 in this volume). To catch the sustained interest of organizational behavior analysts, these claims need stronger empirical support, in our view—inferences need to rest on more compelling empirical evidence. As Buss (1995, 12) notes, some of the more robust evolutionary psychology does just this: "The power of a theory rests with its ability to explain known facts and to generate new predictions, which are then subjected to empirical test." However, this challenge can prove difficult, because evolutionary theoretical claims are not always stated in ways that make them readily or easily falsifiable. Moreover, compelling evidence on the evolution of social or cultural traits may need to span decades or even centuries into the past, eras for which relevant records appear sparse at best.

A particular challenge involves overcoming criticism of so-called *form to function* theories (Tooby and Cosmides 1992), in which a pattern of descriptive effects is discovered, and researchers subsequently search for explanations of their evolved function. These theories are often disparaged as "just so" theories, because of the relative ease with which a post-hoc explanation can be recruited from a trove of possibly evolved mechanisms, many of which may not be falsifiable. However, some attempts to build new theory rooted in robust evolutionary findings from observable behavior have succeeded, such as sex differences in jealousy (e.g., Buss et al. 1992). These findings may be reminiscent of *form to function* findings in other fields, such as geologists developing theories of plate tectonics after discovering patterns of continental drift (see Buss 1995, 12). However, evolutionary psychology at times apparently suffers from a lack of such robustness.

In work that would be more akin to *function to form* theories, researchers might follow Weick's (1974) advice about formulating creative organizational theories. He advises scholars to search for intriguing questions in everyday behavior and situations instead of searching for new ideas directly within organizational contexts. The Biological Foundations Project could profit by taking established insights from biological and evolutionary fields and developing rich ideas to test in organizational contexts. This approach would also have the benefit of predicting novel mechanisms to explain certain patterns of behavior, but it would do so in a forward-looking manner.

Family Business as an Example

Consider again the theory and research on biology and family firms reviewed by Nicholson in chapter 10. (As with the entrepreneurship example above, we choose this chapter for illustration because of its strength and clarity, as well as the familiarity of its topic to us.) He describes studies that show the impressive prevalence of family businesses in all economies, and their pronounced persistence and occasional dominance in advanced modern economies. Throughout his analysis, Nicholson maintains that something is different in the family firm because it involves kin with shared genes, making it a primal unit. The primal family business possesses potential advantages because of its "capacity for fast and flexible decision making, indelible high-trust relationships with all their stakeholder groups, and powerful, positive family bonds and values suffused throughout the business" (236). Yet Nicholson's analysis of the family firm is wide-ranging; he outlines a set of unique features, each of which provides potential advantages as well as disadvantages, including co-ownership by kin, intergenerational ownership transmission, teamwork between kin and non-kin, and genetic wildcard inheritance.

In Nicholson's analysis, the somewhat involuntary central involvement of kin in the family firm also means that both the sources of disagreement and the bonds of affiliation will be stronger, in his view. For instance, he writes (248) that family firms will have "more extreme centrifugal and centripetal forces than other kinds of organization." He describes the centrifugal as "the scope for disagreements among people who did not choose each other as associates" and the centripetal as "the bonds of genetic relatedness that give them an overriding, shared genetic interest" (248). The two forces are seen as offsetting—the stronger disagreements can be tolerated because the solidarity bonds are firmer.

Nicholson elaborates with what he calls the Darwinian dynamics of the family firm. In essence, he argues (249) that successful firms are those that possess a "healthy family dynamic" despite the risks involved. He further claims that in modern societies, the biggest challenge to getting it right on the family dynamics involves merging the rational social order of work with the emotional social order of non-work. Here he sees four forms of tension common to family firms: nepotism, parent-offspring conflict, affinal bond unions among unrelated persons, and sibling rivalry. In each instance, he draws on biological patterns and findings about other species to inform his discussion, and makes something of a continuity-of-nature argument.

Nicholson attributes many of the relevant features in the healthy family dynamic to genetics and highlights the role of randomness in inheritance, referring to a "gene lottery." This observation leads him to the "expectation of extreme variation in the form, functioning, and success of family firms. One can infer that some families will be lucky. . . . Others are cursed" (255). He continues by noting that two interrelated, external contingencies moderate these effects: cultural norms and interfamilial processes.

This is a wealth of theory, and even ignoring some lines of argument (like that about the self in the latter sections of the chapter), we are presented with more theory than exists in some areas of social science. Yet, as Nicholson makes clear in his conclusion, he does not think that evolutionary theory has yet taken hold in OB as it concerns the family firm. His chapter is intended to show that it "has considerable explanatory power, along with the *capacity* to integrate current theorizing" (259; emphasis added).

In that regard, we think that the mission has been fully accomplished. But, looking at the claims in the chapter and the careful weighing of opposing forces and tensions on various elements of the family firm, we also see a theory that is highly malleable and capable of explaining many possible phenomena. Malleable theory has many attractive advantages— witness the power of rational action theory. Yet the predictive value of such a theory may be limited unless it is sharpened with stronger assumptions and leads to more clearly falsifiable positions. At the same time, when it comes to areas like family firms, we also recognize that at the moment there may not be many strong reasons to come down on one side or another of any specific issue—the evidentiary basis is not especially strong and is hard to develop.

A Role for Empirical Research on Family Business

Accordingly, progress on these kinds of evolutionary ideas might best be achieved through the collection and analysis of pertinent, systematic, empirical evidence. This will not always be easy, given the types of arguments made about adaptiveness of various structural arrangements. But relevant evidence can be developed, as shown by Ingram and Lifschitz's (2006) analysis of family shipbuilders in the Clyde River region of England. They find that network ties to shipbuilders are beneficial, especially when the families do not use a corporate structure. Further, the possibility for more falsifiable predictions may be quite available for general, mid-level, and specific evolutionary theories, as evolutionary theorists often use exactly the same kinds of methods as any other social scientist, including archival analysis, experimental manipulations, field studies, observational data, and others (see Buss 1995).

In our view, an intriguing direction here may reside in something even simpler: statistical descriptions of various populations in specific times and places, including breakdowns of family forms by various features and environmental conditions. These data would allow analysts to search for recurrent contingent patterns that might provide clues to form-environmental interactions on viability. They could form the basis for more positive theory about evolution and the organizational behavior of family firms, which would increase the impact of this research program. At a minimum, we can see how such a development might lead to further progress on the topics in the component of the evolutionary project.

THE INTEGRATED BIOLOGICAL FOUNDATIONS PROJECT

In its fullest vision, the Biological Foundations Project proposed in this book seeks to combine and integrate the organic research program with the evolutionary program. That is, the project sets as its goal the tying together of biological research on organic matter and evolutionary theory to speak to important issues in organizational behavior. It is not clear to us exactly what form the integration is envisioned to take. We imagine there are many possibilities, and we read the editors and authors here as being somewhat agnostic (or at least not single-minded) about this form. But we also think that many of them would not object to seeing genetics serve as a link or bridge across the two programs. In any event, integration of the kind suggested faces many challenges, but in our view none is greater than specifying and studying the aggregation mechanisms involved.

Aggregating processes across levels of analysis is always difficult, and, despite much rhetoric, efforts to do so often do not live up to claims. While there is no shortage of claims of cross-level integration, they are typically very messy affairs conceptually, such as so-called meso-level organizational behavior. Or, they are hegemonic claims of integration accomplished by highjacking the issue in favor of one level or discipline, such as when someone claims to be able to explain institutional phenomena by using simple theories of individual rational action. But if success is defined as elegant abstraction and requires endorsement (or at least acceptance) by scientists who normally work at each of the various levels involved, then the magnitude of the challenge becomes clearer. As White and Pierce argue in chapter 11, the possibility of a coherent system of analysis at different levels may already have a strong basis in sociobiology, such as multilevel selection theory. For instance, evolutionary biologists have moved from focusing on the individual as the unit of analysis to the idea of group selection with a focus on cooperative decision making at the group level. While these multilevel approaches in related fields show promise for OB and OT scholars attempting to do the same, the challenges in doing so are not trivial.

Consider, for instance, the problems of integrating ideas across sociology and economics, two disciplines with much common interest in certain phenomena such as organizations, work, consumption, and the like. A key problem in transferring ideas from one discipline to the other involves the very different ways in which economists and sociologists aggregate from the individual level to other social entities. As Baron and Hannan (1994, 1114) explain it, "Economics, at least in its neoclassical micro variants, relies on a highly simplified model of individual action (rational choice) and a simple mechanism (market equilibrium) to aggregate individual actions to derive system-level implications." By contrast, they suggest that "most sociology uses complicated models of individual action (including effects of values, prior experience, commitments, location in social networks, context) and complicated aggregation mechanisms to aggregate interests and actions" (1114). As a result, economists and sociologists often talk past one another, if they talk at all. Moreover, antipathy too often characterizes some of the informal exchanges that do occur.

It is important to note that the difficulties of finding and specifying aggregation mechanisms across levels of analysis are not peculiar to social science. Indeed, the paragon discipline of this volume, biology, faces an identical challenge in the core topic of concern here: the integration of models of genetic and physical evolution and associated evidence. Genotypic evolution involves how gene pools change over time in response to various environmental conditions and with different inheritance rules. Phenotypes are the observable characteristics of organisms, and phenotypic evolution concerns how distributions of these features change over time in response to environmental variations. (In chapter 1, Colarelli and Arvey also discuss extended phenotypes, a major wrinkle used by some social scientists.)

Renowned evolutionary theorist Richard Lewontin (2011) offers insight into the problems of integrating genotypic and phenotypic evolution. He starts by noting that there would be no real problem if every change in a genotype resulted in a corresponding phenotypic change, reflecting a one-to-one relation across the two levels that could be reconstructed by analysts in mechanical fashion. As he observes, "However, the actual correspondence between genotype and phenotype is a many-many relation in which any given genotype corresponds to many different phenotypes, and there are different genotypes corresponding to a given phenotype. The current state of the study of organismic development ignores this many-many relationship" (n.p.).

He further explains that current scientific practice mistakenly treats the relation as a mechanical problem. Why? As he elaborates,

> It is not that developmental biologists are unaware of the many-many relationship between genotype and phenotype. Rather, pragmatic considerations dictate that the understanding of the mechanisms of development will best be achieved by first concentrating on those developmental outcomes that have an unambiguous relationship between genotype and phenotype, leaving for the future the issues posed by the many-many relation. An unintended side product of this strategic decision is that the language used to describe the problematic, and the results of the research, create and reinforce an overly simple view of the relationship between genes and characters. Lewontin (2011, n.p.).

Note that this genotype-phenotype problem is itself embedded in the Biological Foundations Project of organizational behavior, if genetics are to serve as the bridge linking the levels.

Moreover, the severity of the aggregation problem is compounded when we add on top of that one or both of the aggregation problems already found in organizational behavior: (1) the person-situation interaction for predicting micro organizational behavior in groups or organizations, and (2) the micro-macro divide of the field between individual behavior and the structure and functioning of collectives, such as organizations. So, in the end, we wind up with a set of research questions involving three, maybe four, distinct levels of analysis, each of them challenging in its own right, given endogenous factors, interactive effects and measurement difficulties. Chapters by Price and Van Vugt (chapter 4), by Nicholson (chapter 10), and by White and Pierce (chapter 11) all explicitly recognize some aspects of this levels-of-analysis challenge. Recall that in chapter 1, Colarelli and Arvey mention that Darwin developed the (macro) theory of natural selection, even though he used an incorrect (micro) theory of genetics; it was not until Mendelian genetics were rediscovered that the two levels could be reconciled. If this incident proves telling, then perhaps the current practice of working on single levels of analysis may not be so debilitating in the long run.

As if all that were not enough of a challenge, consider too that the "owners" of the various levels involved come from distinct disciplines (biology, psychology, sociology, and economics), where different concepts, assumptions, and methods are brought to bear on research problems. The chapters by Song, Li, and Wang (chapter 2), Ilies and Dimotakis (chapter 3), Zhang and Zyphur (chapter 7), Nicholson (chapter 10), and White and Pierce (chapter 11) all recognize this challenge and explicitly call for more multidisciplinary or interdisciplinary research. Yet, with such strongly held core conceptual beliefs emanating from their home discipline, one has to wonder how the various analysts can avoid talking past each other. In recognizing this challenge, Baron and Kreps (2013) recount a lovely story about James March explaining to an audience that economists have been well socialized to stay away from "the saloons of sociology." They also describe their own efforts in attempting to foster interdisciplinary dialogue with respect to employment issues as "facing incredulous economists over the years" (338). To put a final flourish on the point, we note that, despite the calls herein for such discipline-spanning and inclusion, the vast majority of the authors of these chapters work and reside in the discipline of psychology, albeit broadly defined. We do not intend this observation as a criticism but as an illustration of the difficulty of the challenge: even scientists advocating multidisciplinary approaches tend to clump around a focal discipline in order to be able to make progress.

Our point in highlighting this challenge is not to suggest that it is insurmountable or to cast a gloomy cloud over the Biological Foundations Project. Rather, we aim to call attention to these important issues so as to encourage theorists and other analysts to work on them. In our view, connections between biology and organizational behavior will likely continue to develop in the coming years, but we do not think the full potential will be achieved until at least some explicit attention is paid to the aggregation issues.

CONCLUSION

The Biological Foundations Project presents an intriguing challenge to organizational scholars. As with any new challenge, the first question to ask is whether the challenge will be joined or ignored. While we think it would be a great loss if ignored, we also think that work remains to be done before traditional analysts will wrestle in earnest with the issues raised by the project. At the risk of oversimplification, our basic view is that, on the one hand, the organic component of the foundations project needs greater theoretical development while, on the other hand, the evolutionary component needs better systematic empirical support. These are challenging demands, to be sure, but they are things that social scientists clearly know how to do. In contrast, the main challenge we see for the integrated program is something for which there is less readily available equipment: it needs theory and evidence about aggregation across levels, one of science's most challenging problems. Overall, the Biological Foundations Project represents an ambitious vision that contains audacious challenges. These kinds of things have never stopped science from progressing, and we do not think they should do so in this context.

Notes

1. As March and Simon (1958, 5) wrote decades ago, "Any attempt to bring together this scattered and diverse body of writing about organizations into a coherent whole must surmount two serious problems. The literature leaves one with the impression that after all not a great deal has been said about organizations, but it has been said over and over in a variety of languages."

2. Some of these divisions are readily apparent in many top business schools today, in which two highly disciplinary subgroups exist under the greater departmental umbrella of OB. This challenge posed by level of analysis and focus may be compounded by the challenge of each discipline to develop itself as a strong paradigm field (Pfeffer 1993), with high consensus about theory, methodology, vocabulary, and other important scientific factors. It is perhaps not surprising that each subfield may have more paradigmatic consensus with its respective discipline (sociology; psychology) than it has within organization studies more generally.

3. However, it must be noted that social context often plays a key role in mating and the inducement of nonrandom conception (and, of course, situational features may influence genetic expression).

4. It is perhaps instructive to compare our proposed approach to that of Hambrick (2007), who pleads for a greater appreciation of management-oriented studies that pursue goals other than the advancement of novel theory. He is especially forceful in advocating empirical research that advances important new facts. However, Hambrick also describes an interesting fact as one for which: "all obvious covariates

and endogenous relationships have been controlled for; and the effect size is big" (1349). In other words, he is insisting on relevance and high rigor, standards that might not encourage biological research at this point.

References

Allport, G. W. 1937. *Personality: A psychological interpretation*. New York: Holt, Rinehart and Winston.

Arvey, R. D., Bouchard, T. J., Jr., Segal, N. L., and Abraham, L. M.. 1989. Job satisfaction: Environmental and genetic components. *Journal of Applied Psychology* 74 (2): 187–92.

Arvey, R. D., Zhang, Z., Avolio, B. J., and Krueger, R. F. 2007. Developmental and genetic determinants of leadership role occupancy among women. *Journal of Applied Psychology* 92:693–706.

Baron, J. N., and Hannan, M. T. 1994. The impact of economics on contemporary sociology. *Journal of Economic Literature* 32:1111–46.

Baron, J. N., and Kreps, D. M. 2013. Employment as an economic and social relationship. In *Handbook of organizational economics*, ed. R. Gibbons and D. J. Roberts, 315–41. Princeton, NJ: Princeton University Press.

Barrick, M. R., and Mount, M. K. 1991. The Big Five personality dimensions and job performance: A meta-analysis. *Personnel Psychology* 44 (1): 1–26.

Bazerman, M. H., Loewenstein, G., and Moore, D. A. 2002. Why good accountants do bad audits. *Harvard Business Review* 80 (11): 87–102.

Bearman, P. 2008. Exploring genetics and social structure. *American Journal of Sociology* 114 (S1): v–x.

Bernheim, B. D. 2009. The psychology and neurobiology of judgment and decision making: What's in it for economists? In *Neuroeconomics: Decision making and the brain* , ed. P. W. Glimcher, C. F. Camerer, E. Fehr, and R. A. Poldrack, 115–25. New York: Elsevier.

Blau, P. M., and Scott, R. W. 1962. *Formal organizations: A comparative approach*. San Francisco: Chandler.

Buss, D. M. 1995. Evolutionary psychology: A new paradigm for psychological science. *Psychological Inquiry*, 6 (1): 1–30.

———, Larsen, R., Westen, D., and Semmelroth, J. 1992. Sex differences in jealousy: Evolution, physiology, and psychology. *Psychological Science* 3 (4): 251–55.

Carney, D. R., and Mason, M. F. 2010. Decision making and testosterone: When the ends justify the means. *Journal of Experimental Social Psychology* 46:668–71.

Carroll, G. R., and Hannan. M. T. 2000. *The demography of corporations and industries*. Princeton, NJ: Princeton University Press.

———, and Khessina, O. 2005. The ecology of entrepreneurship. In *Handbook of entrepreneurship: Disciplinary perspectives*, ed. R. Agrawal, S. A. Alvarez, and O. Sorenson, 167–200. New York: Kluwer.

Caspi, A., McClay, J., Moffitt, T. E., Mill, J., Martin, J., Craig, I. W., et al. 2002. Role of genotype in the cycle of violence in maltreated children. *Science* 297 (5582): 851–54.

Clegg, S. R., and Hardy, C. 1996. Introduction: Organizations, organization, and organizing. In *Handbook of organization studies*, ed. S. R. Clegg, C. Hardy, and W. R. Nord, 1–28. Thousand Oaks: Sage.

Cosmides, L., and Tooby. J. 1996. Are humans good intuitive statisticians after all? Rethinking some conclusions from the literature on judgment under uncertainty. *Cognition* 58 (1): 1–73.

Davis-Blake, A., and Pfeffer, J. 1989. Just a mirage: The search for dispositional effects in organizational research. *Academy of Management Review* 14 (3) :385–400.

Delacroix, J., and Carroll, G. R. 1983. Organizational foundings: An ecological study of the newspaper industries of Argentina and Ireland. *Administrative Science Quarterly* 28 (2): 274–91.

Derbyshire, S. 2009. How has neuroimaging been applied to economics and politics? Why is association not cause? Available online at http://www.slideshare.net/sderbysh1/derbyshireiasi.

Digman, J. M. 1990. Personality structure: Emergence of the five-factor model. In *Annual Review of Psychology*, ed. M. R. Rosenzweig and L. W. Porter, 41:417–40. Palo Alto, CA: Annual Reviews.

Dobrev, S. D., Kim, T. Y., and Hannan. M. T. 2001. Dynamics of niche width and resource partitioning. *American Journal of Sociology* 106:1299–1337.

Dunbar, R. I. M. 1998. The social brain hypothesis. *Evolutionary Anthropology* 6 (5): 178–90.

Fleeson, W. 2004. Moving personality beyond the person-situation debate the challenge and the opportunity of within-person variability. *Current Directions in Psychological Science* 13, (2): 83–87.

———, and E. Noftle. 2008. The end of the person-situation debate: An emerging synthesis in the answer to the consistency question. *Social and Personality Psychology Compass* 2:1667–84.

Freese, J. 2008. Genetics and the social science explanation of individual outcomes. *American Journal of Sociology* 114 (S1): S1–S35.

Funder, D. C. 2006. Towards a resolution of the personality triad: Persons, situations and behaviors. *Journal of Research in Personality* 40 (1): 21–34.

———. 2009. Persons, behaviors and situations: An agenda for personality psychology in the postwar era. *Journal of Research in Personality* 43 (2): 120–26.

Goldberg, L. R. 1990. An alternative "description of personality": The Big-Five factor structure. *Journal of Personality and Social Psychology* 59:1216–29.

Guo, G., Tong, T., and Cai, T. 2008. Gene by social context interactions for number of sexual partners among white male youths. *American Journal of Sociology* 114 (S1): S36–S66.

Hambrick, D. C. 2007. The field of management's devotion to theory: Too much of a good thing? *Academy of Management Journal* 50:1346–52.

Hannan, M. T., and Freeman, J. H. 1977. The population ecology of organizations. *American Journal of Sociology* 82:929–64.

———, Pólos, L., and Carroll, G. R. 2007. *Logics of organization theory: Audiences, codes, and ecologies*. Princeton, NJ: Princeton University Press.

Holland, J. L. 1973. *Making vocational choices: A theory of careers*. Englewood Cliffs, NJ: Prentice-Hall.

House, R. J., Shane, S. A., and Herhold, D. M. 1996. Rumors of the death of dispositional research are vastly exaggerated. *Academy of Management Review* 21 (1): 203–24.

Hsu, G. 2006. Jacks of all trades and masters of none: Audiences reactions to spanning genres of feature film production. *Administrative Science Quarterly* 51:420–50.

Ingram, P., and Lifschitz, A. 2006. Kinship in the shadow of the corporation: The interbuilder network in Clyde River shipbuilding, 1711–1990. *American Sociological Review* 71 (2): 334–52.

Kenrick, D. T., and D. C. Funder. 1988. Profiting from controversy: Lessons from the person-situation debate. *American Psychologist* 43 (1): 23–34.

Lewin, K., Lippit, R., and White, R. K. 1939. Patterns of aggressive behavior in experimentally created "social climates." *Journal of Social Psychology* 10 (2): 269–99.

Lewontin, R. 2011. The genotype/phenotype distinction. In *The Stanford encyclopedia of philosophy*, Summer 2011 edition, ed. E. N. Zalta. Available online at http://plato.stanford.edu/archives/sum2011/entries/genotype-phenotype/.

McCrae, R. R., and Costa, P. T., Jr. 1987. Validation of the five-factor model of personality across instruments and observers. *Journal of Personality* and *Social Psychology* 52 (1): 81–90.

March, J. G., and Simon, H. A. 1958. *Organizations.* New York: John Wiley.

Mischel, W. 1968. *Personality and assessment.* New York: John Wiley.

———. 1973. Toward a cognitive social learning reconceptualization of personality. *Psychological Review* 80 (4): 252–83.

Myers, C. S. 1977. *Industrial psychology.* New York: People's Institute. Orig. pub. 1925.

Münsterberg, H. 1913. *Psychology and industrial efficiency.* Boston: Houghton Mifflin.

Negro, G., Hannan, M. T., and Rao, H. 2010. Categorical contrast and audience appeal: Niche width and critical success in winemaking. *Industrial and Corporate Change* 19:1397–1425.

Nicholson, N. 1998. How hardwired is human behavior? *Harvard Business Review* 76 (4): 134–47.

O'Reilly, C. 1991. Organizational behavior: Where we have been, where we're going. *Annual Review of Psychology.* Palo Alto, CA: Annual Reviews.

Pfeffer, J. 1993. Barriers to the advance of organizational science: Paradigm development as a dependent variable. *Academy of Management Review* 18:599–620.

Plassmann, H., O'Doherty, J., Shiv, B., and Rangel, A. 2008. Marketing actions can modulate neural representations of experienced utility. *Proceedings of the National Academy of Sciences* 105:1050–54.

Ree, M. J., and Earles, J. A. 1992. Intelligence is the best predictor of job performance. *Current Directions in Psychological Science* 1 (3): 86–89.

Roberts, B. W., and Caspi, A. 2001. Personality development and the person-situation debate: It's déjà vu all over again. *Psychological Inquiry* 12 (2): 104–9.

———, and Pomerantz, E. M. 2004. On traits, situations, and their integration: A developmental perspective. *Personality and Social Psychology Review* 8:402–16.

Roethlisberger, F. J., and Dickson, W. J. 1939. *Management and the worker.* Cambridge, MA: Harvard University Press.

Scott, R. W. 1998. *Organizations: Rational, natural, and open systems.* 4th ed. Upper Saddle River, NJ: Prentice Hall.

Sloan, P. 2010. Evolution. In *The Stanford encyclopedia of philosophy* , Fall 2010 edition, ed. E. N. Zalta. Available online at http://plato.stanford.edu/archives/fall2010/entries/evolution/.

Staw, B. M. 1984. Organizational behavior: A review and reformulation of the field's outcome variables. *Annual Review of Psychology* 35:627–66.

———, and J. Ross. 1985. Stability in the midst of change: A dispositional approach to job attitudes. *Journal of Applied Psychology* 70:469–80.

Sternberg, R. J., and Wagner, R. K. 1993. The g-centric view of intelligence and job performance is wrong. *Current Directions in Psychological Science* 2 (1): 1–5.

Stogdill, R. M. 1974. *Handbook of leadership: A survey of theory and research.* New York: Free Press.

Tooby, J., and Cosmides, L. 1992. Psychological foundations of culture. In *The adapted mind*, ed. J. Barkow, L. Cosmides, and J. Tooby, 19–136. New York: Oxford University Press.

Weick, K. 1974. Amendments to organizational theorizing. *Academy of Management Journal* 17:487–502.

Zhang, Z., Ilies, R., and Arvey, R. 2009. Beyond genetic explanations for leadership: The moderating role of the social environment. *Organizational Behavior and Human Decision Processes* 110 (2): 118–28.

Richard D. Arvey
Department of Management
    and Organization
School of Business
National University of Singapore
Mochtar Riady Building #08-55
15 Kent Ridge Drive
Singapore 119245

Glenn R. Carroll
Stanford Graduate School of Business
Knight Management Center
655 Knight Way
Stanford, CA 94305-7298
USA

Stephen M. Colarelli
Department of Psychology
Central Michigan University
Mt. Pleasant, MI 48859
USA

Peter DeScioli
Department of Political Science
Stony Brook University
Stony Brook, NY 11794
USA

Nikolaos Dimotakis
J. Mack Robinson College of Business
Georgia State University
Atlanta, GA 30303
USA

Robert Hogan
Hogan Assessments
Tulsa, OK 74114
USA

Remus Ilies
Department of Management and
    Organization
School of Business
National University of Singapore
Singapore 119245

Timothy A. Judge
Mendoza College of Business
University of Notre Dame
Notre Dame, Indiana 46556
USA

and

Division of Psychology and Language
    Sciences
Faculty of Brain Sciences
University College London
Gower Street
London WC1E 6BT
UK

Robert Kurzban
Department of Psychology
University of Pennsylvania
Philadelphia, PA 19104
USA

Wendong Li
Department of Psychological Sciences
Kansas State University
492 Bluemont Hall
Manhattan, KS 66506
USA

Jayanth Narayanan
Department of Management and
    Organization
School of Business
National University of Singapore
Singapore 119245

Nigel Nicholson
Department of Organizational Behavior
London Business School
London NW1 4SA
UK

Nicos Nicolaou
Department of Business and Public
    Administration
University of Cyprus
1678 Nicosia
Cyprus

and

Cass Business School
City University London
106 Bunhill Row
London EC1Y 8TZ
UK

Kieran O'Connor
McIntire School of Commerce
University of Virginia
Charlottesville, VA 22904
USA

Barbara Decker Pierce
School of Social Work
King's University College
Western University Canada
London, Ontario, N6A 2M3
CA

Smrithi Prasad
Department of Psychology
University of Oregon
Eugene, Oregon 97402
USA

Michael E. Price
Department of Psychology
School of Social Sciences
Brunel University
Uxbridge, Middlesex UB8 3PH
UK

Scott Shane
Weatherhead School of Management
Case Western Reserve University
Cleveland, Ohio 44106
USA

Zhaoli Song
Department of Management and
    Organization
School of Business
National University of Singapore
Singapore 119245

Peter M. Todd
Cognitive Science Program
Department of Psychological and Brain
    Sciences
Indiana University
Bloomington, IN 47405
USA

Mark Van Vugt
Department of Social and Organizational
    Psychology
VU University
1081 BT Amsterdam
The Netherlands

Nan Wang
PhD Program Office
School of Business
National University of Singapore
Singapore 117592

Roderick E. White
Richard Ivey School of Business
Western University–Canada
London, Ontario N6A 3K7
CA

Zhen Zhang
W. P. Carey School of Business
Arizona State University
Tempe, AZ 85287
USA

Michael J. Zyphur
Faculty of Business and Economics
University of Melbourne
Parkville 3010 VIC
AUS

Note: Page numbers in *italics* indicate figures.

biochemical processes and functions, 27–29, *28*

Biological Foundations Project: approaches in, 311–15; biological data and research design, 328–29; challenges in, 318, 325, 335–36; entrepreneurship example, 325–28; evolutionary processes program, 313, 329–34; family firms example, 332–34; integration of organic and evolutionary in, 334–37; organic (basis of behavior) program, 313, 321–29; research design advantages, 323–25; summary, 338

biology: diversity of field, 313; economics as branch of, 274; family as entity in, 238–41; fight for survival among siblings, 253–54; "fit" in, 9–10; future studies in, 15–16; information-processing studies in, 205–6; "observable" descriptors in, 323; propositions on influence of, 73–74; research design levers from data in, 328–29; social behaviors influenced by, 119–20; social sciences unified with, 270–71; social scientists' attitudes toward, 314; theoretical mechanisms in phenomena of, 325. *See also* biology in organizational behavior; evolution by natural selection; genetics

biology in organizational behavior: approaches and themes, 6–8, 313; assessment of development and themes, 8, 311–15; challenges in, 2–4, 325; conceptual congruence in, 8–10; guide to OB research and, 315–21; organizational ecology and, 288–89, 318–21; practice and theory in, 4–6; research design issues, 323–25, 328–29; scope of, 10–15; summary, 15–16. *See also* Biological Foundations Project; organizational behavior (OB)

birds, 253

Bismarck, O. von, 107

Blau, P. M., 316

blood pressure (BP): demands-control-support model and, 148–49, 152–53; employee response to work events and, 152; as predictor, 145

BMI (body mass index), 103

Boehm, C., 141, 286

Bollinger, M., 76

Bono, J. E., 155

Borlaug, N., 98

Bouchard, T. J., 24, 27, 51, 61, 100

bounded rationality concept, 207–8

Bowles, S., 107

Boyd, R., 185, 241, 284, 285

BP. *See* blood pressure (BP)

brains: entrepreneurial behaviors and function of, 77; mirror neurons in, 299; physiology of, 122–23, *125*, 125–26; size of, 278–79, 282. *See also* cognitive ability; neurobiological systems

Brondolo, E., 151–52

Bugental, D. B., 223

Burt, A., 36

Buss, D. M., 51, 290, 331

Butner, J., 223

Byrne, Z. S., 153–54

Cable, D. M., 102, 103–4

Cai, T., 323–24

Cameron, K., 93

Campbell, D., 275

candidate gene approach, 38, 82

Caplan, R. D., 157

cardiovascular processes: demands-control-support model and, 148–49, 152–53; employee health and, 145–47

Carney, D. R., 131

Carroll, G. R.: chapter, 311–42; referenced, 8

Caspi, A., 37

Cates, D. S., 60

cerebral cortex, 122–23, 125, 126

Chance, N., 176

cheater detection, 292–93

Chen, E., 144

Cherry, T. L., 220–21

Chiao, J. V., 37

children: conflict with parents, 251; genetics of obesity and, 329; sibling rivalry, 253–54. *See also* adoptive children; parents and parenting styles; social context and systems; twins

China: entrepreneurship in, 327; individualism in, 149; job satisfaction in, 149

Chorney, M. J., 35

Chun, J. U., 299

Clausen, J. A., 52

Clegg, S. R., 312

Cloninger, C. R., 32

CNV (copy number variation), 25, 28, 38

Coase, R. H., 297

Coats, G., 105

coevolution: family systems in, 239–41; of genes and cooperative instinct, 285–87

cognitive ability: attractiveness and, 105; behavioral imitation as, 299; cultural evolution and, 284–89; as deep-level trait, 108–9; emotional intelligence concept and, 110–11; entrepreneurial behaviors and, 78; evolution of capacity for cooperation, 278–82; friendship and mechanisms in, 227–29; general vs. specific abilities, 110; heritability of, 34, 38; incentive-seeking vs. strategy selecting in, 205–6, 217; information processing mechanisms (toolkit) in, 203–4, 225; molecular genetics linked to variables in, 34–35; preferences for leaders with, 179; role of, 31; selecting appropriate tools, 216–22; strategy and innovation linked to, 97. *See also* cooperation; decision-making dynamics; evolutionary psychology (EP); heuristics

cognitive neuroscience approach, 83. *See also* imaging technologies

cognitive prototypes, 95, 96–97, 105

Cohen, S., 151

Colarelli, S. M.: chapter, 1–21; referenced, 313, 314, 337

Cole, S. W., 144

collective action, 12, 185–86. *See also* cooperation

collective self-identity concepts, 258

Collins, M. A., 105

Colonel Blotto game, 212

communication skills: blood pressure and, 152; cooperation and, 280; difficulties with, 159; organizational size and, 15; organization's vision and, 300; preferences for leaders with, 179. *See also* language

competition and competitiveness: altruism and, 177, 183; cooperation and, 274–77, 299; density dependence, niche width, and, 319–20; intergroup, 91, 93–94, 96, 97, 170, 212, 239, 303; in key life outcomes, 106, 107–8; kinship and family, 251, 253–54; in organizational environment, 213–14, 229–30, 237–38, 247; testosterone levels in, 127

COMT val158Met, 36

Connolly, J. J., 53

conscientiousness, 32, 53–54, 78, 95, 96, 103, 106, 317, 325

consilience concept, 270

Conway, L. G., 58

cooperation: altruistic, 272, 274–75, 283, 293; approach to studying, 8, 269–71; attractiveness and, 105; evolution of cognitive capacity for, 278–82; evolution of culture and, 284–89; in evolved systems, summarized, 274–75; of kin and non-kin in family firms, 247; on larger scale, 282–83; leadership and, 298–301; multilevel character of, 272–74; as multilevel phenomenon, 287–89; among organisms, 276–78; organizations as system of, 271–74; reputation-based, 279–80; social glue as, 10–12; social sensitivity linked to, 107; in status hierarchical settings, 142; summary, 301–4; warfare and, 92. *See also* leader-follower relations; multilevel selection theory (MLST)

cooperative instinct hypothesis, 286–87

copy number variation (CNV), 25, 28, 38

Cordes, C., 297

cortisol: employee stress levels and, 144–45; entrepreneurial behaviors and, 77; immune system affected by, 146; salivary levels of, 139, 152, 153; threat/reward systems and, 120–24, *122*, 131

Cosmides, L., 2, 216, 217, 292, 314, 329

creativity, 78, 83, 96

Crick, Francis, 24

Crockett, M. J., 126–27

Cuddy, A. J. C., 131

cultural evolution: concept, 284–85; cooperative instinct and, 285–87; multilevel cooperation and, 287–89

culture: assumptions in SSSM, 2–3, 270, 314; celebrity influence in, 98; decision making and, 221–22; drivers of, 94; evolution of, 241–42, 284–89; of family firms, 247; family firms and contingencies in, 255–56; family systems in relation to, 239–41, 255–56, 258; institutional ecology differences and, 288–89; mate selection and, 252; physical attractiveness in, 104–5; political sex scandals in, 181; reflexive self-consciousness evidenced in, 256; sports teams and managers in, 182; weight perceptions in, 103–4, 112–13n5. *See also* cultural evolution; kinship; social context and systems

CYP2A6, 36

Darwin, C.: on adaptive advantages, 107, 172; on human morality as group adaptation, 195n1; limits of, 16n2; multilevel perspective of, 273–75; on status hierarchy, 108. *See also* evolution by natural selection

Davis-Blake, A., 317

Dawkins, R., 8–9, 195n2, 275, 276, 283, 304n3

Day, M., 83

Deater-Deckard, K., 59–60

decision-making dynamics: adaptive toolkit of simple heuristics in, 206–16; approach to studying, 8, 203–4, 206; behavioral decision theory and, 328; chronic stressors in, 14–15; coordinating other agents with mechanisms of, 222–28; demands-control-support model in, 147–49, 152–53; ethical, 157; evolution and specialization in relation to, 204–5; evolutionary psychology toolkit in, 216–22; mind as incentive-seeker vs. strategy selector in, 205–6, 217; molecular genetics linked to variables in, 36; multilevel selection theory applied to, 291–98; neuroscience research on, 83; summary, 228–30

Dennett, D. C., 271

density dependence (theory fragment), 319

De Pater, I. E., 149, 153, 155, 158, 159

Derbyshire, S., 322

Descent of Man, The (Darwin), 195n1

DeScioli, P.: chapter, 203–35; referenced, 8, 313

Dickson, H. A., 315

Dictator game, 220–21

Dimotakis, N.: chapter, 47–69; referenced, 7, 12, 149, 153, 155, 158, 159, 313, 326, 337

diseases and disorders: GWA studies of, 27; heritability of, 23–24; phenotypes and, 25–26

—specific: ADHD, 77–78, 82, 85; autism, 6; coronary heart disease, 146; dyslexia, 77, 78, 85; Huntington's disease, 25; obesity, 103–4, 112–13n5, 329

dispositional approach: entrepreneurship and, 72, 76–79; job satisfaction and, 52; situational approach vs., 316–18, 322

distribution systems: meritocratic vs. equality-based, 184–85. *See also* organizational justice; wages

DIT (dual inheritance theory), 239–40, 255

DNA (deoxyribonucleic acid): defined, 24–25; sequencing of, as genotyping method, 26. *See also* molecular genetics and genomic methods

dopaminergic system: COMT val158Met polymorphism, 36; entrepreneurial behaviors and, 72, 82; receptor gene DRD4, 32–34, 36–37, 326; reward system and, 121, *125*, 125–26

DRD2, 36

DRD4 (or D4DR), 32–34, 36–37, 326

dual inheritance theory (DIT), 239–40, 255

Dunbar, R. I. M., 278

Durkheim, Emile, 10–11, 15

Dutta, R., 105

Dutton, J. E., 160

Dwyer, D. J., 124, 139, 144, 149, 153

dyslexia, 77, 78, 85

Eastern Europe, entrepreneurship in, 327

Ebstein, R., 30, 31, 32, 34, 35

ecological rationality, 208, 209–11, 330

ecology, organizational. *See* organizational ecology

economics: as branch of biology, 274; divergence from classical models in, 221; double auction model of, 218–19; family firms and contingencies in, 255–56; implications of global collapse (2008–9), 269–70, 303; incentive-seeking view in, 205–6; integrating sociology with, 335; production and transaction costs in, 297; psychological processes as trumping, 242; traditional rational approach in, 211–12, 213. *See also* family firms; neuroeconomics

EEA (environment of evolutionary adaptedness), 140–43, 249. *See also* mismatch theory

EEG (electroencephalography), 83

Einstein, A., 1

Eisenberger, R., 155

Elofsson, S., 152

emotional traits and states: decision making and, 216–17; effects of stress on, 257; emotional intelligence concept and, 110–11; employee response to work events and, 151–53; genetic basis of, 58–59; job satisfaction and, 52–53; proposed studies on, 83; rational order of family firm and, 249; reciprocal altruism regulated by, 281–82. *See also* affectivity; psychological traits and

emotional traits and states (*continued*)
functions; work attitudes, behaviors, and emotions; work/life/love

empathy, 106–7, 121, *128*, 128–30

employee health and physiological functioning: approach to studying, 7, 139–40; biological mechanisms noted, 2; cardiovascular processes, 145–47; coworker and supervisor support and, 152–53, 154–56; demands-control-support model in, 147–49, 152–53; evolutionary psychology and, 140–43; framework overview, 143–44, *144*; group-level analysis in, 158–59; measurement issues in, 159; organizational justice in relation to, 150–51, 159; outcomes of, 153–56; practical implications of, 159–60; proposed "untoughening" hypothesis of, 149; summary, 160; theoretical frameworks proposed, 156–57; within-individual analysis in, 158; work events in relation to, 151–52; workplace mismatch in, 14–15, 140–43. *See also* hormones

endocrinological system: dual hormone hypothesis on, 131; HPA (hypothalamic-pituitary-adrenal) axis, *122*, 123, 131, 132; HPG (hypothalamic-pituitary-gonadal) axis, 131; person-environment interactions and, 145. *See also* hormones

Eneroth, P., 153

Engel, C., 296

Ensminger, J. E., 222

entrepreneurship and entrepreneurial behaviors: approach to studying, 7, 12, 71–72; Biological Foundations Project example of, 325–28; definitions of, 85n3; direct genetic effects on physiology and, 76–78; GE interplay and, 79–81; gender differences in, 60–61; genetic covariation with individual attributes and, 78–79; genetic factors in variations of, 72–73; heritability of, 75–76; "liability of newness" in, 244; measures of, 75; personality traits mediating, 62; serial type of, 82; summary, 84–85. *See also* family firms

—specific approaches: boundaries of biological perspective, 73–74; cognitive neuroscience, 83; hormone research, 83–84; molecular genetics, 82–83; quantitative genetics, 81–82; targeted treatments, 84–85

environmental factors: appropriate measures in response to, 216–17; cultural development in context of, 241–42; decision making and representations of, 207–11, 224, 229; family systems in relation to, 239, 255–56; genetic expression in relation to, 323, 338n3; shared and unshared, 49; specific genes in relation to, 39–40. *See also* gene-environment (GE) interplay

environment of evolutionary adaptedness (EEA), 140–43, 249. *See also* mismatch theory

EP. *See* evolutionary psychology (EP)

epistasis, defined, 35

Eskimo (Inuit) people, 176

Etzioni, A., 11

eugenics, 3

Evans, O., 146

"everyday speech" method, 31–32

evolutionary psychology (EP): anthropometric (surface-level) traits and, 98–105, 112–13n5; approach to studying, 94–97; assumptions about reciprocity and leadership in, 171–74; development and acceptance of, 289; employees' physiology and, 140–43; functionally specialized mechanisms in, 170–71; function of, 5; on hierarchy, 13; implications for OB/OMT, summarized, 301–4; information-processing studies in, 205–6; key themes in, 91–94, 292; leadership theory based in, 169–70; limits of, 290; personality (deep-level) traits in, 105–11; role in Biological Foundations Project, 329–34; social sensitivity (empathy) in, 106–7. *See also* employee health and physiological functioning; leader-follower relations; multilevel selection theory (MLST)

—toolkit: basics, 216–17; Dictator games in, 220–21; double auction in, 218–19; public goods in, 217, 219–20, 221–22; summary, 221–22

evolutionary synthesis, 65n1

evolution by natural selection: adaptation, selection, and transitions in, 276–78; basics, 9–10; family firm dynamics in, 248–54; functionality in, 170–74; inheritance, behavioral genetics, and, 50–51; intelligence and health in, 109; kinship systems in relation to, 238–41;

mechanisms for survival and reproduction in, 204–5; multilevel nature
of, 273–75; organizational ecology
and, 288–89, 318–21; organizations in
context of, 301–4; practical advances
based on, 1–2; variation/selection/re-
tention (VSR) process in, 301. *See also*
appearance; biology in organizational
behavior; coevolution; cultural evolution; fit (adaptation); fitness (match);
individual differences and attributes;
multilevel selection theory (MLST);
neo-Darwinian theory
extended phenotype concept, 8–9
extraversion, 32–33, 53–54, 58–59, 78–79,
95, 96, 317, 325

factionalization, 183–84
families: adaptation and dysfunction in,
242–43; behavioral genetics and functioning of, 248, 255–56; as biological
entity, 238–39; coevolution and forms
of, 239–41; cross-cultural differences
in, 8, 149, 258; uniqueness of, 255–56;
work and, 243. *See also* children; kinship; parents and parenting styles
family firms: affinal bonds in, 252–53; approach to studying, 8, 237–38; Biological Foundations Project example
of, 332–34; changing context of, 243;
collective self-identity concepts and,
258; co-ownership of, 245, 246, *246*;
Darwinian dynamics of, summarized,
248–49, 332–33; development models
of, 257; emotions and rational order
in, 249; empirical research on, 333–34;
genetic wildcard inheritance of, *246*,
248, 254, 255; institutional trust and,
289; intergenerational transmission
of, 244, *246*, 246–47; kin and non-
kin teamwork in, 11, 247; mediating
self and leadership in, 241, 256–58; as
microcosm of social experimentation,
240; nepotism in, 249–50; parent-
offspring conflict in, 251; preferences,
persistence, and success of, 244–45;
scandal involving, 237; sibling rivalry
in, 253–54; summary, 258–60. *See also*
entrepreneurship and entrepreneurial
behaviors; kinship
Fehr, E., 280, 281
Fernet, C., 149
Ferrie, J. E., 159

FFM (Five-Factor Model). *See* Big Five
factors
"field theory" (Lewin), 11
"fight or flight" responses, 98–99, 122–24.
See also cortisol
Finkel, D., 59
Fischbacher, U., 280, 281
fish, leader-follower relations in, 171
Fisher, P. J., 35
Fiske, A. P., 223, 226
fit (adaptation): adaptive problem, defined,
170; biology and OB's assumptions of,
9–10; Darwinian concept, 3, 276–77;
in families, 242–43; founding new
organizations and, 288; for leadership
and followership, 169–72; of mind
and environment in decision making,
207–9; multilevel nature of, 274–75.
See also cooperation; environment of
evolutionary adaptedness (EEA); leader-
follower relations; multilevel selection
theory (MLST)
fitness (match): challenges to, 170; deep-
level characteristics of, 105–11; in organizational effectiveness, 92–93; social
models in, 224–26; surface-level characteristics of, 98–105. *See also* family
firms; mismatch theory
Five-Factor Model (FFM). *See* Big Five
factors
5-HTTLPR (serotonin transporter genetic
marker), 32–34, 35, 36–37, 38
5-HT2A (serotonin receptor), 34, 36
5-HT2C (serotonin receptor), 34
fMRI (functional resonance imaging), 33,
83, 132
Ford, M. T., 150–51
Ford Motor Company, 245
form to function theories, 331–32
Fowler, J. H., 36
Fox, M. L., 124, 139, 144, 149, 153
framing effects, 206
Fredrickson, B. L., 155
Freedman, D. G., 103
Freeman, J. H., 288, 320, 321
"free-rider problem," 185–86, 280–82
French, J. R. P., Jr., 157
Freud, S., 6, 91, 107, 244
friendship vs. exchange, 226–29
Frykblom, P., 220–21
Fukuyama, F., 288–89, 303
functional resonance imaging (fMRI), 33,
83, 132

height: as anthropometric trait, 102–3; fitness in relation to, 98–99; of leaders in small-scale societies, 178–79
Heinrichs, M., 132
Heller, D., 54
Henley, N., 106
Henrich, J., 221, 285
Herhold, P. M., 318
heritability, defined, 75. *See also* genetics; *and specific traits*
Hershberger, S. L., 55–56
Herzberg, F., 112
heuristics: behavioral imitation, 299; bounded rational, 207–8; defined, 207; ecological rational, 208, 209–11, 330; hiatus, 211; lexicographic, 211; over-fitting problem in, 212; recognition, 207, 208–9, 210; satisficing, 210, 214; selecting appropriate, 216; sequential searches and decisions, 213–16; take-the-best, 211. *See also* adaptive toolbox of simple heuristics
hierarchy. *See* status hierarchy
Hobbes, T., 274
Hochwarter, W. A., 153, 154
Hoffman, E., 220, 221
Hoffsteader, R., 3
Hogan, J., 108
Hogan, R.: chapter, 91–118; referenced, 7, 13, 14, 191, 313
Holland, J. L., 317
Homans, G. S., 273
homophily phenomenon, 250. *See also* family firms
hormones: employee health and, 144–45; entrepreneurial behaviors and, 76–77, 79–80, 83–84; interactions of systems, 131; motivational systems and, 120–21. *See also* cortisol; endocrinological system; oxytocin (neuropeptide); testosterone
Hosoda, M., 105
hostility-related traits, 60. *See also* aggression
House, R. J., 318
HPA and HPG axes. *See under* endocrinological system
Hulin, C. L., 52–53
human behavior and behavioral traits: biological explanations for, 4–6; genetic models linking attitudes and, 61–63; genetic transmission of, 23–24, 248; innate drivers of, 91–94; social glue

in, 10–12; Tinbergen's typology of, 7; work and non-work, 57, 59–61. *See also* emotional traits and states; humans; motivational systems; organizational behavior (OB); psychological traits and functions; work attitudes, behaviors, and emotions; *and specific traits*
Human Genome Project, 23
humans: affinal bonds of, 252–53; coevolution and, 239–41; decision making and relations among, 222–24; function of friendship for, 227–29; GE interplay and longitudinal developmental studies, 40–41; group-level adaptations of, 276–78; key features of, 241; oxytocin and physical contact among, 129–30; reflexive self-consciousness of, 241, 256–58; sociality of, 92, 240–41, 273, 286–87; themes important to society, 91–94; warfare among, 92–93. *See also* families; human behavior and behavioral traits; hunter-gatherer societies; indigenous peoples; individuals; kinship
hunter-gatherer societies: collective action problem in, 185–86; cooperation in, 171–72, 282; decision making in, 216, 294–95; dietary needs in, 175–76, 188–89; different leaders for different roles in, 181–82; family systems and adaptations of, 239–41; group size in, 187–89, 192–93, 282, 331; in-group advantage of leaders in, 182–83; leadership and followership adaptations in, 91, 169–72; leadership in, 187–89, 192–93; leaders preferred in, 176–79, 183–85; male status striving and using status for sex in, 180–81; motivational systems in, 120; self-interest constrained in, 300; sequential search problems for, 213; social structure of, 13, 141, 286; stress responses, 14; work of, 243
Huntington's disease, 25
Hurst, C., 96, 104, 105

IgG, 153
Iliad, The (Homer), 97
Ilies, R.: chapter, 47–69; referenced, 7, 12, 79, 100, 149, 153, 155, 158, 159, 313, 326, 329, 337
imaging technologies: in entrepreneurial studies, 83; research advantages of, 32–34, 323
—specific: EEG, 83; fMRI, 33, 83, 132

immune systems, 146
in- and out-group factors: competition and, 276–78, 286–87; cooperation and, 223, 283–85; dispute resolution and, 182–83; factionalization and, 183–85; generosity and, 130; relationships in context of, 224; selection pressures and, 303
incentives: opportunistic behavior and, 298; opposite of desired effects of, 203–4; strategy selection vs. seeking, 205–6, 217
indigenous peoples: different roles for different leaders among, 181; fairness norms among, 183–85; group size and type of leadership in, 188–89; leaders preferred by, 176–79; slavery among, 189
individual differences and attributes: in altruism, implications of, 219–20; anthropometric (surface-level) traits, 98–105; approach to studying, 7, 91–97; Chinese traditionalism and, 149; deep- and surface-level, distinguished, 112n2; in employee health organizing framework, 143–44, *144*; evolutionary perspective on, 50–51; general vs. specific abilities, 110; genetic basis of, 51–61; genetic disposition to entrepreneurship linked to, 72, 76–79; intelligence (deep-level) trait, 108–11; organizational justice in relation to, 151; personality (deep-level) traits, 105–8; personnel selection and, 63–64; summary, 111–12. *See also* emotional traits and states; physiological traits and functions; psychological traits and functions
individuals: leader-follower adaptations as benefit to, 169–72; mechanical vs. organic solidarity among, 10–11; mediation and self-consciousness of, 241, 256–58; multilevel selection theory and decision making of, 292–93; OB's focus on, 275; phenotypes and genotypes of, 8–9, 13, 14; reciprocal altruism between, 172–73; selfish and altruistic factors in, 275. *See also* humans
industrial and organizational (IO) psychology, 29, 110, 259, 315–16
Ingram, P., 334
inheritance: of behavioral genetics in family firms, 248; complexity of attitudes

linked to, 51–61; evolution, behavioral genetics, and, 50–51; of learned behaviors, 284–89. *See also* genetics; *and specific traits*
insects, 10, 171, 278
intelligence. *See* cognitive ability
Irlenbusch, B., 281
Israel, S., 30, 31, 35

Jackson, C. N., 153
James, W., 91, 108
Japan: motherhood in, 255; oldest family firm in, 243, 244
Jermier, J. M., 190
job characteristics: demands-control-support model of, 147–49, 152–53, 154–55; distributional and procedural justice, 150–51, 159, 184; employee's self-determination, 149; job satisfaction in relation to, 39; lack of exit options, 192–93; proposed redesign of, 159–60. *See also* work environment (workplace)
job demands–decision latitude model, 147–49, 152–53
job performance and success (factors): age, 101–2; agreeableness, 95–96; conscientiousness, 95; height, 102; intelligence, 109; openness, 96
job satisfaction: affectivity as mediating, 62; behavioral genetics research on, 55–56; change frequencies and, 59–60; heritability of, 23, 24; job characteristics in relation to, 39; personality factors in, 52–55, 61; as quantitative trait, 26
Johnson, W., 56
Joseph, D. L., 111
Judge, T. A.: chapter, 91–118; referenced, 7, 13, 14, 52–53, 54, 61, 62, 313

Kahn, R. L., 273
Kaiser, R. B., 191
Kamarck, T. W., 148
Karasek, R. A., 145, 147–48
Katz, D., 273
Keeley, L. H., 92
Keller, L. M., 56
Keltikangas-Järvinen, L., 79–80
Kendler, K. S., 60
Kenrick, D. T., 223, 292
Kerr, N. L., 294–95
Kerr, S., 190
kinship: adaptation and dysfunction in

Necker cube analogy, 8–9
Neeleman, D., 78
negative affectivity (NA), 53, 58–59
Nelson, R. R., 287–88
neo-Darwinian theory, 271, 304n1. *See also* evolution by natural selection; multilevel selection theory (MLST)
NEO Personality Inventory, 32
nepotism, 249–50
nervous system, *122*, 123, 217
Nesse, R. M., 142, 154
Nettle, D., 51, 54, 205
Neuberg, S. L., 292
neurobiological systems: approach to studying, 7, 119–20; complexities of, 133–34; social behavior and, 11–12, 119–20. *See also* brains; cognitive ability; imaging technologies; motivational systems
neuroeconomics: concept, 119, 125–27, 128, 133; mentioned, 7; research design and, 324
neuroendocrine system. *See* endocrinological system; hormones
neuropeptides. *See* oxytocin (neuropeptide)
neuroticism, 32–33, 35, 53–54, 58–59, 95, 158, 317
Newman, D. A., 111
News Corporation International (NewsCorp), 237, 238
Newton, I., 1
niche construction, 240. *See also* environmental factors
niche width (theory fragment), 319–20
Nicholson, N.: chapter, 237–67; referenced, 8, 11, 119, 313, 320, 332–33, 337
Nicolaou, N.: chapter, 71–89; referenced, 7, 12, 313, 325–26
nomadic foraging societies. *See* huntergatherer societies
non-kin cooperation theory, 172. *See also* leader-follower relations
Nootka people, 189
North, D. C., 288
Nowak, M. A., 280, 282–83

OB. *See* organizational behavior (OB)
obesity, 103–4, 112–13n5, 329
occupational health and stress. *See* employee health and physiological functioning
occupational health psychology, 139, 144, 159
O'Connor, K.: chapter, 311–42; referenced, 8

On the Origin of Species (Darwin), 172, 274
openness to experience, 32, 53–54, 78–79, 95, 96, 317, 325
opportunity recognition measures, 75, 79
organizational behavior (OB): defined, 312; dispositional vs. situational effects in, 316–18, 322; fit and mismatch in, 9–10, 14–15, 140–43; genetic transmission of, 23–24; hierarchy in, 12–13; multilevel selection theory applied to, 290–91, 297–98; perceptions of, 259; social glue in, 10–12. *See also* biology in organizational behavior; cooperation; decisionmaking dynamics; employee health and physiological functioning; family firms; motivational systems; multilevel selection theory (MLST); work attitudes, behaviors, and emotions; workrelated outcomes
organizational behavior research (organizational theory, OT): adding biological lens to, 4–6; brief guide to, 315–21; on employee well-being and health, 139–40, 156–57; extended phenotype view in, 8–9; group-level analysis in, 158–59, 295–96; implications of multilevel selection theory for, summarized, 301–4; input-process-output (I-P-O) model in, 143–44, *144*; micro- and macro-levels in, 312, 316–17, 325, 336–37, 338nn1–2; molecular genetics approach in, 37–41; organizational ecology and, 288–89, 318–21; SSSM's dominance in, 2–3, 270, 314; theory development in, 301–2; within-individual analysis in, 158. *See also* behavioral genetics research; Biological Foundations Project; organizational management theory (OMT)
organizational ecology: bioecology models in, 320–21; evolutionary theory of, 318–20; institutional differences and, 288–89
organizational justice: employee health and, 150–51, 159; fairness norms and, 183–85; as intervention in employee health, 154
organizational management theory (OMT): control discourse in, 3; information as tool in, 4; multilevel selection theory applied to, 290–91, 297–98, 301–4. *See also* cooperation; leaders and leadership; multilevel selection

organizational management theory (OMT) (*continued*)
theory (MLST); organizational behavior (OB)

organizations: biology and ecology of, 320–21; communicating vision of, 300; as cooperative systems, 271–74; decision making and relations in, 222–24; decreased productivity and absenteeism in, 153–54; distributional and procedural justice in, 150–51, 159, 184; effectiveness of, 92–93, 105, 111–12; employee health interventions and costs, 153–56; employee health organizing framework and interventions by, 143–44, *144*; entrepreneurship and rate of founding within, 326–27; friendship vs. exchange relationships in, 226–29; as goal-seeking machines, 229–30; incentives and opportunistic behavior in, 298; in institutional ecology, 288–89; multilevel selection theory and decision making in, 297–301; personnel selection and training in, 63–64; populations and ecology of, 318–20; profitability of, 139; routines in, 287–88; traditional economic approach to, 203; use of term, 304n5

Orma people (Kenya), 222

Orth-Gomér, K., 152, 153

OT. *See* organizational behavior research (organizational theory, OT); organizational management theory (OMT)

oxytocin (neuropeptide): affiliation system and, 121, *128*, 128–30, 132; employee health and physiology in relation to, 157; entrepreneurial behaviors and, 77; prosocial behaviors linked to, 12, 35–36

PANAS (Positive and Negative Affect Schedule), 58–59

parental investment theory, 180, 253–54

parents and parenting styles: changing strategies of, 242–43; children raised by non-kin, 240; cultural differences, 255; heritability index for, 61; heuristics of decision making, 211; parent-offspring conflict and, 251; sibling rivalry and, 253–54. *See also* families; kinship

Patterson, P., 16n4

PCR (polymerase chain reaction), 26

perceived organizational support (POS), 155

personality traits: assumptions about, 48; biological models and neuroimaging studies, 32–34; as deep-level traits, 105–8; defined, 94–95; five-point model of, 53–54; genetics and attitudes mediated by, 57–58, 61–63; heritability of, 24; job satisfaction linked to, 52–55, 61; measures of, 31–32; path models of, 58–59; as quantitative trait, 26; role of, 30–31; within-group criteria of, 105–6. *See also* Big Five factors; psychological traits and functions; *and specific traits*

person-environment (P-E) fit theory, 156–57

Pfeffer, J., 317

PGG (public goods game), 217, 219–20, 221–22

phenotypes: defined, 25, 335–36; environmental influences on, 48; extended, 8–9; individual differences and distribution of, 50–51; polygenic, 26. *See also* genotypes; physiological traits and functions

phenylketonuria (PKU), 25

physiological traits and functions: as anthropometric (surface-level) traits, 98–105; in employee health organizing framework, 143–44, *144*; genetic disposition to entrepreneurship and, 72, 76–79; genotype changes and, 14; immune system, 146; influence based on, 98–105; as potential genetic pathway in OB, 27–29, *28*; symptoms of poor functioning, 146–47. *See also* appearance; blood pressure (BP); cardiovascular processes; employee health and physiological functioning; neurobiological systems

Pierce, B. D.: chapter, 269–310; referenced, 8, 11, 313, 335, 337

Pillutla, M. M., 123

Pittsburgh Healthy Heart Project, 148

Plomin, R., 29, 75, 80

political attitudes, 36, 58

Pólos, L., 319

polymerase chain reaction (PCR), 26

POS (perceived organizational support), 155

positive affectivity (PA), 53, 58–59

Positive and Negative Affect Schedule (PANAS), 58–59

Prasad, S.: chapter, 119–37; referenced, 7, 313

pre-frontal cortex (PFC), *125*, 125–26
Pressman, S. D., 151
prestige. *See* service-for-prestige transaction
Price, M. E.: chapter, 169–201; referenced, 8, 13, 313, 337
Prisoner's Dilemma (PD) game, 132, 279, 304n2
probability theory, 213–14
psychiatry, 6
psychological traits and functions: entrepreneurial behaviors and, 72; heritability of, 23–24, 38; molecular genetics linked to variables in, 30–37; as polygenetic phenotypes, 26; as potential genetic pathway in OB, 27–29, *28*. *See also* attitudes; cognitive ability; emotional traits and states; personality traits; work attitudes, behaviors, and emotions
psychology: behaviorism in, 3; genotype changes and, 14; on group decision making, 295–96; industrial and organizational (IO), 29, 110, 259, 315–16; occupational health, 139, 144, 159; reciprocal, 220. *See also* Big Five factors; evolutionary psychology (EP)
Psychology and Industrial Efficiency (Münsterberg), 315
psychosocial variables. *See* attitudes; cognitive ability; emotional traits and states; personality traits; psychology
public goods game (PGG), 217, 219–20, 221–22
punishment, 220, 280–82

quantitative genetics approach, 81–82
quantitative trait locus (QTL), 35

rally effect, 182–83
Ramachandran, V. S., 107
Rand, D. G., 281
Rapoport, A., 214
rationality: bounded form of, 207–8; challenges to dominant paradigm of, 270; ecological, 208, 209–11, 330; problematic assumption about, 221; social, 208
Rau, R., 152
reciprocal altruism theory: basics, 172–73; collective-action dilemma in, 185–86; cooperative behavior in, 279; emotions regulating, 281–82; group size and type of leadership in relation to, 187–89, 192–93; leaders imposed on

vs. selected by followers and, 177–78; preferences for altruistic, pro-group leaders and, 190–92; preferences for "fair" leaders and, 183–85; reciprocal-based leadership and, 169–72; summary, 193–95; voluntary leader-follower interaction in, 174–75. *See also* reciprocity
reciprocity: direct and indirect types, described, 279–80; use of term, 173. *See also* reciprocal altruism theory; service-for-prestige transaction
Reeb, D. M., 247
Relational Models Theory, 223, 226
religion: family firms and, 255; function of, 241; society and, 93–94; use of term, 112n1
replication, genes and memes for, 9–10
reproduction: adaptation and, 9–10; collective success and, 94, 97; evolutionary mechanisms for, 204–5; fitness for, 98–100, 103; status and, 93, 108. *See also* sexual selection
reputation: altruistic punishment for poor, 280–82; indirect reciprocity based on, 279–80; measures of, 94–95, 105
resilience, 156
reward system: basics, 121, 124–25, *125*; behavioral manifestations of, 125–28; biological mechanisms of, 125, 126, 127; interaction of affiliation system with, 132; interaction of threat system with, 130–31
Rhoades, L., 155
Richerson, P. J., 185, 241, 284, 285
Riemann, R., 59
Rilling, J. K., 11–12
Robbins, J. M., 150–51
Roberts, G., 205
Rockenbach, B., 281
Roehling, M. V., 103
Roethlisberger, F., 315
Ross, J., 52, 317
Roze, D., 277
Russia, entrepreneurship in, 327

Salmon, C. A., 254
Sapolsky, R., 131
Schaubroeck, J., 149, 150
Schnorpfeil, P., 152–53
Science, 24
Scott, R. W., 316
Scottish Mental Survey, 109

Seale, D. A., 214

self: attractiveness and self-esteem, 104–5; collective self-identity concept, 258; employee's self-determination, 149; future research on, 259–60; reflexive self-consciousness, 241, 256–58

self-interest: appropriate use of, 226; co-operation and, 271–72, 275, 278, 281, 283, 286–87, 303; family firms and, 245, 248, 251; group (or other) interest vs., 299–301; of leader, 195; limits and constraints on, 297–98, 299, 300–301; paradigm of, 269–70; public goods and, 220

Selfish Gene, The (Dawkins), 195n2, 275, 283, 304n3

Selznick, P., 298, 304n5

Sen, S., 35

Senecal, C., 149

sensation-seeking behavior, 12, 32, 72, 78, 82, 325

serotonin system: personality studies and, 32–34, 35; reward system and, 121, *125*, 126–27; social experiences and, 36–37

servant leadership theory, 191–92, 194

service-for-prestige transaction: basics, 170, 173–74; coercive leadership in context of, 187, 189; collective action problem in, 185–86; in early group environments, 176–86; exploitation of followers without exit options in, 192–93; low tolerance for unnecessary leaders and, 189–90; preferences for altruistic, pro-group leaders and, 190–92; summary, 193–95; voluntary leader-follower interaction as, 174–75

Settle, J. E., 36

SEU (subjective expected utility) theory, 205–6

sex differences: attractiveness and self-esteem in, 104–5; evolutionary and biological perspectives on, 5; organizational literature on, 2; in perceptions of weight, 103–4, 112–13n5; in physical traits of leaders, 178–79. *See also* gender differences

sexual selection: affinal bonds and, 252–53; changing criteria for, 240; kinship and, 239; status striving and, 180–81; types preferred in, 178. *See also* reproduction

Shakelford, T. K., 289–90

Shakespeare, W., 251

Shane, S.: chapter, 71–89; referenced, 7, 12, 313, 318, 325–26

Shogren, J. F., 220–21

Shuar people (Ecuadorian Amazon), 177, 186

Simon, H. A., 207, 214, 338n1

Simon, L. N., 104, 105

Singer, T., 132

single-nucleotide polymorphisms (SNPs): association analysis of, 27; boundaries of influence of any one SNP, 74; defined, 25; genotyping and, 26; in longitudinal human development studies, 40; in personality trait studies, 34

Slatcher, R. B., 158

small tandem repeat (STR, or minisatellite), 25

Smith, A., 204

Smith, V. L., 218–19, 220, 221

social context and systems: attitudes in, 31, 35–37; biological data and research design on, 328–29; socialization process, 2–3, 28, 94, 106–7, 239, 297; success/failure of, 241–42; taboos and boundary crossing in, 225–26. *See also* culture; hunter-gatherer societies; psychological traits and functions; social relationships and networks

social Darwinism concept, 3

social relationships and networks: cardio-vascular processes and, 146; decision making and toolkit of, 219–20, 221–24; depression vs. life satisfaction and, 62; family systems in relation to, 240; friendship vs. exchange in, 226–29; genetic influence on, 38–39; matched/mismatched models of, 224–26; sensitivity and, 106–7; status in, 174, 176–78, 180–81. *See also* kinship; social context and systems; status hierarchy

social sciences: biological sciences unified with, 2, 270–71; OB and organizational studies as, 15; SSSM's dominance in, 2–3, 270, 314

social sensitivity concept, 106–7

sociology: on group decision making, 295–96; on human bonds, 10–11; integrating economics ideas with, 335

Song, Z.: chapter, 23–46; referenced, 7, 313, 337

specialization, 204–5, 272–73

Spencer, H., 274

SSSM (standard social science model), 2–3, 270, 314

status hierarchy: challenges of teamwork in, 142; functions and effects of, 12–13, 93; height in relation to, 103; inequality and multiple levels of, 141; realpolitik and competitiveness in, 107–8; threat and reward systems interacting in, 130–31. *See also* leaders and leadership

Staw, B. M., 52, 317

Steptoe, A., 146

Stogdill, R. M., 317

Stone-Tomero, E. F., 105

STR (small tandem repeat, or minisatellite), 25

stress: increased maladies related to, 142, 145–47; job demands, employee health, and, 147–49, 152–53; mismatch theory and, 158–59; organizational interventions in, 154–56; studies of work-related, 124; within-individual analysis for understanding, 158. *See also* cortisol; threat system

Stubbe, J. H., 56

subjective expected utility (SEU) theory, 205–6

substance abuse, 154

Sulloway, F. J., 254

Sundie, J. M., 292

"survival of the fittest," coining of, 274

Swedish Adoption/Twin Study of Aging, 55–56

Syme, S. L., 148

Szathmary, E., 277

taboos and boundary crossing, 225–26

Takahashi, T., 123

Taylor, F. W., 111–12, 312, 315

Temperament and Character Inventory (TCI), 34

Terracciano, A., 34

Tesser, A., 57–58

testosterone: cues to levels, 178; entrepreneurial behaviors linked to levels of, 77, 79, 84; group status in relation to, 158–59; reward system and, 121, *125*, 127–28, 131

Tetrick, L. E., 150–51

thalamus, 121, *122*, 122–23

Theorell, T., 145, 148, 153, 155

Thompson, J. D., 273

Thornhill, S., 77, 79

threat system: basics, 120–22, *122*; behavioral manifestation of, 123–24; biological mechanism of, 122–23; interaction of affiliation system with, 132; interaction of reward system with, 130–31

Timmel, J. J., 296

Tinbergen, N., 7

Tindale, R. S., 294–95

Todd, P. M.: chapter, 203–35; referenced, 8, 313

Tong, T., 323–24

Tooby, J., 2, 216, 217, 292, 314, 329

Toppinen-Tanner, S., 156

Tridimensional Personality Questionnaire (TPQ), 32

Trier social stress task, 123

Trivers, R. L., 172–73, 251

trust: affiliation system and, 121, *128*, 128–30; developing institutional, 288–89; employee health and physiology in relation to, 157; preferences for altruistic, pro-group leaders and, 191–92; in public goods game, 222

Turkheimer, E., 99

twins, monozygotic (MZ) vs. dizygotic (DZ), 85n2. *See also* adoptive children

twins, studies of: co-twin control designs in, 84; entrepreneurial behaviors, 60–61, 75–76, 78–79, 81; genetic influences generally, 23, 49–50, *50*; hostility-related traits, 60; job and life satisfaction, 55–56; job and occupational change frequencies, 59–60; leadership roles, 323; non-work attitudes, 57–58; parental attention to stronger vs. weaker, 253; social support and depression vs. life satisfaction, 62

Ultimatum game, 83, 221

ultrasociality, 286–87

Undén, A.-L., 152

United States: anti-genetic-discrimination legislation in, 64, 65; attitudes toward evolution in, 1; culture of honor in, 241; efficiency studies in, 315; family firms in, 245; Lend-Lease program of, 227; motherhood in, 255; physical weight and earnings in, 104

Van Harrison, R., 157

Van Vugt, M.: chapter, 169–201; referenced, 8, 13, 97, 313, 337